THE MONETARY APPROACH TO THE BALANCE OF PAYMENTS, EXCHANGE RATES, AND WORLD INFLATION

THE MONETARY APPROACH TO THE BALANCE OF PAYMENTS, EXCHANGE RATES, AND WORLD INFLATION

Thomas M. Humphrey
Robert E. Keleher

Praeger Studies
in International Monetary Economics and Finance
General Editors: J. Richard Zecher
D. Sykes Wilford

PRAEGER

PRAEGER SPECIAL STUDIES • PRAEGER SCIENTIFIC

Library of Congress Cataloging in Publication Data

Humphrey, Thomas M.
The monetary approach to the balance of payments, exchange rates, and world inflation.

(Praeger studies in international monetary economics and finance)
Bibliography: p.
1. Balance of payments. 2. Foreign exchange problem. 3. Inflation (Finance) I. Keleher, Robert E. II. Title. III. Series.
HG3882.H85 332.4'5 81-19979
ISBN 0-03-055956-1 AACR2

To Mitzi and Jane

Published in 1982 by Praeger Publishers
CBS Educational and Professional Publishing
a Division of CBS. Inc.
521 Fifth Avenue, New York, New York 10175 U.S.A.

23456789 145 987654321

Printed in the United States of America

FOREWORD

D. Sykes Wilford *J. Richard Zecher*

The monetary approach to the balance of payments and/or exchange rate determination is both a young and an ancient body of literature. That is, its modern day proponents began to influence the profession only in the last ten years. As for its antiquity, one has only to refer to David Hume to see that this way of viewing balance of payments determination has been around for some time.

Two elements of the professional scope of the monetary approach have been missing. One, a complete synthesis of the recent literature, and two, the links of the approach to earlier authors. In this volume Thomas M. Humphrey and Robert E. Keleher have taken up these challenges and more than met them. The integration of recent developments of monetary models into historical policy debates provides a new and better understanding of the general monetary approach.

Humphrey and Keleher have addressed the history of monetary approach thought in a way that will benefit the general business, academic, and government audiences. Their erudite exposition of the various debates make this volume important to a wide audience as a tool to be used in exchange rate and balance of payments understanding, planning, or forecasting. All practitioners of this dismal portion of the "dismal science" must express their gratitude to these authors for presenting their analysis in a fashion that will enable its users to easily gain a broad understanding of, what is to many, a difficult set of concepts.

By searching antiquity Humphrey and Keleher have shed new light on the monetary approach and knitted distinct threads of past thought together in a unique fashion. Their effort has been successful. It is up to the reader to use what they have provided.

PREFACE

This volume examines the monetary approach to the balance of payments, exchange rates, and world inflation—an approach that highlights the role of excess money supplies and demands in the international adjustment process. Since its reemergence in the late 1960s and early 1970s, the monetary approach has been proclaimed as the single most significant theoretical development in international monetary economics in the past 30 years. In tracing this development the book has three objectives.

First, it identifies the three component models of the monetary approach and specifies the monetary adjustment mechanism embodied in each. These models refer (1) to the closed aggregate world economy, (2) to the individual small open economy operating under fixed exchange rates, and (3) to the individual small open economy operating under freely floating exchange rates. In the first model, prices adjust to equilibrate money supply and demand. By contrast, in the second and third models, monetary equilibrium is achieved through balance of payments and exchange rate adjustments, respectively. In recognizing and giving equal weight to each of these three cases, this book differs markedly from other surveys of the monetary approach, most of which examine only one, or at best two, of the three cases.

This book also demonstrates that classical monetary theorists fully understood and distinguished between the three component models of the monetary approach and that a full recognition of their understanding resolves some apparent contradictions in their work. In documenting this point, the book provides a novel interpretation of some earlier monetary writers and historical episodes.

Another distinguishing feature of the present volume is its emphasis on the historico-evolutionary credentials of the modern monetary approach. In particular, this volume demonstrates that, far from being new, all the major building blocks of the monetary approach were enunciated and integrated into a coherent analytical framework by earlier generations of economists. As a result, the monetary approach should be regarded not so much as a radical new development but rather as a return to an earlier mainstream view of the international adjustment mechanism, a view in which money supplies and demands occupy center stage. To be sure, this point has been made often enough before. But it has not heretofore received the degree of documentation provided in the text. That documentation, together with a description of the role of the monetary approach in a succession of celebrated historical policy controversies, constitutes perhaps the principal contribution of this volume.

ACKNOWLEDGEMENTS

Special thanks go to Audrey Gable, Donna Pollard, and Brenda Womble for expert typing assistance; to Patricia Rhodes for proofreading and checking sources; and to Donna Pollard for overseeing the manuscript through innumerable successive drafts.

CONTENTS

Part One

CLOSED WORLD ECONOMY

1

INTRODUCTION

In the last ten to fifteen years, a unique approach to balance of payments and exchange rate analysis has emerged. This approach has been referred to as the monetary approach to the balance of payments and the monetary approach to exchange rates. It has also been characterized as the "global" or "world" monetarist position.

THE EMERGENCE OF THE MONETARY APPROACH

The monetary approach has become popular among economists in recent years in large part because of the repeated policy failures of various alternative approaches in the post-World-War-II period. In particular, the prevalent nonmonetary (real), partial balance of payments models simply failed to fit the factual evidence. Existing balance of payments frameworks (such as the elasticities model) could not explain or reconcile "a mounting accumulation of awkward failures of prescription and prediction with respect to devaluations and revaluations and other balance of payments policies."[1] Notable among these was the failure of the British devaluation of 1967 to improve the British balance of payments as well as the failure of revaluations of the mark and yen to eliminate external surpluses.[2] Moreover, the predictions of prevalent theories emphasizing a direct relationship between income growth and balance of payment deficits seemed to conflict with the coexistence of high growth rates and external surpluses in Germany and Japan throughout much of the 1960s and 1970s.[3] In addition, movements in interest rates sometimes affected capital flows in the direction opposite to that predicted in conventional theory.[4] Furthermore, the experience of inflation in all countries at the same time, together with simultaneous business cycles among many of the world's economies, seemed to be at variance with received doctrine.[5]

These observations and policy failures led to a rethinking and reformulation of various balance of payments and exchange rate theories. At the same time, it came to be realized that the world was becoming more and more integrated and that most economies were much more open than had commonly been believed. Moreover, with economic growth, as well as technological developments in transportation, communication, and data processing, for example, it was expected that the world would continue to become more integrated. This realization, together with the reformulation-rethinking process, ultimately led to the emergence of the monetary approach, an approach that was premised on integrated world markets and seemed to explain many of the above-cited anomalies. This explanatory power, together with the simplicity of the model, tended to enhance greatly the popularity of the monetary approach. The successive stages of the reformulation of balance of payments theory in the post-World-War-II period have been carefully outlined by Johnson.[6] He indicates that balance of payments models evolved from the elasticities approach, to the Keynesian multiplier approach, to the absorption approach, to the Meade-Tinbergen-Mundell policy approach, and, finally, to the monetary approach.[7] Once exchange rates had been allowed to float in the early 1970s, the monetary approach to the balance of payments was easily converted to its counterpart, the monetary approach to exchange rates.

UNIQUE CHARACTERISTICS OF THE MONETARY APPROACH

The monetary approach has several unique characteristics that clearly differentiate it from these other approaches. Most importantly, the approach stresses the direct influence of the supply and demand for money on the overall balance of payments rather than the relative price aspects of balance of payments adjustment.[8] As indicated above, it is an approach for analyzing well-integrated economies. Conceptually, therefore, it is quite different from those models of segmented or loosely related closed economies in which foreign repercussions are considered to be of a second order of magnitude.

Moreover, the monetary approach views commodity and capital markets as being relatively competitive, whereas the other models often perceive these markets as imperfectly competitive. In addition, the monetary approach is a general monetary model rather than a partial, relative price or real model of the balance of payments or exchange rates. Emphasis in the monetary approach is placed on the entire balance of payments rather than on certain of its components such as the balance of trade (as is stressed in alternative models). As Johnson has argued:

> The essence of the [monetary] approach is to put at the forefront of the analysis the monetary rather than the relative price aspects of international adjustments. . . . The approach . . . places the emphasis not on relative price changes but on the direct influence of excess demand for or supply of money . . . on the overall balance of payments.[9]

> The [monetary] approach differs radically from the standard Keynesian approach to international monetary economics in placing its emphasis fully on the application of monetary theory and taking it off relative national price levels and interest rates as determinants of international flows of goods and capital.[10]

As suggested by Johnson, the monetary approach maintains that interactions between closely interdependent economies—in the form of balance of payments adjustments and/or exchange rate movements—are largely monetary in nature and, as such, should be analyzed within a monetary framework, that is, a framework comprised of the supply of and the demand for money. The major distinguishing characteristic of the monetary approach, then, is its emphasis on the role of money supply and money demand in the international adjustment process.

According to the monetary approach to the balance of payments, for example, the balance of payments is a monetary (rather than real) phenomenon representing a "disequilibrium in the market for money."[11] That is, assuming a given demand for money, the monetary approach to the balance of payments "postulates a direct relationship between the balance of payments and the money supply."[12] An increase in the money supply such that actual cash balances exceed desired cash balances will cause the balance of payments to go into deficit as individuals exchange excess money for foreign goods. Exogenous disturbances, then, "whatever their nature and origin, can best be analyzed via the relationship between the demand for and supply of money."[13] In short, balance of payments adjustments involve, and should be analyzed as, adjustments between actual and desired stocks of money and not as merely current account adjustments as depicted in some alternative approaches. The demand for and supply of money constitute the "central theoretical relationships around which to organize thought concerning the balance of payments."[14]

The monetary approach also places emphasis on the role of monetary forces in analyzing exchange rate movements. Exchange rates, in this approach, are regarded as the relative prices of different national monies rather than as the relative price of national outputs, as in some alternative approaches.[15] Consequently, in analyzing movements in these prices, the monetary approach emphasizes the relationship between the demand for and supply of (relative) national monies. In a similar vein, devaluation is regarded as "foremost a monetary phenomenon."[16] In sum, the monetary approach maintains that interactions between interdependent economies in the form of either balance of payments adjustments or exchange rate movements are largely monetary in nature and should be analyzed within a monetary framework that highlights the role of the demand for and supply of money.

As a result of this different emphasis, some predictions of the monetary approach conflict with those of various other frameworks. For example, the monetary approach to *exchange rates* predicts that an increase in income and a decrease in interest rates (of the small open economy) will lower the domestic currency price of a unit of foreign exchange, that is, it will cause the exchange rate to appreciate. These predictions are contrary to those of alternative models. They result from the focus on the demand for and supply of money—namely, given the nominal supply of money, increases in income and decreases in interest rates will produce an excess demand for money balances. Given the money supply, prices will begin to fall in order to increase the real money stock to its higher equlibrium level. With these prices getting out of line internationally, an exchange rate appreciation is required to restore purchasing power parity.[17] Important differences also exist between the monetary approach to the *balance of payments* and alternative frameworks for balance of payments analysis (see Chapter 2). The monetary approach, then, is a unique approach to balance of payments and exchange rate analysis, and one that has produced alternative views as to predicted relationships between some important economic variables and to the balance of payments adjustment mechanism.

In developing the monetary aspects of international adjustment, the monetary approach extends several fundamental monetary propositions to the model of the open economy. For example, the monetary approach demonstrates that monetary disturbances in the open economy can be analyzed as discrepancies between actual and desired real money balances, which are equilibrated by adjustments made by the public in determining the real money stock it wishes to hold. The monetary approach, then, can be viewed as an extension of the real balance effect to the open economy.

The theory of real balance adjustments to monetary disequilibrium in the closed economy was provided by Patinkin in his general equilibrium model.[18] In that framework, it was demonstrated that discrepancies between desired real money balances and actual real money balances lead to changes in spending behavior. In a closed economy, this change in spending behavior ultimately affects the general price level. This change in the price level works to equate desired and actual real money balances and, consequently, serves as the equilibrating adjustment mechanism.

The monetary approach extends this theory of real balance adjustment to the open economy. In the case of the small open economy under fixed exchange rates, for example, discrepancies between actual and desired real money balances are eliminated by adjustments in actual nominal money balances. In particular, the equilibrating adjustments in real balances take the form of movements or flows of nominal money balances through the balance of payments rather than through price movements.

In the case of the small open economy under flexible exchange rates, discrepancies between actual and desired real money balances are eliminated through exchange rate and price level changes. These exchange rate/price level alterations are part of the same adjustment mechanism that serves to equilibrate actual and desired real money balances. An exchange rate depreciation/price level increase has the same effect on real money balances as does a nominal monetary contraction.

The monetary approach indicates that devaluations (or revaluations) should also be analyzed as a monetary (rather than real or relative price) phenomenon and examined within a monetary framework.[19] According to the monetary approach, the function of a devaluation is to deflate real balances and thereby induce domestic residents to attempt to restore an equilibrium level of real balances by exporting more and importing less through the international commodity and security markets.[20] That is, devaluation is a form of monetary policy that operates via the real balance effects on absorption. The monetary approach, then, views devaluations as being equivalent to or a substitute for domestic monetary contraction in the sense that both devaluation and monetary contraction cause a temporary real balance effect (reduction), which operates to bring desired real balances into equality with actual real balances.[21]

The monetary approach, therefore, analyzes monetary disequilibrium and the consequent monetary adjustment process and in so doing extends the analysis of real balance effects to the open economy. *The monetary approach in this sense, then, can be characterized as an extension of the real balance effect to the international setting.*[22]

Another monetary proposition that the monetary approach has extended to the open economic framework is the concept of *monetary neutrality.*[23] That is, it is demonstrated by the monetary approach that in international economic relations as well as domestically, monetary disturbances are neutral with respect to relative prices and, hence, to real variables in the long run.[24] It is a well-established contention of classical monetary theory of the closed economy, for example, that monetary disturbances will not permanently affect real variables or relative prices.[25] Although it was recognized that the price level is a function of both monetary variables and real output, a monetary disturbance such as an increase in the money supply was not believed to affect real variables permanently.

The monetary approach extends this proposition to the open economy. In the case of the small open economy under fixed exchange rates (where all goods are tradable), for example, monetary disturbances such as an increase in the money supply cannot affect relative prices (and, hence, real variables) in the long run, since all prices are determined in world markets. Any such increase will eventually be eliminated via monetary flows through the balance of payments. Consequently, the ultimate monetary adjustment will be neutral.[26]

In the case of the small open economy under flexible exchange rates, the monetary approach asserts that an increase in the money supply will affect prices and exchange rates in a proportional manner so that, in the long run, no real variables or relative prices are affected. Changes in both exchange rates and domestic prices are part of the adjustment process affecting the prices of both tradables and nontradables and bringing about neutrality. Accordingly, the purchase power parity theorem (discussed below) is characterized by several authors as analogous to the quantity theory of money in the sense of being a neutrality theory.[27] Purchasing power parity, for example, indicates that the terms of trade will not be affected by monetary disturbances such as a change in the money supply. Mundell, for example, has endorsed this neutrality interpretation of purchasing power parity:

> . . . the homogeneity postulate has two children. One is the quantity theory of money, and the other is purchasing power parity on the international scene.[28]

The monetary approach also extends the concept of neutrality to exchange rate changes under a system of pegged exchange rates. That is, devaluation is viewed by the monetary approach as being neutral in the long run with respect to real variables and relative prices. Dornbusch, for example, contends that it is a well-known and unchallengeable fact "that an exchange rate change in and of itself will exert no real effects."[29] This implies that, in the long run, devaluation will not improve the balance of trade but will only affect the price level.

Any arbitrary monetary disturbance, according to the monetary approach, then, will have neutral effects in all the principal monetary models. Or, as stated by Grubel:

> . . . in the long run money is only a veil and monetary policy cannot influence the real variables determining comparative advantage, long-run capital flows, real terms of trade and average unemployment rates. Instead, it can only influence the price level and exchange rate of individual countries and inflation in the world as a whole.[30]

The monetary approach, therefore, extends the concept of neutrality as well as real balance effects to the open economy. Whereas both of these concepts are well-known and established propositions in the modern monetary theory of the closed economy, their extension to the open economy in a sense provides a complete picture of monetary theory.

The monetary approach can be described from several other perspectives. Another way of characterizing the monetary approach, for example, is as a framework for analyzing monetary aspects of small open economies within the closed world economy. The world economy is here viewed as a closed system of well-integrated, interdependent open national economies rather than as the collection of loosely related closed national economies portrayed by some alternative interpretations. The monetary approach indicates that different monetary models must be employed in analyzing the small open economy as distinct from the larger, closed world aggregate. Moreover, different exchange rate regimes call for the use of alternative monetary frameworks for examining individual small open economies.

The monetary approach, then, carefully sets out these alternative monetary models for the individual components of an integrated world aggregate as well as for the aggregate itself. Moreover, it indicates how these models fit together or interact with one another. In a sense, then, the monetary approach constitutes a synthesis of various monetary theories as well as a revival of the view that countries belong to a world economy.

Viewed in this vein, the monetary approach can also be described as a theory of the generation and transmission of world inflation. The monetary approach describes the generation of inflation for the single integrated closed world aggregate as well as for its well-integrated component parts, the small open economies. In so doing, the monetary approach distinguishes between alternative money-price relationships in these economies. In the closed world economy, for example, the familiar propositions of the monetary theory of the closed economy are applicable. In particular, an increase in the supply of money—relative to money demand—will ultimately result in an inflationary rise in the price level. World inflation, then, is brought about by an excess supply of world money. An elaborate description of the monetary transmission mechanism, however, is not provided by the closed economy monetarist model because it is believed to involve so many variables as to be too complex for simple representation.

In analyzing monetary interactions between the aggregate and its component parts, the monetary approach also discusses the determinants of and the transmission of inflation between individual small open economies. The determination and transmission of inflation between individual small open economies is quite different for alternative monetary frameworks or exchange rate regimes. Under fixed exchange rates, for example, rates of inflation for individual small open economies will be similar to or closely tied to the world rate of inflation. Since each small open economy is a price taker on world markets, each small open economy will also take the world inflation rate as its own. In this case, the monetary approach maintains that commodity arbitrage assumes a central role in the transmission of inflation, and local monetary authorities have little, if any, control over inflation or the domestic money supply. Hence, inflation in any individual small open economy will be largely determined in world markets, that is, by world inflation, which, in turn, is determined by world monetary growth. Fixed exchange rates, therefore, ensure that single-country inflation will not significantly differ from the world inflation rate.

The monetary approach insists that under flexible exchange rate regimes, however, it is possible for individual small open economies to have quite different inflation rates, depending on the behavior of the monetary authorities in the individual small open economy. Under these circumstances, although individual small open economies are not completely insulated from world price conditions, domestic monetary authorities acquire an important degree of influence over domestic inflation via their control over the domestic money supply. In large measure, then, inflation is domestically determined rather than exogenously given to the individual small open economy. Moreover, in the case of the small open economy under flexible exchange rates, alternative versions of the monetary approach endorse different monetary transmission mechanisms. That is, some versions of the monetary approach argue that changes in the domestic money supply affect domestic prices before exchanges are affected, whereas other versions indicate that exchange rates are affected before prices. Still other versions contend that a change in the domestic money supply simultaneously affects prices and exchange rates. Whatever the chronological order of price and exchange rate adjustment, however, all advocates of the monetary approach agree that causation runs from money to exchange rates. Nonetheless, simple, general versions of monetary transmission may be misleading, since various countries may have quite different transmission mechanisms, depending on their size, openness, the time period involved, the effectiveness of arbitrage, the ratio of traded to nontraded goods, and alternative expectation formation mechanisms. Therefore, as stated by Mussa:

> The monetary approach takes an eclectic view of the process of adjustment because it seems unlikely that any single model of the process of adjustment will be relevant to all countries, at all time periods, and under all institutional arrangements. The monetary approach seeks to combine a relatively general theory

> of long-run behavior with a number of different models of the process of adjustment.[31]

In this sense, the monetary approach is similar to the domestic closed economy monetarist view, which also emphasizes the complexity of the transmission process and the difficulty of its analysis and prediction. In sum, the monetary approach describes the determinants of inflation as well as suggesting various ways in which inflation is transmitted among the economies of the world. The monetary approach, therefore, can be characterized as a theory of the generation and transmission of world inflation.

THE MONETARY APPROACH IS NOT NOVEL

Although the monetary approach is unique, it is not novel. It will be shown in subsequent chapters of this volume that all of the principal building blocks of the approach have been laid down by earlier generations of economists. A primary purpose of this study is to demonstrate that the monetary approach to the balance of payments and exchange rates constitutes a return to earlier frameworks for analyzing monetary matters. In particular, it will be shown that the fundamental components of all three monetary models—the closed model, the model of the small open economy under fixed exchange rates, and the model of the small open economy under flexible exchange rates—were well recognized and articulated by earlier generations of economists. Hence, the "new" monetary approach should be viewed as being part of an evolutionary process rather than being, in any sense, revolutionary. Other economists have endorsed this interpretation. Johnson, for example, indicated that the tradition of the monetary approach "has dominated international economics for most of the two centuries during which economics has existed as a scientific system of thought."[32] The argument, however, has never been fully developed and examined.

Although the fundamental concepts of the monetary approach were well known in the nineteenth and early twentieth centuries, they apparently fell into disfavor after that. This was due, in part, to the world monetary and economic instability during the interwar period, which encouraged the development of economic models and policies for closed, segregated, compartmentalized economies. (Keynesian closed economy and later Monetarist closed economy models, for example, directed the attention of economists away from the analysis of open economies.[33]) The recent development of the monetary approach, therefore, constitutes a reemergence of these earlier views.

WHY KNOWLEDGE OF THE HISTORICAL DEVELOPMENT OF THE MONETARY APPROACH IS IMPORTANT

As mentioned above, a principal purpose of this volume is to outline the historical evolution of the monetary approach. This objective raises several questions. For example, what purpose or what value does a study of the history of economic analysis or monetary analysis serve? Why is a study of the history of monetary theory important or relevant? If we already understand the theory, of what value is the knowledge of its historical evolution?

Cogent answers to these questions are not easily stated, yet they are of crucial importance to a relatively new social science such as economics. A thorough knowledge of the evolution or history of theory is essential for several reasons. First, in economics, old mistakes seem often to be made over and over again. Several factors are responsible for this. For one thing, simple, naive, easy-to-understand views may be more readily accepted and supported than more difficult, complex theories, and, hence, the former tend to crop up repeatedly. Moreover, economists and policymakers are often subject to fads and fashions that tend to run in cycles and to respond to differing economic circumstances.[34] These factors, consequently, often lead to the recurrent appearance of discredited views. (As Johnson has recently shown, an excellent example of this phenomenon is the regular reemergence of mercantilist views related to commercial trade.)[35]

Given these recurrent mistakes, a great amount of effort and resources is often wasted in rediscovering long-established truths and in duplicating efforts.[36] Thus, a thorough knowledge of the unsuccessful erroneous theories of the past may help economists to avoid endorsing them and, hence, repeating the same errors, and to recognize that "new" innovations are frequently not new and have been argued unsuccessfully before. Similarly, as pointed out by Ekelund and Hebert, "a knowledge of past 'dead-ends' in analysis is also important in lowering the probability of error in the development of contemporary analysis."[37] These arguments have been supported by economists such as Schumpeter:

> . . . it is, I believe, the fact that most of the fundamental errors currently committed in economic analysis are due to lack of historical experience more often than to any other shortcomings of the economists' equipment.[38]

Einzig has also endorsed the same position:

> Much theoretical knowledge and practical experience acquired by our forerunners is being largely wasted by being allowed to fade into oblivion. It is rediscovered from time to time through trial and error, at the cost of mistakes which could and should have been avoided.[39]

A knowledge of what has failed in the past can, therefore, help the economist to avoid detours, blind alleys, or dead ends and, hence, may prevent the wasted resources and effort involved in the "reinvention of the wheel" every generation or so. This contention may be particularly relevant today, since the profession has placed less and less emphasis on the history or evolution of economic theory and so much more on modes of analysis that are entirely divorced from the historical underpinnings of the theory, such as mathematical modeling and econometrics.

In addition to a knowledge of what has failed in the past, a knowledge of previous successful theories is important as well. An understanding of the significance of this statement requires an appreciation for what might be labeled the evolution of economic theories. Progress within a science may be thought of as a process of the formulation and modification of theories, that is, of discarding the fallacious theories and adopting and reformulating those that have not been refuted.[40] In discussing such a process, Hayek contends that "all scientific knowledge is knowledge not of particular facts but of hypotheses which have so far withstood systematic attempts at refuting them."[41] This evolutionary view, to paraphrase Hayek, is based on the insight that the result of the experimentation of many generations of economists may embody more experience and knowledge than any one economist or group of economists possesses.[42] In other words, the fact that a seasoned theory is a product of evolution implies that it has been intellectually challenged and empirically tested, and it has withstood attempts by successive generations of economists to refute it. It is a product of many minds, many institutional arrangements, and many historical periods.[43] In short, it is time-tested and it has prevailed because it is successful. A new, unseasoned theory, on the other hand, although often considered to be "general," may apply only to a limited set of circumstances. The premises upon which the theory is constructed, for example, often reflect current conditions that are not universal. Consequently, the theory may be correct or applicable in certain periods (or to particular or institutional arrangements), but not in others.[44] As conditions change over time, the theory may well be refuted. The simplified textbook version of the Keynesian macromodel is an obvious example of such a theory.

An understanding of this complex evolutionary process of the development of theory is important to the economist because it lends to the time-tested, mature theory a degree of robustness or additional credibility not availabile in unseasoned theories. Moreover, a knowledge of the details of this evolutionary process may enable the economist to reject or accept readily "new" ideas in the literature. That is, he may be better able to judge when a "new" idea is original or whether it is a repetition of an older, disproven view. In addition, an economist who has knowledge of the historical development of theories will be less apt to be swayed by fads and accept new theories hastily, without careful, extended consideration. The benefits of studying the history of economic theory were well articulated by Haney:

> Standing at the highest point yet reached after centuries of economic thought, and looking back over the path of truth, strewn with fallacies and truisms though it be, the student feels his judgment broadened, and a well-balanced and reasonable conservatism, or a wise progressivism, may fill his mind. He is not so apt to be swept off his feet by fads, nor to be made confused and hopeless when controversies rage around him; for he knows that fads and controversies have come and gone, while so substantial a body of economic truth has been established that progress in it must come, not through revolution, but through evolution.[45]

All of the above considerations are particularly relevant to monetary theory. For "few aspects of modern economic discussion have their roots so deeply in the past as the theory of money."[46] A knowledge of the historical evolution of monetary theory and, consequently, of the monetary approach is indispensable for the monetary economist to be able to properly evaluate contemporary monetary writers, to resolve monetary controversies, to present appropriate policy prescriptions, and to avoid being "swept off his feet" by the latest monetary fads and fashions.

RATIONALE AND OUTLINE OF THE STUDY

As the monetary approach emerged, it became obvious to the present authors that the theory sounded familiar. Since we both have a strong interest in the history of thought and especially the history of monetary theory, we began investigating and rereading the writings of monetary writers of earlier generations. We were both impressed with the often virtually identical arguments of the contemporary proponents of the modern monetary approach and those of earlier writers. Although some of the "originators" of the contemporary monetary approach made casual reference to the historical underpinnings of the theory, its historical development has never been rigorously documented. Consequently, one purpose of the study is to present a more in-depth examination of the origins, historical underpinnings, and historical development or evolution of the monetary approach than has been previously presented. The present study, then, seeks to reexamine and in some cases reinterpret these earlier views and to present an interpretation of the historical evolution of modern monetary theory.

There is yet another purpose of the study. It has become obvious to the authors that in assessing and evaluating contemporary monetary problems, many modern economists either have not studied the history of their discipline or have forgotten the body of knowledge that was passed on to them by earlier generations of economists. The present authors sincerely believe that there is much in this body of knowledge that can be helpful in assessing contemporary problems. The present study, then, does not attempt to expand the theoretical frontiers of the monetary approach as much as to present earlier views in which, we believe, lie many of the answers to contemporary monetary problems.

Any study of the history of economic thought can focus on particular economists, on particular time periods and the social, political, and economic events during these periods that may have shaped the theories, or on the evolution of the ideas or theories themselves. In accordance with the above evolutionary view of economic theories, the present study is intended to be a history of ideas rather than of particular economists or of their times.[47] There are advantages to such an approach. For example, a logically consistent framework need not be constructed for each economist. (His ideas need not be presented as a whole.) Moreover, inconsistencies in a particular economist's thought can be ignored. This facilitates a smoother, continuous presentation as well as the comparison of ideas.[48] Presentations of the historical evolution of theories, however, may necessarily be repetitious at times. This is especially true when a particular theory is endorsed by generation after generation of a profession's leading thinkers.

In view of these considerations, Chapter 2 sets out a skeletal outline of the major components of the monetary approach. These major components and their historical evolution are fully developed in subsequent sections and chapters. In particular, the major frameworks in monetary theory—the closed economy, the small open economy under fixed exchange rates, and the small open economy under flexible exchange rates—are each discussed in turn. This three-framework view not only aids in describing the evolution of monetary theory, but helps to clarify some muddled interpretations of certain episodes (such as, for example, the Currency School/Banking School debate) as well as certain authors who analyzed more than one framework.

As subsequent chapters will demonstrate, each of the major frameworks in monetary theory developed somewhat differently. The closed framework, being the oldest, served as the basis from which important elements of the other models developed, and, hence, it is presented in Chapters 3 and 4. Chapters 5 and 6 describe the development of the monetary model of the small open economy under fixed exchange rates (that is, a convertible currency regime). These chapters emphasize the law of one price as well as the balance of payments adjustment mechanism of such an economy. The remainder of the study deals with the monetary model of the small open economy under flexible exchange rates (that is, an inconvertible currency regime). The development of this model has been more spasmodic than that of the other models. In part, this is because, historically, experiences of inconvertible currency regimes have often consisted of isolated, disconnected episodes rather than of a long-lasting and continuous development. Detailed analysis of devaluations is not emphasized, for two reasons. First, since, historically, devaluation had not been regarded as a viable policy option, it was not until managed international monetary arrangements such as Bretton Woods (or crawling peg systems) came into existence that analysis of devaluation and its effects became important and consequently developed. Secondly, the evolution of the theory of devaluation and its effects during the Bretton Woods period has been well elaborated elsewhere (particularly by Johnson).[49]

NOTES

1. Harry G. Johnson, "Money, Balance of Payments Theory and the International Monetary Problem," *Essays in International Finance* No. 124 (Princeton: Princeton University Press, November 1977), p. 13.

2. See, for example, Harry G. Johnson, "The Monetary Approach to Balance of Payments Theory," *Journal of Financial and Quantitative Analysis* (March 1972):1555, and Mordechai Kreinin and Lawrence Officer, "The Monetary Approach to the Balance of Payments: A Survey," *Princeton Studies in International Finance* No. 43 (Princeton: Princeton University Press, 1978), p. 33.

3. Ibid., p. 32.

4. Ibid., p. 33.

5. Johnson, "Money, Balance of Payments Theory," p. 13.

6. See, for example, ibid.; Harry G. Johnson, "Elasticity, Absorption, Keynesian Multiplier, Keynesian Policy, and Monetary Approaches to Devaluation Theory: A Simple Geometric Exposition," *American Economic Review* (June 1976); Harry G. Johnson, "The Monetary Approach to Balance of Payments Theory and Policy: Explanation and Policy Implications," *Economica* (August 1977); and Harry G. Johnson, "The Monetary Approach to the Balance of Payments: A Nontechnical Guide," *Journal of International Economics* 7 (1977).

7. Ibid.

8. Johnson, "Monetary Approach to Balance of Payments Theory," pp. 1555–6.

9. Ibid.

10. Harry G. Johnson, *Inflation and the Monetarist Controversy* (Amsterdam: North-Holland, 1972), p. 84.

11. Jacob Frenkel and Harry G. Johnson, "The Monetary Theory of Balance of Payments Policies," in *The Monetary Approach to the Balance of Payments* ed. Jacob Frenkel and Harry G. Johnson (Toronto: University of Toronto Press, 1976) p. 262

12. Marina von Neumann Whitman, "Global Monetarism and the Monetary Approach to the Balance of Payments," *Brookings Papers on Economic Activity* 3 (1975):505. See also Jacob Frenkel and Harry G. Johnson, "The Monetary Approach to the Balance of Payments: Essential Concepts and Historical Origins." Frenkel and Johnson, op cit., p. 37, where they indicate that "an excess supply of money should be reflected in all of the other accounts of the balance of payments."

13. Whitman, op. cit., p. 505. Whitman also asserts that the monetary approach to the balance of payments "regards the relationship between the stock demand for and supply of money as the critical determinant of the balance of payments," ibid., p. 514. Elsewhere, Mussa has argued that "the effects of a tariff on the balance of payments cannot be analyzed except in an explicitly monetary model," Michael Mussa, "A Monetary Approach to Balance of Payments Analysis," *Journal of Money, Credit, and Banking* (August 1974): 334.

14. Mussa, op. cit., p. 335. A similar view of the balance of payments is taken by Harry G. Johnson: "The balance of payments is a monetary phenomenon . . . and can only be understood by the application of monetary theory." Harry G. Johnson, "Money and the Balance of Payments," *Banca Nazionale del Lavoro Quarterly Review* (March 1976):3. See also Johnson, *Inflation and Monetarist Controversy*, p. 84. Other economists have noted that without money, there would not be a balance of payments.

15. See, for example, Kreinin and Officer, op cit., p. 21 and Whitman, op. cit., p. 499.

16. Rudiger Dornbusch, "Devaluation, Money, and Nontraded Goods," in Frenkel and Johnson, op. cit., p. 185.

17. Rudiger Dornbusch, "Monetary Policy under Exchange Rate Flexibility," *NBER Working Paper Series*, Working Paper No. 311 (January 1979), p. 8. See also, for example, John Bilson, "Recent Developments in Monetary Models of Exchange Rate Determination." *IMF Staff Papers* 26 (June 1979):203, and Herbert Grubel, "International Monetarism and the Explanation of World Inflation," *Weltwirtschaftliches Archiv* 114 (1978):180–81.

18. Don Patinkin, *Money, Interest, and Prices* (New York: Harper & Row, 1965).

19. Other contemporary models of devaluation such as the elasticity approach are real models and not monetary models. See, for example, Johnson, *Inflation and Monetarist Controversy*, p. 82.

20. Johnson, "Monetary Approach to Balance of Payments Theory," p. 1570. Elsewhere, Johnson stated similarly: ". . . The effect of devaluation is transitory, working through the restoration of the public's actual to its desired real balances with the impact of an excess demand for money in producing a surplus on the current or capital accounts, or both on the balance of payments. . . ." In Johnson, *Inflation and Monetarist Controversy*, p. 91.

21. Johnson, for example, strongly expresses this view: ". . . devaluation [in the small open economy] is strictly equivalent to a reduction in the domestic real balances, and revaluation to an increase in domestic real balances; and the effect will be in the one case trade and balance of payments surpluses and in the other deficits, in each case the difference between income and consumption and the overall imbalance of the balance of payments dwindling asymptotically towards zero as equilibrium between actual and desired real balances is restored." In Harry G. Johnson, "The Monetary Approach to Balance of Payments Theory: A Diagrammatic Analysis," *The Manchester School* (September 1975):227.

22. Grubel, for example, voices this interpretation: "In International economics there had been an analytical development equivalent to Patinkin's demonstration of the importance of the real-balance effect [p. 177]. . . . At the purely theoretical level, the monetary approach to the balance of payments may be interpreted as filling the gap which had existed because the role of the real-balance effect had never been made explicit theoretically, as it had been in Patinkin's and other domestic models in the monetarist tradition [p. 182]." In Grubel, op. cit., pp. 177, 182.

23. The proposition of monetary neutrality contends that real variables are invariant to monetary disturbances.

24. See, for example, Grubel, op. cit., p. 178.

25. This statement is better known as the homogeneity postulate. This postulate indicates that commodity excess demand functions are homogeneous of degree zero in money prices, which implies that real demands depend on relative prices but not money prices. Since a change in the money supply is believed to cause all prices to change in proportion, it will not affect real variables.

26. This case could be made more complicated with the addition of nontradables. Although the adjustments would be more complicated, the ultimate results remain the same (see below).

27. See, for example, Lance Girton and Don Roper. "The Evolution of Exchange Rate Policy," in *The Monetary Approach to International Adjustment*,

ed. Putnam and Wilford (New York: Praeger, 1978), p. 223, and Dornbusch, "Monetary Policy under Exchange Rate Flexibility," p. 3.

28. Robert Mundell, "General Discussion: What Have We Learned? What Are the Fundamental Conflicts of Opinion?" *Scandinavian Journal of Economics* 78 (1976):398.

29. Rudiger Dornbusch, "Alternative Price Stabilization Rules and the Effects of Exchange Rate Changes," *The Manchester School of Economic and Social Studies*, No. 3 (September 1975):275. See also Jacob Frenkel and Carlos A. Rodriguez, "Portfolio Equilibrium and the Balance of Payments: A Monetary Approach," *American Economic Review* (September 1975):685.

30. Grubel, op. cit., p. 182.

31. Mussa, op. cit., p. 338.

32. Harry G. Johnson, "Money, Balance of Payments Theory and the International Monetary Problem," *Essays in International Finance* No. 124 (Princeton: Princeton University Press, 1977):3. See also Frenkel and Johnson, "The Monetary Approach to the Balance of Payments: Essential Concepts and Historical Origins."

33. See, for example, Johnson, *Inflation and Monetarist Controversy*, p. 76, where Johnson states that "The development of monetary theory since the 1930's, and more specifically since the Keynesian revolution, has tended to focus professional and policy attention on the unique circumstances of individual countries, to the neglect of the international monetary system as an integrated unit."

34. See, for example, F. A. Hayek, *The Constitution of Liberty*, (Chicago: University of Chicago Press, 1960), p. 404.

35. Harry G. Johnson, "Mercantilism: Past, Present, and Future," *The Manchester School* (March 1974).

36. See, for example, C. Iverson, *Aspects of the Theories of International Capital Movements* (London: Oxford University Press, 1935), p. 259. Schumpeter expressed a similar view when he stated that "We learn what succeeds and how and why from a study of the past. Of course, we do learn from the past but mostly when it is too late, and this seems to be inevitable in economics. There are many cases of duplicated effort in our history." In D. N. Winch, "What Price the History of Economic Thought," *Scottish Journal of Political Economy* (November 1962):197.

37. Robert B. Ekelund, Jr., and Robert F. Hebert, *A History of Economic Theory and Method* (New York: McGraw-Hill, 1975), p. 11. Furthermore, Ekelund and Hebert point out that because of an awareness of previous "dead ends," positive avenues of research are often suggested by the economist familiar with the historical development of theory.

38. J. A. Schumpeter, *The History of Economic Analysis* (New York: Oxford University Press, 1954), p. 13.

39. Paul Einzig, *The History of Foreign Exchange* (London: Macmillan, 1979), p. 4.

40. Schumpeter refers to a similar process, "The Filiation of Scientific Ideas—the process by which men's efforts to understand economic phenomena produce, improve, and pull down analytic structures in an unending sequence." In Schumpeter, op. cit., p. 6.

41. F. A. Hayek, *Law, Legislation, and Liberty, Volume I: Rules and Order* (Chicago: University of Chicago Press, 1973), p. 17.

42. Hayek, *Constitution of Liberty*, p. 62.

43. See Schumpeter, op. cit., p. 4.

44. See, for example, Einzig, op. cit., p. 3, where he contends that the student of economics who is unfamiliar with the history of his discipline "may be inclined to regard his conclusions as being founded on immutable economic laws and is oblivious of the possibility that [economic variables] may obey to some extent a different set of laws amidst totally different circumstances or against a totally different institutional background."

45. Lewis H. Haney, *History of Economic Thought* (New York: Macmillan, 1949), pp. 6, 7.

46. Arthur Eli Moore, *Monetary Theory Before Adam Smith* (New York: Augustus M. Kelley, 1966), p. vii.

47. Ibid., p. vii.

48. Ibid., p. vii.

49. See note 32 above.

2

THE MAJOR COMPONENTS OF THE MONETARY APPROACH: A SKELETAL OUTLINE

INTRODUCTION

As indicated above, the monetary approach to the balance of payments and exchange rates can be characterized as a framework for analyzing open economies within a larger closed world economy. That is, this approach views the world aggregate as a closed system of smaller, integrated open economies. Elaborations of the monetary approach have established that different models must be employed in analyzing the small open economy as distinct from the larger, closed aggregate. Moreover, different exchange rate regimes call for the use of alternative frameworks for examining individual small open economies. Thus, in examining monetary aspects of various economies, the monetary approach indicates that three fundamental cases exist that must be clearly distinguished from one another: namely, the closed economy, the small open economy under fixed exchange rates, and the small open economy under flexible exchange rates.

In this chapter, these three fundamental monetary models will be briefly outlined in skeletal form.[1] Hence, the models presented here will constitute the ground upon which more elaborate discussions of the models, as well as their historical evolution, will be made in subsequent chapters. The three models presented here constitute pure-form cases that are, admittedly, oversimplified. That is, complicating factors such as the existence of "impure" exchange rate systems (managed "dirty float" or "crawling peg" systems), as well as the existence of nontraded goods in open economies, tend to make real world circumstances more complex. The fundamental principles set out here, however, are not invalidated by these complicating factors. Consequently, by presenting these admittedly oversimplified cases, the basic ideas of the monetary approach can be well understood, and the groundwork for more complex and elaborate discussions can be established.

In outlining these three models, emphasis will be placed on (a) setting out the alternative mechanisms by which discrepancies between actual and desired real money balances are ultimately eliminated and equilibrium restored (that is, real balance adjustments to monetary disturbances will be analyzed), (b) examining the causal relationship between money and prices, and (c) demonstrating the neutrality of monetary disturbances. These aspects of the monetary approach are stressed because they are the key ingredients (essentials) of that approach.

THE CLOSED WORLD ECONOMY

Since both monetarist and Keynesian economists have extensively studied theories of the closed economy in the post–World-War-II period, the analysis of monetary disturbances in the closed economy is well known to most economists. Advocates of the monetary approach contend that since the world is the only truly closed economy, the theory of the closed economy is directly applicable to it but not to its component parts (which are all, to some extent, open economies). Moreover, since the world is the only truly closed economy, it can be analyzed as an economy in which all goods are nontraded (that is, domestically produced and consumed). Hence, the types of adjustments to monetary disturbances that are made in the closed economy are related to those made in the nontraded sectors of open economies, which will be discussed below.

In the case of monetary disturbances in the closed economy, the familiar propositions of the conventional monetarist (and Patinkin) position hold.[2] That is, any (exogenous) increase in the nominal money stock such that actual money balances exceed desired money balances causes households and businesses to increase their rate of spending by exchanging money for goods and securities.[3] Although some *temporary* real output gains may immediately follow, in the long run, growth in real output is determined by real (that is, nonmonetary) economic variables such as growth in technology and factors of production and, hence, is independent of the money stock. Consequently, in the long run, this increased spending will cause prices of all commodities to increase proportionately.[4] Thus, as emphasized by Patinkin, "The causal relationship between money and prices is not at all a mechanical one, but is instead the economic consequence of the prior effect of changes in the quantity of money on the demand for commodities."[5] These price increases occur in the closed economy because there are no external sources of supply to accommodate these increased demands (as in the open economy under fixed exchanges), and, consequently, supply or capacity constraints eventually become binding. In the long run, once all adjustments have been completed, relative prices and, consequently, real economic activity remain unchanged; only the price level has been permanently altered. That is, monetary disturbances of this type are neutral in their effect on real economic variables in the closed economy.[6] In the case of monetary expansion in the closed economy, then, this price level increase serves to deflate actual real money balances and, consequently, works to equate actual real money balances with desired real money balances as required for the attainment of monetary equilibrium.

Similar arguments apply when the money stock falls short of desired money holdings. In this case, households and businesses are induced by the shortage of desired cash balances to accumulate money balances by exchanging (supplying) goods and services for money. The resulting fall in spending and hence in the price level serves to increase actual real money balances and, consequently, works to equate actual and desired real money balances. It should be noted that, as these examples indicate, real monetary balances are endogenous and determined by the public, even though nominal money balances may be controlled by the monetary authority.

In the case of the closed economy, then, movements in the general price level serve as the adjustment mechanism that equates actual and desired money balances. That is, the price level clears the market for real money balances and, moreover, is considered to be an endogenous or passive element in this closed economy formulation.[7] Thus, the quantity theory of money—in the sense of causality running from the (exogenous) stock of money to prices—applies in the case of the closed economy. Since advocates of the monetary approach contend that the only purely closed economy is the world economy, they maintain that the quantity theory of money applies to the world economy. In the world economy, therefore, *world inflation is caused by excessive world monetary growth.*

THE SMALL OPEN ECONOMY UNDER FIXED EXCHANGE RATES

Before discussing various monetary aspects of the integrated small open economy under fixed exchange rates, a discussion of some basic assumptions of this framework is in order. In examining this case, it will be assumed initially that all goods are tradable (that is, produced or consumed in international markets) and that a fully integrated world economy exists. The assumption that all goods are tradable will be subsequently relaxed with the incorporation of nontraded goods into the analysis. Secondly, in discussing the integrated small open economy, it is normally assumed that such economies are a relatively small proportion of the world aggregate of which they are a part. In particular, the small open economy is usually assumed to constitute such a small proportion of the total world market for goods and securities that any alteration in its supplies or demands for goods (or credit) has no effect on world market prices or world interest rates. That is, the small open economy is too small in both production or consumption to influence either interest rates or prices; it is dominated by world commodity and capital markets. In the vernacular of economic analysis, the small open economy is a price taker in world markets.

Third, prices of traded commodities are assumed to be equalized the world over by the working of commodity arbitrage. That is, any discrepancy between prices (and in rates of price change) of a homogeneous good in different countries or locations is assumed to be quickly removed by the operation of arbitrage. For example, if the market for a particular commodity in one country yields prices that are momentarily too high relative to world prices of that commodity, prices in that particular country will be quickly driven back to the world level by an inflow of those commodities matched by an outflow of other commodities, assets, or money.[8] Hence, prices of tradable goods cannot differ by more than the sum total of freight, insurance, and customs duties. If prices were not equalized in this sense, arbitragers would make virtually unlimited profits by purchasing goods in one location and selling them in another. This equalization of prices (and rates of price change) across countries has been referred to as the "law of one price." It states that different units of the same goods cannot be sold at different prices when denominated in the same currency. The law also applies to interest rates across countries. It implies that price movements are transmitted or propagated geographically by the operation of commodity arbitrage.

The important implication of these three assumptions (tradable goods, smallness, and the law of one price) for the small open economy under fixed exchange rates is that prices, interest rates, and inflation are determined in world markets and, hence, given exogenously to the small open economy. Under such conditions, the small open economy is a price taker in the world marketplace. Single country inflation is impossible, and inflation can only be imported. In these circumstances, therefore, inflation is clearly a world problem.

Before analyzing monetary adjustments for the small open economy under fixed exchange rates, one additional assumption should be mentioned. Specifically, growth in real income is considered to be determined by real factors such as growth in technology and factors of production and, hence, independent of the money stock. This assumption, together with those mentioned above, implies that in the case of the small open economy under fixed exchange rates (and unlike the case of the closed economy), all of the principal arguments in the demand for money function (prices, interest rates, and income) are considered to be exogenous.

These observations have major implications for the analysis of monetary aspects of such a small open economy. In particular, both adjustments to monetary disturbances and causal relationships between money and prices are quite different in the case of the small open economy under fixed exchange rates from that in the closed economy case. Specifically, in the fixed-rate small open economy an increase in the nominal money stock such that actual money balances exceed desired money balances causes households and businesses to increase their rate of spending, just as in the closed economy. However, this increased spending cannot alter prices, interest rates, or real income, since, as indicated above, these are all exogenous to the small open economy under fixed exchange rates. Instead of affecting these variables, increased spending in the open economy leads to increased purchases of foreign commodities (or securities). That is, the public can export excess nominal money stocks through the balance of payments in exchange for goods and securities; that is, the excess money stock "leaks out" through a balance of payments deficit. This "leakage" or reduction in actual money balances continues until actual and desired money balances are equated (that is, by importing or exporting money in exchange for goods and securities, each nation uses the mechanism of the balance of payments to bring actual money balances into line with desired money balances). In short, therefore, an increase in actual (over desired) money balances creates a balance of payments deficit, which itself causes the excess (actual) supply of money to contract as these excess balances are traded for foreign goods or securities.[9] This contraction of actual money balances (and balance of payments deficit) will continue until actual and desired money balances are equated and a sufficient redistribution of the world's money reestablishes an equality of expenditure and income.[10] Hence, an excessive quantity of money cannot persist in a single small open economy under fixed exchange rates, since any such excess sets into motion corrective mechanisms that eventually cause this same nominal money increase to reverse itself so as to restore monetary equilibrium.[11,12] In this case, then, actual real money balances are equated to desired real money balances by nominal money flows through the balance of payments rather than by the price level changes that serve as the adjustment mechanism in the case of the closed economy.

There are important implications of this formulation that deserve mention. First, assuming the absence of monetary contraction abroad, persistent balance of payments deficits in any small open economy under fixed exchange rates are a symptom of excessive growth in its money supply. Such deficits can be eliminated with an appropriate slowing in that growth rate (or in an actual money supply contraction).

Secondly, since one-time increases in the money supply of any single small open economy under fixed exchange rates soon reverse themselves by being drained out through the balance of payments and since all relative prices are determined in world markets, and consequently are unaffected by single country monetary disturbances, changes in the money supply in this case do not affect real variables and therefore are neutral in the long run. Neutrality, then, holds in the case of the small open economy under fixed exchange rates as well as in the closed economy.

Another implication of this framework is that the demand for money is exogenous, since all of its arguments are exogenous. Moreover, the fact that actual money balances can be freely imported or exported like any other commodity implies that the supply of money is passive (or endogenous). That is, the supply of money quickly adjusts to exogenous changes in real income, world prices, or world interest rates and, hence, to the demand for money via the balance of payments as the public adjusts its expenditures and receipts. Thus, in an open economy under fixed exchange rates, "The public can and does determine the total stock of money through its ability to convert domestic money into goods and securities in the international markets."[13] The central bank or monetary authority, on the other hand, has no central control over the nominal stock of money in the small open economy as long as exchange rates remain fixed. The quantity of money in this case, then, is determined by demand and not supply.[14] And the distribution of world money across nations is determined by relative national money demands and, hence, is proportional to relative national income levels. In other words, the balance of payments is the allocation mechanism that serves to distribute a given amount of world money across nations consistent with the requirements of monetary equilibrium in each country. This formulation is in sharp contrast with the case of the closed economy, where the demand for money adjusts to an exogenously determined money supply. The upshot of these considerations is that the quantity of money in any single small open economy under fixed exchange rates is a *dependent* variable, a conclusion that is often forgotten by many contemporary economists who are trained to think in terms of closed economy models.

Fourth, because prices are given exogenously to the small open economy under fixed exchange rates and because the supply of money adjusts (via the balance of payments) to changes in the demand for money (and its determinants), causal relationships between money and prices in this case are quite different from those in the closed economy. In particular, changes in money cannot affect prices (or real income) because those variables are exogeneous. Hence, causality cannot run from money to prices, as in the closed economy. Instead, causality runs in the opposite direction. That is, nominal money balances adjust via the balance of payments to exogenous changes in world prices (and exogenous changes in real income) in order to accommodate the demand for money. Thus, money serves to accommodate (validate) or support inflation rather than to cause it in this case. Consequently, the direction of causality between money and prices (or money and nominal income) tends to be from prices to money (or from income to money), that is, the reverse of that in the closed economy. In this case, then, the quantity theory of money (in the sense described above) does not apply. This point is well recognized by McCloskey and Zecher, who state that:

> The quantity theory, in the sense of a theory arguing that changes in the money supply cause prices . . . and incomes to change, may well apply to the world economy . . . as a whole, but for individual countries, the monetary theory [of the balance of payments] turns the quantity theory on its head: prices . . . and incomes determine national supplies of money rather than the other way around.[15]

Thus, the case of the small open economy under fixed exchange rates provides theoretical support for the so-called reverse causation hypothesis.[16]

When nontradables (that is, those commodities that are too perishable, bulky, or otherwise expensive to trade profitably over space) are added to this framework, the adjustment process becomes somewhat more complicated. Nonetheless, the long-run conclusions set out above are not invalidated by this extension of the model. In the long run, for example, it is assumed that enough intercommodity substitution in production and consumption exists between tradables and nontradables so as to make nontradable prices move in line with the prices of tradables. That is, "competitive labor and domestic goods markets bring the inflation rates of wages and nontradable goods prices into alignment with . . . the world rate of inflation."[17] In short, prices of nontraded goods are kept within bounds by their ultimate (long-run) degree of substitutability in production and consumption with tradable goods. Consequently, the contentions of the traded goods formulation discussed above still tend to apply, at least as a first approximation, when nontraded goods are incorporated into the analysis.

THE SMALL OPEN ECONOMY UNDER FLEXIBLE EXCHANGE RATES

The case of the small open economy under flexible exchange rates (the monetary approach to exchange rates) may be viewed as a dual relationship to or an exact counterpart of the case of the small open economy under fixed exchange rates (the monetary approach to the balance of payments).[18,19] That is, money plays an important role in the determination of exchange rates under this approach, just as it is important in determining the balance of payments in the case of the small open economy under fixed exchange rates. In the monetary approach to exchange rates, an exchange rate is viewed as the relative price of two monies. An equilibrium exchange rate is attained when the outstanding stocks of the two money supplies are willingly held. Consequently, under the monetary approach, exchange rates and their determinants are analyzed in terms of the supply and demand for these monies.[20] That is, just as in the case of the small open economy under fixed exchange rates, the demand for and supply of money constitute the central theoretical relationship around which to organize analysis and discussion of exchange rates. Thus, a method of analysis analogous to that of the fixed exchange rate case is employed when examining adjustments to monetary disturbances in the case of the small open economy under flexible exchange rates. In spite of this similar method of analysis, however, the specific adjustments to monetary disturbances are quite different for the flexible exchange rate case and for the case of fixed exchange rates. Moreover, in the flexible rate case, alternative versions of the adjustment process exist in the literature.

For example, one version of this case assumes that all goods are traded and that arbitrage is so efficient that adjustments are instantaneous and price differences are never observed for homogeneous goods (ignoring transportation costs, tariffs, and so forth).[21,22] This version contends that an increase in the nominal money stock of a single small open economy, such that actual money balances exceed desired money balances, causes households and businesses to increase their rate of spending. This spending increase is concentrated on imported traded goods. Under these conditions (with the assumptions cited above), the prices of these traded goods cannot increase until the exchange rate has depreciated. With this concentration of spending on imported traded goods, an excess demand for foreign currency and a corresponding excess supply of domestic money appear in the foreign exchange markets. This induces the exchange rate on domestic money to depreciate, which, in turn, causes all prices and hence, the price level to increase. Thus, the chronological order or time sequence of adjustment is from changes in money to changes in the exchange rate to changes in prices. Exchange rates in this version are viewed as being directly determined by relative money stocks, and exchange rate movements are interpreted as an adjustment mechanism serving to offset differing monetary growth rates.

In another version (associated with the purchasing power parity doctrine), an increase in the domestic money supply induces individuals and businesses to increase their spending on commodities located in the domestic economy. That is, the excess money stock remains at home to induce an equiproportionate rise in the domestic price level. This domestic price level increase makes foreign commodities more attractive and, hence, induces an exchange rate depreciation as expenditures switch to imports and consequently increase the excess demand for foreign currencies. In this version, then, the chronological order or time sequence of adjustment is from changes in money to changes in prices to changes in the exchange rate. Exchange rates adjust subsequent to adjustments in the price level in this version because of differing underlying assumptions. In particular, arbitrage is not instantaneous, and/or there are nontraded goods. The exchange rate in this version is viewed as being determined by relative price levels, and changes in the exchange rate are seen as an adjustment mechanism that serves to equalize price levels or maintain purchasing power parities of the relevant currencies. That is, "exchange rate changes are interpreted as a mechanism by which pressures resulting from different rates of inflation among countries are relieved."[23]

In a third version, exchange rates and inflation are simultaneously determined. In all of these versions, both exchange rate changes and price level changes are caused by changes in the money supply. That is, whatever the causal mechanism between exchange rates and prices, all advocates of the monetary approach agree that causation runs from money to exchange rates and from money to prices.[24] In other words, both prices and the exchange rate are unanimously recognized as endogenous variables determined by the exogenous relative stocks of money. Moreover, proponents of the monetary approach all agree that both changes in exchange rates and changes in prices are part of a complex adjustment process, whereby actual real money balances are equated to desired real money balances. For example, in the case of a monetary expansion such that actual real money balances exceed desired real money balances, both exchange rate changes and price changes serve as part of an adjustment mechanism that equates actual and desired real money balances. This mechanism works by the exchange depreciation/price level increase deflating the value of actual real money balances. Thus, the exchange rate depreciation/price level increase is part of a real balance effect that works to remove discrepancies between actual and desired real money balances. According to the monetary approach, this exchange depreciation/price level increase is equivalent to domestic monetary contraction in that both bring about temporary real balance effects that operate to bring desired real money balances into equality with actual real money balances. Note that the specific adjustments to monetary disturbances in the case of the small open economy under flexible exchange rates differ markedly from those in the case of fixed exchange rates. In the latter, equilibrium is restored via quantity adjustments, namely, international flows of money. In the former, however, equilibrium is restored by price adjustments, namely, changes in the domestic price level. Nonetheless, both adjustments entail or involve real balance effects, and, in this sense, the monetary approach can be viewed as an extension of the real balance effect to the open economy.

There are several important implications of this model of the small open economy under flexible exchange rates that merit attention. First, according to this view, sustained depreciation of a currency is a symptom of excessive monetary growth, just as are persistent balance of payments deficits under a fixed-rate regime. That is, although short-run and temporary exchange rate fluctuations may result from nonmonetary disturbances, long-run and sustained currency depreciation is viewed as the result of excessive monetary growth.

Secondly, the adjustment mechanism described above serves to equalize foreign and home country general price levels measured in terms of a common currency unit in the long run. That is, a representative bundle of goods will cost the same everywhere measured in terms of either currency. Since the value of money is simply the inverse of the general price level, another way of saying the same thing is to say that the above mechanism works to equalize the value of money or to maintain its purchasing power parity. If this were not the case, goods would be cheaper in one country relative to the other. Consequently, individuals and businesses would be induced to buy in the low-price country and sell in the high-price country. The resulting excess demand for the currency of the low price country and the corresponding excess supply of the currency in the high-price country would force the exchange rate into purchasing power parity equilibrium, thereby eliminating the price disparity (and, hence, the discrepancy between the values of the two monies).[25]

A third implication of this formulation is that monetary disturbances (such as an increase in the money supply) in the small open economy under flexible exchange rates are neutral. That is, for example, any exogenous increase in the money supply results in an equiproportionate change in the (nominal) exchange rate as well as in the price level. These equiproportionate changes leave all real (exchange-rate-adjusted) relative prices unaltered, including the terms of trade.[26] Consequently, in the long run, there are no changes in the value of all real quantities (real economic magnitudes), including real output, exports, imports, and the trade balance. In short, all real variables are unaffected by such monetary disturbances. The real value of money balances is also one of these real magnitudes that is unaffected. After all, it is these proportional price level/exchange rate changes that alter the value of actual real money balances and bring it back into equality with desired real money balances. Since this adjustment involves both the price level and the exchange rate, the relative prices of traded and nontraded goods also remain unaffected by such monetary disturbances. Neutrality, with respect to monetary disturbances, then, applies to the small open economy under flexible exchange rates as well as to both the closed economy and the small open economy under fixed exchange rates. This is the reason why purchasing power parity is viewed as a theory of neutrality.

Another implication of this framework is that the nominal stock of money is inconvertible, under the control of the monetary authority, and, hence, exogenously determined. Therefore, in this model the price level and exchange rate are endogenous elements that serve to clear the market for money balances. Consequently, the demand for money is endogenous (as in the closed economy), since price level/exchange rate movements cause money demand to adapt to the exogenously determined supply of money. The quantity of money in this case is determined by supply rather than demand, and, hence, it can be interpreted as an independent variable (as in the closed economy case). Under these conditions, inflation rates can differ among countries and are largely under the control of the monetary authorities. As a result, a certain degree of insulation from monetary disturbances originating abroad is possible under a flexible exchange rate regime.[27] A corollary to this, however, is that, under flexible exchange rates, a country must suffer the consequences of its inflationary policies, since it cannot export its inflation abroad.

A final implication of the model described above is that the quantity theory of money (in the sense of causality described above) applies to the case of the small open economy under flexible exchange rates, since changes in money will precede changes in the price level. That is, whatever the causal mechanism between exchange rates and prices, all proponents of the monetary approach concur that in this case causation runs from money to prices. Hence, the monetary approach to exchange rates constitutes an extension of the quantity theory of money to the open economy.[28]

CONCLUSION

This chapter has outlined in skeletal form the fundamental monetary frameworks of the monetary approach. In particular, it has been established that the monetary approach extends the notion of the real balance effect, as well as the concept of monetary neutrality, to the open economy under both fixed and flexible exchange rate regimes. Moreover, although real money balances are controlled by the public in all three cases, the specific adjustments made by the public in equating actual to desired real money balances differ. As a consequence of these differing adjustment mechanisms, causal relationships between money and prices also differ in the various frameworks. This brief discussion of the monetary approach lays the groundwork for more elaborate analyses of these models, as well as of their historical evolution, in subsequent chapters.

NOTES

1. More elaborate discussions of the models have been presented elsewhere. See, for example, essays in Jacob Frenkel and Harry G. Johnson (eds.), *The Monetary Approach to the Balance of Payments* (Toronto: University of Toronto Press, 1976), Jacob Frankel and Harry G. Johnson (eds.) *The Economics of Exchange Rates, Selected Studies* (Reading: Addison-Wesley, 1978), and International Monetary Fund, *The Monetary Approach to the Balance of Payments* (Washington: International Monetary Fund, 1977).

2. See, for example, Don Patinkin, *Money, Interest, and Prices* (second ed.,) (New York: Harper & Row, 1965).

3. In describing the case of the closed economy, we will assume exogenous changes in money. The question of whether this assumption is a valid one will be discussed in Chapter 3.

4. The so-called proportionality postulate of the quantity theory of money refers to the contention (of the strict classical version of that theory) that prices will vary in exact proportion as changes in the quantity of money. That is, a given percentage change in the stock of money will result in an identical percentage change in commodity prices. As Humphrey has indicated, "this proposition follows from the assumption that people want to hold for transactions purposes a constant quantity of real (price deflated) cash balances at the economy's full-capacity level of real output. It should be noted that the proportionality postulate implies that the demand for real cash balances and its counterpart, the circulation velocity of money, are completely stable." Thomas Humphrey, "The Quantity Theory of Money: Its Historical Evolution and Role in Policy Debates," *Economic Review* (May/June 1974).

5. Patinkin, op. cit., p. 164.

6. The concept of monetary neutrality is normally described as the proposition that, in the long run, real magnitudes and relative prices, including interest rates, are not permanently influenced by monetary disturbances such as an increase in the money supply. A related issue is the so-called homogeneity postulate. This postulate indicates that commodity demand functions are "homogeneous of degree zero in money prices." That is, if you double all money prices, the equilibrium quantities demanded of commodities are not changed. In other words, real demands do not depend upon nominal (or money) prices but only on relative prices. These various qualities of money (proportionality and neutrality) are characteristics which distinguish it from all other commodities. See, for example, F. W. Taussig, *Principles of Economics* 1 (New York: Macmillan, 1911), p. 236.

7. Although the price level is considered to be the passive element in this closed economy view, this does not imply that it is determined *only* by the money supply. Rather, it is a function of both the money supply and real money demand.

8. Donald McCloskey and J. Richard Zecher, "How the Gold Standard Worked, 1880–1913," paper presented at the annual Cliometrics Conference, University of Wisconsin, April 27, 1973, p. 14.

9. If international reserves are traded for foreign goods, the outflow of these reserves will effect a contraction of the nominal money stock to its equilibrium level.

10. As Aghevli and Khan indicate, "In the framework of the monetary approach, the balance of payments position of a country is considered a reflection of decisions on the part of its residents to accumulate or run down their stock of money balances. It is this process of adjustment to the desired stock of money balances that results in balance of payments deficits and surpluses." Bijan B. Aghevli and Mohsin S. Khan, "The Monetary Approach to the Balance of Payments Determination: An Empirical Test," paper presented at the American Economic Association convention, San Francisco, December 1974, pp. 1–10, as quoted in D. Sykes Wilford, *Monetary Policy and the Open Economy: Mexico's Experience* (New York: Praeger, 1977), p. 10.

11. This observation—that an excessive quantity of money cannot persist in a single small open economy—has led some economists to maintain that it makes little sense to talk of an "exogenous" change in money, since this is not possible in a framework where the quantity of money is a dependent and endogenous variable and not an independent exogenous variable. See, for example, Lance Girton and Don Roper, "J. Laurence Laughlin and the Quantity Theory of Money," *Journal of Political Economy* 86 (August 1978).

12. Similar arguments hold for decreases in the nominal money stock. That is, if a country's actual money stock is smaller than its desired money stock, households and businesses will decrease their spending in an effort to replenish their actual money balances. Resources will be released for the export trade, thus generating a balance of payments surplus. That is, goods will be exported and money imported until the gap between actual and desired money balances is eliminated.

13. Jacob Frenkel and Harry G. Johnson, "The Monetary Approach to the Balance of Payments: Essential Concepts and Historical Origins," in Frenkel and Johnson, *The Monetary Approach*, p. 23.

14. These arguments were well stated by Johnson: ". . . in an open economy the money supply is in the long run endogenous and not exogenous, because the public can import or export nominal money through the balance of payments and so adjust the money supply to what it wants to hold, by a mechanism alternative to the classical quantity theory's adjustment of actual to desired real balances through movements of the price level in face of a policy determined nominal stock of money. . . . On the assumptions of the model, the public can adjust the nominal supply of money to what it wants by exporting or importing money through the balance of payments. This is in contrast to the theory of money in a closed economy, in which the monetary authority controls the nominal quantity of money and the public adjusts its real balances to what it wants through spending behavior affecting the price level." In Harry G. Johnson, *Inflation and the Monetarist Controversy*, (Amsterdam: North-Holland, 1972), pp. 47, 89.

15. McCloskey and Zecher, op. cit., p. 7.

16. This contention was well stated by Jonson: "In pointing out that the domestic money supply of an open economy which maintains fixed exchange rates is adjusted to demand through the balance of payments, this . . . casts doubt on the findings of Friedman and Meisselman–type tests for open economies. In

effect, the monetary approach to the balance of payments presents a powerful reason why reverse causation is likely to be particularly important." In P. D. Jonson, "Money and Economic Activity in the Open Economy: The United Kingdom, 1880-1970," *Journal of Political Economy* 84 (October 1976):981.

17. Michael Parkin, "A 'Monetarist' Analysis of the Generation and Transmission of World Inflation: 1958-1971," *American Economic Review* 67 (February 1977):168.

18. See, for example, Jacob A. Frenkel, "A Monetary Approach to the Exchange Rate: Doctrinal Aspects and Empirical Evidence," *The Scandinavian Journal of Economics* 78 (1976):200.

19. Until recently, the experience of both the closed world economy and the small open economy under fixed exchange rates has not been associated with periods of serious inflation. Episodes of serious inflation, however, have been associated with flexible exchange rate regimes. Consequently, expectations of inflation and theories of inflationary expectations have played a more prevalent role in the development of the monetary approach to exchange rates than in either of the other two models. Discussions of this aspect of the monetary approach to exchange rates will not be made in this chapter but will be examined in Part III of this volume.

20. See, for example, Frenkel, "Monetary Approach to Exchange Rate," p. 201.

21. In this case, arbitrage is assumed to be so rapid that the law of one price holds continuously. That is, homogeneous traded goods cannot be sold at different prices when denominated in the same currency (ignoring transportation cost, tariffs, etc.).

22. Another assumption that is sometimes made in conjunction with this version is that expectations in exchange markets are formed rationally. See Part III of this volume for a discussion of expectations and models of their formation in foreign exchange markets.

23. Donald S. Kemp and D. Sykes Wilford, "Exchange Rates and the Balance of Payments in Latin America," *Business Economics*, 14 (September 1979):31.

24. The question as to whether causality runs from exchange rates to prices or vice versa in the small open economy under flexible exchange rates cannot be adequately resolved. This is because both changes in exchange rates and changes in prices are part of the same general response to an increase in the supply of money. That is, in the final analysis both prices and the exchange rates are endogenous variables jointly determined by the exogenous money stock. After the money supply has been increased, the specific sectors or commodities that will initially be affected are difficult or impossible to predict. That is, the particular path or transmission mechanism that this monetary impulse takes in ultimately affecting all prices is difficult or impossible to accurately forecast; it is simply too complex. Consequently, simple generalizations of the monetary transmission mechanism or of the time sequence of adjustment for exchange rates and prices may be misleading, since various countries operate under differing circumstances and institutional environments. In particular, the time sequence of adjustment for exchange rates or prices may differ in various countries, depending on the country's size, openness, institutions, effectiveness of arbitrage, ratio of traded to nontraded goods, and alternative expectation formation mechanisms. Therefore, as stated by Mussa: "The monetary approach takes an eclectic view of the process of adjustment because it seems unlikely that any single model of the process of adjustment will be relevant to all countries, at all

time periods, and under all institutional arrangements. The monetary approach seeks to combine a relatively general theory of long-run behavior with a number of different models of the process of adjustment." In Michael Mussa, "A Monetary Approach to Balance of Payments Analysis," *Journal of Money, Credit, and Banking* 6 (August 1974):338. In this sense, the monetary approach is similar to the domestic closed economy's monetarist view, which also emphasizes the complexity of the transmission process and the difficulty of its analysis and prediction.

25. See Thomas M. Humphrey, "The Purchasing Power Parity Doctrine," *Economic Review* 65 (May/June 1979):4.

26. Although the nominal exchange rate moves in proportion to the change in the money supply, the real exchange rate is unaffected by such monetary disturbances. See, for example, Lance Girton and Don Roper, "The Evolution of Exchange Rate Policy," *The Monetary Approach to International Adjustment*, ed. Bluford Putnam and D. Sykes Wilford (New York: Praeger, 1978), p. 223. This will be further discussed in Part III of this volume.

27. This insulation, however, it not complete, as has been demonstrated by the literature on currency substitution. See, for example, Marc Miles, "Currency Substitution: Perspectives, Implications, and Empirical Evidence," *The Monetary Approach to International Adjustment*, ed. Putnam and Wilford (New York: Praeger, 1978) and the bibliography therein.

28. This contention is in accordance with those who maintain that the purchasing power parity doctrine constitutes an extension of the quantity theory to the open economy.

I

CLOSED WORLD ECONOMY

3

THE HISTORICAL DEVELOPMENT OF THE MONETARY MODEL OF THE CLOSED ECONOMY: PART ONE

INTRODUCTION

Like all of the principal monetary frameworks, the monetary model of the closed economy was well known to earlier generations of economists. Indeed, of the three monetary models briefly described in Chapter 2, the closed economy model has the earliest origins. As a consequence, a presentation of the development of the closed model, especially prior to that of the other models, is important for several reasons. First, such a presentation enhances our understanding of the monetary aspects of the closed world economy that forms the environment in which all small open economies operate. Since the closed economy model has the earliest beginnings and, hence, the longest history, it served as the base from which other monetary models of small open economies developed as offspring. Historically, for example, it was only once the closed world model was understood that explanations of the operation of component small open economies were developed. Consequently, the closed economy framework serves as the foundation from which comparisons and contrasts of alternative monetary models can be made. Moreover, presentation of the development of the closed model prior to that of the others simplifies the description of the subsequent evolution of the offspring, small open economy frameworks.

Secondly, in the small open economy under fixed exchange rates, the price level, as well as inflation, is determined in world markets. In this case, then, in order to understand the determinants of the value of money, as well as changes in its value, an understanding of the operation of the closed world economy is essential.

This chapter as well as the following one will describe the development of the monetary model of the closed economy. As indicated in Chapter 1, an objective of this study is to emphasize the evolution of ideas rather than the thinking of particular economists. Consequently, when discussing the writings of various economists, their contributions to the model's evolution will be stressed, whereas inconsistencies in their thinking will, in general, be ignored. In describing the model's evolution, the development of certain components of that model will be emphasized. In particular, the concepts of causality, exogeneity, and neutrality, as well as the real balance effect, will be stressed where appropriate.

Because of the several components of the model, as well as the evolutionary nature of its development, it is not meaningful to search for or contend that a single economist was "*the* originator" of the model. Rather, the several components of the model were developed by various economists. Thus, the first writer to synthesize all of the components of the closed model was not necessarily the originator of its ideas but rather the first to state it in comprehensive form.

The chapter is organized according to the chronological development of the model. First, the period prior to the writings of David Hume will be discussed. This was the period in which mercantilist views predominated in the thinking of most economic writers. Hume and Smith's recognition and acceptance of the model are then established. Moreover, their use of the model in examining the small open economy under fixed exchange rates is alluded to. Similarly, the acceptance and use of the closed model in the analysis of bullionist, as well as Currency School and Banking School, writers are demonstrated. The further restatement of the model by both James Mill and John Stuart Mill is then documented.

RELEVANT WRITINGS PRIOR TO JOHN LOCKE

As indicated above, the closed monetary framework, as described in Chapter 2 (above), has the earliest historical origins of any of the monetary frameworks described in this study. Indeed, certain elements of this view are so simple that they were recognized at a very early date. It did not require any profound knowledge, for example, to realize that in a closed economy, a large increase in money would lead to a fall in its value. Both Hegeland and Marget have documented the fact that crude forms of this idea were recognized at least as early as 500 B.C. by the Chinese.[1] This is certainly not surprising in view of the fact that in this period the Chinese not only lived in a relatively closed economy, but had developed a currency system prior to most other countries.[2] Thus, for example, Hegeland contends that:

> The idea that there is a causal relation between changes in the quantity of money and its value . . . goes back at least as far as to the Chinese in 500 B.C., who used it in their recommendations for influencing the price level. . . . The Chinese maintained that an increase or decrease of the circulation would raise or lower prices.[3]

Several researchers have established that similar views related to causality were voiced by Greek and Roman writers.[4] According to Heckscher, Hegeland, and Marget, for example, the notion that if the supply of money changes, prices will change in the same direction was endorsed by Xenophon, Julius Paulus, and others.[5] Thus, several authors in the period between 500 B.C. and A.D. 200, writing in the context of a closed framework, recognized primitive versions of the concept of causality. That is, they recognized that, just as with any other good, an increase in the supply of money (*ceteris paribus*) would lead to a decrease in its value. Moreover, at least one interpreter of these early writings has indicated that they embodied the concept of a real balance effect. That is, Heckscher contends that:

> The quantity theory in its primitive form—i.e., prices determined by demand for goods on the part of the holders of money—is so simple an idea that it occurred at a very early date; the Roman jurist Paulus . . . [is] among the many who have been named as its originator.[6]

Thus, the origins of some elements of the closed framework were established even prior to the Medieval period.

Information relating to both monetary thought and its development, as well as to economic and monetary conditions during the Middle Ages, is relatively scarce and unreliable. It is known, however, that as the world gradually became more integrated over time, the acceptable international means of exchange came to be precious metals—notably gold or silver. That is, gold and silver came to be regarded as international money (or the base of international money). Thus, discussions of world money always pertained to gold or silver standards (that is, commodity standards). In the following discussions of gold or silver standards, therefore, it should be recognized that mention of gold or silver supplies refers to the *world* money supply and, hence, to the money supply of a closed economy. Other information that exists for this period tends to indicate that prices remained relatively stable over extended periods of time. Precious metals, then, apparently maintained their value for long periods. Because of this stability literally over centuries, it came to be believed that gold (and, to some extent silver) had a fixed value. Hegeland points out that this view—that the value of the precious metals was fixed—stemmed from and "was also supported by the circumstances that there had been very few significant changes in the price level before the sixteenth century."[7] These long periods of relatively stable prices are related to the fact that, under precious metal standards (such as gold or silver standards), automatic mechanisms were at work, which stabilized world prices in the long run. Under a gold standard, for example, if world prices begin to fall (due, for example, to increases in world real output and, hence, to increases in the demand for gold), gold becomes more valuable in terms of goods (that is, each unit weight of gold exchanges for more goods) and at the same time the cost of producing gold decreases. Because of this increased profitability of gold production, the current rate of gold production tends to increase. At the same time, gold becomes relatively expensive in nonmonetary uses, and consequently, the fraction of the existing stock used for monetary purposes tends to increase.[8] Both effects tend to increase the monetary gold supply and, hence, slow or reverse the fall in world prices. This mechanism, then, works to stabilize world prices. Similar effects in the opposite direction work to slow or reverse world price increases. Hence, over extended periods of time, shifts in the world monetary demand for gold induce accommodating changes in the world monetary gold supply, which results in relatively stable world prices.[9] The stable world prices through much of the Middle Ages were undoubtedly due, at least in part, to the functioning of this mechanism.

However, the discovery of America—or, in the language of the day, the discovery of the "New World"—affected this stability. In this case, the supply of precious metals increased drastically relative to their demand. Rist, for example, indicates that:

> 'The ten centuries which preceded the discovery of America brought to light ten cubic metres of gold, less than one cubic metre a century.' The discovery of the mines of Mexico and South America brought into circulation, in little more than one century . . . 39.1 cubic metres.[10]

Similarly, Taussig indicates that with the discovery of America, silver production increased almost *sevenfold*![11] Although this increased supply arrived via Spain, it quickly made its way into circulation over all of Europe.[12] Following this sudden enormous (and what may be legitimately labeled exogenous) increase in the world supply of gold and silver in the sixteenth century, European ("Old World") prices increased substantially. Rist, for example, contends that "there is uncontested evidence that in the sixteenth century there was . . . an enormous rise in prices . . . in Europe."[13] Similarly, Taussig states that by the middle of the seventeenth century, prices had increased as much as threefold (largely during the preceding century).[14]

In view of this significant world inflation, several authors attempted to provide explanations for it. Although it has been documented that several authors predated him, the French social philosopher, Jean Bodin (1568), is generally recognized as one of the first and most influential writers to provide an adequate explanation.[15] In responding to M. de Malestroict's contention that the price increase was due to debasement, Bodin indicated that the world inflation was "chiefly and almost solely" attributable to an increase in the world money supply.[16] In particular, Bodin stated that:

> The principal reason which raises *the price of everything, wherever one may be*, is the abundance which governs the appraisal and price of things. . . . It (is) the abundance of gold and silver. . . .[17]

In short, Bodin provides a recognition of the importance of changes in the supply of money *as a determinant of* changes in the general level of prices (or changes in the value of money).[18] That is, Bodin's explanation came to be "taken as evidence of a *direct causal relation* between variations in money and prices."[19] Since the enormous money supply increase was a result of the discovery of the "New World" and its rich mines, it can legitimately be interpreted as an exogenous increase in the world money supply.[20] Hence, Bodin's explanation was properly viewed as describing a causal relationship between an (exogenous) increase in the world money supply and an increase in world prices within a closed world economy. (The general price level, then, assumes the role of a passive, dependent variable in Bodin's framework.) Although Bodin clearly recognized that he was not the first to notice this causal relationship, his writing "attracted enormous attention," and, consequently, he is generally viewed as "the first to make it widely known and accepted."[21]

In explaining the significant world price increases, other writers soon endorsed the same or similar views. Bernardo Davanzati (1588), for example, also recognized the importance of changes in the quantity of gold (or world money), such as that resulting from the discovery of America, and in determining the level of prices (or the value of money). In explaining the exchange value of world money, Davanzati equated the stock of goods with the stock of money:

> Now all these [earthy things which satisfy men's wants] . . . are worth all the gold (comprehending also the silver and copper) that is wrought *in the world.*[22]

It follows logically from this view that the more money that exists, *ceteris paribus*, the less each unit's exchange value will be.[23] Moreover, although Davanzati did not explicitly state so, the concept of proportional movements in the price level is implicit in his position. This has led Hegeland to name Davanzati as the founder of the proportionality proposition "because it is inherent in his monetary theory."[24]

Louis Molina (1593), Gerard Malynes (1622), and Thomas Mun (1664) are additional examples of writers cited for their support of the concept of causality running from money to prices. Malynes, for example, states that:

> . . . the enhancing of our monies will increase the prices of all things.[25]

> . . . plenty of money maketh generally things dear, and scarcity of money maketh likewise generally things good cheap.[26]

Furthermore, contends Malynes, inflation during the sixteenth and early seventeenth centuries was due, in his opinion, to the "oceans of monies which had come from the West Indies."[27] Mun (1664—written about 1630) indicates that such views relating to causality were common in his day:

> It is a common saying that plenty or scarcity of money makes all things dear or good or cheap. . . .[28]

Vaughan, writing about 1630, set out a framework analogous to that of Davanzati in which a proportionality relationship between goods and money was implied.[29] The proportionality postulate, however, was stated quite explicitly by William Potter (1650):

> . . . an increase of money would occasion an increase in the price of commodities, *proportionable* to such increase of money (that is, if the money were twice as much, commodity would be twice as dear)

> consequently . . . would not occasion any increase in the sale of commodity. Therefore not any increase of trade. . . .[30]

This statement by Potter, claims Hegeland, "may be the first in which proportionate price changes are (explicitly) mentioned."[31] Moreover, in indicating that changes in money not only would bring about proportionate price changes but would also have no effect on trade, Potter was among the first to recognize that proportionality implies neutrality; that changes in the supply of money have no permanent effects on real economic activity.

In 1683, the Italian writer, Geminiano Montanari, elaborated and extended the earlier work of his fellow countryman Davanzati. In so doing, Montanari clearly indicated that these views pertained to the *closed* economy. For example, he contended that:

> . . . if a city . . . were *cut off from all commerce with outsiders for a long time*, and as a result found itself with fewer commodities, but with much gold and silver, it is plain that people would have to pay high prices. If only certain commodities were scarce, their price alone would rise, but the whole supply of goods would still be equal to all the money. Similar reasoning applies to the case of *an isolated province*; and since commerce is now so widespread that the most remote provinces are 'linked together by a chain of gold and gems,' we may say that all the gold, silver, and copper coined and in circulation is the price of all the commodities bought and sold among these nations.[32]

Thus, by the late seventeenth century, several of the major components of the monetary framework of the closed economy as described in Chapter 2 had been voiced by important monetary writers of the day. In particular, the significant price increases that afflicted the world during this period led to advances in the theory of the value of money. These advances related to the concept of exogenous shifts (increases) in the supply of world money and, as a consequence, to increases in world prices. Hence, the causal nature of the relationship between money and prices in the closed economy came to be accepted by most writers of the period, and, as emphasized by Viner, "there were few who rejected it once they became aware of it."[33] Moreover, although not as widely accepted, the concepts of proportionality between money and prices, as well as monetary neutrality, had also been expressed by at least one monetary writer in this period. This is not to say that any one of the above-cited writers endorsed all of the components of the closed framework or held a complete view of the closed framework consistently in all of his works. Instead, the point to be made is that several of the individual components of the closed framework had been voiced by monetary writers prior to 1690.

JOHN LOCKE

In 1691, however, John Locke presented the most lucid, complete, and refined version of the closed economy monetary framework written to that date. Locke, for example, strongly endorsed the view of an inverse relationship between the quantity of world money and its purchasing power. Despite the fact that the money-price causality proposition was a standard part of the thinking of his day and was "old even in 1691," Locke stated it repeatedly and consistently in his writings.[34] In elaborating this view, Locke contended that changes in the value of money were determined by changes in its supply because the demand for money was relatively constant.[35] Specifically, Locke indicated that:

> He that will justly estimate the value of anything, must consider its quantity, in proportion to its vent, for this alone regulates the price. . . . But because the desire of money is constantly, almost everywhere the same, its vent varies very little; but as its greater scarcity enhances in price and increases the scramble, there being nothing else that does easily supply the want of it. The lessening of its quantity, therefore, always increases its price, and make an equal portion of its exchange for a greater of any other thing.[36]

Thus, Locke recognized that the value of money is governed by quantity of money supplied *relative to its demand*. Since demand was seen as relatively constant (or stable), changes in the supply of money would always alter its value.[37] Thus, the implicit corollary of the causality proposition—that the demand for money is relatively stable—was made explicit by Locke.[38]

What is particularly relevant to this study is that Locke indicated that the money-to-prices causality proposition was applicable to the closed economy or to the world as a whole, but that it did not apply to the case of the open economy. This interpretation of Locke has been endorsed by Leigh (1974). Leigh, for example, emphasized Locke's "application of [the causality] principle to a closed economy *or to the world as a whole* and his denial that it works out in practice in a nation engaging in trade with the rest of the world."[39] In analyzing the relationship between money and prices in the closed economy, then, Locke recognized that when the supply of money (exogenously) increases, the price level passively adapts to this change. In the open economy under fixed exchange rates, however, Locke realized that domestic prices were related to and, hence, constrained by prices in other countries. (The case of the open economy under fixed exchange rates will be developed below.)

In addition to recognizing the money-to-prices causality proposition in the closed economy. Locke was one of the first to state the proportionality postulate forcefully and explicitly. This view—that changes in the world money supply will cause proportional changes in its value—was implicit in the work of several earlier writers but, with the exception of Potter, had never been stated explicitly. Moreover, although Potter had stated it earlier, Locke's statement received much more attention and, consequently, was much more influential. In stating this view, Locke indicated that:

> There being ten times as much silver now *in the world* (the discovery of the West Indies having made the plenty) as there was then [in Henry VII's time] it is nine-tenths less worth now than it was at that time; that is, it will exchange for nine-tenths less of any commodity now, which bears the same proportion to its vent as it did 200 years since. . . .[40]
>
> . . . the value of money in respect of those [commodities] depends *only* on the plenty or scarcity of money *in proportion to* the plenty and scarcity of those things; and not on what interest shall, by necessity, law, or contract be at that time laid on the borrowing of money. . . .[41]
>
> The value of money in general, is the quantity of *all the money in the world in proportion to all the trade. . . .*[42]

In stating his views of money in the closed economy, then, Locke simply indicated that the level of prices would vary in proportion to the quantity of money; the quantity of money being understood to take into consideration the velocity of its circulation (or the demand for money).[43] In describing his position, Locke employed the case of an isolated island economy (that is, a closed economy). In such a closed economy framework, he contended, the quantity of money didn't matter, since the price level would always adjust proportionately to any monetary change (that is, real balances wouldn't change). Hence, any quantity of money would serve to drive any proportion of trade in the closed economy, and consequently, "the adequacy of the money supply is therefore of no concern."[44] In Locke's own words:

> That supposing any island separate from the commerce of the rest of mankind, . . . any quantity of that money (if it were but so much that every body might have some) would serve to drive any proportion of trade, whether more or less; there being counters enough to reckon by. . . .[45]

The implication here was that changes in the quantity of money would affect all prices proportionately and, therefore, would have no effect on relative prices and, hence, on real economic activity. Since any quantity of money in the closed economy would be adequate to drive any proportion of trade and since changes in the quantity of money would have no real effects, Locke's proportionality postulate implied monetary neutrality. This interpretation is supported by Hegeland, who indicates that in Locke's view an increase in the world money supply would not increase the world's real wealth:

> . . . [Locke] mentions that nobody would get richer if the quantity of gold and silver were doubled *in all countries*. . . . Consequently, a variation in its quantity [money] does not mean any change in the total wealth of *the world*. . . . Locke's intention was to point out that the quantity itself of gold and silver, as means of exchange and disregarding their industrial uses, was of no importance to *an isolated economy or to the world as a whole*. . . . Locke was evidently correct . . . as long as he dealt with macroeconomics in *an isolated economy*.[46]

In presenting these views, Locke was very explicit in indicating that they pertained to the case of the closed economy; he stressed that they applied either to the isolated island economy (with no commerce with the rest of the world) or to the world as a whole. Thus, in his closed economy monetary views, Locke recognized the concepts of causality from (exogenously given) changes in money to changes in prices, proportionality, as well as monetary neutrality. His views on the latter constituted a contribution and advance over previous writers.[47] In view of these refinements, as well as his wide influence, it is no wonder that Locke is often credited with the first English formulation of the quantity theory of money.[48]

EARLY EIGHTEENTH-CENTURY WRITERS

By the end of the seventeenth century, therefore, most of the fundamental elements of the monetary model of the closed economy, such as causality (and exogeneity), proportionality, and neutrality, as described in Chapter 2, were established in the monetary literature. A contribution of many of the eighteenth-century monetary writers to this closed monetary framework was to restate, elaborate, refine, and, to some degree, extend this monetary model.

Isaac Gervaise (1720), for example, restated views relating to the value of money previously set out by Davanzati, Montanari, and Locke. In particular, he indicated that:

> The value or proportion of all things useful, or necessary, is to gold and silver, *in proportion* to the quantity of gold and silver that is *in the world*; so that the more gold and silver is *in the world*, the greater the value of things will be.[49]

As indicated above, this view implies that an increase in the quantity of world money effects a proportional increase in the level of world prices. Like Locke, Gervaise attributes this to a steady or stable demand for money.[50] Vanderlint (1734) is another monetary writer during this period who endorsed the "rigid proportion version of the quantity theory of money."[51]

Restatement of the concepts of causality as well as proportionality was provided by Montesquieu (1748). In discussing the value of money, for example, he compared the total of all the world's commodities to the "mass of gold and silver *in the whole world*," just as several previous writers had done.[52] Similarly, Montesquieu's explanation of the great increase in the actual price level is analogous to that provided by earlier writers cited above:

> If since the discovery of the Indies, gold and silver have increased in Europe in the proportion of 1 to 20, the price of provisions and merchandizes must have been enhanced in proportion of 1 to 20. But, if, on the other hand, the number of merchandizes has increased as 1 to 2, it necessarily follows, that the price of these merchandizes and provisions, having been raised in proportion of 1 to 20, and fallen in proportion of 1 to 2, it necessarily follows, I say, that the proportion is only 1 to 10.[53]

As indicated by Hegeland, Montesquieu's "method of demonstrating the proportionate changes in the price level by using figures, [had] only one purpose: to emphasize proportionality."[54]

Richard Cantillon, writing in 1734 (not published, however, until about 1755), was one monetary writer who not only restated many of the above views but extended them in several important respects. Cantillon explicitly indicated that he had read Locke and endorsed several of Locke's arguments. For example, he restated what was apparently common knowledge in this period, namely, that an exogenous increase in world money leads to an increase in world prices. That is, he recognized the closed economy version of causality:

> Everybody agrees that the abundance of money or its increase in exchange, raises the price of everything. The quantity of money brought from America to Europe for the last two centuries justified this truth by experience.
>
> M. Locke lays it down as a fundamental maxim that the quantity of produce and merchandise in proportion to the quantity of money serves as the regulator of market price. I have tried to elucidate his idea in the preceding chapters: he has clearly seen that the abundance of money makes everything dear. . . .[55]
>
> The quantity of money, as of all other commodities, determines its value. . . .[56]

In addition to restating several of the components of the monetary model of the closed economy, Cantillon developed and extended elements of the framework. For example, Cantillon indicated not only that a world money supply increase would affect world prices, but he also spelled out how this would occur. That is, he traced the various channels by which an increase in world money would ultimately affect all world prices. In particular, he indicated how an increase in the gold supply works to increase prices first in one sector or one country and then in another, until eventually all prices are affected or until the prices of products are raised in "all the channels of circulation which [money] enters."[57] In short, he developed the specifics of the world monetary transmission mechanism as well as its corollary that the effects of a world money supply increase is independent of its place of origin. Moreover, Cantillon (according to Schumpeter) "was the first to speak of *vitesse de la circulation*" as well as "the first to state in so many words that increase in the velocity of money was equivalent to increase in its quantity."[58]

Another important extension of the closed economy monetary model made by Cantillon was his explicit description of real balance effects. In particular, Cantillon contended that the causal relationship between money and prices in the closed economy was the consequence of prior changes in the quantity of money on the demand for commodities or expenditures on consumption. That is, he demonstrated that a new gold discovery (or an exogenous increase in the world money supply) would constitute a fresh source of demand, and, via increased expenditures, result in an increase in world prices. Specifically, he stated that:

> Increased money will bring about *increased expenditure* and this will cause an increase in market prices. . . . I consider in general that an increase of actual money causes . . . a corresponding increase in consumption which gradually brings about increased prices.[59]

Even Patinkin contends that Cantillon had a real balance effect. He, for example, lists Cantillon among those "early expositions of the quantity theory which make it clear that an increase in the quantity of money raises prices through its prior effect in increasing demand. . . ."[60] Patinkin, however, concedes that other writers may have thought "this causal relationship to be too obvious for comment."[61] Cantillon's influence in this matter upon subsequent writers seems to have been considerable. One writer so influenced, for example, was James Stuart (1767), who essentially restated Cantillon's views on the real balance effect.[62] In particular, Stuart indicated "that mere changes in the quantity of money would not have any effect on prices if they did not have any effect on demand."[63]

By the time David Hume's (1752) writings appeared, then, all of the fundamental components of the closed economy monetary framework had been assembled. Specifically, the concepts of causality (from an exogenous increase in the world money supply to world prices) and neutrality (proportionality), as well as real balance effects, had been established in the literature. Moreover, these concepts had been formulated so as to apply explicitly to the closed economy. As indicated by Viner, on certain of these issues there was virtual consensus among the period's monetary writers. (In particular, there was a large consensus among writers in attributing a world price increase to an exogenous increase in world money, that is, the influx of precious metals stemming from the discovery of the "New World.") It should be noted that most of the writers in this period were considered to be mercantilists (at least to some degree). In analyzing the closed world economy, then, mercantilists endorsed the essential building blocks of the closed economy monetary framework described in Chapter 2. This interpretation of the mercantilists has been supported by Viner, Heckscher, Wu, and others and, hence, is by no means novel. Viner, for example, indicates that:

> . . . a quantity theory of the value of money . . . was held by many of the mercantilists, and there were few who rejected it once they became aware of it.[64]

Heckscher also indicated that the causality proposition began at a very early date and was widespread during the mercantilist period.[65] Moreover, Wu suggests that:

> Considering the mercantilist writers as a whole, it must be noted that they furnished most of the materials out of which the classical theory . . . was evolved. For example, they provided a quantity theory of money, a doctrine of a due proportion between the national stock of money and the monetary needs of a nation. . . .[66]

Although the mercantilists recognized the various elements of the closed monetary framework, they failed to recognize their implications. Specifically, they failed to realize the important inconsistencies of these views with other major aspects of their doctrine—specifically those relating to trade and to the small, open economy.[67] This point will be developed below in subsequent chapters relating to the small open economy.

In any case, the closed framework—the elements of which had all been established in the literature by the mid-eighteenth century—provided the foundation for others to use as a base for extensions of monetary theory to the small open economy. That is, the closed monetary framework formed the source from which other monetary frameworks took root.

EARLY CLASSICAL WRITERS—HUME AND SMITH

Early classical writers in the eighteenth and early nineteenth centuries generally accepted all the essential elements of the monetary model of the closed economy as described above. Most of these writers were very familiar, for example, with the writings of Locke as well as other writers such as Cantillon.[68] Their contributions, if any, to this closed framework were to synthesize the already existing components of the model. In any case, as indicated by Schumpeter, the closed framework was so well accepted and commonplace by this time that it was frequently taken for granted by monetary writers of the day.[69] Consequently, although these early classical writers did consistently restate these well-accepted principles, they often did so very briefly. This commonplace acceptance of the closed monetary framework led to its use as a backdrop or base for extensions of monetary theory.

In particular, during the period prior to the British suspension of convertibility in 1797, extensions were made in applying monetary theory to the small open economy under a convertible currency (or under a fixed exchange rate regime). That is, early classical writers went beyond accepting the monetary model of the closed economy and extended their analysis to the small open economy under fixed exchanges. In so doing, they removed themselves from mercantilist views and, indeed, forcefully demonstrated the fallaciousness of mercantilist doctrine. Although they used the closed model as a foundation for extensions to the open economy, these economists all clearly and explicitly recognized the differences between the closed and open monetary models. In short, they were able to synthesize the monetary model of the closed world—which they had essentially inherited from earlier writers—with that of a model for the small open economy under fixed exchange rates. That is, they were able to formulate a model for the small open economy which was not only consistent with the older closed model, but which actually was a model of the building blocks or components of which the closed aggregate was made.

In describing the workings of the small open economy under fixed exchanges (which will be developed below), they indicated the importance played by global or world considerations. That is, they demonstrated that the closed model continued to have an important role in any examination or analysis of the small open economy with fixed exchange rates. In particular, by the time of the writings of these early classical economists, a framework had been established which was employed, albeit implicitly in analyzing prices and inflation. In analyzing inflation, it should be remembered, there were no reliable general price indices available to monetary writers in this period;[70] consequently, in their discussions relating to money and prices, indirect proxies were frequently employed. To these early classical economists, a convenient proxy involved the price of bullion.[71] In particular, the product of the currency price of gold (a fixed rate of exchange when currency is convertible) and the price of goods in terms of gold was employed, albeit implicitly, as a proxy for the level of commodity prices. In terms of an algebraic equation:

$$(1) \quad P_{£/goods} = \bar{p}_{£/gold} \cdot P_{gold/goods}$$

In this equation, the price of gold in terms of domestic currency is represented by $\bar{p}_{£/gold}$. Under a convertible currency, this price is determined and *fixed* by the weight of gold that a unit of domestic currency is deemed to represent.[72] The price of goods in terms of gold, $P_{gold/goods}$ (or the reciprocal of the price of gold in terms of goods), is determined in *world* markets. It can be viewed as the *world* price of commodities denominated in terms of gold or as a proxy for the world price level.[73] Since the individual small open economy is assumed to be too small in both production and consumption to affect world markets, this price is viewed as being given exogenously to the small open economy. Therefore, since $\bar{p}_{£/gold}$ is fixed and $P_{gold/goods}$ is exogenously determined in world markets, domestic prices in the small open economy, $P_{£/goods}$, are determined in world markets. That is, the prices of goods in terms of domestic currency—or, to generalize, the domestic price level—is determined by world prices.[74] Thus, in a world of fixed exchange rates (or under a gold standard regime), it is the quantity of world money (relative to world goods) that determines the general price level in each individual small open economy. As such, the causes of domestic inflation must be sought at the *world* rather than at the national level; that is, *the closed monetary model has a high degree of relevance to the open economy under fixed exchange rates.*[75]

Given this importance of the closed model to their analysis of the small open economy, early classical economists explicitly restated important elements of the closed framework. David Hume, for example, who made important contributions to the monetary theory of the small open economy under fixed exchange rates (as well as to the international adjustment mechanism of such an economy), explicitly restated all of the fundamental components of the closed model as described above. Moreover, he differentiated the closed from the open monetary framework. The concepts of causality, proportionality, and the long-run monetary neutrality in the closed economy are all evident in the following quotations from Hume's essay, "Of Money":

> If we consider *any one kingdom by itself*, it is evident, that the greater or less plenty of money *is of no consequence*; since the prices of commodities are always *proportioned* to the plenty of money. . . .

> Where coin is in greater plenty; as a greater quantity of it is required to represent the same quantity of goods; *it can have no effect*, either good or bad, *taking a nation within itself*. . . .

> In my opinion, it is *only* in this interval or intermediate situation,

between the acquisition of money and rise of prices, that the encreasing quantity of gold and silver is favorable to industry.

It seems a maxim almost self-evident, that the prices of everything depend on *the proportion between commodities and money*, and that any considerable alteration on either has the same effect, either of heightening or lowering the price. Encrease the commodities, they become cheaper; *encrease the money, they rise in their value*. As, on the other hand, a diminution of the former, and that of the latter have contrary tendencies.[76]

Thus, in restating the closed economy views inherited from earlier writers, Hume indicates that in the long run not only does the general level of prices vary directly and proportionately with changes in the quantity of money, but that monetary neutrality is implied in the analysis. Hume, then, endorses a quantity theory of the value of money and its several corollaries; namely, the propositions of money-to-prices causality, proportionality, and long-run monetary neutrality.[77] Hume's views on long-run monetary neutrality are underscored in his essay, "Of Interest." In this essay, Hume denies that a change in the quantity of money will affect the interest rate in the long run.[78]

In addition to endorsing these monetary propositions relevant to the closed economy, Hume also recognized the real balance effect; that is, he indicates that an increase in the money supply causes those merchants and artisans who receive it before others to increase their demands for and spending on commodities.[79] Thus, Hume recognized and endorsed all of the major components of the closed monetary model described above.

Hume and his writings undoubtedly had an important influence on Adam Smith.[80] It is known, for example, that "Smith was intimately acquainted with Hume and his works."[81] Hume and Smith, it will be recalled, were close friends, were often in correspondence with one another, and as indicated by Taylor, "mutually influenced each other's thinking."[82] Indeed, Taylor contends that:

There can be little doubt that Smiths close intimacy with Hume . . . exercised a powerful influence on his economic philosophy. . . . Hume was both the perceptive anticipator of Adam Smith and his acute critic, and Smith benefited greatly from almost thirty years of close relationship with him.[83]

Moreover, Hume and Smith had an influential mutual friend, James

Oswald, who was also their confidant and, to some extent, the adviser of both writers.[84] Both Smith and Hume "held Oswald's enlightened economic opinions in high regard and they often sought out his views on their respective economic ideas."[85] In view of their association with Oswald, it is interesting to note that Oswald believed that "the prices of an *isolated economy* would rise *in proportion* as the supply of money increased."[86]

It should not be surprising, therefore, that the monetary views of the closed economy adopted by Adam Smith were also those of Hume and Oswald. In discussions relating to the closed world economy, for example, Smith explicitly endorsed the view that changes in the money supply directly and proportionately affected changes in prices:

> The discovery of the abundant mines of America, reduced in the sixteenth century, the value of gold and silver in Europe to about a third of what it had been before.[87]

> So far . . . as the increase of the quantity of the precious metals in any country arises from the increased abundance of the mines, it is necessarily connected with some diminution of their value.[88]

> The discovery of the abundant mines of America, seems to have been the sole cause of this diminution in the value of silver *in proportion to* that of corn. It is accounted for accordingly in the same manner by everybody; and there never has been any dispute either about the fact, or about the cause of it. . . . The increase of the supply had, it seems, so far exceeded that of the demand, that the value of that metal sunk considerably.[89]

> Any rise in the money price of goods which proceeded altogether from the degradation of the value of silver, would affect all sorts of goods equally, and raise their price universally a third, or a fourth, or a fifth part higher, according as silver happened to lose a third, or a fourth, or a fifth part of its former value.[90]

Smith also endorsed the corollary of monetary neutrality in the closed economy. For example, he indicated that:

> . . . degradation of the value of silver which is the effect of the fertility of the mines, and which operates equally, or very near equally, through the greater part of the commercial world, is a matter of very little consequence to any particular country. The consequent rise of all money prices, though it does not make those who receive them really richer, does not make them really poorer. A service of

> plate becomes really cheaper, and *everything else remains precisely of the same real value as before.*[91]

A change in the quantity of money is of little consequence in the closed economy, contended Smith, because money is neither wealth nor capital but a medium of exchange and, consequently, in the long run affects absolute prices but not relative prices and real economic activity.[92] That is, once a given change in the money supply has been absorbed into the economy and prices have adjusted accordingly, there is no reason to expect real variables to be any different than they had been initially.[93] This view was clearly set out by Smith:

> Any increase in the quantity of silver, while that of the commodities circulated by means of it remained the same, would have no other effect than to diminish the value of that metal. The nominal value of all sorts of goods would be greater, *but their real value would be precisely the same as before.*[94]

Elsewhere, Smith explicitly indicated that, in the long run, changes in money would not affect variables such as real wages, employment, the rate of interest, the capital stock, and profits.[95]

In sum, while both Hume and Smith made substantial contributions to the monetary theory of the small open economy under fixed exchange rates (as will be demonstrated below), they always recognized the important relevance of the monetary theory of the closed world economy to this open framework. Consequently, they explicitly endorsed the monetary model of the closed economy and all of its important components and, moreover, employed this closed model as a backdrop or foundation from which they extended monetary theory.

BULLIONIST WRITERS AND THE CLOSED MODEL

Since Hume and Smith endorsed the closed model and because their work was so widely read and influential, the monetary model of the closed economy was even more widely known and commonplace by the end of the eighteenth century. At the end of this century, events occurred in Britain in which other important British monetary theorists had occasion to employ the monetary model of the closed economy. Known as the Bullionist Controversy, this debate will be more thoroughly analyzed in subsequent chapters. Here, however, the relevance of the closed model to the analysis of these bullionist writers, as well as their recognition and endorsement of the model, will be briefly outlined.

The events that occurred in Britain were related to the war that broke out between France and Britain in 1793. As a consequence of problems associated with financing the war, the British were soon unable to maintain the convertibility of their currency and, consequently, in 1797 enacted legislation restricting cash payments. Although intended to be only a temporary restriction, the inconvertible paper currency (or flexible exchange rate regime) lasted until 1821. During this period, it was soon recognized that Britain was experiencing a significant increase in prices. Although almost everyone recognized that "something was happening to prices, there existed no consensus regarding the method of index numbers whereby the behavior of groups of commodities might be evaluated; at best only intelligent guesses could be made regarding general prices."[96,97] At the same time, no established theoretical monetary framework existed for analyzing the open economy under flexible exchange rates. In view of these major uncertainties, it is not surprising that the well-known and well-accepted closed model played a role in analyzing these circumstances as well as in aiding in the formulation of a monetary model of an inconvertible currency. Bullionist writers recognized the relevance of the closed monetary framework in analyzing the problems of their day, just as Hume and Smith had done earlier.

Specifically, the closed model was employed by bullionist writers, such as Wheatley, Thornton, Ricardo, and others, as a kind of comparative reference point by which to analyze price relationships. Of prime concern during this period of restriction, for example, were the cause and measurement of inflation. In examining price increases in Britain, it was necessary for the bullionists to formulate a method by which they could ascertain whether such inflation was caused by world or domestic factors. That is, an important objective was to distinguish between domestic and external sources of inflation. The methods devised by the bullionist writers to answer this question involved an indirect use of the closed world framework. In particular, with the aid of a few simple price relationships, bullionist writers were able to relate prices that were known to be determined in world markets to other prices known to be domestically determined under an inconvertible currency regime. As a consequence, they were able to ascertain whether inflation was determined domestically or by world factors. To illustrate this, the simple price relationship described in equation (1) above was used, albeit implicitly, by bullionist writers in this analysis:

$$(1) \quad P_{£/goods} = p_{£/gold} \cdot P_{gold/goods}$$

According to this relationship, bullionists recognized that the domestic price of commodities, $P_{£/goods}$, was determined by the product of the domestic currency price of gold and the gold price of commodities. The sterling price of gold (or the market price of bullion denominated in domestic currency), $p_{£/gold}$, was flexible under an inconvertible currency and consequently determined by the supply of inconvertible currency bidding for the world supply of gold. Since the supply of inconvertible currency is determined by the issuer of domestic currency, this price is largely domestically determined. The gold price of commodities, $P_{gold/goods}$, was known to be determined by the supply of gold relative to that of the *world* supply of commodities and, hence, determined in world markets.[98] Thus, by observing that (1) domestic bullion prices had increased substantially above the official mint price of gold and (2) that the gold price of commodities had remained relatively stable, bullionists were able to infer that the inflation in Britain was in large part caused by an excessive issuance of domestic inconvertible currency and not by world factors.[99]

Since gold was viewed as world currency, equation (1) was also interpreted to indicate that, in these circumstances, sterling had depreciated relative to both commodities and world currency. Factual data of the period indicated not only that the sterling price of bullion had increased and that the world currency price of commodities had remained relatively stable, but that the sterling price of foreign exchange had increased for those currencies maintaining a fixed or stable gold value. Sterling, then, had depreciated against commodities, world currency, and those currencies that had retained their world purchasing power. Consequently, the depreciation of the pound, the high price of bullion, and the domestic inflation were all rightly viewed by bullionist writers as the result of an overissue of inconvertible currency.[100] That bullionist writers made these price comparisons is indicated in the following remarks by the most well-known bullionist, David Ricardo (1810–11):

> In saying . . . that gold is at a high price, we are mistaken; it is not gold, it is paper which has changed its value. *Compare an ounce of gold*, or, 3£ 17s $10\frac{1}{2}$d *to commodities, it bears the same proportion to them which it has before done*. . . . But if we compare the substitute of an ounce of gold, 3£ 17s $10\frac{1}{2}$d in banknotes, with commodities, we shall then discover the depreciation of the banknotes. *In every market of the world*, I am obliged to part with 4£ 10s

in banknotes to purchase the same quantity of commodities which I can obtain for the gold that is in 3£ 17s 10½d of coin.[101]

Moreover, the *Bullion Report* (1810) to which Henry Thornton was an important contributor indicated that:

> . . . it does not appear that during the period when the price of gold was rising here, as valued in our paper, there was any corresponding rise in the price of Gold Bullion in the market of the Continent, as valued in their respective currencies. . . . The actual prices of gold in the foreign markets are just so much lower than its market price here, as the difference of exchange amounts to. . . . The prices of all commodities have risen and gold appears to have risen in its price only in common with them. If this common effect is to be ascribed to one and the same cause, that cause can only be found in the state of the currency of this country . . . a general rise in all prices, a rise in the market price of gold, and a fall of the foreign exchanges, will be the effect of an excessive quantity of circulating medium in a country which has adopted a currency not exportable to other countries. . . .[102]

Thus, in analyzing the circumstances in Britain during the period of restriction, the bullionist writers were able to employ profitably relevant aspects of the closed monetary model. In so doing, they were able to demonstrate that the inflation, the high sterling price of gold, as well as the depreciation of the exchanges were largely caused by domestic and not external world factors; in particular, by an overissuance of inconvertible currency. In establishing these conclusions, the bullionists not only recognized but endorsed and restated the closed model as well as its important corollaries.[103] In briefly documenting this contention, the writings of three of the most well-known and influential bullionists will be emphasized, namely, Wheatley, Thornton, and Ricardo.

The concepts of money-to-prices causality as well as monetary neutrality in the closed economy, for example, were specified by John Wheatley in the following remark:

> . . . the greater the quantity [of money] in circulation the lower will be its standard as the measure of equivalency, the greater will be the quantity given in exchange between produce and produce, and the higher will be the price of all things: but as an advance in the price of produce, and a reduction in the value of money are convertible terms, an increase of money has no other effect than to cause its own depression. This effect was sensibly experienced in the reign of Elizabeth, when the remittances from America considerably

> augmented the currency of Europe, and proportionally added to the specie of this country in common with the rest. But this increase had no other operation than to raise the price of produce, and augment the nominal incomes of all, without making any addition to their real opulence, as their incomes exchanged for no more subsequently to the increase than before it, and exchanging for no more, could be of no greater value. . . . [Universally] high prices are in reality only a test that the aggregate currency of the world has increased in a greater proportion than its aggregate produce.[104]

These views were also restated by David Ricardo. Specifically, Ricardo endorsed the concept of money-to-prices causality in the closed economy: "If the quantity of gold and silver *in the world* employed as money were exceedingly small, or abundantly great, . . . The variation in their quantity would have produced no other effect than to make the commodities for which they are exchanged comparatively dear or cheap. . . ."[105] Moreover, Ricardo contended that "the discovery of a gold mine, resulting in an increase of circulating coins" would produce "a proportionate price increase."[106] Henry Thornton also expressed similar views. He indicated, for example, that "it was unquestionably true," that the quantity of the precious metals influenced their value, "for the augmented supply obtained from the mines of the new world, was acknowledged to have produced that general lowering of the value of money, which had been experienced in Europe for many years."[107]

The concepts of monetary neutrality as well as real balance effects were also endorsed by both Thornton and Ricardo. Ricardo, for example, citing the views of both Hume and Smith, denied that changes in the quantity of money affected relative prices or real economic activity in the long run. This denial was made repeatedly with respect to the rate of interest.[108] Thornton made similar denials.[109] As Patinkin indicates, real balance effects were also recognized by Ricardo as well as Thornton. That is, these writers indicated that an increase in the quantity of money raises prices not mechanically but rather through its prior effect in increasing the demand for commodities.[110,111]

Thus, bullionist writers endorsed the closed monetary model and all of its corollaries, which were established and well known by this period. In addition to restating these arguments, however, these writers also refined the closed model to some extent; that is, they indicated their awareness of the closed model and its implications in another way. In particular, they demonstrated that, under a convertible currency regime, if *all countries* increased their note issue simultaneously and in proportion, the *total world money supply* would likewise increase, causing prices to rise in all countries (and, hence, in the world). Under these conditions, this could occur without any single country necessarily experiencing checks or constraints to this expansion in the form of international reserve drains. Thus, bullionists recognized that the world money stock could (exogenously) increase not only because of gold discoveries and new gold mining technologies, but also as a result of a simultaneous and proportionate increase in note issues by the various monetary authorities in the world. Thornton, Wheatley, and Ricardo all explicitly specified this view.[112] However, as in many other instances, although Ricardo was not the originator or architect of these views, they received their most lucid form under his pen.[113] Specifically, Ricardo indicated that:

> . . . if the circulation of England were ten millions, that of France five millions, that of Holland four millions, etc. etc. whilst they kept their proportions, though the currency of each country were doubled or trebled, neither country would be conscious of an excess of currency. The prices of commodities would every where rise, on account of the increase of currency, but there would be no exportation of money from either.[114]

In addition to this refinement, the bullionists contributed to the closed model in another way. Specifically, they were aware of the significance of the size of an economy within this closed framework. That is, they recognized that if an economy were large enough relative to the world aggregate, an expansion in its money supply could influence the world money supply. Suppose, for example, that under a convertible currency regime, a large country (with large gold reserves) expanded its paper issue, thereby inducing a large outflow of bullion. If this gold outflow were large enough, it could affect the bullion price of commodities and, hence, of the world price level. Thus, a money supply expansion in a large country could affect the world money supply and, therefore, world prices. Both Thornton and Ricardo recognized this view.[115] In one passage, for example, Ricardo indicated that if England were a large enough country, an English note expansion could influence the world money supply, and hence, the note expansion would not be fully offset by specie drains (since England would retain its share of the world money supply increase).[116] This recognition was a harbinger of similar views formulated in the twentieth century, when the U.S. economy and its currency played a key role in influencing the world economy as well as in international monetary arrangements.

The bullionists, then, were fully aware of the closed model, its corollaries, as well as some of its important implications. Because these writers were so well known and influential, their restatements and endorsements of the closed model enhanced its acceptance to later monetary writers in the nineteenth and twentieth centuries.

CURRENCY AND BANKING SCHOOL WRITERS AND THE CLOSED MONETARY MODEL

The writings of Thornton, Wheatley, Ricardo, and other bullionists served as the foundation from which the positions of both the so-called currency school and banking school developed. The currency school/banking school controversy (sometimes referred to as the Bank Charter Debate) related to alternative monetary interpretations of the functioning of the small open economy.[117] That is, these two schools posited alternative views as to the international adjustment mechanism as well as to the appropriate operating procedures for the central bank of an open economy under a convertible currency (fixed exchange rate) regime. (Since the controversy in general pertains to the open economy, it will be more thoroughly discussed and analyzed in subsequent chapters.) Discussions related to the closed economy, then, were not the primary focus of attention in this debate. When currency school and banking school writers did explicitly analyze the monetary theory of the closed economy, they were in full agreement.[118] Both schools fully endorsed and restated the closed model as described above. Indeed, this closed model was accepted by most monetary writers of the period. Consequently, when mention of the closed model was made, it was normally very brief; its content was often taken for granted or considered almost too obvious for comment.

In any case, the closed model and its corollaries were recognized and endorsed by writers associated with both the currency school and banking school positions. Banking school writers (such as Tooke, Fullarton, Wilson, and Gilbart), for example, clearly indicated that an increase in the world money supply—due, for example, to exogenous increases in the world gold stock—would bring about an increase in world prices.[119] That is, in the case of the closed world economy, they endorsed money-to-prices causality. Similar views of the closed world economy were stated by currency school writers such as Torrens, Norman, and Overstone. Torrens, for example, stated that:

> . . . the value of gold in relation to commodities must rise and fall as its quantity is diminished or increased. . . . An increase in the quantity and fall in the value of gold, in relation to commodities, is the same thing as an increase in the quantity, and fall in the value of the currency in relation to commodities—is the same thing as a rise of prices.[120]

Writers associated with the banking school went out of their way to emphasize that whereas they did *not* view causality to operate this way in the small open economy under a convertible currency regime (see below), they endorsed money-to-prices causality in the case of the closed world economy. That is, these writers repeatedly stressed that increases in the domestic money supply that reflected increases in the world money supply (that is, an increased gold supply) were inflationary, whereas increases in the domestic money supply arising from redistribution of the existing world supply (due, for example, to a favorable balance of payments) would not be inflationary (see below).[121] Fullarton, for example, emphasized the distinction "between the effects of an influx of gold from the mines [which it was contended would raise prices] and the effects of an influx of gold which was part of the previously existing supply [which it was said could not have a causal effect on prices]."[122]

Other corollaries of the closed model were also supported by these writers. Tooke, for example, in discussing the closed model, explicitly endorsed the view that an increased supply of gold "would soon increase prices *in proportion* to the new supplies of the metals."[123] That is, in the context of the closed economy, Tooke supported the proportionality postulate.[124] The view that changes in the quantity of money had no permanent effect on real economic activity was also supported by writers of both the currency and banking schools, who "harboured no doubts that the level of the rate of interest . . . could certainly not be influenced by an increase or diminution in the quantity of money or other media of payment in circulation. . . ."[125] Tooke, for example, explicitly endorsed Ricardo's view that the "rate of interest was independent of the quantity of money, except for temporary influences.[126] Finally, the real balance effect was recognized by these writers. Newmarch, in his writings with Tooke, for example, showed that as gold production increased, gold miners would increase their expenditures on various commodities, which initiated a process that ultimately resulted in an increase in the prices of all goods. Following Cantillon, he described the mechanism by which increased gold production ultimately affects all prices. Specifically, he contended that "it is . . . by the increased expenditure either at home or abroad of those who get the gold from the mines" that prices are increased over the world.[127] In summary, then, the closed model was essentially restated and endorsed by writers of both the currency and banking schools. With respect to their views on the closed model, therefore, these two schools were in full agreement.

OTHER NINETEENTH-CENTURY MONETARY WRITERS AND THE CLOSED MODEL: JAMES AND JOHN STUART MILL

Other monetary writers in the nineteenth century also discussed and analyzed the closed model. Many of these writers are not normally associated with any particular monetary school of thought; nonetheless, their restatements and endorsements of the closed monetary model further enhanced its tenability.

James Mill, for example, was one of the important monetary writers of this period who restated the closed monetary model. Mill contended that the quantity of money determined its value and thereby endorsed money-to-prices causality.[128] This is evident in a section of his *Elements* (first published in 1821) entitled "What Regulates the Value of Money."[129] It is also evident in his discussion of how an increase in gold production increases prices in "the whole connected chain of the commercial world."[130] The corollaries of proportionality and neutrality are also restated by Mill.[131] He states, for example, that changes in the supply of money do not affect relative prices:

> An alteration in the value of money, it is obvious, alters the relative value of nothing else. All things—bread, cloth, shoes, etc., rise in value as compared with money; but not one of them rises in value as compared with any other.[132]

The essentials of the closed model, then, were clearly recognized and reaffirmed by James Mill. Given his endorsement, it is not surprising that his son, John Stuart Mill, also supported the closed monetary model. For, as Ashley has indicated, James Mill had a strong influence on the economic (and monetary) opinions of his son. This influence, contends Ashley "was deep and indelible. . . . John [Stuart] Mill's economics remained those of his father down to the end of his life."[133]

John Stuart Mill's endorsement of the closed monetary model, as well as its important corollaries (such as money-to-prices causality, proportionality, and neutrality), is illustrated in the following quotations from Mill's *Principles of Political Economy* (first published in 1848). Assuming that the money supply had been exogenously increased, for example, Mill contended that:

> Prices would have risen in a certain ratio, and the value of money would have fallen in the same ratio. . . . This ratio would be precisely that in which the quantity of money had been increased. If the whole money in circulation was doubled, prices would be doubled. If it was only increased one-fourth, prices would rise one-fourth. . . . When there had been time for the increased supply of money to reach all markets, or (according to the conventional metaphor) to permeate all the channels of circulation, all prices would have risen one-fourth. . . . So that the value of money, other things being the same, varies inversely as its quantity; every increase of quantity lowering the value, and every diminution raising it, in a ratio exactly equivalent.[134]

> That an increase of the quantity of money raises prices, and a diminution lowers them, is the most elementary proposition in the theory of currency, and without it we should have no key to any of the others. In any state of things, however, except the simple and primative one which we have supposed, the proposition is only true other things being the same. . . .[135]

In the following remarks, Mill leaves no doubt that these views pertained to the closed world economy. Assuming a sudden exogenous increase in the supply of (metallic) money, Mill contends that:

> . . . the newly acquired stock of money would diffuse itself over all countries . . . through all parts of the commercial world. The money . . . would spread itself to an equal depth over all commercial countries . . . until . . . the money had diffused itself so equally that prices had risen in the same ratio in all countries, so that the alteration of price would be for all practical purposes ineffective, and . . . [real economic variables], though at a higher money valuation, would be exactly as they were originally. . . . the discovery of the treasure would thus produce only temporary [real] effects . . . until the treasure had disseminated itself through the world. . . .[136]

The real balance effect was also explicitly described by John Stuart Mill. That is, Mill indicated that changes in the quantity of money affected prices through its prior effect in altering demand.[137] John Stuart Mill, then, fully supported the closed model and its important corollaries. The documentation of Mill's endorsements is particularly important because he was so widely cited and influential.

It is well known, for example, that "all through the second half of the 19th century Mills' *Principles of Political Economy* was the undisputed bible of economists. . . . As late as 1900, Mill's work was still the basic textbook in elementary courses in both British and American universities."[138] Because of Mill's notoriety, then, his reaffirmation of the closed model further enhanced its credibility and served to further propagate these principles through the nineteenth century. This continued development and reaffirmation of the model will be described in the following chapter.

NOTES

1. Hugo Hegeland, *The Quantity Theory of Money* (Goteborg: Elanders Boktryckeri Aktiebulag, 1951), pp. 24, 180-82, and Arthur W. Marget, *The Theory of Prices*, Volume 1 (New York: Augustus M. Kelley, 1966), pp. 9-10 (footnote).
2. Hegeland, op. cit., p. 24.
3. Ibid., pp. 180, 182; see also p. 24, where Hegeland indicates that the Chinese "displayed the idea of regulating the value of money by changing its quantity."
4. Ibid., pp. 24, 151; Marget, op. cit., pp. 9-10 (footnote); and Eli Heckscher, *Mercantilism*, Volume II (London: Allen and Unwin, 1931), p. 225.
5. See, for example, Hegeland, op. cit., p. 151. See also Heckscher, op. cit., and Marget, op. cit. Hegeland indicates that this concept was also endorsed by Henry of Ghent as well as Antonine of Florence (Hegeland, op. cit., p. 151.)
6. Heckscher, op. cit., p. 225.
7. Hegeland, op. cit., p. 24.
8. See, for example, Milton Friedman, "Commodity Reserve Currency," in *Essays in Positive Economics*, ed. Milton Friedman (Chicago: University of Chicago Press, 1953), p. 207. See also Lester Chandler, *The Economics of Money and Banking* (New York: Harper, 1948), ch. 29.
9. These views have been associated with various theories of money often referred to as cost of production theories of money, commodity theories of money, or metallism, a particular version of the commodity theory of money. See, for example, Friedman, op. cit., and Chandler, op. cit.
10. Charles Rist, *History of Monetary and Credit Theory*, (New York: Augustus M. Kelley, 1966), p. 110. The imbedded quote is from de Foville.
11. Frank Taussig, *Principles of Economics*, Volume I (New York: MacMillan, 1911), p. 256.
12. Ibid., p. 256.
13. Rist, op. cit., p. 110.
14. Taussig, op. cit., p. 257. Specifically, Taussig indicated that "By the middle of the seventeenth century, prices had risen to double or triple what they were at the opening of the sixteenth century. The change worked itself out chiefly during the hundred years from 1550 to 1650. . . ."

15. It has been documented that the Polish astronomer, Nicolas Copernicus, as well as several Spanish authors, gave essentially the same explanation as Bodin before his work was published in 1568. In addition to Copernicus (see Hegeland, op. cit., pp. 14, 15, 182), the Spanish writers were identified as Francisco Lopez de Gomara (cited in Hegeland, op. cit., p. 15) and the Salamancian theologian, the Dominican Martin de Azpilcueta Navarro, in Murray Rothbard, "New Light on the Prehistory of the Austrian School," *The Foundations of Modern Austrian Economics,* ed. Edwin Dolan (Kansas City: Sheed and Ward, 1976), p. 56. For references citing Bodin, see Marget, op. cit., Volume I, p. 9; J. Schumpeter, *History of Economic Analysis* (New York: Oxford University Press, 1954), pp. 311–12; and Hegeland, op. cit., pp. 15–16.

16. See, for example, Heckscher, op. cit., p. 225.

17. Jean Bodin, "Jean Bodin's Reply to the Paradoxes of Malestroit Concerning the Dearness of All Things and the Remedy Therefore," *Early Economic Thought,* ed. Arthur E. Monroe (Cambridge: Harvard University Press, 1924), p. 127 [emphasis added].

18. See, for example, Marget, op. cit., Volume I, p. 10 (footnote), and Volume II, p. 13.

19. Hegeland, op. cit., p. 169 [emphasis added].

20. This does not imply that money was exogenous in the sense of a policy control variable.

21. Hegeland, for example, indicates that Bodin's statement "suggests that he by no means considered himself to be the first to establish the causal relation as such for he refers to the same relation experienced during the reign of the Roman Emperors Paulus Aemilius and Julius Caesar." (Hegeland, op. cit., p. 16.) See also Hegeland, op. cit., pp. 24, 152–53, and Schumpeter, op. cit., p. 312.

22. B. Davanzati, as quoted in Chi-Yuen Wu, *An Outline of International Price Theories* (London: Routledge, 1939), p. 22.

23. Hegeland, op. cit., p. 18.

24. Ibid., p. 25.

25. Malynes, quoted in Heckscher, op. cit., p. 228.

26. Malynes, quoted in Jacob Viner, *Studies in the Theory of International Trade* (New York: Augustus M. Kelley, 1965), p. 41. See also Schumpeter, op. cit., p. 314 (footnote).

27. Heckscher, op. cit., p. 225.

28. Mun, quoted in Viner, op. cit., p. 41. Mun's work was written in 1630 but was not published until 1664. See Viner for additional quotes of writers during this period.

29. Although written about 1630, Vaughan's writings were not published until 1675.

30. W. Potter, *The Key of Wealth* (1650), p. 13, quoted in Hegeland, op. cit., p. 31 [emphases added].

31. Hegeland, op. cit., p. 31.

32. Arthur E. Monroe, *Monetary Theory before Adam Smith* (New York: Augustus M. Kelley, 1966), p. 109.

33. Viner, op. cit., p. 75.

34. Arthur Leigh, "John Locke and the Quantity Theory of Money," *History of Political Economy* 6 (Summer 1974):204, 207.

35. Heckscher, op. cit., p. 225.

36. John Locke, "Some Considerations of the Consequences of the Lowering of Interest and Raising the Value of Money (1691)," *Several Papers*

Relating to Money, Interest and Trade (New York: Augustus M. Kelley, 1968), pp. 61-26.

37. In other words, changes in the value of money were determined more by changes in supply than by changes in demand. See, for example, Wu, op. cit., p. 48.

38. See, for example, Hegeland, op. cit., p. 29. Locke, in analyzing the demand for money, gave a ". . . remarkably thorough and quantitative analysis of the transactions demand for money, in this instance clearly a stock demand, not a flow demand." (Leigh, op. cit., p. 205.) In this regard, Locke also explicitly indicated the importance of the velocity of money. See, for example, Wu, op. cit., p. 48.

39. Leigh, op. cit., p. 207 [emphasis added]. The reason why it does not apply to the open economy, as well as Locke's views pertaining to the open economy, will be developed in subsequent chapters.

40. Locke, op. cit., pp. 73-74 [emphasis added and second parenthesis added]. This passage is also quoted in Hegeland, op. cit., p. 29. See also Monroe, *Monetary Theory*, p. 112.

41. Locke, op. cit., p. 46 [emphasis added]. See also Douglas Vickers, *Studies in the Theory of Money, 1690-1776* (New York: Augustus M. Kelley, 1968), p. 62.

42. Locke, ibid., p. 77 [emphasis added]. See also Vickers, op. cit., p. 67, and Leigh, op. cit., p. 208.

43. Thus, Locke's proportionality postulate implicitly assumes a stable demand for money. See, for example, Hegeland, op. cit., p. 29; Marget, op. cit., p. 17 (footnote); and Wu, op. cit., p. 47-48.

44. Leigh, op. cit., p. 208. See also Heckscher, op. cit., p. 239.

45. Locke, op. cit., pp. 75-76. See also Leigh, op. cit., pp; 207-08.

46. Hegeland, op. cit., pp. 27, 82, 167 [emphasis added].

47. This contention is especially emphasized by Hegeland.

48. See, for example, Viner, op. cit., p. 40, and Monroe, *Monetary Theory*, p. 111.

49. Isaac Gervaise, *The System or Theory of the Trade of the World* (Baltimore: Johns Hopkins, 1954), p. 5 [emphasis added].

50. See, for example, Monroe, *Monetary Theory*, p. 213.

51. Thomas T. Sekine, "The Discovery of International Monetary Equilibrium by Vanderlint, Cantillon, Gervaise, and Hume," *Economia Internazionale XXVI* 2 (1973):265.

52. Montesquieu, *The Spirit of Laws*, translated by T. Nugent, New York, 1949, Volume I, pp. 378-79, quoted in Don Patinkin, *Money, Interest and Prices* (second ed.) (New York: Harper & Row, 1965), pp. 529-30.

53. Montesquieu, op. cit., Chapter VIII, Book XXII, quoted in Hegeland, op. cit., p. 33.

54. Hegeland, op. cit., p. 34.

55. Richard Cantillon, *Essai sur la nature du commerce en général*, ed. Henry Higgs (London: Macmillan, 1931), p. 161.

56. Cantillon, as quoted in Joseph Spengler, "Richard Cantillon: First of the Moderns," *Essays in Economic Thought*, eds. Joseph Spengler and William Allen (New York: Rand McNally, 1960), p. 122.

57. Cantillon, op. cit., p. 161.

58. Schumpeter, op. cit., p. 317.

59. Cantillon, op. cit., pp. 161, 163.

60. Patinkin, op. cit., p. 529.

61. Ibid., p. 530. See also Hegeland, op. cit., p. 16 (footnote), and Heckscher, op. cit., p. 255, where Heckscher indicates the view that changes in prices are determined by changes in the demand for goods on the part of the holders of money is "so simple an idea that it occurred at a very early date. . . ."

62. See, for example, Spengler, op. cit., p. 106.

63. Hegeland, op. cit., p. 159.

64. Viner, op. cit., p. 75.

65. See, for example, Heckscher, op. cit., pp. 225-27. See also Leigh, op. cit., p. 207 (footnote).

66. Wu, op. cit., p. 74.

67. See, for example, Viner, op. cit., p. 41.

68. See, for example, references to Locke and Cantillon in Adam Smith, *An Inquiry into the Nature and Causes of the Wealth of Nations,* ed. Edwin Cannan (New York: Random House, 1937) as well as Spengler, op. cit., p. 106, who indicates that Smith was appreciably influenced by Cantillon.

69. See, for example, Schumpeter, op. cit., p. 315.

70. As Viner has ably pointed out: "Hume wrote before the first attempt in England, that of Evelyn in 1798, to measure price levels by means of statistical averages. Even after 1798, the leading economists until the time of Jevons either revealed no acquaintance with the notion of representing, by means of statistical averages, either a level of prices, or changes in such level, or found it unacceptable for various reasons. . . . While a number of crude index numbers were constructed during the first half of the Nineteenth Century, none of the classical economists . . . would have anything to do with them. . . ." In Viner, op. cit., pp. 312-13.

71. See, for example, Oswald St. Clair, *A Key to Ricardo* (New York: Kelley and Millman, 1957), p. 298; Dennis P. O'Brien, *The Classical Economists* (Oxford: Clarendon Press, 1975), pp. 148-49; Johan Myhrman, "Experiences of Flexible Exchange Rates in Earlier Periods: Theories, Evidence, and a New View," *Scandinavian Journal of Economics,* 78 (1976):171; and Robert V. Eagly, "The Swedish and English Bullionist Controversies," *Events, Ideology and Economic Theory,* ed. Robert V. Eagly (Detroit: Wayne State University Press, 1968), p. 26.

Torrens, for example explicitly asserted that "an increase in the quantity and fall in the value of gold, in relation to commodities, is the same thing as an increase in the quantity and fall in the value of the currency in relation to commodities is the same thing as a rise of prices." In Lionel Robbins, *Robert Torrens and the Evolution of Classical Economics* (London: MacMillan, 1958), p. 125. See also J. Laurence Laughlin, *The Principles of Money* (New York: Scribners, 1903), p. 417.

72. This price indicates how much domestic currency is worth in terms of gold. As long as the domestic price of currency remains convertible, the market price of bullion must closely approximate the official mint price. That is, it can only vary between relatively narrow bands—i.e., between the gold export and import points.

73. Another way of interpreting the price of goods in terms of gold is to view it as the reciprocal of the world price of gold. Adam Smith clearly indicated that this price was determined in world markets: "The proportion between the value of gold and silver and that of goods of any other kind, depends in all cases, not upon the nature or quantity of any particular paper money, which may be current in any particular country, but upon the richness or poverty of the mines, which happen at any particular time to supply the great market of the commercial *world* with those of metals." In Smith, op. cit., 349-50 [emphasis added].

74. Note that in equation 1, gold units cancel so that goods in terms of domestic currency appear on both sides of the equation.

75. This was recognized at least as early as 1695 by Simon Clement, who indicated that a small open economy under a gold standard could do nothing to prevent inflation in the face of world inflation. Specifically, he indicated that: "Nothing that any nation can do will raise the value of bullion in the face of the great supplies that have come from America." In Monroe, *Monetary Theory*, p. 105.

76. David Hume, "Of Money," *Writings on Economics,* ed. Eugene Rotwein (Freeport: Books for Libraries Press, 1955), pp. 33, 37, 38, 42 [emphasis added]. In his essay, "Of Interest," Hume again indicates that: "The greater or less plenty of (money) is of no consequence, if we consider a nation within itself. . . ." In David Hume, "Of Interest," *Writings on Economics* (Freeport: Books for Libraries Press, 1955), p. 48.

77. See, for example, Vickers, op. cit., p. 226, and Hegeland, op. cit., p. 157, where Hegeland indicates that one of Hume's conclusions was that "*changes* in the quantity of money, *ceteris paribus*, will *cause* proportionate price variations."

78. Hume, "Of Interest," pp. 48, 51, 56, 57. See also Thomas Sowell, *Classical Economics Reconsidered* (Princeton: Princeton University Press, 1974), pp. 56-57.

79. Specifically, Hume states that the artisan who receives money before others "carries his money to market, where he finds everything at the same price as formerly, but returns with greater quantity and of better kinds, for the use of his family." In David Hume, "Of Money," p. 38. Hume indicates that, ultimately, this process leads to an increase in all prices.

80. See, for example, the references to Hume in Adam Smith, *Wealth of Nations.*

81. W. L. Taylor, *Francis Hutcheson and David Hume as Predecessors of Adam Smith* (Durham: Duke University Press, 1965), p. 131.

82. Ibid., p. 35. See also p. 39.

83. Ibid., p. 51.

84. Ibid., p. 50.

85. Ibid., p. 38. See also J. M. Low, "An Eighteenth Century Controversy in the Theory of Economic Progress," *The Manchester School* (September 1965):312, where he indicates that both Smith and Hume knew Oswald and both "valued him highly as an economist. . . ."

86. Ibid., p. 314 [emphasis added].

87. Smith, op. cit., p. 37.

88. Ibid., p. 209.

89. Ibid., p. 213.

90. Ibid., p. 266.

91. Ibid., Volume 2, p. 16 [emphasis added].

92. See, for example, ibid., pp. 372-76, 379, 450-51.

93. Sowell, op. cit., p. 56-57.

94. Smith, op. cit., p. 377 [emphasis added].

95. Ibid., pp. 376-78.

96. Samuel Hollander, *The Economics of David Ricardo* (Toronto: University of Toronto Press, 1979), p. 416. Hollander also indicates that "the general fact of price inflation was certainly recognized by contemporaries," including, for example, Henry Thornton. Moreover, "primative index numbers had been devised. In fact, John Wheatley, *Remarks on Currency and Commerce*

(London 1803), utilized the index published in 1798 by Sir George Shuckburgh Evelyn (1798)," Hollander, op. cit., p. 416 (footnote).

97. As a consequence of the lack of data related to general price indexes, the bullionists directed much of their formal analysis on readily quantifiable magnitudes such as the price of bullion and the foreign exchange rate. See, for example, Hegeland, op. cit., p. 416.

98. As Hollander has indicated, this view was forcefully set out by Adam Smith. Smith stated, for example, that: "'A paper currency which falls below the value of gold and silver coin, does not thereby sink the value of those metals, or occasion equal quantities of them, to exchange for a smaller quantity of goods of any other kind.' The gold price of commodities 'depends in all cases, not upon the nature or quantity of any particular paper money, which may be current in any particular country, but upon the richness or poverty of the mines, which happen at any particular time to supply the great market of the commercial world with those metals.'" Adam Smith, *Wealth of Nations,* pp. 312-13. Quoted in Hollander, op. cit., p. 428.

99. The increase in the sterling price of bullion could have been caused by an increase in the world demand for gold, as contended during this period by the Bank of England. However, bullionists pointed out that the price of gold in terms of foreign currencies had not increased, that commodity prices in terms of gold had remained relatively stable, and that sterling prices of commodities had increased. Taken together, these facts demonstrated that the British price disturbances during this period were in large part caused by an excessive issuance of inconvertible currency.

100. Since no index numbers were available, the premium on bullion was viewed as *the* measure of inflation caused by the excessive issuance of inconvertible currency. See Karl H. Niebyl, *Studies in the Classical Theories of Money* (New York: Columbia University Press, 1946), p. 114.

101. David Ricardo, "The High Price of Bullion, a Proof of the Depreciation of Bank Notes," *The Works and Correspondence of David Ricardo,* ed. Piero Sraffa, Volume III (Cambridge: Harvard University Press, 1951), p. 80 [emphasis added].

102. Edwin Cannan ed., *The Paper Pound of 1797-1821, The Bullion Report* (1810) (New York: Augustus M. Kelley, 1969), pp. 6, 7, 12, 16.

103. Bullionist writers were well aware of and familiar with the earlier works of Hume and Smith. They accepted the closed economy views of Hume and Smith and often explicitly referenced both of these earlier classical monetary theorists.

104. John Wheatley, *An Essay on the Theory of Money and Principles of Commerce* (London: T. Cadell and W. Davies, Strand, St. James, 1807), pp. 37-38, 51. These concepts of causality and monetary neutrality were also specified elsewhere by Wheatley. For example, Wheatley indicates that in investigating the depreciation of money from the period of Elizabeth to William The Third, "no controversy has ever arisen, either on the fact of the depression, or on the cause that led to it, the influx of money from America." (Wheatley, op. cit., pp. 266-67.) Wheatley also explicitly states that in the long run, when all prices have adjusted, an increase in money can have no effect on real economic activity. (Wheatley, op. cit., p. 40.)

105. David Ricardo, op. cit., p. 53 [emphasis added].

106. Hegeland, op. cit., pp. 59-60. See also Ricardo, op. cit., p. 90. In citing a letter from Ricardo to Malthus, Hollander contends that, in a technical

sense, Ricardo did not support proportionality because of nonmonetary demands for gold. Ricardo, however, tended to neglect this technical qualification in formal statements relating to the determination of general price. (Hollander, op. cit., pp. 477-78.)

107. Henry Thornton, "Two Speeches of Henry Thornton on the Bullion Report," Appendix III, *An Enquiry into the Nature and Effects of the Paper Credit of Great Britain*, ed. F. A. Hayek (Fairfield: Augustus M. Kelley, 1978), p. 328.

108. See, for example, Ricardo, op. cit., pp. 25-26, 89-92, 137, 143, 150, 341, 374-76.

109. See, for example, Thornton, *An Enquiry into the Nature and Effects of the Paper Credit of Great Britain* (Fairfield: Augustus M. Kelley, 1978), pp. 255-56. See also Thomas Sowell, op. cit., p. 58.

110. Don Patinkin, op. cit., pp. 164, 529.

111. See, for example, Thornton, *An Enquiry*, p. 195, footnote, pp. 250-67, and Ricardo, op. cit., pp. 91, 217, 362-63, 390.

112. See, for example, Thornton, *An Enquiry*, p. 266; Wheatley, op. cit., pp. 285-87, 331, 375; and Ricardo, op. cit., pp. 56-57.

113. In concluding his classic essay. "The High Price of Bullion," Ricardo himself explicitly indicated that he was well aware that he had ". . . not added to the stock of information with which the public has been enlightened by many able writers on the same important subject." (Ricardo, op. cit., p. 99.)

114. Ricardo, op. cit., pp. 56-57.

115. See, for example, Thornton, *An Enquiry*, pp. 269-70, and Ricardo, op. cit., pp. 56-57.

116. Ricardo, op. cit., p. 57 (footnote).

117. See, for example, O'Brien, op. cit., p. 153.

118. See, for example, Viner, op. cit., p. 221.

119. See, for example, Frank W. Fetter, *Development of British Monetary Orthodoxy, 1797-1875* (Cambridge: Harvard University Press, 1965), pp. 190-91; T. E. Gregory, "Introduction," *A History of Prices*, Volume I, Tooke and Newmarch (New York: Adelphi, 1928), p. 30; Thomas Tooke, *A History of Prices*, Volume IV (New York: Adelphi, 1928), pp. 206-09, 462; Marion R. Daugherty, "The Currency-Banking Controversy: Part I and II," *Southern Economic Journal* 9 (July 1942-April 1943); and Lionel Robbins, *Robert Torrens and the Evolution of Classical Economics* (London: Macmillan, 1958), p. 125.

120. Robert Torrens, *Principles and Practical Operation of Sir Robert Peels Act of 1844, Explained and Defended*, pp. 191-92, as quoted in Robbins, op. cit., p. 125.

121. See, for example, Fetter, op. cit., pp. 190-91; Tooke, op. cit., pp. 206-09, 462; and Gregory, op. cit., p. 30.

122. Daugherty, op. cit., pp. 245-46.

123. Tooke, op. cit., p. 208 [emphasis added]. (Here Tooke is endorsing the views of Wilson.)

124. Moreover, in answering questions before the Committee on Banks of Issue in 1840, Tooke indicated that if the value of gold in the commercial world were affected by an extensive substitution of paper for gold, then prices of commodities would undergo a variation *proportionate to* the increase in notes. (Tooke, op. cit., p. 462.)

125. Ludwig von Mises, *The Theory of Money and Credit* (New York: Foundation for Economic Education, 1971), p. 343.

126. Hegeland, op. cit., p. 186. See Tooke, *An Inquiry into the Currency Principle* (London: London School of Economics, 1959), p. 124, and *A History of Prices,* Volume III (New York: Adelphi, 1928), p. 245; Volume IV, p. 200; and Volume V, p. 345.

127. Charles Rist, op. cit., p. 288. See Tooke, *A History of Prices,* Volume IV, pp. 234–35.

128. Mill, it should be pointed out, also endorsed a cost of production theory of money. This view is not irreconcilable with the theory that emphasizes money-to-prices causality, since the former explains the intrinsic and long-run value of money, whereas the latter view explains the market value of money within the context of a shorter time frame. See, for example, Chi-Yuen Wu, op. cit., p. 126.

129. James Mill, *Elements of Political Economy* (New York: Augustus M. Kelley, 1965), pp. 131–35. In this section, Mill indicates that: "This, it is evident, is a proposition universally true. Whenever the value of money has either risen or fallen, [the quantity of goods, against which it is exchanged, and the rapidity of circulation, remaining the same] the change must be owing to a corresponding diminution or increase of the quantity; and can be owing to nothing else." (p. 134; see also p. 136 and Hegeland, op. cit., p. 161.)

130. Mill, *Elements,* p. 178.

131. See, for examples, Mill, *Elements,* pp. 133, 163.

132. Ibid., p. 163.

133. W. J. Ashley, "Introduction," John Stuart Mill, *Principles of Political Economy* (London: Longmans, Green, 1926), p. VIII. In his autobiography, John Stuart Mill indicated that monetary theory was introduced by his father, ibid., p. V.

134. John Stuart Mill, *Principles,* pp. 492–93.

135. Ibid., p. 495.

136. Ibid., p. 630. The neutrality of money was also described elsewhere by John Stuart Mill. He indicated, for example, that changes in money would have no long-run effect on the rate of interest. See, for example, ibid., p. 645. See also Sowell, op. cit., p. 56.

137. That is, Mill contended that an increased demand for commodities and an exchange of money for commodities are identical activities that bring about an increase in prices. In his own words: "Money acts upon prices in no other way than by being tendered in exchange for commodities." (John Stuart Mill, *Principles,* p. 524. See also pp. 491–93, 496.)

138. Mark Blaug, *Economic Theory in Retrospect* (Homewood: Richard D. Irwin, 1968), p. 180.

4

THE HISTORICAL DEVELOPMENT OF THE MONETARY MODEL OF THE CLOSED ECONOMY: PART TWO

THE CALIFORNIA AND AUSTRALIAN GOLD DISCOVERIES AND THE CLOSED MONETARY MODEL

In the middle of the nineteenth century, events occurred that continued to enhance the credibility of the closed model, particularly as it applied to the world economy. In particular, important gold discoveries were made in California (1848) and in Australia (1851). As Fetter has indicated: "By 1850 annual production [of gold] was . . . nearly fifteen times what it had been at the turn of the century, and five times what it had been in 1848. In the five years 1849–1853, gold production exceeded the world's total production between the time of Columbus's discovery of America and the discovery of California gold."[1] Among other things, these large discoveries stimulated discussion as to the relationship between the world money supply and world prices. John E. Cairnes, W. Stanley Jevons, and others made significant contributions to this discussion.[2] In particular, these economists analyzed the effect of the gold discoveries on world prices.

Cairnes, for example, wrote four essays between 1858 and 1860 on the inflationary effects of the gold discoveries. (These essays were republished in 1873 under the title, *Essays in Political Economy*.)[3] In analyzing the increase in world money, Cairnes forcefully asserts that the world is a closed economy and should be analyzed as such. He indicated, for example, that ". . . the world, as a whole, has no foreign trade; it has no means of exchanging for the productions of other planets the gold which it produces."[4]

After establishing the closed context of his analysis, Cairnes, following Cantillon, examined the transmission mechanism of an increased world money (gold) supply on world prices. That is, he analyzed the process by which increases in gold production increase prices first in one sector or country and then in another, until ultimately all "prices throughout the world . . . rise in proportion."[5, 6] In examining these effects of the gold discoveries, Cairnes forcefully restated the closed model and its corollaries of money-to-prices causality, proportionality, and neutrality. This is demonstrated, for example, in Cairnes' following remarks:

> It is not indeed denied . . . by anyone pretending to economic knowledge, that the enlarged production of gold now taking place has a tendency to lower its value. . . . I am quite prepared to admit that *an increase of money tends ultimately*, where the conditions of production remain in other respects the same, *to affect the prices of all commodities and services in an equal degree*; but before this result is attained a period of time, longer or shorter according to the amount of the augmentation and the general circumstances of commerce, must elapse. In the present instance the additions which are being made to the monetary systems of the *world* are upon an enormous scale, and the disturbance effected in the relation of prices is *proportionally* great.[7]

Moreover, Cairnes indicated that, in the long run, an exogenous increase in world money "would tend to lower the value of money, but [unless so far as it affected fixed contracts] would not alter the relative purchasing power of individuals, nor therefore the distribution of commodities, nor the interests of mankind"; in short, it would not affect real economic activity.[8] Finally, Cairnes explicitly recognized the real balance effect: "When an increased amount of money comes into existence, there is, of course, an increased expenditure on the part of those into whose possession it comes, the immediate effect of which is to raise the prices of all commodities which fall under its influence.[9]

As indicated by Bordo, the various contentions made by Cairnes were for the most part substantiated by the empirical evidence.[10] In particular, Cairnes, "through a systematic analysis of the data," demonstrated that there was in fact "a substantial worldwide increase in prices," which followed a substantial increase in the quantity of world money.[11] In sum, therefore, Cairnes not only restated the closed monetary model (and its important elements), but supported his claims with empirical evidence.

Further evidence tending to support the closed monetary model was also provided by other economists examining the empirical data of the period. In particular, W. Stanley Jevons made estimates of the depreciation of the value of gold, using price data he had compiled and price indices he had constructed. On the basis of his estimates, he contended that the gold discoveries had significantly depreciated the value of gold.[12] Jevons, then, reaffirmed the view that with an (exogenous) increase in the world money supply, world prices would increase shortly thereafter, that is, that causality in this case runs from money to prices. In supporting this view, Jevons was led to endorse corollaries of the closed model, as is indicated in the following remarks:

> . . . it is almost a matter of indifference, within certain limits, whether there is much gold or little. Prices having once settled themselves, it is only a question of carrying a little more metal or a little less in your pocket. As Cantillon, and subsequently, but independently Hume, remarked, if the money in the world were suddenly doubled or halved trade would go on as before, all prices being approximately doubled or halved.[13]

Thus, the closed monetary model was supported not only by economists who employed deductive methods but by empirically oriented economists intimately familiar with the data and circumstances of the mid-nineteenth century.

THE PERIOD BETWEEN 1873 AND 1896 AND THE CLOSED MONETARY MODEL

The period between about 1873 and 1896 also attracted a great deal of attention on the part of monetary economists interested in problems of the day.[14] During this period (of more than 20 years), world prices declined substantially.[15] At the same time, however, the introduction of new methods, technological advancements, new raw material sources, and increased competition led to increases in productivity, real wages, and world output.[16] In short, the period witnessed substantial increases in the supply of commodities on world markets, or an increase in world aggregate supply.[17] Although gold production slowed from the extraordinarily high rates of production experienced during the 1850s and 1860s, production remained positive.[18] In light of these circumstances, various monetary economists of the period analyzed the causes of the existing deflation and recommended remedies for it as well. In so doing, they directed attention to *world* determinants as well as to *world* remedies. Nicholson, for example, argued that any analysis of movements in general prices required an examination of world variables rather than those of an individual country:

> . . . it becomes clear that the general level of prices in any one country [under a gold standard] depends on causes beyond the power of that country to control, and a fall in prices cannot be explained without a wide survey . . . movements in general prices can only be explained by taking into account the causes which affect the demand for, and the supply of, gold [i.e., world money].[19]

As a result of the various analyses during this period, there arose among monetary economists a controversy relating not only to the interpretation of the period but to the proposed remedies for world deflation as well. These proposed remedies were directed at adopting alternative world monetary standards. In particular, one group of monetary economists advocated international bimetallism, whereas another group endorsed the gold standard, or gold monometallism. The controversy, therefore, is often referred to as the Bimetallist–Monometallist debate. Since the controversy is marred by problems of semantics, the creation of straw men, as well as a confusion between the short run and the long run, a lucid summary of the debate has never been published. In the brief discussion that follows, the relevance of the controversy in the evolution of the closed monetary model will be emphasized.

In analyzing the period between 1873 and 1896, economists recognized the above-cited increase in aggregate supply, the slowdown in gold production, and the substantial world deflation. These factors in and of themselves might have implied an increase in the demand for gold (for transactions purposes) relative to gold supply, and, consequently, could be viewed as explaining the world deflation. In addition to this reason for an increased demand for gold, however, several other important events developed during the period. Several economies, such as the United States, Italy, and Austria, for example, emerged from paper money regimes and returned to the gold standard. (The United States resumed specie payments at the pre-Civil War basis.) The implication of these changes in money standards was an increased demand for gold. In addition to alterations from paper to gold standards, however, several economies changed from silver—or bimetallic—to purely gold-based standards, further increasing the demand for gold.[20] A list of the dates on which various countries adopted gold as a single standard is provided in Table 1.[21]

According to the closed model, an (exogenous) increase in the demand (relative to the supply) of gold would have the same depressing effect on *world prices* as would a decrease in the supply of gold. This is the essence of what occurred in the period under consideration. Consequently, the period constitutes additional evidence that tends to support the closed monetary model. That is, these substantial increases in the demand for gold were enough to bring about the world-wide deflation observed during the period.[22]

Whereas these facts were recognized by the analysts of the period, bimetallists and monometallists emphasized different factors and, hence, presented alternative interpretations of the period as well as differing remedies. Bimetallists, such as Walker, Nicholson, and Wolowski, for example, emphasized the short run and premised their analysis on the quantity theory of money.[23] They attributed the world price deflation of 1873–96 to the fact that the gold standard prevented the supply of money from increasing in line with the rapidly growing demand for money.[24] Moreover, they indicated that the abandonment of silver and the limitation of free coinage to gold alone contributed to the current deflation.[25] These monetary economists recommended the adoption of an international bimetallic standard, which would, they argued, "increase the supply of the

TABLE 1. Dates of Adopting Gold Standard

Germany	1871	Italy	1874
Sweden	1873	Greece	1874
Norway	1873	Holland	1875
Denmark	1873	Uruguay	1876
France	1874	United States	1879
Belgium	1874	Austria	1892
Switzerland	1874	Chile	1895

From Lester Chandler, *The Economics of Money and Banking* (New York: Harper, 1948), p. 94. Chandler indicates that these "dates are approximate only, for some of the countries made the change from bimetallism or monometallism [silver] to gold in several steps." (Ibid., p. 93, footnote.)

precious metal available for currency purposes and thus prevent a further fall in the prices of commodities."[26]

Monometallists, on the other hand, emphasized the long run as well as the cost of production theory of money (sometimes referred to as the commodity theory of money).[27,28] However, as Rist has indicated: ". . . advocates of gold monometallism . . . too believed in the quantity theory and would not for a moment have denied the influence on prices of changes in the quantity of bullion."[29]

As to the monometallist interpretation of the period, some analysts indicate that monometallists largely attributed the world deflation to the increase in world aggregate supply. Although some monometallists (such as Laughlin) may have adopted this view, other monometallists (such as Giffen and Jevons) fully recognized all the aspects of the supply and demand for money which work to determine general prices. Rist, for example, demonstrates that monometallists "did not deny that in theory the price level depends on [both] the quantity of goods offered for sale and on the output of the previous metals."[30] Moreover, monometallists "freely admitted that the suspension of silver coinage and the increased demand for gold due to the wider adoption of the gold standard . . . contributed to the fall in prices; this opinion was held by Marshall, Jevons, Sir Robert Giffen (and others)."[31] While recognizing these various factors, monometallists believed that the relative scarcity of gold—the effects of which they did not dispute—would soon be succeeded by a period of abundance.[32] As a result, they advocated international gold monometallism.[33]

Despite the characterizations of the literature of the day, which tended to exaggerate the differences between monometallists and bimetallists, the fundamental dissimilarities between the two groups were not as great as is often indicated. In addition differences between the two groups often involved questions of semantics as well as a confusion between a short-run and a long-run emphasis.[34] As indicated above, for example, economists in both groups ultimately came to recognize that the deflation of 1873–96 was due to a slowdown in gold production, together with a substantial increase in the demand for gold resulting from (1) the adoption of the gold standard by various countries and (2) the increased trade and transactions resulting from rapid increases in aggregate supply and real growth.[35] In short, both groups recognized that the supply of gold had decreased relative to its demand and, hence, implicitly accepted the causal role of the supply of gold relative to its demand in determining world prices.[36]

Moreover, both bimetallists and monometallists were advocates of commodity standards. As such, they did not disagree as to the workings of commodity standards, which, in part, necessarily involves the recognition that rapid increases in the supply of the commodity reserve relative to its demand implies a fall in its value. Where their positions differed related, of course, to the relative merits of the particular commodity each wished to employ as a standard. Both groups contended that the particular commodity standard they endorsed would best serve to supply the *world* with an adequate quantity of money and, consequently, would work to stabilize *world* prices.

Finally, although bimetallists emphasized the quantity theory of money and monometallists stressed the cost of production theory of money, these positions are not necessarily inconsistent with one another. As clearly indicated by such economists as J. S. Mill, Wicksell, and others, the cost of production theory of money applies to the long run, whereas the quantity theory of money (in the closed economy under a commodity standard) pertains to a shorter-run time frame. The two positions are not, however, necessarily in conflict with one another.[37] As an illustration of this, no economist —even monometallists who ardently supported the cost of production theory of money (such as Laughlin or Giffen)—denied that a sudden discovery of gold (or a technological innovation leading to a sudden increase in gold production) would cause the value of gold to fall—or general prices to rise.[38] Indeed, monometallists such as Laughlin or Giffen often used such cases as examples by which to illustrate the effect of a sudden large increase in gold production on general prices.[39]

Interpreted in this way, then, the differences between the two views are not nearly as significant as is sometimes suggested in the literature. Indeed, there are many important areas of agreement between the two positions. What is important here, however, is to note that the positions of both bimetallists and monometallists can be viewed as being fully consistent with the closed monetary model as described above. Because of this consistency, together with the fact that (1) the bimetallist-monometallist controversy directed attention to the relationship between the *world money supply* and *world prices*, and (2) interpretations of the period served to support and, hence, to further bolster the credibility of the closed monetary model, the bimetallist-monometallist debate served to further reaffirm the closed monetary model as well as to pass it down to later generations of monetary economists.

THE SOUTH AFRICAN AND KLONDIKE GOLD DISCOVERIES AND THE CLOSED MONETARY MODEL

Beginning in the mid 1890s, world monetary circumstances changed once again. Gold was discovered in the Klondike-Yukon area and in South Africa. Moreover, the cyanide process of refining gold was introduced.[40] The exploitation of these mines and the enormous influx of gold that followed dominated other events relating to world monetary circumstances during this period.[41] As Taussig has indicated,

> the total production of gold was as great during the eighteen years 1891-1908, as it was during the forty years, 1850-1890; and during each of these periods it was much greater than it has been during the centuries that elapsed between 1493 and 1850. . . . The production of gold may be grouped as follows:
>
> aggregate during 257 years, 1493-1850—152 million ounces
> aggregate during 40 years, 1850-1890—232 million ounces
> aggregate during 18 years, 1891-1980—240 million ounces.[42]

This large increase in the supply of world money (gold) was followed by a rise in world prices.[43] Thus, the prolonged world price decline of 1873-96 was succeeded by a marked rise in world prices. This rise both in world gold supplies and in world prices eased the worldwide transition to the gold standard and effectively eliminated the bimetallic case against gold.[44] The controversy over the monetary standard, then, ceased to be an important issue.[45] At the same time, various monetary economists of the period were able to analyze the reasons for this reversal from falling world prices (1873-96) to rising world prices (after 1896). As a result of the availability of improved data during this period, it was possible, for example, to make more objective statistical investigations of the relationship between price movements and world gold output.[46] Those who conducted such investigations found it difficult to attribute the reversal of world price movements "to any other cause than the sudden abundance of the precious metals after their relative scarcity."[47] Thus, these economists found strong support for the closed monetary model—for the dependence of the world price level on the world money (gold) supply.[48] Consequently, "the traditional doctrine of the direct influence of an influx of the precious metals on [world] prices regained its former prestige."[49]

Monetary writers of the day who examined this particular period and found strong support for the view that changes in world money (gold) had a direct effect on world prices included such luminaries as Walras, Taussig, Wicksell, I. Fisher, Cassel, and others. As early as 1895, before any price effects of these gold discoveries were visible, for example, Walras accurately predicted the world price effects of these large gold discoveries. Specifically, Walras indicated that "Deducting the 14 or 15 milliards of gold which should come from the Witwatersrand alone as the value of the gold which will be used for industrial and luxury purposes, the price rise which will take place within the next ten years or so as a result of the increase in the output of gold may, without exaggeration, be put at 12 or 15 percent."[50]

Illustrations abound of monetary economists who, after examining the period's empirical evidence, endorsed the closed world monetary model. Frank Taussig, for example, indicated that "This vast addition to the stock of gold has been the foundation of the rise in prices which has taken place in the western nations, and indeed the world over, during the last decade [1900–10]."[51]

Similarly, Knut Wicksell, in the preface to his *Lectures on Political Economy* indicated that "the change in price tendency after 1895 is associated with the rapid increase in the quantity of gold."[52] Both Irving Fisher and Gustav Cassel also examined this particular period and concluded that the increase in world prices was due to an increase in the world money (gold) supply. Fisher, for example, stated that:

> From 1896 to the present (1911), prices have been rising because of the extraordinary rise in gold production. . . . The gold of South Africa combined with the gold from rich mines of Cripple Creek and other parts of the Rocky Mountain Plateau, and reinforced by gold from the Klondike, caused, and is still causing, a repetition of the phenomenon of a half a century ago.
>
> That there has been a distinct rise in prices is evident from the figures of *all* index numbers. Those of *The Economist*, Sauerbeck, Dun, the Labor Bureau Reports, and Bradstreet are given. . . . That the rise in prices has been *world wide* is evidenced not only by index numbers, which are only available for a limited number of countries, but by general impressions of consumers and by special reports and investigations.[53]

In examining this period, Cassel also drew analogous conclusions. Specifically, he contended that the world price movements occurring during the period could be attributed to divergencies between the actual and the normal stock of world money (gold).[54]

Indeed, in interpreting this period, no reputable monetary economist denied the effect that the increase in gold supplies had upon prices, that is, that an increase in the supply (relative to demand) of world money (gold) brought about an increase in world prices. Thus, in general, the proposition of causality from money to prices in the closed world economy was endorsed by the monetary writers of the day. This period, then, constitutes additional empirical support for the closed monetary model.

LATE NINETEENTH- AND EARLY TWENTIETH-CENTURY MONETARY WRITERS AND THE CLOSED ECONOMY

In addition to the accumulation of empirical support from periods in the late nineteenth and early twentieth centuries, several monetary theorists of this period reaffirmed and fully endorsed the monetary theory of the closed economy as spelled out above. In so doing, they provided still more theoretical support for the model. The monetary writers of this period who will be briefly discussed here include Wicksell, Laughlin, Fisher, Cassel, Taussig, Mises, and Pigou.

Knut Wicksell

In any examination of Wicksell's monetary writings, it is evident that Wicksell fully recognized the important contributions to monetary theory of earlier economists. In particular, the contributions of Smith, Ricardo, the Banking School writers, J. S. Mill, and Jevons are quoted extensively throughout Wicksell's discussions of monetary theory.[55] It should not be surprising, then, that Wicksell was influenced by these earlier monetary writers and that his views often closely correspond to their positions.

In his monetary writings, Wicksell clearly understood the importance of distinguishing the closed from the open economic framework. He very explicitly noted in several passages that the only truly closed economy is the world economy.[56] In discussing the closed world economy, Wicksell endorsed the idea of the direct action of world money (gold) on world prices.[57] Moreover, he analyzed the specific mechanisms by which gold discoveries ultimately affected all world prices.[58] Hence, in analyzing the closed economy, Wicksell endorsed the view that changes in the supply of money (relative to its demand) bring about changes in prices, that is, he reaffirmed the concept of causality from money to prices in the closed economy. Wicksell, then, held that the quantity theory of money—in the sense of causality running from the stock of money to prices—applied to the case of the closed economy.[59]

That Wicksell endorsed the concept of money to prices causality in the closed economy is manifest in another way. While he recognized that currency convertibility ensured the impossibility of single country inflation (see discussion of the open economy below), Wicksell restated the Ricardian position that if *all* countries pursued monetary expansion simultaneously (and, therefore, increased the *world* money supply), inflation could result, despite convertible currency systems.[60] In Wicksell's view of the closed world economy, then, causality runs from money to prices.

In addition to supporting this concept, Wicksell also endorsed other elements of the monetary model of the closed economy. In one passage, for example, Wicksell emphasizes that changes in the money stock necessarily have a proportionate effect on its value.[61] Moreover, Wicksell provided an important discussion of the real balance effect. He explicitly indicated, for example, that "The result of the increase in the quantity of money is a rise in the demand for commodities . . . with the consequence that all prices rise continuously—until cash balances stand once again in their normal relation to the level of prices."[62] Fundamental elements of the closed monetary model, then, were reaffirmed and restated by Wicksell.

J. Laurence Laughlin

Like Wicksell, Laughlin was also familiar with the important contributions to monetary theory of earlier economists, who are often cited throughout Laughlin's discussions of monetary theory. Being familiar with the views of these monetary writers, Laughlin recognized the important distinction they made between the open and closed monetary frameworks.[63] It is not surprising, then, that Laughlin made the same distinction (see below).

When he discussed the *closed world economy*, for example, Laughlin set out a proposition that, he contended, was acceptable to all economists: "We may . . . start from a proposition on which we can all agree. An increase in the quantity of the monetary standard *in the world*—such as gold—would tend, *other things being equal*, to lower its value and thus raise prices."[64]

Moreover, in analyzing the workings of the world gold standard (and a convertible currency system), Laughlin repeatedly emphasized that:

> A variation in prices from causes affecting gold itself can take place only through such effects as may modify its value *throughout the world*,—by alterations in the *world's* supply of, or the world's

> demand for gold. A mere rearrangement of the existing stock of gold by transfer from one place of storage to another would not unless accompanied by a greater total demand than before, be sufficient to change the world value of gold.[65]

In discussing inflation under these conditions, then, Laughlin indicated that: "prices could not increase unless there were a serious fall throughout the world in the value of gold."[66] Laughlin acknowledged in several passages that one important factor that could reduce the value of gold was an increase in its supply.[67]

This relationship between money and prices in the closed monetary framework was also recognized by Laughlin in other ways. He noted, for example, that for an individual country, an inflow of gold reflecting an increase in the world gold stock (and, hence, world money supply) would bring about an increase in prices, whereas a gold inflow reflecting a single country's favorable balance of payments, and hence manifesting a redistribution of the existing world stock of gold, would not affect the level of prices in that country.[68] Moreover, he explicitly noted that, under a convertible monetary regime, an increase in the domestic money supply of a single country could affect its domestic price level only if it were large enough to affect the value of gold and, hence, world prices.[69]

In assessing the historical evidence relating to money and prices in the closed world economy, Laughlin acknowledged that causality could indeed run from changes in world money to changes in world prices. Laughlin indicated, for example, that the increase in "old world" prices in the sixteenth century was due to the importation of precious metals from the "new world":

> . . . it is evident that the importation of specie—which was mainly silver—from the New World created perturbations of a serious nature in the value of silver, and consequently in the prices of all goods, wages, and rents expressed in that standard. . . . Out of the general beliefs thus current the idea that an increased quantity of money led to a higher level of prices was natural and just. Without doubt, an influence such as the opening of rich mines in America must have had a direct effect on lowering the exchange value of the existing stock of silver in Europe. The supply was so large compared with the previously collected stock that the world value was without doubt violently changed. Any operation by which the standard of prices should itself be lowered in value would bring about a rise of prices. . . .[70]

Moreover, in another passage, he indicated that the large gold discoveries in the 1850s also increased world prices: "In 1850 and thereafter the new supply of gold was large relatively to the existing stock, and the value of the standard commodity must have fallen, with a consequent effect of a tendency to higher prices. . . . It may be argued that this increase in gold caused a rise of prices."[71] Similarly, Laughlin admits that large increases in world gold production in the 1890s may also have affected world prices but suggests that other factors may have been at work as well.[72]

With respect to the closed economy, then, Laughlin's theoretical views, as well as his empirical investigations, led him to acknowledge that changes in the world money supply could lead to changes in world prices. Thus, although Laughlin was recognized as an antiquantity theorist [particularly with respect to his views of the open economy under a convertible currency regime (see below)], his views pertaining to the closed world economy are not necessarily inconsistent with the monetary model of the closed economy as described above.

Gustav Cassel

Gustav Cassel was another well-known economist in the early twentieth century whose monetary views of the closed world economy were fully consistent with the framework described here. Cassel indicated, for example, that in analyzing determinants of the general price level under an international gold standard, one must look to the *world* money supply as a principal determinant.[73] With respect to his theoretical views, Hegeland, Ostlind, Schumpeter, and others have indicated that "Cassel has been considered as a rather pronounced quantity theorist," implying that he explained changes in the world price level as caused primarily by changes in the amount of world money.[74]

Moreover, in his empirical work, Cassel emphasized the dependence of the world price level on gold. Cassel, for example, examined the relationship between fluctuations in world money (or gold production) and the price level during the period between 1850 and 1910. In carrying out his analysis, he defined a "normal" increase as a "uniform increase in the gold stock which, after the elapse of a certain period leaves the price level unaltered."[75] In a sense, a "normal" increase in the world gold stock was one that matched changes in the world demand for gold. Cassel then indicated that variations in the general price level were caused by deviations in the actual gold stock from the "normal" gold stock—or changes in what Cassel labeled the "relative" gold stock (that is, changes in what amounted to a demand-adjusted world gold stock).[76] On the basis of this framework, Cassel concluded that:

> For the period under review (1850-1910) *the chief causes of the secular variations of the general price level are to be found in changes in the relative gold stock*, and that the Quantity Theory is correct in so far as the general price-level, although influenced in addition by other factors, is *directly proportional to the relative gold stock. . . . The secular variations of the general price-level are in the main to be ascribed to the fluctuations of the relative gold stock and for the rest to certain irregularities in the otherwise practically uniform rise in the demand for gold.*[77]

Elsewhere, Cassel stated that "In the long run, and when no extraordinary changes in the monetary demand for gold take place, the general price level, as measured in a gold standard, is *directly proportional* to the *world's* relative supply of gold. . . ."[78] As Hegeland has indicated, this view was first presented by Cassel in 1904, but he made no reservations in the last (1938) edition of *The Theory of Social Economy*.[79] With respect to his monetary views of the closed world economy, then, Cassel was fully in accord with the closed monetary framework as described above.

Irving Fisher

Another well-known early-twentieth-century monetary writer was Irving Fisher. In his famous book, *The Purchasing Power of Money* (1911), Fisher both set out the theory and compared it to the available empirical data. Fisher explicitly indicated that this theory pertained "to an isolated community, having no trade relation with other communities."[80] In short, his deductive monetary theory applied to a "hypothetical community" that was a *closed economy*.

Fisher's monetary theory was essentially a restatement of the closed model (as well as all of its important components) described in Chapter 2. That is, he forcefully indicated that an (exogenous) increase in the money supply of the closed economy eventually leads to a proportional rise in general prices, *ceteris paribus*, and does not affect real variables in the long run.[81] According to Fisher, then, causality runs from changes in money to changes in prices in the closed economy and, hence, the price level is an "absolutely passive element in the equation of exchange."[82] Fisher explicitly indicates that this view applies to the world economy as a whole. In one passage, for example, Fisher states that changes in the *world* price level are the effect of changes in the *world's* money supply.[83] As Fisher himself indicated in the preface to *The Purchasing Power of Money*, "the main contentions of (the) book are at bottom simply a restatement and amplification of the old 'quantity theory of money.'"[84]

In addition to the fact that his monetary theory pertained to the closed economy, Fisher's analysis of the statistical data often involved an examination of the relationship between *world* money (gold) and *world* prices. Much of his empirical analysis, then, constituted an examination of money/price relationships in the closed *world* economy. Fisher analyzed, for example, the price increases associated with the gold and silver discoveries in America during the sixteenth century. In examining this episode, Fisher contended that ". . . there can be no doubt that [prices] rose or that the rise was great. The [price] rise between the discovery of America and the beginning of the nineteenth century was several hundred percent. This rise was simultaneous with an increase of the stock of the precious metals, because production outran consumption (i.e., supply increased relative to demand)."[85]

Fisher, in his chapter entitled "Statistical Verification: General Historical Review," also examined the period during which gold was discovered in California and Australia (in 1849-73), the deflationary period 1873-96, as well as the period in which gold was discovered in South Africa (1896 to about 1910). His interpretations of all of these periods are fully consistent with the closed world monetary model as described above. Indeed, they are nearly identical to the interpretations given these periods by the monetary writers cited above. In particular, Fisher indicated that the history of world prices has, in essence, been the history of a race between the increase in world money and the increase in world trade and production.[86] In interpreting these periods, Fisher contended that sometimes the supply of world money increased faster than trade and production, and, hence, world prices increased. "This was undoubtedly the case" in the periods between 1849 and 1873 and 1896 to about 1910.[87] Sometimes, on the other hand, increases in the supply of world money lagged behind trade and production, and world prices fell. This, maintained Fisher, must have been the case in the period 1873-96.[88]

Thus, Fisher's theoretical monetary views, as well as his interpretations of the empirical data, fully support and are consistent with the monetary model of the closed economy (as described in Chapter 2).

Frank Taussig

Frank Taussig was another well-known economist of the early twentieth century. Like Fisher, Taussig reaffirmed the view that in a "hypothetical community" (that is, a closed economy), an increase in the quantity of money would lead to a *proportional* increase in prices—other things being equal.[89] Also like Fisher, Taussig proceeded to relate this view to historical episodes of the world economy. He indicated, for example, that "The great advance in [world] prices [in the sixteenth century]—the fall in the value of [world] money—was due unquestionably to the increase in the quantity of specie."[90] Similarly, Taussig indicated that the world price increase that occurred after 1850 was caused by the increase in world gold production associated with the large gold discoveries in California and Australia.[91] Moreover, he provided an analogous explanation for the world price increase after 1896: "This vast addition to the [world] stock of gold was the foundation of the rise in prices which took place in the western nations and indeed the *world* over, during the first decade of the century [1900–10]. . . . The increase in the gold supply was the dominant cause."[92] Taussig, then, is another of the early-twentieth-century monetary writers reaffirming the closed monetary model.

CAMBRIDGE MONETARY WRITERS

Other noteworthy monetary economists of the early twentieth century include writers associated with Cambridge University. Alfred Marshall is generally recognized as the "father" of this group of writers, which included such luminaries as Pigou, Robertson, and Keynes. Although Marshall did not write as extensively on monetary topics as he did on others, he nevertheless left his mark in this area as well. His monetary views pertaining to the closed economy can be interpreted as paralleling the views presented above. In his evidence before the Committee on Indian Currency, for example, Marshall indicated that in a "hypothetical community" ". . . if everything else remains the same, then there is (a) direct relation between the volume of currency and the level of prices, that, if one is increased by ten percent, the other also will be increased by ten percent."[93]

Marshall's monetary views were influential. It is not surprising, then, that these views were restated in the writings of several of his students. Robertson, for example, indicated that ". . . given the conditions of demand for money, its value *varies inversely* as the quantity available, or in other words the 'general level of prices' varies directly as the quantity of money available."[94]

Similar views were also reaffirmed by other students of Marshall.[95] In addition to presenting his theoretical views of the closed economy, Marshall related this theory to the historical evidence. For example, Marshall asserted that long period fluctuations in general prices "are chiefly caused by changes in the amounts of the precious metals relative to the business which has to be transacted by them. . . ."[96] The implication of this remark, of course, is that changes in world money produce changes in world prices. This view—that changes in world money produce changes in world prices—was also recognized by students of Marshall, such as Pigou, Hawtrey, and Robertson. Pigou and Hawtrey, for example, indicated that if all countries of the world increased their currencies concurrently, a world inflation would result.[97] Similarly, Robertson recognized that if a country were large enough relative to the world, changes in its money supply would affect world prices.[98] Whereas the views of these Cambridge writers were certainly consistent with the closed monetary model outlined above, they did not emphasize the relevance of the model to the closed world economy as forcefully as had the previous writers cited above.

In sum, *prior to World War I, almost all important monetary writers of the day endorsed and reaffirmed the monetary model of the closed economy* (as well as its important corollaries) as described in Chapter 2.[99] The view was stated and restated repeatedly until it came to be taken for granted. In endorsing this position (while under a gold or silver standard), *these monetary economists viewed the closed world economy as a single, integrated economy*. Consequently, so long as currencies were freely convertible into gold (or silver), the economic relevance of political boundaries was minimized and fundamental movements in general prices and monetary aggregates were importantly related to changes in *world* (and not national) variables. This is an important point to recognize, since these conditions changed with the advent of World War I.

THE INTERWAR PERIOD AND THE CLOSED MONETARY MODEL

The focus on the relationship between *world* money and *world* prices, as well as the corollary view of the world as an integrated closed economy, crumbled during the interwar period. The reasons for this disintegration are related to the massive world economic disruptions both of World War I and of the postwar period, as well as to the general disorder of postwar international monetary arrangements. More specifically, once problems associated with financing the war forced most countries off the gold standard, less attention was focused on the *world* monetary aggregates and upon the world as an integrated economy. Rather, the focus of attention was shifted to *national* considerations or to the unique circumstances of individual countries—to the neglect of the world as a whole (that is, emphasis was shifted to what Hayek refers to as "monetary nationalism").

The definitive interpretation of the interwar period has not yet been written and is not in the scope of this chapter. Nonetheless, the period is of critical importance in understanding the evolution of the closed monetary model. Consequently, this section will briefly suggest an interpretation of the period from the perspective of the closed *world* monetary framework. Such a perspective suggests that the worldwide economic disruptions of the interwar period should necessarily be analyzed within a *world* framework rather than from the perspective of an individual national economy. Moreover, this view indicates that the basic underlying cause of the period's economic disruptions was monetary in nature and directly related to international monetary arrangements. This monetary interpretation of the interwar period from the perspective of the world economy is not novel. It has been suggested in skeletal form by several authors, such as Rist, Rueff, Mundell, Roper, Henneberry and Witte, and others.[100]

THE PERIOD FROM WORLD WAR I TO 1924: THE WORLD OFF THE GOLD STANDARD

As a result of the disruptions of World War I, international monetary arrangements changed dramatically from the prewar circumstances. Wartime deficits common to belligerents and nonbelligerents alike were financed to an important degree by paper money expansion, which forced most countries off the gold standard.[101] Gold coins were consequently withdrawn and virtually disappeared from circulation. With currencies no longer convertible into gold, in many cases further monetary expansion occurred. Because of the nearly worldwide abandonment of the gold standard, there was an important decrease in the world monetary demand for gold.[102] This decrease occurred at the same time as a substantial increase in the supply of inconvertible paper money, which necessarily raised commodity prices worldwise.[103] This view was clearly recognized and expressed during the period both by Cannan and by Cassel.[104] In 1920, for example. Cassel indicated that "The present [1920] low value of gold is principally the result of a relatively diminished demand for monetary purposes."[105] "The decrease in the monetary demand for gold in comparison with the more and more abundant supply of paper money has brought the value of gold down to about half its prewar level."[106]

Monetary conditions immediately following the war were consequently characterized by floating exchange rates, increased stocks of inconvertible currencies, and increased levels of commodity prices. Given the high rates of inflation and the generally unstable world monetary conditions following the war, most countries desired a return to stability, which in their view, was synonymous with a return to fixed exchange rates and convertible currencies (that is, a return to an international gold standard). Several ways of restoring the gold standard were possible. One alternative was the institution of a new set of gold parities as advocated, for example, by Charles Rist.[107] Public opinion in several countries—especially in the United States and Great Britain—was, however, "obstinately opposed to a rise in the price of gold."[108] Many countries desired a return to the prewar parity structure, which, however, required a substantial deflation of internal prices via the liquidation of inconvertible currencies. Without such a liquidation, a return to the stability of the earlier parity structure and its readily understood guidelines would be impossible.[109]

Such a liquidation was attempted in the early 1920s. As indicated by Henneberry and Witte, however,

> . . . most Western European nations were reluctant to (fully) deflate because they considered their political and social instability to be sufficiently great that the temporarily high rates of unemployment which must accompany any sizable liquidation of paper money stocks were deemed hazardous to survival. Therefore, the liquidation which began in most countries in 1920 was abandoned in 1921 in most cases, leaving a structure that had not accommodated itself to the prewar parities and retaining a fiat money overhang.[110,111]

By 1921, most countries had abandoned their attempts to soak up excess liquidity following World War I. Further deflation was out of the question. But many countries still strongly desired to return to the prewar parity structure. And a fiat money overhang—relative to gold reserves at prewar parities—still existed.[112] Given these conditions, the world's leading monetary authorities proposed what they considered to be an alternative both to further deflation and to a new parity structure.

Specifically, it was recognized that with the existing large volume of paper money, a return to the gold standard at the prewar parity structure would bring about a substantial increase in the world demand for gold and, hence, a substantial increase in its world value (that is, a substantial *world* deflation). In order to avoid this, it was recommended that countries economize or minimize their monetary demands for gold through international agreement and cooperation. In particular, an alternative form of the gold standard was recommended, which would minimize the use of and, hence, the demand for gold but would require an increased amount of international cooperation and coordination. In order to accomplish this, it was recommended that gold coins not be reintroduced into circulation,[113] gold cover not be increased, a gold exchange standard be adopted (so that substitutes for gold could be employed as reserves), and that countries agree to cooperate and to coordinate their monetary policies.

These recommendations were endorsed by many of the world's leading monetary authorities. Gustav Cassel indicated, for example, that under the circumstances prevailing in the early 1920s, preventing gold from rising in value

> . . . can only be done by some sort of international agreement to keep down the world's monetary demand for gold. A restoration of the use of gold as a circulating medium, and of the former requirements as to gold covering for the liabilities of the central banks, would without doubt mean a violent rise in the value of gold and a corresponding fall in the general price level. These two sources of demand for gold must consequently be laid under a control to be internationally agreed upon.[114]
>
> "Prices," Cassel stressed, "could be maintained at their existing level only if the world's monetary demand for gold were systematically restricted."[115]

Similarly, Ralph Hawtrey contended that it was necessary "in the absence of new and large supplies of gold . . . to reduce the demand for gold, so that the quantity of gold available for payments may correspond with the new price level."[116] The ways of bringing about a reduction in the demand for gold, which were outlined by Hawtrey, included the adoption of the gold exchange standard, a reduction in the legal reserves of banks of issue, and an increased cooperation and coordination of the monetary policies of central banks.[117]

As is well known, the gold exchange standard was eventually adopted in the 1920s. One of the primary reasons for its adoption was to alleviate the perceived gold shortage by allowing foreign exchange as well as gold to be used as international reserves.[118] As Nurkse has indicated:

> The chief recommendation of the Genoa Conference in 1922 was that the gold exchange standard should be established as widely as possible *in order to avoid the scramble for gold that might ensue if all the countries wanting to restore the gold standard were to absorb gold in their central reserve.* . . . The gold exchange standard was successfully extended in the 'twenties, thus meeting a substantial part of the total demand for international currency in the form of foreign exchange reserves instead of gold.[119]

Measures that were adopted were in large part intended to prevent a sharp increase in the world demand for gold and, hence, a world deflation, which would otherwise have been associated with a return to the gold standard (at the prewar parity structure). At the same time, however, these measures worked to reduce gold reserve ratios and, hence, worked to further pyramid notes and deposits on the base of gold. These smaller ratios of gold to notes and deposits increased the vulnerability of the system to an increased demand for gold. It can be said, therefore, that this increased vulnerability of the system resulted from the failure either to adopt a new parity structure (Rist) or to complete the deflation that was begun in the early 1920s (Henneberry and Witte).

THE INCREASED ROLE OF THE UNITED STATES IN INTERNATIONAL MONETARY AFFAIRS

In any case, this increased vulnerability of the system occurred at the same time that the world distribution of gold became unbalanced. This maldistribution of gold was related to the increasingly important role that the United States came to play in international monetary affairs after World War I, which came about because of some peculiar circumstances during and immediately after the war. In particular, because the United States was the primary supplier of the allies, had remained isolated from and made a late entrance into the war, and had maintained a convertible currency (through most of the period), confidence in the U.S. gold parity remained unquestioned.[120] Consequently, the United States was perceived as a relatively safe, attractive haven or repository for gold, and, as a result, large amounts of gold flowed there. Hence, gold came to be concentrated in the United States, and a world gold reserve imbalance or maldistribution was created. Indeed, according to one author, the United States came to possess "considerably more than half of the gold stocks in the world."[121] This concentration of gold, while other currencies remained inconvertible, made it possible for the dollar to remain convertible despite a substantial increase in the U.S. price level.[122] The amount of gold that accumulated was so great, however, that an even larger rise in prices might have taken place if the United States had not altered its monetary policy.[123] In particular, instead of allowing this substantial gold inflow to have its full effect on money and credit and, hence, on general prices, the Federal Reserve (in effect) severed the link between the gold stock and the money supply,[124] allowing the proportion of gold to notes and deposits outstanding to rise to abnormally high levels, that is, as high as 70 to 80 percent.[125] Part of the reason for this was the anticipation of the return to convertible currencies in Europe and a consequent anticipated return of gold flow there. As Hardy indicated: "It had become a commonplace of monetary discussion in the U.S. that the gold which came in just after the war would return to Europe when it was again needed to support gold standard currencies in Europe, hence [it] could not safely be built into our own credit structure."[126]

In addition to these considerations, the United States emerged from World War I not only with a relatively large and healthy economy but with a highly regarded currency relative to available alternatives. Consequently, with the establishment of the postwar gold exchange standard, the dollar acquired the status of a key currency.[127] Some important implications arose as a result of this set of circumstances. In particular, because of the large size both of the U.S. economy and of its gold stock, relative to the rest of the world, as well as the key currency status of the dollar, the U.S. monetary authority acquired a significant influence over the world money supply and price level.[128] Consequently, as other countries returned to the postwar gold exchange standard, they found themselves significantly under the influence of U.S. monetary policy. This was recognized in a remarkable article by Ohlin published in 1927. Ohlin indicated that should the Federal Reserve pursue an expansionary monetary policy, the consequence would be that a portion of its superfluous gold stock would flow to other countries, causing money supplies and, hence, prices to increase everywhere.[129] Similarly, if the Federal Reserve pursued a restrictive monetary policy, other countries would also be compelled to follow suit. Otherwise, their balance of payments would become adverse, inducing an outflow of their limited gold reserves. Since they could not permit this, they would be compelled to follow the United States in pursuing a restrictive monetary policy.[130] Hence, the Federal Reserve acquired an important influence on both world money and world prices.[131, 132]

After World War I, therefore, U.S. monetary policy had assumed an increasingly important role in the international monetary sphere, no longer reacting passively to external events but as a major independent force that assumed a critical role in influencing world money and prices.[133] This influence became particularly important in the late 1920s.

THE PERIOD BETWEEN 1924 AND 1928

Beginning in 1923, countries began to return to the newly instituted gold exchange standard, many at or near their prewar parities.[134] This occurred despite the fact that price levels still remained above those of the prewar years, and an overhang of fiat money remained. By about 1928, most countries had returned to the gold exchange standard. The rapid, widespread, generalized adoption of the gold exchange standard under these circumstances had important implications. As mentioned above, the return to the gold standard of many countries implied an increased world demand for gold; that is, new claims kept accumulating on a relatively constant stock of gold.[135] Other things being equal, this increased world demand for gold would be expected to increase the value of gold and, hence, to bring about a world deflation. This was, however, to be prevented by world cooperation in conserving gold in the various ways mentioned above.

There was, indeed, a great deal of cooperation among the world's major central banks in adopting these measures during this period.[136] Nonetheless, the evidence suggests that world commodity prices began to decline with the widespread adoption of the gold exchange standard in about 1925. Wholesale prices, for example, fell continually through this period in the United States, the United Kingdom, and France, as well as in other countries.[137] Several authors have suggested that this decline in prices was related to the increased world demand for gold, despite the steps that had been taken to minimize this demand.[138] Under circumstances of an international gold standard with exchange rates of various currencies fixed to one another, it will be remembered, deflation is necessarily an international or world phenomenon, related to changes in the supply and demand of world money (that is, with exchange rates fixed, single-country deflation is not possible). Hence, the evidence suggests that this decline in world commodity prices may well have been related to an increase in the demand for world money. Nonetheless, the price declines that occurred through 1928 were relatively mild, leading some economists to contend that the gold-economizing measures and central bank coordination and cooperation had worked reasonably well to restore an international gold standard successfully. Yet the new system, although intact in 1928, remained vulnerable. Under the new arrangements, gold reserves of a key currency country could, for example, be rapidly depleted by a decision of another central bank to demand payment of its foreign exchange claims on gold.[139] Since foreign exchange accounted for about 40 percent of international reserves in 1928, the system was particularly vulnerable to such an event.[140] This vulnerability became evident in the years following 1928.

THE BREAKDOWN OF THE GOLD EXCHANGE STANDARD

Initially, the increased demand for gold associated with the restoration of the postwar gold standard was satisfied without any *severe* contraction in world prices.[141] The gold-conserving measures, along with central bank cooperation, seemed to be working to successfully restore the gold standard. However, the monetary policies of two important countries—France, and the United States—soon altered these circumstances. In particular, the Federal Reserve, responding to speculative activity in the stock market and elsewhere, began to pursue a more restrictive monetary policy in 1928. This action, which had nothing to do with the Federal Reserve's desire to hold gold, effectively halted the supply of U.S. gold reserves to the world.[142] This outward flow of gold from the United States—which was essential in restoring the international gold standard—ceased in late 1928, and an inflow followed. Indeed, the U.S. gold stock rose during the next several years, until August 1931. Despite this gold inflow, the Federal Reserve allowed the money stock to decrease during this same period. At the same time, France stabilized her currency in 1928 and continued to enlarge her gold reserves through 1929.[143] In attracting gold reserves, these actions on the part both of France and of the United States aggravated the world gold scarcity and created a pull on the gold supplies of the rest of the world.[144] As indicated above (and by Ohlin in 1927), because of the special influence of the United States, this induced further monetary contraction by other countries. In particular, other countries were compelled to pursue restrictive monetary policies in order to protect their international reserves.[145]

As Hardy indicated: "The international gold standard makes it practically necessary for small countries to follow where their more powerful neighbors lead. If they do not tighten their money when the larger countries do so, they may lose their entire reserves without much effect on the situation in the larger neighbors markets."[146]

The combined actions of the United States and France, then, worked to bring about restrictive monetary policies in the rest of the world and consequently led to a decrease in the world money supply. This fall in the supply of world money was followed by a depression in world prices. With this deflation—or decrease in the nominal value of all wealth—contracts expressed in terms of money soon could not be honored.[147] Accordingly, bankruptcies became commonplace. Confidence in international monetary arrangements was shaken with the failure in 1931 of the Credit-Anstalt, the largest bank in Austria. Consequently—as frequently happens in such circumstances—the demand for gold increased further. The vulnerability of the gold exchange standard soon became evident. In particular, the possibility of exchange rate instability and, hence, of losses arising from exchange rate movements rendered the holding of foreign balances risky.[148] This, in turn, "led to a further scramble for gold through the liquidation of previously accumulated foreign exchange reserves of central banks."[149] As a consequence, the key currency countries "had to meet the claims of gold which had been deferred by the introduction of the gold exchange standard."[150] These circumstances compelled Britain to call in loans in order to obtain additional foreign exchange reserves. This action, however, further accentuated the deflationary pressures. Eventually, Britain's gold reserves proved inadequate, and, consequently, Britain was forced off the gold standard. (Convertibility was officially suspended on September 21, 1931.[151])

Following the "crisis of September 1931," gold was also withdrawn from the other major key currency country, the United States. This was related to the "wholesale liquidation of foreign exchange reserves, reflecting the complete collapse of the gold exchange standard (in 1931-32)."[152] The U.S. gold stock continued to decline for about a year after the British crisis. Meanwhile, a U.S. banking crisis had been associated with the U.S. monetary contraction and deflation. Two banking crises, in particular, adversely affected the public's confidence in the U.S. banking system. As described by Friedman and Schwartz, circumstances in the United States led to a further contraction in the U.S. money supply—further exacerbating the contraction in world reserves, the collapse of the gold exchange standard, and, consequently, the contraction of the world money supply.[153, 154]

In short, the increased world demand for gold and the consequent collapse of the gold exchange standard caused the contraction of international reserves and media of exchange, that is, a contraction of the world money supply, and this, in turn, brought about a world deflation and a world depression.[155] Instead of eliminating the need for deflation, then, the gold-conserving measures adopted in the early 1920s increased the vulnerability of the system and only postponed the deflation.[156]

THE INTERWAR PERIOD: SOME CONCLUSIONS

The world deflation and world depression of the late 1920s and early 1930s were, therefore, largely a result of a contraction of the world money supply. Although U.S. monetary policy clearly played an important role during this period, an understanding of the period requires an analysis within the context of a *world* framework rather than from the perspective of an individual national economy. Such an examination suggests that the basic underlying cause of these economic disruptions was largely monetary in nature.[157] *These events, therefore, constitute another episode that fully supports the closed monetary model described above.*

Unfortunately (as indicated by Cassel and others), few policy-makers of the period understood this. Many other explanations were given for the period's economic problems.[158] As a consequence, the view of the world as an integrated, closed economy and the policies appropriate to this view were replaced by policies emphasizing the individual domestic economy. In particular, with international monetary arrangements in disarray and with the breakdown of international trade, countries pursued nationalistic monetary policies and beggar-thy-neighbor trade policies designed to stabilize their individual economies and to ensure the survival of their political systems, rather than adopting a world, global perspective. Because of these considerations, the view of the world as a single integrated closed economy, as well as the closed monetary model, fell into dormancy in the 1930s.

MONETARISM AND THE REEMERGENCE OF THE CLOSED MONETARY MODEL

Despite the dormancy of these views, elements of the closed monetary model soon reemerged, especially in the United States. These views were often associated with abstract closed economy versions of the quantity theory of money. There are several reasons for their reemergence. The economy of the United States had, for example, become large and relatively self-sufficient relative to other economies in the world. Since international sectors of the U.S. economy were comparatively small (relative to GNP), the U.S. economy was often viewed as an approximation of the closed economy. Furthermore, because the U.S. dollar was a key currency, balance of payments constraints on monetary policy were not nearly as important to U.S. policymakers as they were in other countries. These particular circumstances of the U.S. economy enabled its money supply to be more of an exogenously controlled policy variable than was the case in other countries.[159] In short, these factors contributed to the relative neglect of international considerations in the monetary and macroeconomic analysis in the United States during the 1940s and 1950s. Although international concerns were discussed during this period, they certainly were a subordinate element of the period's macroeconomic and monetary analysis, which was primarily concerned with the closed economy.

As theoretical models of the closed economy were developed, the importance of the money supply and its control became evident. Elements of the monetary theory of the closed economy, often associated with the quantity theory of money, were emphasized and tested by various U.S. economists during this period. Writers, such as Henry Simons, Lloyd Mints, Clark Warburton, Milton Friedman, Karl Brunner, Allan Meltzer, and others, became associated with this view, which is today referred to as monetarism. Moreover, a powerful theoretical model of the monetary aspects of the closed economy was presented by Don Patinkin, which further bolstered this view.

Although monetarism certainly revived many of the important elements of the closed monetary model, it was normally applied to a particular national economy (especially the U.S. economy) rather than to the only purely closed economy, that is, the world economy. The restatement of an explicit monetary model of the closed world economy came with some important developments in international monetary theory in the 1960s and 1970s as well as with an improved understanding of the Bretton Woods System.

Important developments in international monetary theory, for example, were made in the 1960s and 1970s. As closed economy models were refined with the addition of international sectors, it became evident that international capital markets were well integrated. These markets, then, were seen as world rather than national markets. Consequently, under fixed exchange rates, these markets imposed important international constraints on the monetary policies of individual countries. At the same time, important developments were made in the theory of devaluation of the balance of payments. In particular, as an alternative to other theories of devaluation and the balance of payments (such as the "elasticity," "absorption," or "foreign-income multiplier" approaches), a monetary approach to analyzing devaluation and the balance of payments was presented.[160] According to this view, balance of payments deficits were related to excessive monetary growth. If this monetary growth continued unabated, currency devaluation would not improve a country's balance of payments. Devaluation, in this case, would only produce an increase in the price level as traded goods prices (denominated in the same currency) were equalized across countries. This view emphasized that many commodity markets are integrated world markets rather than compartmentalized, segmented national markets. It was recognized, then, that money and capital, as well as many commodity markets, were integrated *world* markets. These theories led to the revival of the view of the world as a single, integrated closed economy.

During the same period—the latter years of the Bretton Woods System—it was recognized that all countries were experiencing inflation at the same time—inflation had become a world problem. In examining the reasons for this, the role of the dollar—a key currency—in influencing the world supply of reserves and, hence, the world money supply was emphasized. In particular, since the dollar was the system's primary key currency, U.S. monetary growth could continue at relatively high rates without effective balance of payments constraints. That is, since other countries held dollars as international reserves, the United States could continue to expand its money supply in the face of balance of payments deficits—hence, suppliers of the system's key currency (as the source of the rest of the world's reserve currency) could impose inflation (or deflation) on the rest of the world. Apparently, such was the case in the latter period of the Bretton Woods System, when the Federal Reserve allowed the money supply to expand in the face of large external deficits.

In addition to the reserve currency status of the dollar, other factors influencing the growth of world reserves and world money were also recognized. One of these was the role of the IMF. In particular, it was noted that the IMF's creation of SDRs effectively added to the world supply of international reserves and to the world monetary base.[161] In addition, the importance of the size of the U.S. economy and its money supply was noted. Since the U.S. economy was so comparatively large, its monetary expansion could overwhelm the influence of other factors and, hence, affect world monetary growth.

In explaining the world inflation, then, attention was directed to the determinants of world reserves and world monetary growth. Developments and circumstances in the Bretton Woods period led to the revival of the monetary theory of the closed world economy, that is, that increases in world reserves and, hence, world money, had led to world inflation. This view—dubbed "global monetarism"—has subsequently been empirically tested in various studies.[162] The results of these tests have generally supported the theory. The reemergence of the view that the world is a closed, integrated economy, together with the revival of the monetary theory of the closed world economy, then, was essentially complete by the mid-1970s. These views were, of course, simply a return to the earlier views outlined above.

SUMMARY AND CONCLUSION

This chapter as well as the preceding one have described the development of the monetary model of the closed world economy as well as its important corollaries. Repetition is unavoidable in such an outline, since these views were continually restated and reaffirmed. Nonetheless, in documenting this repeated reaffirmation of the closed world monetary model by generation after generation of monetary economists, there can be little doubt as to the model's robustness.

In addition to documenting the repeated endorsement of the closed world framework, it was demonstrated that writers such as Hume and Smith employed the closed world model in analyzing and understanding the small open economy under fixed exchange rates. Similarly, bullionist writers employed the closed world model in analyzing and understanding the small open economy with an inconvertible currency. The use of the closed world model in analyzing and developing models of the small open economy by these writers is prima facie evidence of their thorough understanding of the closed model and its implications.

Moreover, the closed world model was shown to be consistent with a great deal of empirical evidence. In addition to explaining the world inflation following the gold and silver discoveries in the "new world," the model explains all the important movements in world prices during the nineteenth and twentieth centuries. Thus, not only was the monetary model of the closed world economy endorsed by the bulk of the world's leading monetary economists and employed to develop monetary models of the small open economy, but it was shown to be consistent with every major world price movement for which accurate data are available.

Many of the authors cited in this chapter and their views as to the closed economy will be referred to later. In particular, their monetary views of the closed economy will be contrasted with their monetary views of the small open economy. It will be demonstrated that many of these authors made clear and emphatic distinctions between the closed and open economies and, moreover, very clearly described the differing relationships between money and prices under these different circumstances. In short, it will be shown in subsequent chapters that many of these monetary writers clearly recognized and distinguished between the alternative frameworks, as described above in Chapter 2.

NOTES

1. Frank W. Fetter, *Development of British Monetary Orthodoxy, 1797-1875* (Cambridge: Harvard University Press, 1965), p. 240. Earlier, John Cairnes had described several of these facts. See, for example, John E. Cairnes, *Essays in Political Economy* (London: MacMillan, 1873), pp. 115-16.

2. See, for example, Cairnes, op. cit.; W. Stanley Jevons, *Investigations in Currency and Finance*, ed. H. S. Foxwell (London: Macmillan, 1884).

3. Charles Rist, *History of Monetary and Credit Theory* (New York: Augustus M. Kelley, 1966), p. 290 footnote.

4. Cairnes, op. cit., p. 43.

5. Cairnes, ibid., pp. 47-48. That Cairnes followed Cantillon is ably demonstrated by Jevons. Jevons contends that the exposition of the transmission mechanism of gold set out by Cantillon "is exactly the theory which was brought before the British Association in 1858 by the late Professor Cairnes." In W. Stanley Jevons, "Richard Cantillon and the Nationality of Political Economy," reprinted in Cantillon's *Essai Sur La Nature Du Commerce En General*, ed. Henry Higgs (London: Macmillan, 1931), p. 349.

6. This process by which the increased production of gold "is spread from one country to another, in the end embracing the entire economic world" was also described by Levasseur in 1856. (Rist, op. cit., p. 288.)

7. Cairnes, op. cit., pp. 55-56 [emphasis added].

8. Ibid., pp. 113-14.

9. Ibid., p. 57. See also Michael D. Bordo, "John E. Cairnes on the Effects of the Australian Gold Discoveries, 1851-73: An Early Application of the Methodology of Positive Economists," *History of Political Economy* 7 (1975): 345.

10. Bordo, op. cit., pp. 338-39, 342.

11. Ibid., p. 357.

12. See, for example, Jevons, op. cit., pp. 16, 17, 74, 157. Although Jevons' estimate of the depreciation of gold ranged from 9 percent to 30 percent, he indicated that "as likely as not . . . the true alternation of gold lies within $2\frac{1}{2}$ percent of 16 percent or between $13\frac{1}{2}$ and $18\frac{1}{2}$ percent." (Ibid., p. 157.) Moreover, Jevons contended (along with Cairnes) that "The effect of those discoveries is probably much greater than any we can prove, because the course of prices was in previous years decidedly downwards, so that the new gold has prevented a further fall and occasioned a rise in its stead" (Ibid., p. 154). See also Fetter, op. cit., p. 247, and Vincent W. Bladen, *From Adam Smith to Maynard Keynes: The Heritage of Political Economy* (Toronto: University of Toronto Press, 1974), p. 332.

13. Jevons, op. cit., pp. 318-19.

14. This period was known to economic historians as the "Great Depression." See, for example, W. W. Rostow, *British Economy of the Nineteenth Century* (Oxford: Clarendon Press, 1948), p. 58.

15. See, for example, the British and American price data provided in Roy W. Jastram, *The Golden Constant: The English and American Experience, 1560-1976* (New York: John Wiley, 1977), and German, English, and U.S. price data provided in J. Laurence Laughlin, *Money and Prices* (New York: Scribners, 1919), p. 86.

16. See, for example, Rostow, op. cit., p. 58.

17. See, for example, Irving Fisher, *The Purchasing Power of Money* (New York: MacMillan, 1911), p. 242 (and footnote 2).

18. See, for example, the data provided by Francis H. Brownell, *Hard Money* (New York: American Smelting and Refinery, 1944), p. 32.

19. J. Shield Nicholson, *A Treatise on Money* (London: William Blackwood, 1888), pp. 103, 338.

20. The first of the countries to shift from a silver- to a gold-based standard was the newly formed German Empire in 1871. The new German central government soon began to sell some of its accumulated silver in world markets. This fact, together with decreased imports of silver in the Far East, as well as the great increase of silver production in the U.S., led bimetallic countries to fear such a flood of silver into their mints that they would be unable to retain their gold. These bimetallic countries therefore "hastened to end the free coinage of silver and to adopt a single gold standard. The movement was cumulative; every abandonment of the free coinage of silver increased the fear of silver in the remaining bimetallic countries and enhanced their eagerness to follow suit. Silver (soon) was no longer a standard." In Lester Chandler, *The Economics of Money and Banking* (New York: Harper, 1948), p. 93.

21. See Chandler, op. cit., p. 94.

22. As Irving Fisher has demonstrated, the theory described here is further supported by the movement of general prices in countries remaining on silver standards. Fisher indicates, for example, that "the demonetization of silver in gold countries made a greater amount of that metal available for silver countries. Accordingly, we find that prices rose in India from 107 in 1873 to 140 in 1896, in Japan from 104 in 1873 to 133 in 1896, and China from 100 in 1874 to 109 in 1893. These figures . . . agree in indicating a rise of prices." (Fisher, op. cit., pp. 243-44.)

23. See, for example, Will E. Mason, "The Monetary Rule: Whence It Came and Where It Went—and at What Cost Was It Lost?" (Unpublished manuscript, Pennsylvania State University, 1978), p. 11. See also Nicholson, op. cit., and Francis A. Walker, *International Bimetallism* (New York: Holt, 1896).

24. Mason, op. cit., p. 11.

25. Rist, op. cit., p. 250.

26. E. Prime Eshag, *From Marshall to Keynes* (Oxford: Basil Blackwell, 1963), p. 112.

27. Mason, op. cit., p. 191. See also Robert Giffen, *The Case against Bimetallism* (London: George Bell, 1892), pp. 82, 95, 96, 98.

28. Monometallists included economists such as Giffen, Laughlin, Jevons, Walras, Gide, J. S. Mill, Goschen, Cairnes, and Bagehot. See, for example, Mason, op. cit., p. 26. In emphasizing the long run, monometallists often endorsed the neutrality of money. See, for example, Giffen, op. cit., pp. 16-17.

29. Rist, op. cit., p. 252. See also p. 267.

30. Rist, op. cit., p. 252.

31. Rist, ibid., pp. 253-54.

32. See, for example, ibid., p. 254.

33. Monometallists further strengthened this position by contending that some of the recent deflation was caused by one-time shifts from silver and paper standards to a gold standard. These one-time shifts, they asserted, were not a necessary consequence of monometallism.

34. See, for example, Rist, op. cit., p. 254, and Walker, op. cit., 254.

35. See, for example, the interpretations of this period given by Irving Fisher, op. cit., p. 246, and by John M. Keynes, *A Treatise on Money*, Volume II (Cambridge: Macmillan, 1971), p. 146.

36. Although some monometallists denied this position, monometallists such as Giffen clearly stated it and, indeed, criticized those monometallists who did not support the view. That bimetallists and monometallists held such similar views is exemplified by F. A. Walker, a bimetallist, who used the quotations of monometallist writers such as Giffen to illustrate his views. See, for example, Walker, op. cit., p. 265.

37. See, for example, John Stuart Mill, *Principles of Political Economy* (London: Longmans, Green, 1926), Book III, Chapters VIII and IX, and Knut Wicksell, *Lectures on Political Economy*, Volume 2 (New York: Augustus M. Kelley, 1971), p. 149, where Wicksell contends that the cost of the production theory of money is an element of the quantity theory. See also Will E. Mason, op. cit., p. 55; Mark Blaug, *Economic Theory in Retrospect* (Homewood: Richard D. Irwin, 1968), pp. 134, 199; and Phyllis Deane, *The Evolution of Economic Ideas* (Cambridge: Cambridge University Press, 1978), p. 57.

38. Likewise, no one denies that a sudden (exogenous) increase in the demand for money brings about a fall in prices. See, for example, Giffen, op. cit., pp. 218-19.

39. See, for example, Giffen, op. cit., pp. 218-19, and J. Laurence Laughlin,

The Principles of Money (New York: Scribners, 1903), pp. 135-37, 225-26, 388-89.

40. See, for example, Leland Yeager, *International Monetary Relations* (New York: Harper & Row, 1966), p. 254.

41. Rist, op. cit., p. 301.

42. F. W. Taussig, *Principles of Economics, Volume I* (New York: MacMillan, 1911), p. 260 (second edition revised).

43. See, for example, Rist, op. cit., p. 167.

44. See, for example, Yeager, op. cit., p. 254, and Mason, op. cit., p. 27.

45. Mason, op. cit., p. 27.

46. See, for example, Rist, op. cit., p. 270.

47. Rist, op. cit., p. 301.

48. Rist, op. cit., p. 270.

49. Rist, op. cit., p. 301.

50. Rist, op. cit., p. 267.

51. Taussig, op. cit., p. 260.

52. Rist, op. cit., p. 269. (Rist apparently refers here to the French edition.)

53. Irving Fisher, op. cit., pp. 245-46 [emphasis added].

54. See, for example, Gustav Cassel, *The Theory of Social Economy* (New York: Augustus M. Kelley, 1967), p. 472. See also Rist, op. cit., p. 271, and Rostow, op. cit., p. 147. Specifically, Cassel stated that: ". . . for the period under review (1850-1910) *The chief causes of the secular variations in the general price level are to be* found *in changes in the relative gold stock*, and that the quantity theory is correct in so far as the general price level, although influenced in addition by other factors, is *directly proportional to the relative gold stock*." (Ibid., p. 472.)

55. See, for example, Knut Wicksell, *Interest and Prices* (New York: Augustus M. Kelley, 1965) and the author index in Wicksell, *Lectures*.

56. In *Interest and Prices*, for example, Wicksell state that the "The only closed system today is the world as a whole. . . ." (Wicksell, *Interest and Prices*, p. 157.) See also ibid., pp. 82, 85.

57. Rist, op. cit., p. 302.

58. See, for example, Wicksell, *Lectures*, pp. 197-98, 215-16.

59. The view that Wicksell supported the quantity theory of money (in this sense) is held, for example, by Blaug, Marget, and Patinkin. See, for example, Blaug, op. cit., p. 628; Don Patinkin, *Money, Interest, and Prices* (New York: Harper & Row, 1965), pp. 587-88; and Arthur W. Marget, *The Theory of Prices* Volume I (New York: Augustus M. Kelley, 1966), Chapter VI-X. In one passage, for example, Wicksell stated that: "The Quantity Theory is correct in so far as it is true that an increase or relative diminution in the stock of money must always tend to raise or lower prices. . . ." (Wicksell, *Interest and Prices*, p. XXVIII.) That Wicksell believed the quantity theory applied to the closed world economy is supported by the fact that the money that Wicksell associated with the quantity theory was metallic currency. (Patinkin, op. cit., p. 588; Wicksell, *Interest and Prices*, pp. 59-62; and Wicksell, *Lectures*, Volume II, pp. 67-70, 168-69.)

60. See, for example, Wicksell, "The Influence of the Rate of Interest on Prices," *Economic Journal* 17 (1907), reprinted in *Economic Thought*, ed. James Gherity (New York: Random House, 1965), p. 551; Wicksell, *Interest and Prices*, pp. 81-83, 85; and Wicksell, *Lectures*, Volume II, p. 171.

61. Wicksell, *Lectures*, p. 141. See also Patinkin, op. cit., p. 583.

62. Wicksell, *Interest and Prices*, p. 41. See also ibid., pp. 39–40, and Wicksell, *Lectures*, Volume II, pp. 142–43.

63. See below. See also Robert Keleher, "Of Money and Prices: Some Historical Perspectives." *The Monetary Approach to International Adjustment* eds. Bluford Putnam and D. Sykes Wilford (New York: Praeger, 1978).

64. Laughlin, *Money and Prices*, p. 90.

65. Laughlin, *Principles of Money*, p. 338 [emphasis added].

66. Laughlin, ibid., p. 393 [emphasis added].

67. J. Laurence Laughlin, "A Theory of Prices," *American Economic Association Publications* 6 (February 1905):69, 72.

68. See, for example, Laughlin, *Principles of Money*, pp. 103, 379, 388–89, 393, 417.

69. See, for example, ibid., pp. 135–37, 389. In addition, Laughlin indicates that changes in one country's demand for gold will affect prices only if the world demand for gold is thereby affected. See, for example, ibid., pp. 135–37, 388, and Laughlin, "Theory of Prices," pp. 68–69, 72.

70. Laughlin, *Principles of Money*, pp. 225–26. See also Lance Girton and Don Roper, "J. Laurence Laughlin and the Quantity Theory of Money," *Journal of Political Economy* 86 (August 1978):609 footnote.

71. Laughlin, "Theory of Prices," p. 76 footnote.

72. Laughlin, *Money and Prices*, p. 135.

73. Cassel indicated, for example, that: "The analysis of the factors which produce changes in the price level, as long as the gold standard comes into consideration, cannot stop at the quantity of gold money, but must be extended to the *total gold supply of the world*." In Gustav Cassel, *The Theory of Social Economy* (New York: Augustus M. Kelley, 1967), p. 46 [emphasis added].

74. Hugo Hegeland, *The Quantity Theory of Money* (Goteborg: Elanders Boktryckeri Aktiebulag, 1951), p. 143. See also Schumpeter, p. 1101. Hegeland further indicates that "A. Ostlind, who has studied Cassel's monetary discussions and recommendations very closely, characterizes Cassel as being more influenced by the quantity theory than any other contemporary Swedish economist." (Hegeland, op. cit., p. 143.)

75. Cassel, *Theory of Social Economy*, p. 470.

76. Changes in the actual gold stock as a percentage of the "normal" stock were referred to by Cassel as the "relative" gold stock. (It measured the relationship between the actual gold stock to the "normal" gold stock.)

77. Cassel, *Theory of Social Economy*, pp. 472, 493 [emphasis in original]. As Cassel indicated (ibid., p. 470), "In so far as changes in the general price level for the period 1850–1910 may be traced to changes in the gold stock, they refer exclusively to deviations of the actual gold stock from the *normal stock*." See also Rist, op. cit., p. 271, who, in commenting on Cassel's results, contends that "The method Cassel used has been criticised because of its arbitrary choice of the years designed to serve as a basis for calculating the 'normal' increase in gold; but the striking contrast between the movement of prices before and after the discovery of the Transvaal mines would not be weakened whatever years were chosen."

78. Gustav Cassel, *Post-War Monetary Stabilization* (New York: Columbia University Press, 1928), p. 55 [emphasis added].

79. Hegeland, op. cit., p. 139.

80. Irving Fisher, op. cit., p. 90. Fisher assumed that "we shall . . . ignore foreign trade and thus restrict ourselves to trade within a hypothetical community." Ibid., p. 16.

81. Ibid., pp. 157-58, 183. Fisher readily acknowledged that changes in money affect real variables in the short run.

82. Ibid., p. 172.

83. Ibid., p. 172.

84. Ibid., p. vii.

85. Ibid., p. 236.

86. Ibid., p. 246. Indeed, Fisher indicates that "It is the relation of gold to trade that chiefly affects prices. Even if the stock of gold should increase for many years, prices may not rise; for trade may increase still faster." Ibid., p. 248.

87. Fisher, for example, explicitly indicated that the gold discoveries in Alaska, Colorado, and South Africa in the period between 1896 and about 1910 ultimately contributed to an increase in *world* prices. Ibid., pp. 159, 245-46.

88. Ibid., pp. 247-48.

89. Taussig, op. cit., p. 236.

90. Ibid., p. 257.

91. Ibid., pp. 258-59.

92. Ibid., p. 260.

93. Quoted from Eshag, op. cit., p. 4. Also reprinted in Alfred Marshall, *Money, Credit, and Commerce* (New York: Augustus M. Kelley, 1965), p. 45.

94. Dennis H. Robertson, *Money* (New York: Harcourt, Brace, 1922), p. 33.

95. See for example, J. M. Keynes, *A Tract on Monetary Reform* (London: Macmillan, 1971), p. 61, where he indicates that the quantity theory of money "is fundamental. Its correspondence with fact is not open to question." He also indicates that his views follow those of Marshall and Pigou and "come to the same thing" as those of Fisher (ibid., p. 63, footnote). This interpretation is supported by that of Patinkin, who indicates that Keynes endorsed the quantity theory of money in his writings through the *Treatise on Money*. See, for example, Don Patinkin, *Keynes' Monetary Thought* (Durham: Duke University Press, 1976), pp. 18, 119.

96. Alfred Marshall, "Remedies for Fluctuations of General Prices," *Memorials of Alfred Marshall* ed. Arthur C. Pigou (New York: Augustus M. Kelley, 1966), p. 192.

97. See, for example, Arthur C. Pigou, "Inflation," *Economic Journal* 27 (1917):487-88 and Ralph G. Hawtrey, *Currency and Credit* (London: Longmans, Green, 1934), p. 110.

98. See, for example, Robertson, *Money,* p. 86.

99. Many writers not cited here (as, for example, Walras and Aftalion) also endorsed the same theory.

100. See, for example, Charles Rist, *History of Monetary and Credit Theory* (New York: Augustus M. Kelley, 1966); Charles Rist, *The Triumph of Gold* (New York: Philosophical Library, 1961); Jacques Rueff, *The Monetary Sin of the West* (New York: Macmillan, 1972); Robert A. Mundell, "The Monetary Consequences of Jacques Rueff: Review Article," *The Journal of Business* 46 (1973); Don Roper, "Peter Temin, Did Monetary Forces Cause the Great Depression? A Review Article," *Journal of Monetary Economics* 4 (1978); Barbara Henneberry and James Witte, "The I.M.F. Gold Auction: More Bitter Fruit from Bretton Woods?" paper presented at the Annual Meetings of the American Economic Association, September 18, 1976.

101. See Henneberry and Witte, op. cit., p. 4.

102. See, for example, Edwin Cannan, *Money: Its Connexion with Rising and Falling Prices* (London: P. S. King, 1935), p. 92, where he indicates

that World War I "tended to diminish the value of gold by enormously reducing the demand for it." Similarly, Gustav Cassel contended that "the great changes that occurred in the sphere of money during the war, and more especially after it, have completely interrupted the continuity in the development of the world demand for gold. As a result of the competition of paper money issued with little or no gold backing, and particularly as a result of the withdrawal of gold coins from circulation, there arose a superfluidity of gold, which raised the price level, after the resumption of the gold standard, by roughly 50 percent as compared with the pre-war level." (Cassel, *Theory of Social Economy*, p. 477.)

103. That is, increased commodity prices were related to an increase in the quantity of inconvertible currencies. See, for example, Henneberry and Witte, op. cit., p. 4.

104. For Cannan's views, see footnote 102 above. See also Jacques Rueff, op. cit.

105. Cassel, *Theory of Social Economy*, p. 505.

106. Gustav Cassel, "Further Observations on the World's Monetary Problem," *Economic Journal* (March 1920):39.

107. See, for example, Rueff, op. cit., p. 33.

108. Rueff, op. cit., pp. 33, 51.

109. See Henneberry and Witte, op. cit., p. 5.

110. Ibid., p. 5.

111. The immediate postwar period, then, was characterized by highly volatile price fluctuations in most countries. It was during this period of flexible exchange rates and highly unstable *world* prices that several well-known monetary writers (such as Keynes and Pigou) presented alternative monetary policy prescriptions for the open economy. In particular, these authors took note of the prevailing unstable *world* monetary conditions and asserted that the policy choice open to the monetary authorities of various countries was a choice between stable prices and stable exchanges. See, for example, Arthur C. Pigou, *Industrial Fluctuations* (New York: Augustus M. Kelley, 1967), pp. 303–4, and Keynes, *Monetary Reform*. This view fostered the association of fixed exchange rates with unstable prices. That is, it came to be accepted that fixed exchange rates were synonymous with fluctuations in the general price level. This view, in turn, led many economists to advocate flexible exchange rates or what Hayek refers to as "monetary nationalism." Support for the flexible exchange rate view contributed to the further deterioration of the view of a single, integrated world economy.

112. As indicated by Mundell: "Inflation lowered real gold balances and tightened liquidity ratios, particularly the ratio of gold stocks to world output and the ratio of gold reserves to money. International liquidity became too low relative to internal liquidity. . . ." (Mundell, op. cit., p. 385.)

113. Keeping gold in bank reserves is a method of economizing on gold usage. Gold in bank reserves can support a higher price level than gold in circulation.

114. Cassel, "Further Observations," p. 40.

115. Cassel, *Theory of Social Economy*, p. 504.

116. Rist, *History of Monetary and Credit Theory*, p. 281.

117. Ibid., p. 281.

118. As Rueff has indicated: "Resolution 9 of the Genoa Conference, which in 1922 recommended that it be introduced, states expressly that the gold exchange standard, 'makes for savings in the use of gold by maintaining reserves in the form of foreign balances.'" (Rueff, op. cit., p. 49.)

119. Ragnar Nurkse, *International Currency Experience* (Geneva: League of Nations, 1944), p. 7.

120. See, for example, Rueff, op. cit., p. 50, and Mundell, op. cit., p. 385.

121. Bertil Ohlin, "The Future of the World Price Level," *Index*, Stockholm (1927):7.

122. See, for example, Cassel, *Theory of Social Economy*, p. 477. Some authors contend, however, that this continued U.S. convertibility despite a higher price level was made possible only at the cost of the inconvertibility of all other major currencies. See, for example, Rueff, op. cit., p. 50.

123. As Cassel has indicated: ". . . the superfluity of gold [in the United States] was so great that an even greater rise of prices would have taken place if the United States had not kept a part of the surplus gold as a reserve for the future, the Federal Reserve System allowing its gold stocks to reach the abnormally high level of 70–80 percent of the notes and deposits outstanding." (Cassel, *Theory of Social Economy*, p. 477.)

124. See, for example, Ohlin, "Future of World Price Level," p. 7. As Ohlin indicated: "The influx and efflux of gold in the United States . . . lost all influence upon the monetary purchasing power and the price level in that country."

125. See Cassel, *Theory of Social Economy*, p. 477.

126. Charles O. Hardy, *Is There Enough Gold?* (Washington: Brookings Institution, 1936), p. 154.

127. See, for example, Milton and Rose Friedman, *Free to Choose* (New York: Harcourt, Brace, Jovanovich, 1980), pp. 76–77.

128. See, for example, Ohlin, op. cit., p. 7, where he states: "The control of the development of the world price level has passed entirely into the hands of the Federal Reserve Board and Governors."

129. Ohlin, op. cit., p. 7. Because of both the superfluous U.S. gold stock and the key currency status of the dollar, any balance of payments deficit resulting from expansionary monetary policy would not constitute the constraint on monetary policy that would otherwise be the case. See, for example, Thomas Humphrey, "Monetarist Model of the World Inflation and the Balance of Payments," *Economic Review*, Federal Reserve Bank of Richmond, 62 (November/December 1976):21–22.

130. Ohlin, op. cit., pp. 7–8.

131. See, for example, Milton and Rose Friedman, op. cit., pp. 76–77, where they indicated that: "By the end of the war . . . the world was effectively on a dollar standard and remained so even after a weakened version of the prewar gold standard was reestablished. The Federal Reserve System was no longer a minor body reacting passively to external events. It was a major independent force shaping the world monetary structure."

132. In a remarkable quote, Ohlin indicated *in 1927* that "the development of the world price level during the next decade is a question of American monetary policy. The decision regarding its stabilization lies in the hands of the leaders of that policy. It is a tremendous responsibility." (Ohlin, op. cit., p. 9).

133. See Milton and Rose Friedman, op. cit., p. 77.

134. See, for example, the chart in Lester V. Chandler, *The Economics of Money and Banking* (New York: Harper & Row, 1948), p. 106.

135. See, for example, Rueff, *The Age of Inflation* (Chicago: Henry Regnery, 1964), p. xii.

136. See, for example, Cassel, *Theory of Social Economy*, p. 506, and Milton Friedman, "The Political Economy of International Monetary Arrange-

ments," in *Dollars and Deficits*, ed. Milton Friedman (Englewood Cliffs: Prentice-Hall, 1968), p. 273.

137. See, for example, the data provided in Roy Jastram, *The Golden Constant* (New York: John Wiley, 1977), as well as in Charles Kindleberger, *The World in Depression* (Berkeley: University of California Press, 1973), pp. 88–89, 106.

138. See, for example, Don Roper, op. cit., p. 147; Ohlin, op. cit., p. 8; G. F. Warren and F. A. Pearson, "Relationship of Gold to Prices," *Journal of the American Statistical Association*, Supplement, 28 (1933):118, 122–23; and Rist, *History of Monetary and Credit Theory*, p. 273.

139. See, for example, Chandler, op. cit., pp. 109–10.

140. Mundell, op. cit., p. 386.

141. Hardy, op. cit., pp. 154–55.

142. Hardy, op. cit., p. 157.

143. Hardy, op. cit., pp. 157, 159.

144. Cassel, *Theory of Social Economy*, p. 506, and Hardy, op. cit., p. 160.

145. See, for example, Hardy, op. cit., pp. 160, 162.

146. Hardy, op. cit., p. 162.

147. Rueff, *The Monetary Sin of the West*, p. 54.

148. Ragnar Nurkse, *International Currency Experience*, p. 39.

149. Ibid., p. 39.

150. Rueff, *The Monetary Sin of the West*, p. 55.

151. Francis H. Brownell, *Hard Money* (New York: American Smelting and Refining, 1944), p. 7. Nurkse, op. cit., p. 39, indicates that after Britain went off gold, central banks were often forced to liquidate foreign exchange reserves: ". . . the withdrawal of balances from the United Kingdom after September 1931 was often imposed on central banks by their statutes, requiring them to hold their exchange reserves exclusively in gold standard currencies. To remain eligible as legal cover, these balances therefore had to be converted into gold or into a gold standard currency."

152. Nurkse, op. cit., p. 33.

153. For a description of circumstances in the United States, see Milton Friedman and Anna Schwartz, *A Monetary History of the U.S.* (Princeton: Princeton University Press, 1963).

154. When a key currency country (such as the United States) allows its domestic money supply to fall, this causes world reserves to fall. As imports, for example, of the key currency country fall, the reserve balances of other countries fall and the liquidity of holders of foreign exchange reserves diminishes. Nurkse, for example, indicated that: "The pressure resulting from the collapse of the gold exchange system was passed on from London and New York to the world's debtor countries, mainly through the abrupt cessation or even reversal of capital movements and through the fall in prices of primary commodities. . . . (The) debtor states . . . suffered a heavy reduction in gold reserves as well as in foreign exchange, though the proportionate decline was considerably greater in foreign exchange than in gold. . . . It is clear that when debtor countries used up their foreign exchange reserves for payments to the centers in which the reserves were held, there occurred an extinction and not simply a transfer of central banks' international currency reserves. . . . Thus the breakdown of the gold exchange standard involved a sharp reduction in the aggregate of international currency reserves not only through the conversion of exchange reserves

into gold but also through the absorption of exchange reserves by payments to the reserve centers." (Nurkse, op. cit., pp. 40–41.)

155. See, for example, Hardy, op. cit., p. 150, and Rueff, *The Monetary Sin of the West*, p. 84.

156. See, for example, Mundell, op. cit., p. 386, and Nurkse, op. cit., p. 41.

157. Cassel, writing in the period, emphasized these points: "The fundamental importance of a stable monetary system for the well-being of mankind has never been so obviously demonstrated as in these hard times. But even now the explanation of the causal connection and of the essentially monetary character of the whole crisis has met with strong opposition. All possible kinds of explanations for the fall in prices have been advanced, but wide and influential circles have obstinately refused to see that the explanation lies in a defective monetary policy." (Cassel, *The Theory of Social Economy*, p. 507.)

158. See footnote 157.

159. See, for example, Harry G. Johnson, *Inflation and the Monetarist Controversy* (Amsterdam: North-Holland, 1972), p. 89, and Marina Whitman, "Global Monetarism and the Monetary Approach to the Balance of Payments." *Brookings Papers on Economic Activity* (1975):523.

160. The modern development of these views on devaluation is outlined elsewhere. See, for example, Harry G. Johnson, "Money, Balance of Payments Theory, and the International Monetary Problem," *Essays in International Finance* No. 124 (Princeton: Princeton University Press, 1977).

161. See, for example, David Meiselman, "Worldwide Inflation: A Monetarist View," *The Phenomenon of Worldwise Inflation*, ed. David Meiselman and Arthur Laffer (Washington: American Enterprise Institute, 1975), pp. 72–73.

162. See, for example, Meiselman, op. cit.; H. Robert Heller, "International Reserves and World-Wide Inflation," *IMF Staff Papers* 23 (1976); Mohsin Khan, "Inflation and International Reserves," *IMF Staff Papers* 26 (1979); Michael Parkin, "A 'Monetarist' Interpretation of the Generation and Transmission of World Inflation: 1958–71," *American Economic Review, Papers and Proceedings* 67 (1977) and Michael Parkin, I. Richards, and G. Zis, "The Determination and Control of the World Money Supply Under Fixed Exchange Rates, 1961–1971," *The Manchester School of Economics and Social Studies* (September 1975).

II

OPEN ECONOMY UNDER FIXED EXCHANGE RATES

5

THE HISTORICAL DEVELOPMENT OF THE MONETARY MODEL OF THE SMALL OPEN ECONOMY UNDER FIXED EXCHANGE RATES: PART ONE

INTRODUCTION

As indicated above, the closed monetary model served as the base from which monetary models of the small open economy developed as offspring. That is, as various writers became familiar with the workings of the closed world framework, they began to develop models of the behavior of the world's smaller components, the small open economies. Since most early currencies were freely convertible into international money (gold or silver), it came to be recognized that a country's money as well as its value were closely connected to events affecting world money and world prices. Eventually, a framework for understanding the individual small open economy with a convertible currency gradually emerged. (Since most early currencies were convertible, this model predates that for the small open economy with an inconvertible currency, which will be discussed in subsequent chapters.) With the development of the convertible currency model—the model of the small open economy under fixed exchange rates—it became apparent that under these circumstances the relationship between money and prices was quite different from that under conditions of a closed economy. Of the frameworks described above in Chapter 2, the model of the small open economy under fixed exchange rates has often been misrepresented by historical interpreters. Among contemporary economists, it is the least understood of the three basic models, and its historical development has not been adequately documented. Consequently, the documentation of the development of this model is the subject of this chapter.

In describing the model's evolution, the development of its implications and key components will be emphasized. In particular, the concepts of causality, endogeneity, neutrality, and purchasing power parity (or the law of one price), as well as the balance of payments adjustments mechanism, will be stressed where appropriate. Throughout the chapter, it will be shown that various authors clearly recognized other monetary frameworks and their important (and differing) implications for the relationship between money and prices. Specifically, many writers of the period explicitly recognized the distinction between the open and closed monetary frameworks and their differing implications with respect to money/price causality and monetary adjustment.[1] Thus, references will often be made to the above-cited closed economy views of authors who contributed to the development of the monetary model of the small open economy under fixed exchange rates.

The chapter is organized according to the chronological development of the model. First, the period prior to the writings of David Hume will be discussed. During this period mercantilist views of monetary theory generally dominated the thinking of most economic writers; despite this influence, several writers of the period, notably Locke, Gervaise, and Cantillon, recognized important elements of the model. Hume and Smith's full recognition and elaboration of the model are then established. The reaffirmation of and use of the model by bullionist writers are then demonstrated.

WRITERS PRIOR TO DAVID HUME

The period prior to the monetary writings of David Hume was an era during which mercantilist views of monetary theory strongly influenced the thinking of most monetary writers. Although some mercantilist writers recognized and endorsed the closed world monetary model (as shown above), mercantilists generally did not fully understand the workings of the small open economy under fixed exchange rates. Mercantilists, for example, contended that a nation should always strive to increase its stock of precious metals via foreign trade. Since money was equated with wealth (or capital), the accumulation of money was seen as the means by which to increase the nation's wealth and power.[2] Despite their recognition of the effect of money on prices in the closed world economy, mercantilists emphasized the effect of increases in the money supply on wealth (and trade), but neither on prices nor on the balance of payments in the context of the small open economy.[3] That is, mercantilists believed that increases in the money supply—secured through a balance of payments surplus—would enrich a country but would not adversely affect its balance of payments.[4] More specifically, although (some) mercantilists understood the relationship between prices and foreign trade as well as that a favorable trade balance would increase the stock of specie, they failed to recognize the effect of domestic monetary accumulation on the balance of payments.[5] Indeed, some mercantilists believed that an increased domestic money supply would *improve* the balance of payments.[6] In short, mercantilist writers had little understanding of the monetary nature of the balance of payments adjustment mechanism.[7] Mercantilists, then, did not understand the essentials of the monetary approach to the balance of payments, or the theory of the small open economy under fixed exchange rates.

Whereas mercantilist writers had little understanding of the complete version of this model, elements of this view were developed by certain writers during the mercantilist era. Later, these elements or components would be synthesized into a complete monetary model of the small open economy under fixed exchange rates by Hume and others. In any case, several monetary writers prior to Hume developed components—but not a complete version—of the monetary approach to the balance of payments. Indeed, several of these writers came close to integrating some of these elements into a complete and consistent theory, but they remained, to some extent, wedded to inconsistent mercantilistic views.

One early writer who recognized an element of the monetary theory of the small open economy under fixed exchange rates was Thomas Mun. Writing in the early seventeenth century, Mun identified a link between a country's money supply and its balance of payments. Specifically, Mun indicated that an increase in the money supply (secured through a balance of payments surplus) would work to increase domestic prices. This increase in domestic prices, he maintained, would adversely affect foreign trade and, hence, lead to a deterioration of the foreign balance.[8] Implicitly, he recognized that the demand for exports and imports was price elastic and that domestic prices were to some extent related to prices abroad.

There is fragmentary evidence that some elements of the monetary theory of the small open economy were also identified by various writers in the late seventeenth century. Despite their insights, none of these writers held a fully consistent theory. When they attempted to provide such a complete view, their presentations were confused, inconsistent, and often incoherent. Nonetheless, their vague notions provided important clues for later writers. One of these seventeenth-century writers was William Petty. Petty has been credited with identifying rudiments of the "natural distribution of specie" hypothesis; that is, he presented the concept of a "due proportion between the national stock of money and the monetary needs of a country."[9] Dudley North hinted at a similar view, in which he indicated that the proper distribution of money was brought about automatically, "without any aid of Politicians."[10] These were isolated insights, however, rather than lucid, well-developed theories. Similar isolated insights were made by other seventeenth-century authors, such as Barbon, Clement, and others.[11]

One seventeenth-century writer who recognized elements of the monetary approach to the balance of payments and whose contributions are worthy of special mention was John Locke. What was unique about Locke was that—partly as a result of his philosophic training—he was able to present his arguments in a more lucid form than other writers of this period.[12] As indicated in earlier chapters, Locke clearly acknowledged the monetary model of the closed economy (see Chapter 3 above). Moreover, Locke well recognized that the monetary model of an isolated economy was not applicable to an open economy trading with other nations; that is, that different frameworks were required in the analysis of the open vis-à-vis the closed economy.[13] In particular, Locke indicated that, whereas the general price level is determined by the supply of money in the closed economy, this relationship is not applicable in an open economy.[14] That Locke recognized the differing relationship between money and prices in the open vis-à-vis the closed economy is demonstrated in the following remarks made in 1691:

> [In] any island separate from the commerce of the rest of mankind . . . any quantity of . . . money . . . would serve to drive any proportion of trade. . . ."
>
> . . . in a country, that hath open commerce with the rest of the world, and uses money made of the same materials with their neighbors, any quantity of that money will not serve to drive any quantity of trade; but there must be a certain proportion between their money and trade. The reason whereof is this, because to keep your trade going without loss, your commodities amongst you must keep an equal, or at least near the price of the same species of commodities in the neighboring countries. . . .[15]

Here Locke contends that, whereas the price level will adjust to any quantity of money in the closed economy (and, hence, is endogenously determined in the case of the closed economy), commodity prices in the small open economy must bear a certain relationship to the prices of the same goods in other countries in order for trade to be maintained. Hence, in the small open economy, domestic prices (and therefore the price level) are closely related to prices (and the price level) in foreign countries or the rest of the world and are not necessarily (endogenously) determined by the domestic money stock. In a recent interpretation of Locke, for example, Leigh (1974) contends that the price level in the Lockean scheme of the small open economy is best described as being "determined exogenously by its necessary relationship to price levels in other countries."[16] Locke, then, clearly acknowledged that the relationship between money and prices was different in the closed vis-à-vis the open economy—that is, different frameworks were essential in analyzing the closed as distinguished from the open economy.

In addition to this important observation, the above passage by Locke contains a statement that amounts to an early, albeit rudimentary, presentation of the law of one price—that is, that prices of homogeneous commodities are equalized over space when denominated in the same currency (neglecting tariffs, transport costs, etc.).[17] Implicit in the above passage is also the suggestion of a theory of a world distribution of money.[18] That is, in indicating that "there must be a certain proportion between their money and trade," Locke alludes to a "natural distribution of specie" hypothesis. Locke, therefore, not only differentiated between the open and the closed economy, but he identified some very important elements of the monetary model of the small open economy under fixed exchange rates.

Although he identified these important points, however, Locke provided neither a coherent theory of international prices nor a theory of an equilibrating balance of payments adjustment mechanism. That is, although he visualized a resulting world distribution of money, he said nothing of the (automatic) adjustment mechanism that provides this result. More specifically, he said nothing of the commodity and specie flows that maintain domestic prices in harmony with world prices and provide a natural distribution of specie.[19] Sympathetically interpreted, Locke may be credited with identifying an element of an adjustment process but not with developing an international price/specie flow mechanism or, for that matter, with the development of any theory of international prices.[20]

Progress in developing an explanation for such an equilibrating balance of payments adjustment came in the early years of the eighteenth century. In particular, Isaac Gervaise—although not well known and therefore not influential—contributed to an understanding of the workings of the small open economy under fixed exchange rates.[21] Gervaise's contribution came in the form of a single pamphlet published in 1720.

As documented in Chapter 3 above, Gervaise explicitly acknowledged and reaffirmed the monetary model of the closed economy. In addition to recognizing the closed monetary model, Gervaise indicated that a different framework was necessary in order to analyze the small open economy as distinct from that of the closed economy. In describing his interpretation of the workings of the small open economy under fixed exchange rates, for example, Gervaise developed what may be the first complete—or at least the earliest—thorough statement of the monetary approach to the balance of payments. In particular, Gervaise presented what Viner described as a "closely-reasoned exposition of the nature of international equilibrium and of the self-regulating mechanism whereby specie obtained its 'natural' or proper international distribution."[22] Other authors (such as Letiche and Sekine) also credit Gervaise with the most thoroughgoing statement of the monetary approach to the balance of payments to that date.[23]

One of the most outstanding features of Gervaise's presentation is his discussion of the automatic self-regulating nature of the international adjustment mechanism.[24] According to his analysis, this mechanism serves to distribute specie among various countries of the world in certain "proper" or "natural" proportions. Gervaise's presentation, then, amounts to an early but thorough discussion of what has come to be called the natural distribution of specie hypothesis. According to Gervaise, the existing world supply of specie would be distributed to the various countries of the world according to (what amounts to) their relative levels of real economic activity (or real income).[25] In Gervaise's own words:

> A nation can naturally draw and keep unto itself, but such a proportion of the real [money stock] of the world as is proportion'd to the quantity of its inhabitants, because the [money stock] can be attracted but by [production] only; and as the whole world tend to the same end, the [production] of each nation is continually opposed, by all the [production] of the rest of the world. . . . Thus as [production] draws the [money stock] of the world, also the [money stock] draws [production] from the world; so that if the particular [money stock] of any nation be greater than its just proportion, it will draw

> from other nations, a portion of [production] proportion'd to its excess; and if its [money stock] be less than its just proportion, it will draw a portion of gold and silver, proportion'd to what it wants of its just proportion. . . . A [money stock] under its proportion, draws part of all other [money stocks], till it hath attained its proportion; also a [money stock] above its proportion, draws the [production] from other nations, till it be lessen'd to its proportion. . . . A nation cannot retain more than its natural proportion of what is in the world; and the balance of trade must run against it. . . . Time [will] bring all trading nations of the world into that equilibrium, which is proportioned, and belongs to the number of their inhabitants.[26]

This natural distribution of specie hypothesis is among the central propositions of the monetary approach to the balance of payments. It has several important implications, all of which are alluded to in Gervaise's pamphlet. In addition to indicating that the distribution of specie is accomplished automatically by self-regulating free market forces, the natural distribution of specie hypothesis implies that under a fixed exchange rate regime, the money supply of any small open economy is endogenous. Since the money stock is determined by relative levels of economic activity (or real income), it can be said that in this case the money supply is demand-determined. The mechanism by which this endogeneity is affected—or through which the demand for money is accommodated—is via the balance of payments.[27] Accordingly, the money supply is directly linked to the balance of payments and any analysis of the international adjustment mechanism must consider monetary policy as well as any resultant excess flow demand or supply of money.[28] Indeed, Gervaise contended that persistent balance of payments deficits in any particular country were indicative of overly expansive monetary policy. He stated, for example, that "When the balance of trade runs, and continues running, against a Nation, we may conclude its [money stock] exceeds its natural proportion."[29]

This natural distribution of specie hypothesis (or endogeneity of the money stock) also implies that, under certain conditions, causality may run from nominal income to money rather than from money to income as in the closed economy; the relationship between money and prices may be quite different in the small open economy with a convertible currency from that in the closed economy.

Gervaise employs two examples to illustrate this natural distribution of specie hypothesis as well as its implications. He describes the adjustment process, for example, that would occur (1) if gold (silver) mines were discovered in a particular small open economy (with a convertible currency) or (2) if excessive credit expansion occurred in such an economy. In both cases, he indicates that excessive monetary growth would create a balance of payments deficit. This deficit would work to eliminate the excessive money stock as money was exchanged for foreign goods and services (or securities) and, hence, flowed out until the stock of money contracted and thereby returned to its "proper" or "natural" proportion. These examples enabled Gervaise to demonstrate that "no nation can retain more (or less) money than is proportional to its real wealth."[30] In Gervaise's own words: "When a nation has attracted a greater proportion of the [money supply] of the world than its proper share . . . that nation cannot retain the overplus of its proper proportion of the [world money stock]."[31]

Another implication of Gervaise's natural distribution of specie hypothesis relates to prices. This hypothesis, it will be remembered, contends that in all trading countries of the world, a certain similar "natural" proportion is maintained between the stock of money and the stock of goods (or production). Consequently, if this money-to-commodities ratio is the same for all trading countries, the value (or purchasing power) of money will also be the same in all nations. The natural distribution of specie hypothesis, then, implies that price levels (the reciprocal of the price of money) will be similar across countries; that is, it implies a purchasing power parity relationship between the (convertible) currencies of various countries.[32]

In addition to describing the consequences and alluding to some implications of the natural distribution of specie hypothesis, "the first extended (and in-depth) analysis of the process of international adjustment came from Isaac Gervaise."[33] In particular, unlike earlier writers, Gervaise spelled out the specifics of a balance of payments adjustment process that is fully in accord with "modern" versions of the monetary approach to the balance of payments. In delineating this specific adjustment process, Gervaise contended that monetary disturbances in any country would induce changes in the balance of payments through cash (or real) balance effects.[34] That is, he indicated that the effect of an excessive growth rate of cash balances in a nation—whether brought about by an accidental maldistribution of the precious metals or by a deliberate creation of credit—would be to increase the nation's aggregate expenditure on imports. This, in turn, would lead to a trade deficit and, consequently, to an outflow of precious metals (or international reserves), which would eventually remove the excess of cash balances.[35] Thus, Gervaise described balance of payments adjustments as being affected by changes in real money balances, without mentioning price changes as being part of the adjustment mechanism.[36] Consequently, he was one of the first writers to describe balance of payment adjustments as being determined by divergencies between expenditures and income and not necessarily by changes in relative prices.[37] His presentation, then, is remarkably similar to "modern" interpretations of the monetary approach to the balance of payments, whereby the small open economy exists in a fully integrated world economy. According to these "modern" versions, balance of payments adjustments take place via the rapid arbitrage of securities, commodities, and money rather than by divergent movements in general price levels. Gervaise's theory, then, is a notable presage of later developments.

In sum, Gervaise provided in 1720 the most thorough discussion of the monetary model of the small open economy under fixed exchange rates to that date. Elements of this model, such as the automaticity of the adjustment process, the endogeneity of the money supply, and the real balance effect nature of the balance of payments adjustment process, as well as the implication of purchasing power parity, were all ingredients of Gervaise's work. Gervaise, then, was one of the first writers approaching a full understanding of the monetary approach to the balance of payments. Unfortunately, despite the path-breaking nature of Gervaise's analysis, his work was ignored and went virtually unrecognized for nearly a century. Perhaps the obsolete terminology employed by Gervaise contributed to this lack of recognition. In any case, his work apparently had little if any influence on other monetary writers in the eighteenth century, who, because of this, had to reconstruct and rediscover many of the ideas that had earlier been laid out by Gervaise. Writers who contributed to this reconstruction included Vanderlint, Cantillon, and others.

Jacob Vanderlint's tract (published in 1734), for example, provides evidence of a recognition of some elements of the monetary model of the small open economy under fixed exchange rates. In particular, Vanderlint identified certain aspects of a price-specie-flow mechanism. It is clear, however, that he had only a partial and incomplete understanding of the full equilibrium view described in Chapter 2. Consequently, several of his interpreters have labeled him a "semiequilibrium theorist."[38] Nonetheless, Vanderlint indicated that an increase in the money supply would increase aggregate expenditure and consequently lead to an increase in domestic prices.[39] This domestic price increase would discourage exports, encourage imports, and, hence, produce a balance of trade deficit—thus conflicting with the mercantilist objective of maintaining a trade surplus.[40] The trade deficit would, in turn, cause money to flow out via the balance of payments. Although divergent movements in prices were part of the balance of payments adjustment mechanism according to Vanderlint, he recognized that these price movements were internationally constrained.[41] He, for example, "saw clearly . . . that . . . a country which trades with others could not have a price level permanently higher than that of foreign countries."[42] Vanderlint, however, did not indicate that prices would be equalized by this process. Moreover, he did not recognize an equilibrium "natural distribution of specie."[43] Consequently, he fell short of formulating a complete theory of international equilibrium.[44]

Vanderlint, then, is not generally regarded to be as competent a theorist as Gervaise. In addition to being a "semiequilibrium theorist," his analysis is marred in that it contains several inconsistencies and is mired in mercantilist thought. (Vanderlint, for example, endorsed the policy of "artifically keeping imported specie from going into active circulation."[45]) Nonetheless, he recognized elements of a price-specie-flow mechanism and was, hence, a forerunner of the monetary approach to the balance of payments.

There were several other contributors to the construction of a consistent monetary model of a convertible currency system during the early to mid-eighteenth century. Harris, Steuart, and Berkeley, for example, reemphasized that there is a certain proportion between money and the "monetary needs of a nation" and that the demand for money determined its quantity.[46] Steuart, moreover, clearly recognized that if a country had trade with other countries, its domestic prices were largely constrained by international competition. He indicated, for example, that an excessive growth of a nation's money supply would result in money migrating abroad, an inflow of foreign commodities, and, hence, a return of domestic prices to their previous levels.[47] Price levels in separate countries, therefore, were kept in line by international competition, together with a self-balancing mechanism.[48] Although many of the arguments of these authors were consistent with the convertible currency model described in Chapter 2, aspects of their arguments were often inconsistent with this model, and, to some degree, their views were still influenced by mercantilist theories.[49]

One writer of this period whose contributions merit special attention was Richard Cantillon. Cantillon, writing in the early 1730s (not published, however, until 1755), clearly distinguished between the open and closed economies. Spengler, for example, lauds Cantillon's "use of [the] concepts of both closed and open states [that is, economies]."[50] As documented in Chapter 3, Cantillon very explicitly acknowledged the monetary model of the closed economy and several of its implications. As will be shown here, he also recognized and developed many important elements of the monetary model of the small open economy under fixed exchange rates. Cantillon's discrimination between the open and closed economies is manifest in his distinguishing between the effects of increases in the money supply arising from increased gold production (world money supply increases) as opposed to increases in the money supply arising from balance of payments surpluses (redistributions of the existing world money supply). This discrimination between the open and closed economies is also manifest in his emphasis of the different adjustment mechanisms of traded goods (associated with open economies) vis-à-vis nontraded goods (associated with the closed portions of economies). In discussing traded goods, for example, Cantillon recognizes—albeit implicitly—that the markets for these goods are integrated world markets and not compartmentalized or segmented markets. He acknowledges, for example, that the markets of various countries are closely interconnected, and, hence, he recognized the interdependence of the world's trading economies.[51] Cantillon clearly indicates, moreover, that traded good prices are governed—or at least highly constrained—by foreign competition and, hence, suggests that such prices are determined in world markets.

In analyzing the effects of monetary expansion, Cantillon carefully delineated various balance of payments responses and indicated that money creation has a direct effect on the balance of payments. His description of the balance of payments adjustment process was by far the most thorough to that date. Given an increase in the money supply, for example, Cantillon described various transmission mechanisms by which the economy adjusted to this increased stock of money. He concerned himself with "the problem of the actual path through which a change in the volume of money led to changes in price [and other economic variables]."[52] In discussing the adjustment process, Cantillon often distinguished between traded and nontraded goods. He indicated, for example, that, whereas the prices of nontradable goods would increase in response to increases in the money supply, the prices of traded goods "would not rise to a level in excess of its foreign cost plus its cost of transport."[53] Cantillon, then, stated the "law of one price" for traded goods—that is, traded good prices will differ only by the costs of transport when denominated in the same currency.[54] Cantillon recognized, therefore, that price differences for (homogeneous) traded goods were limited or constrained by arbitrage.

In describing these various adjustment processes, Cantillon gave an excellent account of a self-regulating specie flow mechanism. That is, he indicated that an increase in the money stock would lead to temporary domestic price increases. These price increases would quickly induce domestic consumers to purchase cheaper foreign products and exports to become less competitive in international markets. Hence, the money supply increase would result in an increase in imports and a decrease in exports—that is, a balance of payments deficit. This deficit would necessarily lead to an outflow of gold (or international reserves). Thus, Cantillon showed that an increase in the money supply inevitably leads to an outflow of specie and, hence, to a subsequent decrease in the money supply via the balance of payments; that is, he described the essentials of a self-regulating specie flow adjustment mechanism.

Although Cantillon's discussion incorporates much of what is described as a self-regulating mechanism of adjustment, his exposition did not include a formulation of the concept of monetary equilibrium. In particular, Cantillon's writings do not include a theory of an international distribution of specie; equilibrium, the "natural distribution of specie hypothesis," was not part of Cantillon's *Essai.*[55] It is convenient, then, as Sekine has indicated, to refer to Cantillon as a "semiequilibrium theorist," for "despite [his] penetrating insights into the adjustment mechanism, [he] fell a step short of formulating a complete theory of international equilibrium."[56]

There were two basic reasons for Cantillon's incompleteness. First, Cantillon was preoccupied with the details of various monetary transmission mechanisms—which, by their very nature, involve the description of (short-run) stages of monetary disequilibrium rather than long-run monetary equilibrium. Secondly, despite his contributions and various insights, Cantillon still held views consistent with mercantilism. Several writers maintain, for example, that Cantillon was a mercantilist.[57] As illustrated in the following quotation, for example, he continued to equate money with wealth: "I assume always that the comparative wealth of states consists principally in the respective quantities of money which they possess."[58] This mercantilist view prevented Cantillon from developing a complete and general theory of international monetary equilibrium. That is, although he recognized that an increase in the money supply would create a balance of payments deficit and, hence, lead to a monetary drain or outflow, Cantillon's mercantilist leanings prevented him from acknowledging that such an outflow was part of an equilibrating adjustment process that would continue only until an equilibrium was attained. Cantillon—because he equated money with wealth—viewed such a monetary drain as weakening (or reducing the wealth of) a nation rather than as the other side of an equilibrium process.

Thus, he was unable to recognize that such a monetary drain would in and of itself turn a country's balance of payments back in its favor (and adversely affect the balance of payments of specie recipients).[59] Because of his mercantilist bias, Cantillon indicated that the state should intervene in order to preserve an abundance of money, that is, that it should "withdraw money from circulation, keep it for emergencies, and try to retard its circulation"[60] instead of allowing equilibrating forces to operate.

Despite his shortcomings, however, Cantillon's contributions to the theory of the small open economy under fixed exchange rates were substantial. His differentiation of the closed and open economic frameworks (and related differentiation of traded and nontraded goods) and his recognition of both the law of one price and integrated traded commodity markets, as well as his demonstration of the monetary character of the balance of payments and its self-regulating specie-flow adjustment process all make Cantillon an important contributor to the development of the convertible currency model.

In sum, many contributions to the theory of a self-adjusting international monetary equilibrium emerged in the early and mid-eighteenth century.[61] As demonstrated here, several authors contributed to this development of the monetary model of the small open economy under fixed exchange rates. This was the period, it will be remembered, in which "mercantilist doctrine was about to be superseded by classical political economy"[62] Indeed, the emergence of the completed model of the small open economy under fixed exchange rates provided the final blow to the mercantilist view. Although many elements of the model were presented by the above-cited authors, none of them constructed a complete and fully consistent model. All of them were influenced to some degree by mercantilist thought. It remained for a monetary writer to synthesize the available components into a complete whole. That writer was David Hume.

DAVID HUME

By the time David Hume's writings appeared, many of the essential ingredients of the monetary model of the small open economy with a convertible currency had been assembled. By this time, moreover, monetary writers were intimately familiar with the operational aspects of the functioning of the gold (silver) standard. In order to understand better the contributions of Hume, some of these considerations should first be briefly reviewed.

One of these, for example, was the fact that under a convertible currency, exchange rates were not absolutely fixed but rather, as *modus operandi*, varied between relatively narrow bands (between gold import and export points).[63] Secondly, there were no reliable general price indexes available to the monetary economists writing during this period;[64] consequently, in their discussions relating to money and prices, indirect proxies were frequently employed. To these writers, a convenient proxy involved the price of bullion.[65] That is, the product of the currency price of gold and the price of goods in terms of gold (determined in world markets for tradable commodities) was employed, albeit implicitly, as a proxy for the level of commodity prices (see Chapter 3 above). During periods when currency was convertible, the level of domestic prices could vary for either of two reasons: (1) because of changes in the world price of commodities in terms of gold, or (2) because of variations in the exchanges between the gold points. During normal periods and within moderate time frames, changes in the former factor were not observed because of large outstanding world stocks of gold (relative to current production possibilities of gold). The latter, although it could be affected by banking and monetary policies, could only vary between relatively narrow bands. Consequently, sizable amounts of inflation in any single country were regarded as impossible as long as convertibility was maintained. Nonetheless, because of high price elasticities related both to supplies (demands) of foreign exchange at gold export (import) points and to foreign demand (and supply) of tradable products, slight (and temporary) movements in prices could have strong influences on commodity and asset flows and thereby could serve as the *modus operandi* of the system.[66] These considerations have important implications for the interpretation of the classical economists such as Hume, to which we will now turn.

By the mid-eighteenth century, then, the above aspects of the operation of a commodity standard were known and various ingredients of the monetary model of the small open economy under fixed exchange rates had been published in the literature. It remained for someone to synthesize these elements into a complete and consistent monetary model of a convertible currency. As several writers have indicated, this person was David Hume.[67] Hume is generally viewed as the first well-known English writer to formulate such a complete version of this model, which became widely recognized by subsequent monetary theorists. Hume, then, was not so much the originator but rather the influential and successful synthesist and propagator of the model.[68] More specifically, as will be shown below, Hume integrated the elements that came to form the core of the classical monetary theory. That is, the natural distribution of specie hypothesis, the law of one price, the self-adjusting specie-flow mechanism, and various implications of these elements were integrated by Hume into a complete monetary model of the small open economy with a convertible currency.

In accomplishing this, Hume removed himself from mercantilist views—he carefully distinguished, for example, between money and wealth—and, indeed, forcefully demonstrated the fallaciousness of mercantilist doctrine.[69] As indicated by Johnson:

> Hume was concerned about refuting the concentration of the mercantilists on the objective of accumulating precious metals within the country, and their consequent recommendations of policies designed to bring about a surplus on the balance of payments. His analysis . . . showed that the amount of money in a country would be adjusted automatically to the demand for it (through surpluses and deficits in the balance of payments). . . . Hence the mercantilist desire to accumulate 'treasure' was in conflict with the basic mechanism of international monetary adjustment and could only be emphemerally successful.[70]

Hume showed, therefore, that the very inflow of specie advocated by the mercantilists—by its effect in creating an increase in expenditure on imports and a lessening of exports—contained the seeds of its own destruction.[71] Thus, his specie-flow mechanism "rang the death knell of mercantilism."[72] In addition to this, Hume gained attention because he presented his theory "with a degree of clarity, ability of exposition, emphasis on its importance, and consistent incorporation with the remainder of his economic views, which most of the earlier writers did not even distantly approach."[73]

In examining Hume's contributions, virtually all interpreters of Hume recognize his presentation of the natural distribution of specie hypothesis, whereby world money is distributed via an automatic balance of payments mechanism according to the relative demand for money balances.[74] In these interpretations, the balance of payments is the channel by which the equilibrium or "natural" money stocks are maintained. The quantity of specie in any one country is a function of real factors normally associated with the demand for money, such as the volume of transactions, population, and income—that is, the money stock is demand-determined (or endogenous). On this point, there is virtual consensus. However, certain important implications of this framework for the individual small open economy have received emphasis in only a few of these interpretations. First, for example, Hume's natural distribution hypothesis implied that money would be distributed *in proportion* to these real variables. Hume indicated that, in each country, money would automatically seek a natural "level" equal to that in other countries. In particular, Hume stated that "It must carefully be remarked, that throughout this discourse, wherever I speak of the level of money, I mean always its proportional level to the commodities, labour, industry and skill which is in the several states."[75] In explaining his position, Hume often resorted to an analogy of how water seeks its "natural" level: "It does not seem that money any more than water can be raised or lowered anywhere much beyond the level it has in places where communication is open, but that it must rise and fall in proportion to the goods and labor contained in each state."[76] This equality of level, as Viner has shown, related to *prices* and not to absolute quantities of money: "The equality of level which Hume posited was not between absolute quantities of money but between the proportions of quantities of money to quantities of commodities, i.e., prices. . . ."[77] Thus, an implication of the natural distribution hypothesis for the small open economy is the natural equalization of prices between it and all other countries or, in short, the automatic (and exogenous) determination of prices.[78] Hume, then, although not using modern terminology, was embracing the concept of purchasing power parity (that is, the equalization of the purchasing power or value of money across countries).

Another implication of the natural distribution hypothesis relevant to the small open economy is that the quantity of money in such an economy is a *dependent* variable not subject to discretionary manipulation.[79] According to this view, the supply of precious metals to any individual country "would come in the ordinary course of trade, as opposed to the mercantilist view that special (governmental) action was necessary to that end."[80] For this reason, suppositions of large exogenous changes of the domestic money supply of the small open economy are acceptable only for pedagogical purposes but not for practical examinations of the international monetary adjustment mechanism.[81] Most interpreters of Hume would have little difficulty with these propositions.

However, discussions of the adjustment mechanism—the price-specie-flow mechanism—have produced sharp differences in the interpretation of Hume. Specifically, many interpreters contend that the price-specie-flow mechanism works such that monetary adjustment proceeds by divergent movements in national price levels. That is, it is contended by these interpreters that variations in the price level serve as the adjustment mechanism.[82] If this were the case, the view would contradict the law of one price, except in long-run equilibrium. On rereading Hume, we prefer to adopt an alternative interpretation of the adjustment mechanism.[83]

According to this alternative interpretation, Hume endorsed the law of one price. This law, it will be remembered, implies that any tendency for home prices to change is (mainly) checked by arbitrage across geographic boundaries, that is, prices are equalized such that there exists no advantage in buying in one geographic location over another.[84] Hume essentially outlined a model of price equalization that he explicitly stated would make it impossible for the value of money to vary between provinces of the same kingdom. In Hume's own words: "How is the balance [i.e., monetary equilibrium] kept in the provinces of every kingdom among themselves, but by the force of this [price equalization] principle, which makes it impossible for money to lose its level, and either to rise or sink beyond the proportion of the labour and commodities which are in each province?"[85] Hume goes on to say that in addition to provinces within a country, this price equalization principle applies between countries as well:

> What happens in small portions of mankind, must take place in greater. The provinces of the Roman empire, no doubt, kept their balance with each other, and with Italy, independent of the legislature; as much as the several counties of Great Britain, or the several parishes of each county. And any man who travels over Europe at this day, may see, *by the prices of commodities, that money*, in spite of the absurd jealousy of princes and states, *has brought itself nearly to a level; and that the difference between one kingdom and another is not greater in this respect, than it is often between different provinces of the same kingdom.*[86]

Hume also explicitly endorsed the law of one price elsewhere in his writings:

> The merchant, who exports the cloth, cannot raise its price, being limited by the price which it yields in foreign markets.[87]

> There cannot be two prices for the same species of labour. This extends to all commodities of which there is any part exported, that is to almost every commodity. Even were there some commodities of which no part is exported, the price of labour employed in them, could not rise; for this high price would tempt so many hands to go into that species of industry as must immediately bring down the prices.[88]

In endorsing the law of one price or the concept of price equalization across countries, Hume affirmed support for what is today known as purchasing power parity. In symbolic terms, this view is commonly represented as follows:

$$P_{\$/\text{goods}} = \bar{p}_{\$/£} \cdot P_{£/\text{goods}}$$

That is, the prices of goods denominated in one currency are equal to the product of the (fixed) ratio of exchange (or the fixed exchange rate) and the prices of the same goods denominated in any other currency. This implies that prices in the two countries are the same when denominated in a common currency (ignoring costs of transfer).

That Hume had come to endorse this position by the time his views on the balance of payments adjustment mechanism were published is evident in his correspondence with his friend and critic, James Oswald. After having reviewed a preliminary manuscript of Hume's essay, "Of the Balance of Trade," Oswald wrote Hume a letter dated 10 October 1749 (prior to publication) and explicitly indicated that, unlike the case of the closed economy, prices in the small open economy were directly tied to foreign (world) prices rather than to alterations in the domestic quantity of money.[89] In the words of one interpreter:

> Oswald conceded that the prices of an isolated [closed] economy would rise in proportion as the supply of money increased, but he did not think that Hume was justified in applying this proposition mechanically in the case of an internationally trading society. He based his argument on [the assumption that] '. . . *all transportable commodities will ever be nearly all the same price . . . because they may be transported from one country to another with the addition only of the charge of transportation*'. . . . Hume replied one month later and willingly conceded Oswalds point . . . and he agreed to amend the [preliminary unpublished] draft accordingly.[90]

In his response, then, Hume indicated that he agreed with Oswald's position that prices in the small open economy were directly related to prices in world markets rather than to alterations in the domestic quantity of money, and he indicated that his essay would be restated accordingly.[91]

In discussing his contrived examples of balance of payments adjustments, Hume repeatedly emphasized the *very rapid* workings of arbitrage (price equalization). Hume, for example, used the word "immediate" or similar adjectives to describe price adjustments in at least five of his essays or letters.[92] Indeed, he held that in practice no important price level differences between countries would be observable,[93] as is evident in a passage of his essay, "Of the Balance of Trade." Here, Hume supposes for pedagogical purposes that four-fifths of all the money in Great Britain is miraculously annihilated overnight. He then discusses the adjustment process. Then, again for pedagogical purposes, he supposes that all the money in Great Britain is miraculously multiplied fivefold in one night, and he examines the adjustment process. *In the very next paragraph*, Hume follows this up by stating:

> Now, it is evident, that the same causes, which would correct these exorbitant inequalities, were they to happen miraculously, must prevent their happening *in the common course of nature, and must for ever, in all neighboring nations, preserve money nearly proportionable to the art and industry of each nation*. All water, wherever it communicates, remains always at a level. Ask naturalists the reason; they tell you, that, were it to be raised in any one place, the superior gravity of that part not being balanced, must depress it, till it meet a counterpoise; and that the same cause, which redresses the inequality when it happens, *must for ever prevent it*, without some violent external operation.[94]

Here Hume is stating that, although he assumed (for pedagogical purposes) "miraculous" changes in money, the forces that determine the natural distribution of specie are so strong as to preclude significant inequalities in the natural proportion of money to commodities and, hence, observational differences in prices "in the common course of nature," that is, in reality. Balance of payments adjustments, then, can occur quickly without noticeable divergencies in general price levels; *if* prices diverge, they do so only ephemerally.[95] To clarify this point further, Hume likens money to water; in making this analogy, he indicates that all money, "wherever it communicates"—that is, where it is in international media of exchange—always works to maintain price equality.[96]

This affirmation of the law of one price or purchasing power parity has several important implications. First, it implies that Hume recognized, albeit implicitly, a high degree of price elasticity for tradable commodities, and, therefore, that movements in commodities and money were the *modus operandi* of the system. Second, it implies that, in Hume's view, world markets were significantly integrated so as to ensure these results. Moreover, it implies that trading countries—such as Great Britain—that exist in this integrated world economic system could not pursue independent (nationalistic) monetary policies like those prescribed by the mercantilists.

More specifically, since Hume recognized that money in a small open economy with a convertible currency is a dependent variable and not subject to discretionary manipulation (by virtue of his natural distribution hypothesis), he held that any excessive quantity of money could not long persist in a single country. Hume's view on this matter is illustrated by his remark that "it is impossible to heap up money, more than any fluid, beyond its proper level."[97] An excessive quantity of money could not persist in a single country, according to Hume, not because its price level would rise, because single country inflation was regarded as impossible under a gold standard, but because an excess of spending over income would lead to a trade deficit and specie outflow.[98] Balance of payments adjustments, then, were carried out by money flows—that is, real balance effects.[99] Hume also stressed repeatedly that internal creation of bank credit in any one country would result in a trade deficit, together with offsetting outflows of specie on a one-to-one basis with the quantity of credit produced, rather than in domestic inflation.[100] Hume's recognition of this relationship (Gresham's Law) is epitomized in the following remark: "What a pity Lycurgus did not think of paper credit when he wanted to banish gold and silver from Sparta; it would have served his purpose better than the lump of iron he made use of as money."[101]

Hence, domestic monetary and credit policy does not determine the domestic money supply but rather the proportion of international reserves to domestic credit.[102] And monetary and credit policies are directly linked to the balance of payments. In view of these considerations, then, Hume's supposition of an enormous and exogenous alteration of the quantity of money in a small open economy with a convertible currency can only be viewed as a pedagogical device.[103]

An implication of Hume's position, therefore, is that the quantity theory of money—in the sense of causality running from changes in money to changes in prices—does not apply to the small open economy under fixed exchange rates. Yet, Hume recognized the applicability of the quantity theory to the closed economy, as clearly documented in Chapter 3. When Hume employed his water analogy, for example, it is evident that he recognized this difference between the open and the closed economy. That is, he indicated that in the closed economy, prices were not at all tied to world prices (as in the case of the open economy) but were determined by the proportion between domestic money and domestic commodities. He stated, for example, that: "As any body of water may be raised above the level of the surrounding element, *if the former has no communication with the latter*; so in money, if the communication be cut off, by any material or physical impediment, there may, in such a case be a very great inequality of money."[104] If communication were open (that is, if a country trades internationally), however, Hume indicated that such price inequality could not exist: prices would be directly related to foreign prices and determined in world markets. In the open economy, then, Hume indicated that "it does not seem that money, any more than water, can be raised or lowered anywhere much beyond the level it has in places *where communication is open*, but that it must rise and fall in proportion to the goods and labour contained in each state."[105] Schumpeter underscored Hume's acknowledgement of this difference between the open and closed monetary frameworks when he indicated that: "Hume [showed that] on the one hand, any quantity of money, however small, will do in an isolated [closed] economy; on the other hand, with perfect gold currency all round [i.e., under fixed exchange rates] every country will always tend to have the amount appropriate to its relative position in international trade."[106]

Hume, then, not only outlined a consistent version of the monetary model of the small open economy under fixed exchange rates, but also described how it differed from the monetary model of the closed economy. Two of the three models described in Chapter 2, then, were clearly recognized by Hume.

ADAM SMITH

Hume undoubtedly had an important influence on Adam Smith,[107] as was documented in Chapter 3. Hume and Smith were close friends over an extended period of time and often corresponded with one another.[108] Moreover, both of them were strongly influenced by a mutual friend, economist James Oswald.[109] Consequently, Smith was eminently familiar with the writings of Hume and, like Hume, directed his efforts at a refutation of mercantilist doctrine. Moreover, Smith always wrote, as did Hume, in the context of convertible currencies.[110] Thus, it should not be surprising that Smith endorsed most of the positions relevant to the convertible framework that were set out by Hume (and Oswald). For example, Smith clearly viewed money as a dependent variable and, as such, indicated that it would be automatically supplied to the small open economy in the ordinary course of trade:

> The quantity of money . . . must in every country naturally increase as the value of the annual produce increases. The value of the con-

> sumable goods annually circulated within the society being greater will require a greater quantity of money to circulate them. A part of the increased produce, therefore, will naturally be employed in purchasing, wherever it is to be had, the additional quantity of gold and silver necessary for circulating the rest. The increase of those metals will in this case be the effect, not the cause, of the public prosperity.[111]

Because, in this circumstance, money was viewed as fully endogenous or passive, Smith could not justify or reconcile the assumption of a sudden exogenous change in the quantity of money. To him, this was not possible. Rather, changes in the quantity of money were the effect of changes in other variables.[112] Smith extended this view to the case of (convertible) paper. That is, like Hume, Smith contended in a number of passages that the quantity of convertible paper that is added to the currency is always immediately offset by an equal and direct outflow of specie. Any (exogenous) issuance of convertible paper, then, could not increase a country's quantity of money over and above that quantity which would have otherwise circulated under a pure specie standard. In Smith's own words:

> The whole paper money of every kind which can easily circulate in any country never can exceed the value of the gold and silver, of which it supplies the place, or which [the commerce being supposed the same] would circulate there, if there was no paper money. . . . The channel of circulation, if I may be allowed such an expression, will remain precisely the same as before. One million [for example] we have supposed sufficient to fill that channel. Whatever, therefore, is poured into it beyond this sum, cannot run in it, but must overflow.[113]

In short, the "paper money [that is added] merely changes the form rather than the total of the money supply."[114] Hence, the monetary authority—or the banks—can control only the composition but not the total quantity of money. The following passage is also particularly noteworthy:

> The increase of paper money, it has been said, by augmenting the quantity, and consequently diminishing the value of the whole currency, necessarily augments the money price of commodities. But as the quantity of gold and silver, which is taken from the currency, is always equal to the quantity of paper which is added to it, paper money does not necessarily increase the quantity of the whole currency. From the beginning of the last century to the

> present time, provisions never were cheaper in Scotland than in 1759, though, from the circulation of ten and five shilling bank notes, there was then more paper money in the country than at present. The proportion between the price of provisions in Scotland and that in England is the same now as before the great multiplication of banking companies in Scotland. Corn is, upon most occasions, fully as cheap in England as in France; though there is a great deal of paper money in England, and scarce any in France.[115]

In this denial of overissue, Smith indicates that an increase in convertible paper money will not even temporarily affect prices and, consequently, will not even temporarily alter the value of money.[116] An implication of this position, then, is the endorsement of purchasing power parity as well as the law of one price.[117] In discussing the above passage, for example, Angell rightly notes that Smith's doctrine of offsetting specie flows "must necessarily presuppose fixity of prices, for the time being at least. It conceives of the 'channel of circulation' as being confined within rigid price walls."[118] This interpretation is further supported by noting that Smith, in his elaboration of the specie-flow mechanism, clearly placed emphasis on direct specie outflows (or "overflows," as he put it) and related import purchases, whereas he never stressed divergent price level movements as an adjustment mechanism in the *Wealth of Nations*.[119] Thus, Smith's balance of payments adjustment process took the form of commodity and money flows (real balance effects) instead of price level movements as individuals adjusted their excess (deficient) real cash balances by increasing (decreasing) their net foreign expenditures.[120]

Another implication of Smith's view of offsetting specie flows is that the quantity theory of money (in the sense of changes in the quantity of money causing changes in the price level) does not apply to the small open economy under a convertible currency regime. This implication was explicitly voiced by Angell, who, in discussing Smith's views on this topic, noted that "Smith adopts what seems to be the exact antithesis of the quantity theory view."[121] Smith, of course, in outlining this position, was referring to the open economy. Yet, as has been documented in Chapter 3, in discussions relating to the closed economy, he explicitly adopted a quantity theory view.[122] That Smith recognized the differing relationships between money and prices in the closed vis-à-vis the open framework is particularly evident in his discussion of specie flows. In one passage he was very careful, for example, to make a clear distinction between specie inflows in a single country resulting from increases in its demand for specie, as opposed to autonomous increases in world specie supplies (from new world discoveries of gold and silver mines). He clearly showed that specie inflows caused by increases in the domestic demand for specie were *not* inflationary, since this merely represented a redistribution of world specie supplies, whereas inflows due to new gold and silver discoveries were inflationary. Hence, increases in the domestic money supply (world supplies constant) do not affect prices, whereas increases in the world money supply do affect prices; the quantity theory applies to the closed world economy but not to the small open economy. Smith's view on this matter is epitomized in the following passage: "The quantity of the precious metals may increase in any country from two different causes: either, first, from the increased abundance of the mines which supply it; or, secondly, from the increased wealth of the people, from the increased produce of their annual labour. The first of these causes is no doubt necessarily connected with the diminution of the value of the precious metals, but the second is not."[123]

Smith, then, like Hume, understood the relationship between money and prices in the context of the small open economy under fixed exchange rates and how this relationship differs in the closed economy. In sum, then, Smith (like Hume) recognized two of the three models described above in Chapter 2.

BULLIONIST WRITERS AND THE CONVERTIBLE CURRENCY MODEL

The monetary model of the small open economy under fixed exchange rates and its differences from the closed economy model, then, were recognized and described by both Hume and Smith. Since the writings of both were so influential, these monetary models became well known among subsequent monetary writers. Bullionist writers, for example, who were familiar with both Hume and Smith, recognized and reaffirmed the above-described convertible currency model and carefully differentiated it from the monetary model of the closed economy.[124] It is especially evident that the bullionist writers well understood the monetary models both of the closed economy and of the small open economy with a convertible currency when it is recognized that they were able to employ both of these models profitably in understanding the circumstances in Great Britain during the period between 1797 and 1821. It was during this period, it will be remembered, that bullionist writers were to make their major contribution to the evolution of monetary thought—namely, the formulation of a model of inconvertible currency. The point to be emphasized here, however, is that their knowledge of the previously known models was of great help to them in this formulation. In particular, the bullionists' use of the closed model in understanding the causes of inflation in the inconvertible currency regime of 1797–1821 has already been described above in Chapter 3. In this section, it will be demonstrated that they employed the monetary model of the small open economy with a convertible currency to determine that it was the Bank of England that was directly responsible for the overissuance and, hence, the inflation and exchange rate depreciation of the period, and not the country banks. In view of the fact that they endorsed as well as employed the earlier-cited convertible currency and closed models, it may be noted here that the bullionist writers were the first group of English economists to recognize all three of the monetary models—that is, convertible, inconvertible, and closed—outlined in Chapter 2.

In addition to indicating how the bullionists employed the convertible currency model, this section will document the bullionist reaffirmation and refinement of the monetary model of the small open economy under fixed exchange rates. Two caveats, however, should be noted here. First, the endorsement of this model is made so frequently and so forcefully in the bullionist literature that a comprehensive documentation of it cannot be conveyed here; only a few illustrations can be presented. Secondly, although many writers contributed to the writings of the so-called bullionist school, this section will, in general, focus only on the writings of its most prominent members, namely, Wheatley, Thornton, and Ricardo.[125]

As described in Chapter 3, inflation, exchange rate depreciation, and an increased price of bullion all characterized the circumstances in Great Britain during the period between 1797 and 1821. A contribution of the bullionist writers of this period was to identify the increase in domestic inconvertible currency as the principal cause of these conditions (see Chapter 3, as well as subsequent chapters, for a thorough discussion of this contribution). Another issue of this period, however, was concerned with the identification of the institutions responsible for this excessive issuance of inconvertible currency. Specifically, the issue was whether the country banks or the central bank—the Bank of England—was responsible for this excessive quantity of inconvertible currency. Spokesmen for the Bank of England steadfastly denied that the central bank was responsible. Bullionist writers, however, employed the convertible currency model of the small open economy to demonstrate that the Bank of England was, indeed, responsible.[126]

In analyzing this issue, it is evident that the bullionist writers all had a fairly complete understanding of the operation of a small open economy under a metallic standard.[127] In particular, they understood how convertibility worked to constrain the level of money to its "natural" (equilibrium) proportion, thereby equating the value of money in different countries. Morover, they all recognized the implication that as long as the currency remained convertible, money could not expand more rapidly in the small open economy than in the world as a whole.[128]

As a consequence of this understanding, bullionist writers were able to recognize that if different regions within a country employed a common currency—or used a currency convertible into a common currency—they would behave exactly as different countries under a metallic standard. That is, under these circumstances, regions within a country and regional or country banks operated exactly as if they existed in a fixed exchange rate environment—that is, the natural distribution of money hypothesis applied to commercially connected areas within a country. During this period, bullionist writers noted that, whereas Bank of England notes were no longer convertible into gold, country bank note issue continued to be convertible into (and thus maintained the same value as) Bank of England notes. The supply of country bank notes, then, was constrained by its convertibility into Bank of England notes (which were held by country banks as reserves) and could increase no faster than the growth of this central bank note issue. Since Bank of England notes in essence served as the base for country bank note expansion and were under no convertibility constraint themselves, bullionist writers contended that the central bank was responsible for the overissuance that characterized the period.

Walter Boyd was one of the first writers to emphasize this point. In a letter to Pitt in 1801, for example, Boyd emphatically indicated that country banks were unable to overissue notes because their note issue was still convertible into, and hence, automatically constrained by, demands for Bank of England notes.[129] Boyd went on to say that "the obligation of country banks to redeem in Bank of England notes made their credit operations subject to a limitation comparable to, if not identical with, the limitation that the obligation to redeem in specie had [in times past] placed on the Bank of England."[130] That Boyd believed the overissue was the responsibility of the Bank of England and not the country banks is illustrated in the following passage:

> The circulation of Country Bank-notes must necessarily be proportioned to the sums, in specie *or* Bank of England notes, requisite to discharge such of them as may be presented for payment; but the

> paper of the Bank of England has no such limitation. It is itself now become (what the coin of the country only ought to be) the ultimate element into which the whole paper circulation of the country resolves itself. The Bank of England is the great source of all the circulation of the country; and, by the increase or diminution of its paper, the increase or diminution of that of every Country-Bank is infallibly regulated."[131]

Other writers of the day were not only strongly influenced by Boyd's work but were inspired to elaborate and develop his theme.[132]

One such writer was Henry Thornton. Thornton, for example, developed in detail the workings of the relationship between the central and provincial (regional) banks.[133] In so doing, he explained the mechanism by which country bank note issue was constrained by the note issue of the Bank of England.[134] In order to explain this mechanism, Thornton assumed that a single country bank (or banks in a single region) "issued a very extraordinary quantity of notes" relative to other banks, including the Bank of England. Whether the recipients of these notes desired to make purchases in the local economy or in other areas such as London would not affect the results of the analysis. Thornton indicated that in either case the excessive country bank paper would eventually be returned to the issuers for redemption (that is, to be converted into Bank of England notes). As a result of this redemption and consequent drain of Bank of England note reserves, the country bank (or banks) would be forced to contract their note issue. This would happen immediately if the recipients of the excessive country bank notes desired to make purchases in other regions, such as London, for example. If the excessive country bank note issue was employed to purchase goods in the local economy, however, Thornton stated that:

> The effect of such [local] purchases . . . must be a great local rise in the price of articles. But to suppose a great and merely local rise, *is to suppose that which can never happen* or which, at least, cannot long continue to exist; for every purchaser will discover that he can buy commodities elsewhere at a cheaper rate; and he will not fail to procure them in the quarter in which they are cheap, and to transport them to the spot in which they are dear, for the sake of the profit on the transaction. In order that he may be enabled to do this, he will demand to have the [country bank] notes . . . converted into the circulating medium of the place in which goods are cheap: he will, therefore, require to have his country bank note turned into a Bank of England note.[135]

When these excessive country bank notes are converted into Bank of England notes, Thornton continued, the country bank witnesses a loss of its central bank note reserves and, hence, is forced to contract its note issue.[136] Because of the convertibility of country bank notes, then, these notes can never be oversupplied (relative to Bank of England notes), since convertibility works to continually constrain that supply and to equate the value of these notes to those of the Bank of England. Country banks, therefore, could not have been responsible for the overissuance, since the volume of their note issue was regulated by the note issue of the Bank of England; that is, "The Bank of England was the basis and ultimate controlling influence on the country's entire credit circulation."[137] In Thornton's own words:

> The country paper is rendered, by its exchangeableness with the London paper, almost exactly equal to it in value. . . . It is, moreover, important already to point out that [country bank note and central bank note] value will be equalized, or nearly equalized, . . . by a tendency in the country paper to take exactly the [particular] value which the London paper bears [and not vice versa]. . . . Thus, therefore, the limitation of the supply of . . . London paper . . . is the means both of sustaining the value of London paper, and also of sustaining the values as well as limiting the quantity of the whole paper of the country. . . . The exchangeableness of our country paper for our London paper . . . always in this manner prevent[s] the quantity of paper circulating in one place from being very disproportionate to the quantity circulating in another.[138]

Thornton, in addition to demonstrating that the Bank of England and not the country banks was responsible for the overissuance of paper, noted important implications of his analysis. He indicated, for example, that the mechanism of convertibility, together with the workings of arbitrage, implied that purchasing power parity (or the law of one price for traded goods) was applicable to regions within a country. To assume that the price level in one region would increase relative to others, noted Thornton, was "to suppose that which can never happen." In particular, Thornton stated that the working of convertibility:

> . . . must be such as *always* to check a local rise in the price of commodities . . . *while it is as yet so small as to be scarcely perceptible*. In this manner, therefore, the exchangeableness of country paper for London paper *will never fail* very nearly to equalize the value of them both. . . . [Hence] a very considerable advance in the price of commodities bought and sold in one quarter of this kingdom, while

> there [is] no such rise in any other, [is] not supposable [due to arbitrage]. . . . The exchangeableness of our country paper for our London paper [will] always in this manner . . . preclude any great local rise in the price of commodities within our own island.[139]

Important implications such as these evolved, of course, from the fundamental concept of an equilibrium in the value of money in commercially connected areas within any one country; that is, they evolved from the application of the natural distribution of specie hypothesis to open regions within an integrated national economy.[140]

The above views were reaffirmed and forcefully restated in the Bullion Report and by writers such as Horner and Ricardo. The Bullion Report, for example, emphatically repeated that the Bank of England was fully responsible for the overissuance of paper currency:

> . . . so long as the cash payments of the Bank are suspended, the whole paper of the Country Bankers is a superstructure raised upon the foundation of the paper of the Bank of England. The same check, which the convertibility into specie, under a better system, provides against the excess of any part of the paper circulation, is, during the present system, provided against an excess of Country Bank paper, by its convertibility into Bank of England paper. . . . If the Bank of England paper itself should at any time, during the suspension of cash payments, be issued to excess, a corresponding excess may be issued of Country Bank paper which will not be checked; the foundation being enlarged, the superstructure admits of a proportionate extension.[141]

Ricardo, perhaps the most famous of the bullionist writers, also endorsed these views. In his essay, "The High Price of Bullion." Ricardo indicated that the natural distribution hypothesis, as well as its corollaries, was applicable to regions within a country.[142] Moreover, he reaffirmed the view that the Bank of England rather than the country banks was responsible for the note overissuance that characterized the period.[143]

The bullionist writers, then, employed the monetary model of the small open economy with a convertible currency to small open regions within their country. In so doing, they were able to establish that it was not the country banks but rather the Bank of England that was directly responsible for the overissuance and, hence, the inflation and exchange rate depreciation that characterized the period of restriction.

In addition to applying this model to regions, bullionist writers repeatedly reaffirmed the applicability of this model to trading countries with convertible currencies. After describing its pertinence to regions within a country, for example, Thornton indicated that the model could be usefully applied to commercially connected countries within an integrated world economy: "We may justly extend our views, and conceive of Europe, and even of the world, as forming one great kingdom, over the whole of which goods pass and repass . . . nearly in the same manner in which they spread themselves through this single country."[144]

In indicating that the model pertained to countries with convertible currencies, bullionist writers reaffirmed the natural distribution of specie hypothesis. John Wheatley, for example, contended that "No one nation can possess a greater or less currency than its due proportion, than that proportion which is competent to circulate its produce at par with other countries."[145] This theory of the world distribution of precious metals was also carefully spelled out in detail by Henry Thornton as well as by David Ricardo.[146] Although Ricardo may not have been the original architect of many of the bullionist theories he espoused—since he wrote after several bullionist authors such as Wheatley and Thornton—these views often received their most lucid expression under his pen.[147] This undoubtedly applies to aspects of the convertible currency model such as the concept of an equilibrium (or natural) distribution of the precious metals. Ricardo's version of the theory is well known and is illustrated in the following passage:

> The precious metals employed for circulating the commodities of the world . . . have been divided into certain proportions among the different civilized nations of the earth, according to the state of their commerce and wealth, and therefore according to the number and frequency of the payments which they had to perform. While so divided, they preserved everywhere the same value.[148]

This doctrine of a natural distribution of precious metals has several important corollaries and implications, all of which were wholeheartedly and repeatedly endorsed by bullionist writers. One such implication was that the precious metals were distributed among the various countries according to their relative effective needs or demands and, hence, that the supply of money in any country behaved as an endogenous, dependent variable.[149] This was emphasized by Wheatley, for example, when he indicated that "a nation is not rich because it has money, but it has money because it is rich: The money is the effect, not the cause of wealth."[150] Similarly, Ricardo made this point when he contended that if one country's wealth began to accumulate faster than others "that nation would require and obtain a greater proportion of the money of the world."[151] He reiterated this view when he asserted that money is "exported to find its level, not to destroy it."[152] Moreover, in testimony before the Lords Committee on resumption in 1819, Ricardo illustrated that in the case of the small open economy with a convertible currency, the quantity of money depended on exogenously determined world prices and, therefore, money functioned as a dependent variable.[153]

In addition to indicating that money was distributed according to effective demand, the natural distribution of specie hypothesis indicates that money is distributed *in proportion* to demand, so that the value of money is equal or "on a level" in all countries. The hypothesis, then, implies that money maintains an equal value or a purchasing power parity across space. According to the bullionists, this equal value of money or equalization of price levels was maintained across countries by the workings of arbitrage. That is, if the price of bullion or any other tradable commodity differs in two locations, arbitragers will buy cheap and sell dear until these prices are eventually equalized (ignoring costs of transport). Bullionists, then, acknowledged the international uniformity of the prices of identical (tradable) commodities and thereby endorsed the law of one price and, more generally, the doctrine of purchasing power parity.

Wheatley was one of the first writers to carefully describe this doctrine of price equalization.[154] His statement of the law of one price is probably the most forceful and certainly one of the most elaborate of the bullionist writers. He repeatedly describes how arbitrage works to equate prices of identical commodities both within and across countries. In so doing, he suggests that world commodity markets are well integrated.[155] Moreover, he displays a remarkable awareness of the problems of "testing" the law of one price. For example, in examining empirical evidence, which, he contends, substantiates this law, he explicitly discusses an entire set of complicating factors that should rightfully be taken into account. Wheatley discusses, for example, the existence of nontraded goods, artificial trade barriers, transport costs, and problems associated with identifying homogeneous goods. When these factors are taken into account, Wheatley contends that the evidence tends to support the law of one price and, consequently, the view that money is a "uniform measure of value over the whole world."[156] That Wheatley did, indeed, present such a sophisticated representation of the law of one price is documented in the following passages. His recognition that commodity and money flows (arbitrage) worked to equalize commodity prices across space, for example, is illustrated in the following remark:

> . . . no individual . . . would submit to a material depression in the estimate of his labour or produce in any instance where he could procure a better market. . . . [N]either the peasant nor the manufacturer would sell his labour at one place for less, if by removing to another he could sell it for more of the necessities of life. . . . The same attention to individual interest prevents any particular produce from exchanging at one place for more value than it does at another in the same country. As money is the measure of the value of other produce . . . the proprietor will naturally convey it where it will sell to most advantage. *It is impossible that wheat could be at ten shillings a bushel at Oxford, and fifteen shillings a bushel in London*; as long ere this difference existed, the wheat of Oxford would have been conveyed to London to equalize the price and rectify the measure of value. *It is impossible, therefore, that any local rise can exist in the price of produce*, or that any particular town or district can possess a greater relative currency than others in the same country. . . . The disposition to buy cheap, as well as to sell dear, would make the possessors of the money as ready to part with it to their advantage, as the possessors of the produce to procure it for theirs. . . . The uniformity of the measure of value is thus maintained, and the same commodity is made to exchange for the same quantity of other produce in every part of the same country.[157]

Wheatley qualified his views in that he recognized the existence of nontraded goods:

> I do not mean to contend, that no difference can exist in the price of the same produce at any two district places; but that [there is] a tendency to approximate it so nearly to an equality as to prevent much difference beyond the expense of conveyance. The difficulties of conveyance must always make a certain difference. In commodities that are either of great bulk or are easily perishable, there must always be some variation as there are no means of conveying them from the place where they are cheapest to the place where they are . . . dearest, without great expense. . . . But . . . this difficulty is only experienced in a few commodities.[158]

Wheatley went on to demonstrate that the same commodity and money flows that work to equalize prices within a country function between countries (with convertible currencies) as well. He showed, for example, that if prices momentarily increased in one country relative to others due to a temporary "excessive currency": ". . . foreign produce would be attracted to the rise in [prices] . . . not only foreign produce would be attracted to the country possessing the redundant currency, in order that it might sell dear, but its money . . . would be . . . exported in order that it may buy cheap."[159] Wheatley was sophisticated enough to recognize that, in practice, barriers did exist that could prevent the complete equalization of prices between countries that would otherwise occur:

> Two causes . . . operate in the commercial intercourse of nations to prevent a complete equalization of prices in the same produce—the difficulties of intercourse on account of the distance and . . . restrictions on the freedom of trade. . . . Yet uninterrupted by these disabilities, the action of money, directed by individual interest, has had [a] uniform tendency to make any given quantity of the same produce exchange for the same value in every part of the world.[160]

In analyzing price equalization across countries, Wheatley suggests that this result rests on the integration of world commodity markets. He asserted, for example, that "the facility with which the reciprocal communication of nations is carried on, has a necessary influence on the markets of all and approximates the price of their produce to a general level."[161]

Wheatley was not content to merely present his theoretical views but insisted on "testing" them with the available data of the day.[162] After examining the prices of beef, mutton, veal, pork, bread, and other goods in England, France, Spain, and Italy for the year 1790, Wheatley concluded that the data supported the law of one price—especially when these prices were adjusted for quality differences.[163] After examining this and other data, Wheatley concludes by indicating that the evidence supports Hume's argument that "the value of money is everywhere on a level." Specifically, Wheatley states that the data:

> . . . sufficiently attest the fact of the level of money in Europe; but its equivalency is not confined to Europe alone. . . . The prices of the new world are invariably correspondent with the prices of the old. . . . Both in reason and in fact [then], prices are everywhere the same . . . [and, hence,] it follows as a necessary corollary, that money discharges with fidelity and truth the functions of its office as an uniform measure of value over the whole world.[164]

Another bullionist writer who endorsed this view was Henry Thornton. Thornton recognized, albeit implicitly, that open economies such as Britain's were components of a larger integrated world economy. Consequently, commodities produced in Britain faced competition in world markets. Any increase in the prices of British goods would immediately induce inflows of competing foreign goods, whereas decreases in these prices would foster increased foreign demands.[165] Hence, the (bullion) price of commodities must be uniform for all internationally traded commodities in the world (allowing, of course, for transportation costs):

> The bullion price of articles may be considered to be their general price: because bullion necessarily bears that value, or nearly that value, in each country, in exchange for goods, which it bears in all, allowance being made for the expense of their transmission, inclusive of export and import duties, ordinary profit of the merchant, freight, insurance, and other customary charges. The expense of the transportation of commodities . . . is the measure of the difference subsisting between the bullion prices of the same articles, at the same time, in different parts of the world."[166]

This implied, suggested Thornton, that prices of British traded goods and their substitutes were (exogenously) determined in world markets and, hence, that the value of money in Britain was (exogenously) determined by the world value of money: "The general and permanent value of bank notes must be the same as the general and permanent value of that gold for which they are exchangeable, and the value of gold in England is regulated by the general and permanent value of it all over the world. . . . [given a discrepancy] The gold price must, in a short time, find its level with the gold price over the rest of the world."[167] Thornton, then, acknowledged the law of one price and that the purchasing power of convertible currency was equalized internationally.

These views were also acknowledged by David Ricardo. Ricardo, for example, repeatedly restated "the law which regulates all commodities"—the law of one price.[168] Given this endorsement of the international equalization of (traded) commodity prices, Ricardo also reaffirmed the corollary view that money, when convertible, would always and everywhere maintain an equal value with other convertible currencies. This reaffirmation is illustrated in the following passage: "The currency of one country can never for any length of time be much more valuable, as far as equal quantities of the precious metals are concerned, than any other."[169] Ricardo, while emphasizing the international equalization of the prices of traded goods, recognized that intercountry price differences might exist for some nontraded or "home commodities."[170]

In short, then, the bullionist writers all held the same view as to commodity price determination in the small open economy with a convertible currency; namely, "after allowance for transportation costs, the market prices of identical transportable commodities must everywhere be equal or tend to be equal when expressed in or converted to a common currency."[171] Given this view, together with the bullionist recognition that under these circumstances money behaved as a dependent variable, it is easy to understand Viner's assertion that "bullionists . . . had always explained the mode of operation of a metallic standard as if, under given conditions in the world at large, it dictated to a country adhering to it a specific quantity of currency and a specific range of commodity prices."[172] Indeed, this "specific range of commodity prices" was seen as remaining inviolable, even during disequilibrium situations such as, for example, might exist immediately after an attempt to increase the money supply in one country.[173]

This recognition of an exogenous price level, along with their acceptance of the natural distribution of specie hypothesis, led bullionist writers to emphasize another important implication of this framework—that attempts to control the domestic money supply in such an economy were futile. Refining the views of both Hume and Smith, Wheatley, Thornton, and Ricardo all reaffirmed the view that, under convertibility, "the circulation could never be overfull" in that any excessive increase of convertible paper would result in an offsetting outflow of specie via the balance of payments rather than changes in its value. Wheatley, for example, indicated that if money accidentally increased above its "due proportion," foreign produce would immediately be attracted and "take off the surplus currency" and "that in whatever instance it should be reduced below this proportion, foreign bullion would be attracted . . . and supply the requisite addition" so that "no one nation could possess a greater relative currency than another."[174] Wheatley went on to suggest that, although the total quantity of money could not be controlled by domestic monetary authorities, the proportion of convertible paper to gold in each country could differ and could be influenced by the various central banks.[175] The view that an increase in convertible note issue would induce an outflow of specie and a balance of payments deficit was also repeatedly expressed both by Thornton and by Ricardo.[176]

What is especially significant about these descriptions of monetary and balance of payments disequilibrium is that these bullionist writers did not emphasize divergent movements in price levels (or the value of money) as the adjustment mechanism. Instead, they emphasized the rapidity of arbitrage and, hence, commodity and money flows as performing the adjustment. This emphasis is consistent with the rest of their views, since divergent movements in price levels would have violated the bullionist-supported law of one price. Wheatley especially supported this view. In describing the adjustment mechanism, he continually emphasized the rapid workings of arbitrage. He indicated that adjusting flows of money and commodities would occur immediately and consequently result in little—if any—temporary, and no permanent, differentials in the value of money. In addition, Wheatley indicated that, historically, instead of diverging, price levels in various countries have at all times moved together in lock-step (following the law of one price): "Throughout all ages the prices of this and every other country have maintained a gradual, uniform, and correspondent advancement, which conclusively attests that each country possessed in every period of history the same relative amount of circulation, without any tendency to the exhaustion or repletion. . . ."[177] This interpretation by Wheatley has been endorsed by several "modern" writers;[178] Wu, for example, stated that: "To Wheatley, disturbances arising from the balance of payments automatically adjusted themselves *without any effect on the prices of the countries concerned.*"[179]

Another bullionist who supported this view was Henry Thornton. As indicated above, Thornton supported the law of one price. Since price divergencies would contradict this law (except in long-run equilibrium), such divergencies were not part of the adjustment mechanism, according to Thornton. In one passage, for example, Thornton suggests that unlike the closed economy, in an open economy with a convertible currency, monetary expansion is precluded from causing consequential price level increases because of the constraints imposed by arbitrage and convertibility.[180] In another, Thornton rejects the view that a monetary expansion in one country will cause its entire price level to diverge from that of others. According to Thornton, this view does not sufficiently take into account the tendency of money to go abroad immediately as commodity arbitrage becomes profitable.[181] In short, Thornton believed that specie outflows would occur before price level differentials become evident. Instead of price level divergencies, then, Thornton supported a commodity-money flow adjustment mechanism.[182]

Ricardo's views as to the balance of payments adjustment mechanism were also consistent with the above interpretation. He repeated that under convertibility, any accidental monetary expansion would result in offsetting specie flows via the balance of payments rather than changes in the value of money.[183] This interpretation of Ricardo is forcefully represented by Viner and others.[184] Viner indicated, for example, that "The function of gold movement according to Ricardo is [not to correct an existing imbalance, but rather] to *maintain unaltered* the original relation to each other of the proportion between money and commodities; that is, the price levels, in the two countries. . . . [According to Ricardo] *an export of gold is always the cause never the effect*, of an unfavorable *balance of trade.*"[185] Ricardo's view, therefore, implied that international specie and commodity flows would occur prior to any divergent movement in price levels. Accordingly, Viner states that when "critics of the classical theory have taken it to task on the ground that it explained the adjustment of international balances by the influence on the course of trade of divergent market prices in different markets of identical transportable commodities . . . they have misrepresented the classical doctrine."[186]

A final corollary of the monetary model of the small open economy recognized by bullionist writers should be mentioned. Since bullionist writers emphasized the (exogenous) determination of prices for the individual small open economy, they indicated that the quantity theory of money—in the sense of causation running from money to prices—was not applicable to such an economy. As indicated above, bullionists asserted that, under these circumstances, a monetary expansion would not lead to price increases—since single-country inflation was impossible under a metallic standard—but, instead, would result in an offsetting flow of specie. Hence, they recognized that the causal relationship between money and prices differed for the small open economy under fixed exchange rates vis-à-vis the closed economy. (The bullionist views regarding the monetary model of the closed economy were described in Chapter 3.)

Bullionist views regarding this issue are epitomized in the writings of Ricardo, whose analysis indicated that while a currency was convertible, any domestic alteration in the quantity of money in a single open economy would not be inflationary but would rather involve a redistribution of given quantities of the world stock of precious metals. That is, as long as the world money supply remained unchanged, neither a money supply increase due to a wealth increase nor one due to an increase in bank note issue would cause prices to rise but would, rather, involve a redistribution of world specie stocks.[187] This interpretation by Ricardo has been spelled out by several "modern" writers such as Hegeland: "[according to Ricardo]

The value of coin determined the number of coins that would be employed at a given demand. . . . Thus the causal relation of the value of coin to its quantity is opposite to the proposition of [money to price] causality. Hence the quantity theory, in Ricardo's formulation, cannot be applied to a free circulation of coins."[188]

In analyzing the relationship between money and prices, then, the bullionists understood the important distinction between the closed and open economy. They demonstrated that, whereas the quantity theory did not apply to the small open economy under a convertible currency regime, it was applicable to the closed economy —and, as will be discussed in subsequent chapters, to the small open economy under an inconvertible currency.

In sum, bullionist writers recognized and understood the monetary model of the small open economy with a convertible currency. They were able to apply this model profitably to regions within the British economy and, consequently, to determine that it was the Bank of England that was directly responsible for the over-issuance and, hence, the inflation and exchange rate depreciation of the period, and not the country banks. Moreover, bullionist writers reaffirmed the applicability of this model to countries maintaining convertible currencies. The important corollaries of the model, such as the law of one price (or, more generally, purchasing power parity), money as a dependent variable, the commodity-money flow adjustment mechanism, and alternative causal relationships between money and prices were also delineated by these writers. Since bullionist writers also endorsed the closed model (see Chapter 3) and formulated the monetary model of an inconvertible currency (see chapters below), these writers were the first monetary economists to recognize all three of the monetary models described in Chapter 2.

CONCLUSION

The formulation of the monetary model of the small open economy under fixed exchange rates took place over an extended period of time. Early contributions to this development in the mercantilist era were made by writers, such as Locke, Gervaise, and Cantillon, all of whom recognized the important differences between the closed economy and the small open economy maintaining a convertible currency, which were pertinent to monetary theory. David Hume, although he did not make many original contributions, synthesized the already existing components of the framework into a complete monetary model of the small open economy under fixed exchange rates. Hume's friend, Adam Smith, also endorsed the model, as well as its important corollaries. Moreover, the model, with its implications, was employed and reaffirmed by bullionist writers, such as Wheatley, Thornton, and Ricardo in the early nineteenth century. The essentials of the model, therefore, were well established by the early nineteenth century. Since these authors were so preeminent, most subsequent monetary writers of the nineteenth and early twentieth century were influenced to some extent by their writings. The use of and reaffirmation of this model by these later writers will be the subject of the next chapter.

NOTES

1. A good deal of confusion in interpreting historical monetary controversies relates to the fact that some of the authors failed to spell out explicitly the implicit assumptions and contexts of their views.

2. Eli Heckscher, *Mercantilism*, Volume 2 (London: Allen and Unwin, 1935), pp. 199, 200.

3. See, for example, Mark Blaug, *Economic Theory in Retrospect*, (Homewood: Richard D. Irwin, 1968), p. 19.

4. See, for example, Chi-Yuen Wu, *An Outline of International Price Theories*, (London: Routledge, 1939), p. 7.

5. See, for example, Heckscher, op. cit., p. 250, and Wu, op. cit., p. 7.

6. See, for example, Heckscher, op. cit., p. 250, and Wu, op. cit., p. 7.

7. See, for example, Arthur Leigh, "John Locke and the Quantity Theory of Money," *History of Political Economy*, 6 (Summer 1974):209 footnote.

8. See, for example, Blaug, op. cit., p. 13, and E. A. J. Johnson, *Predecessors of Adam Smith* (New York: Augustus M. Kelley, 1965), pp. 79, 81.

9. Wu, op. cit., p. 72.

10. Dudley North, *Discourses of Trade*, quoted in Wu, op. cit., p. 46.

11. See, for example, Wu, op. cit., pp. 53, 73, and Arthur E. Monroe, *Monetary Theory before Adam Smith* (New York: Augustus M. Kelley, 1966), p. 105. Wu, for example, indicates that Barbon contended that it was differences in the value of money that were the principle inducement for intercountry money flows.

12. As Heckscher has indicated: "What places (Locke) in so unique a position is the fact that his philosophic training enabled him at times to attain a clarity of argument unparalleled among other mercantilist writers." (Heckscher, op. cit., p. 203.)

13. See, for example, Heckscher, op. cit., p. 239, and Leigh, op. cit., p. 207.

14. See, for example, Leigh, op. cit., p. 207.

15. John Locke, "Some Considerations of the Consequences of the Lowering of Interest and Raising the Value of Money," 1691, in *Several Papers*

Relating to Money, Interest, and Trade, 1696 (New York: Augustus M. Kelley, 1968), pp. 75-77.

16. Leigh, op. cit., p. 213.

17. Locke also states the law of one price in another passage. See Locke, "Short Observations on a Printed Paper," in *Several Papers Relating to Money*, p. 17.

18. See, James W. Angell, *The Theory of International Prices* (New York: Augustus M. Kelley, 1965), p. 19.

19. Ibid., p. 19.

20. See, for example, Leigh, op. cit., pp. 211, 218.

21. Unfortunately, Gervaise's pamphlet was almost completely neglected until it was given publicity by Jacob Viner in the 1930s.

22. Jacob Viner, *Studies in the Theory of International Trade* (New York: Augustus M. Kelley, 1965), pp. 79-80.

23. Letiche, for example, contends that: "Gervaise made his greatest contribution toward a general theory of the international mechanism of adjustment. . . . In effect, Gervaise outlined the first theory of general equilibrium in the international field. . . . [He] presents a far more precise and more systematic exposition of the nature of domestic and international equilibrium than does any previous theorist known to me." In John Letiche, "Isaac Gervaise on the International Mechanism of Adjustment," *Journal of Political Economy* 60 (1952):34, 37, 42.

24. Letiche, op. cit., p. 42.

25. See, for example, Viner, *Studies*, p. 80, and Thomas T. Sekine, "The Discovery of International Monetary Equilibrium by Vanderlint, Cantillon, Gervaise, and Hume," *Economia Internazionale*, 26 (1973):271.

26. Isaac Gervaise, *The System or Theory of the Trade of the World (1720)* (Baltimore: Johns Hopkins University Press, 1954), pp. 6, 7, 9. 12, 15. Gervaise defines (p. 6) "Denominator" as gold and silver or the money stock. Moreover, Viner indicates in his foreword (p. vi) that "When Gervaise writes 'labour' this should be read as either 'national production' or 'national productive resources' according to the context, and when he writes 'rich' and 'poor,' this should be read as 'consumers' or 'national expenditures on consumption,' and 'producers' or 'national production,' respectively." The bracketed terms in the text reflect these interpretations.

27. See, for example, Jacob Frenkel, "Adjustment Mechanisms and the Monetary Approach to the Balance of Payments: A Doctrinal Perspective," in *Recent Issues in International Monetary Economics*, ed. Emil Claassen and P. Salin (Amsterdam: North-Holland, 1976), p. 36.

28. Frenkel, op. cit., p. 36.

29. Gervaise, op. cit., p. 15.

30. Sekine, op. cit., p. 270.

31. Gervaise, op. cit., p. 7.

32. Letiche, (op. cit., p. 35) makes the point even more strongly. He, for example, interprets Gervaise as endorsing the law of one price: "Gervaise points out that if certain commodities were transportable and there were no tariffs or transportation costs, identical internationally traded commodities would be sold at the same price in all markets."

33. Frank W. Fetter, *Development of British Monetary Orthodoxy, 1797-1875* (Cambridge: Harvard University Press, 1965), p. 4.

34. See, for example, Sekine, op. cit., p. 271.

35. See Sekine, op. cit., p. 271. In Gervaise's own words: "When a nation has attracted a greater proportion of the [money stock] of the world, than its proper share . . . that nation cannot retain the overplus of its proper proportion of the [money stock], because in that case . . . the number of [consumers] is too great, in proportion to the [producers], so as that nation cannot furnish unto the world that share of [production] which is proportion'ed to that part of [money stock] it possesses: in which case all the [production] of the [producers] will not balance the expense of the [consumers]. So that there enters in that nation, more [production] than goes out of it, to balance its want of [production]: And as the end of trade is the attracting gold and silver, all that difference of labour is paid in gold and silver, until the denominator be lessen'd, in proportion to other nations; which also and at the same time, proportions the [production] to that of [the consumption]. . . . All the profit a nation gains, by unnaturally swelling its [money stock], consists only in the inhabitants living for a time in proportion to that swelling . . . but always at the cost of their coin. . . . A nation cannot retain more than its natural proportion of what is in the world, and the balance of trade must run against it." (Gervaise, op. cit., pp. 7, 12. See also ibid., p. 9.)

36. See, for example, Sekine, op. cit., p. 273, where he indicates that "Nowhere does [Gervaise] explicitly refer to changes in relative prices as being the motivating force of international adjustment. Indeed, the whole discussion can be made perfectly consistent with an assumption of constant relative prices: one country having greater purchasing power buys more at the same price." (Sekine, op. cit., p. 273.)

37. See, for example, Jacob Frenkel and Harry G. Johnson, "The Monetary Approach to the Balance of Payments: Essential Concepts and Historical Origins," in *The Monetary Approach to the Balance of Payments* (Toronto: University of Toronto Press, 1976), p. 37.

38. See, for example, Wu, op. cit., and Sekine, op. cit., p. 265. Sekine, for example, indicates that "It is convenient to classify Vanderlint . . . as (a) 'semi-equilibrium theorist' following Wu's treatment; for, despite (his) penetrating insights into the adjustment mechanism (Vanderlint), fell a step short of formulating a complete theory of international equilibrium." (Sekine, op. cit., p. 265.)

39. See, for example, Jacob Vanderlint, *Money Answers All Things*, 1734 (Baltimore: Johns Hopkins Press, 1914), pp. 16–17.

40. See, for example, Douglas Vickers, *Studies in the Theory of Money, 1690-1776* (New York: Augustus M. Kelley, 1968), p. 183.

41. See, for example, Vanderlint, op. cit., pp. 13, 15.

42. Wu, op. cit., p. 63.

43. See, for example, Sekine, op. cit., p. 267.

44. Sekine, op. cit., p. 265.

45. Wu, op. cit., p. 73. See also Vickers, op. cit., p. 183, and Viner, op. cit., p. 85. Here, Viner, for example, indicates that Vanderlint recommended "hoarding and conversion of bullion into plate as a means of withdrawing bullion from circulation when otherwise an outward drain would ensue."

46. See, for example, Wu, op. cit., p. 10, and Vickers, op. cit., p. 205.

47. See, for example, Monroe, op. cit., p. 203.

48. See, for example, Vickers, op. cit., pp. 282–83, and Monroe, op. cit., p. 203.

49. See, for example, Viner, *Studies*, p. 85, and Wu, op. cit., p. 10.

50. Joseph Spengler, "Richard Cantillon: First of the Moderns," *Essays in Economic Thought*, eds. Joseph Spengler and William Allen (New York: Rand McNally, 1960), p. 109.

51. See, for example, Spengler, op. cit., pp. 126–27, and Sekine, op. cit., p. 209.

52. Wu, op. cit., p. 65.

53. Spengler, op. cit., p. 125. See also Richard Cantillon, *Essai sur la nature du commerce en général* (London: Macmillan, 1931), p. 179.

54. In Cantillon's own words: "Increase of money only increases the price of products and merchandise by the difference of the cost of transport, when this transport is allowed." (Cantillon, op. cit., p. 179. See also ibid., pp. 153, 157, 159.)

55. See, for example, Spengler, op. cit., p. 131.

56. Sekine, op. cit., p. 265.

57. See, for example, Blaug, op. cit., pp. 22–23, and Wu, op. cit., p. 63.

58. Cantillon, op. cit., p. 185.

59. See, for example, Blaug, op. cit., pp. 22–23.

60. Cantillon, op. cit., p. 185. See also Sekine, op. cit., p. 269, and Wu, op. cit., p. 69.

61. See, for example, Sekine, op. cit., p. 262.

62. Sekine, op. cit., p. 262.

63. See, for example, Dennis P. O'Brien, *The Classical Economists* (Oxford: Clarendon Press, 1975), p. 146.

64. As Viner has ably pointed out: "Hume wrote before the first attempt in England, that of Evelyn in 1798, to measure price levels by means of statistical averages. Even after 1798, the leading economists until the time of Jevons either revealed no acquaintance with the notion of representing, by means of statistical averages, either a level of prices, or changes in such level, or found it unacceptable for various reasons. . . . While a number of crude index numbers were constructed during the first half of the Nineteenth Century, none of the classical economists . . . would have anything to do with them. . . ." (Viner, *Studies*, pp. 312–13.)

65. See, for example, Viner, *Studies*, p. 127; Oswald St. Clair, *A Key to Ricardo* (New York: Kelley and Millman, 1957), p. 298; O'Brien, op. cit., pp. 148–49; Johan Myhrman, "Experiences of Flexible Exchange Rates in Earlier Periods: Theories, Evidence, and a New View," *Scandinavian Journal of Economics* 78 (1976):171; and Robert Eagly, "The Swedish and English Bullionist Controversies," in *Events, Ideology, and Economic Theory*, ed. Robert Eagly (Detroit: Wayne State University Press, 1968), p. 26. Later, for example, Torrens asserted that "An increase in the quantity and fall in the value of gold, in relation to commodities, is the same thing as an increase in the quantity and fall in the value of the currency in relation to commodites is the same thing as a rise of prices." In Lionel Robbins, *Robert Torrens and the Evolution of Classical Economics* (London: Macmillan, 1958), p. 125. See also J. Laurence Laughlin, *The Principles of Money* (New York: Charles Scribners, 1903), p. 417.

66. See Viner, *Studies*, p. 333, and Eagly, "Adam Smith and the Specie-Flow Doctrine," *Scottish Journal of Political Economy* 17 (February 1970):64.

67. James Angell, for example, has indicated that: "It must not be forgotten that most of the elements for Hume's work had long lain ready to hand. . . . Hume's role was simply to combine the elements, hitherto more or less separated, into a self-consistent whole." (Angell, op. cit., pp. 25–26.) A similar interpretation is presented by Wu (op. cit., p. 78): "It is true that the essential features

of the [theory] are found in the later mercantilists, but it is only in the hands of Hume that the inevitability of a tendency towards equilibrium and the automatic character of the working of the correctives takes definite form."

68. See, for example, Dietrich Fausten, "On the Humean Origin of the Contemporary Monetary Approach to the Balance of Payments," paper presented at the 53rd Annual Conference of the Western Economic Association, Hawaii, June 1978, p. 28.

69. Hume's essay "Of Money," for example, begins with a clear distinction between money and wealth. See, for example, Marcus Arkin, "The Economic Writings of David Hume—A Reassessment," in *Essays in Economic Thought*, ed. Joseph Spengler and William R. Allen (Chicago: Rand McNally, 1960), p. 146.

70. Harry G. Johnson, "The Monetary Approach to Balance of Payments Theory," *Journal of Financial and Quantitative Analysis* (March 1972):1555–56.

71. See, for example, Vickers, op. cit., p. 237.

72. Blaug, op. cit., p. 23.

73. Viner, *Studies*, p. 84.

74. Rist, for example, indicated that "The theory of the world distribution of the precious metals . . . was worked out with the utmost precision first by Hume." (Charles Rist, *History of Monetary and Credit Theory*, p. 119.) Viner also stated that the "most influential formulation of this theory prior to the Nineteenth Century was by Hume." (Viner, *Studies*, p. 74.)

75. David Hume, "Of the Balance of Trade," in *Writings on Economics*, ed. Eugene Rotwein (Freeport: Books for Libraries Press, 1955), p. 66 footnote.

76. Hume, "Hume to Montesquieu," *Writings on Economics*, April 10, 1749, p. 189.

77. Viner, *Studies*, p. 313, footnote. See also Charles E. Staley, "Hume and Viner on the International Adjustment Mechanism," *History of Political Economy* 8 (Summer 1976):255.

78. Hume was explicit that these considerations were subject to the allowance for transportation costs. See Hume, op. cit., p. 66, footnote. See also Viner, *Studies*, p. 314.

79. See Barbara Henneberry and James G. Witte, "Variable Gold Parities from a Classical Viewpoint: Hume versus the Monetarists," unpublished manuscript, Indiana University, November 1974, p. 1. See also Viner, *Studies*, p. 376.

80. Frank Fetter, *Development of British Monetary Orthodoxy*, pp. 3–4.

81. Lance Girton and Don Roper, "J. Laurence Laughlin and the Quantity Theory of Money," *Journal of Political Economy* 86 (August 1978): 609–12.

82. See, for example, Arnold Collery, *International Adjustment, Open Economies, and the Quantity Theory of Money*, in Princeton Studies in International Finance, No. 28, June 1971, p. 26; Harry G. Johnson, "The Monetary Approach to Balance of Payments Theory," *Journal of Financial and Quantitative Analysis* (March 1972):1555; Harry G. Johnson, "Money, Balance of Payments Theory and the International Monetary Problem," in *Essays in International Finance*, No. 124 (Princeton: Princeton University Press, 1977), p. 5; Deitrich Fausten, "The Humean Origin of the Contemporary Monetary Approach to the Balance of Payments," *Quarterly Journal of Economics* (November 1979) and Sekine, op. cit., p. 278. This view is also implicit in the contention of some contemporary economists that fixed exchange rates and price level stability are incompatible. (See Henneberry and Witte, op. cit., p. 7.)

83. This view has been given elsewhere. See, for example, Rist, op. cit., p. 119; and Robert Keleher, "Of Money and Prices: Some Historical Perspectives," *The Monetary Approach to International Adjustment*, ed. Bluford

Putnam and D. Sykes Wilford (New York: Praeger, 1978); and Viner, *Studies*, pp. 316, 317, 319.

84. See, for example, Henneberry and Witte, "The I.M.F. Gold Auction: More Bitter Fruit from Bretton Woods?" unpublished manuscript, Indiana University, 1976, p. 2.

85. Hume, "Of the Balance of Trade, *Writings in Economics*, p. 65. See also Hume, "Of Money," ibid., p. 35.

86. Hume, "Of the Balance of Trade," ibid., p. 66 [emphasis added]. This hypothesis of Hume—that price differences were no greater between countries than within countries—was empirically supported more than 200 years later by both Genberg and McCloskey and Zecher. See A. Hans Genberg, "Aspects of the Monetary Approach to Balance of Payments Theory," in *The Monetary Approach to the Balance of Payments*, ed. Frenkel and Johnson (Toronto: University of Toronto Press, 1976), and D. N. McCloskey and J. R. Zecher, "How the Gold Standard Worked, 1880-1913," in Frenkel and Johnson, *The Monetary Approach* (Toronto: University of Toronto Press, 1976).

87. Hume, "Of Taxes," *Writings in Economics*, p. 87.

88. Hume, "Hume to Turgot," *Writings in Economics*, p. 208-09.

89. In Oswald's own words: "The increased quantity of money would not necessarily increase the price of all labour and commodities; because the increased quantity, not being confined to the home labour and commodities, might, and certainly would, be sent to purchase both from foreign countries, which importation, unless obstructed by arbitrary and absurd laws, *would keep down the price of commodities to the level of foreign countries*." In Oswald, "Oswald to Hume," *Writings in Economics*, pp. 191-92. See also Charles E. Staley, "Hume and Viner on the International Adjustment Mechanism," *History of Political Economy*, 8 (Summer 1976):254.

90. James M. Low, "An Eighteenth Century Controversy in the Theory of Economic Progress," *The Manchester School* (September 1952):314-16 [emphasis added].

91. See, for example, Hume, "Hume to Oswald," *Writings in Economics*, p. 197, as well as Rotwein's introduction, p. lvi.

92. See, for example, Hume, "Of the Balance of Trade," *Writings on Economics*, pp. 63, 69, 72, 73; Hume, "Of Public Credit," *Writings on Economics*, p. 96 footnote; Hume, "Hume to Montesquieu," *Writings on Economics*, p. 188; Hume, "Hume to Oswald." *Writings on Economics*, p. 197; and Hume, "Hume to Turgot," *Writings on Economics*, p. 209.

93. Hume repeatedly recognized the existence of transportation costs and, hence, the possibility of slight price differences—particularly for nontradable goods. See, for example, Hume, "Of the Balance of Trade," *Writings on Economics*, p. 66, footnote.

94. Hume, "Of the Balance of Trade," op. cit., pp. 63-64 [emphasis added].

95. Hume discusses changes in price levels in his contrived example only as a pedagogical device.

96. This interpretation was endorsed by Rist. See Rist, *History of Monetary and Credit Theory*, p. 119.

97. Hume, "Of the Balance of Trade," op. cit., p. 64.

98. Barbara Henneberry and James G. Witte, "Variable Gold Parities from a Classical Viewpoint: Hume versus the Monetarists," unpublished manuscript, Indiana University, 1974, p. 2.

99. Although the phrase, "real balance effect," was not used by these writers, their explanations were the same.

100. See Henneberry and Witte, "Variable Gold Parities," p. 2. See also Hume, "Of the Balance of Trade," op. cit., pp. 68–70, 72; Hume, "Hume to Oswald," op. cit., p. 198. In his essay, "Of the Balance of Trade," for example, Hume stated that "If you remove these 12 millions [of paper credit], money in this state is below its level, compared with our neighbors; and we must *immediately* draw from all of them, till we be full and saturate, so to speak, and can hold no more." Hume, "Of the Balance of Trade," op. cit., pp. 68–69, emphasis added.

101. Hume, "Of the Balance of Trade," op. cit., p. 70.

102. See Harry G. Johnson, "The Monetary Approach to Balance of Payments Theory," *Journal of Financial and Quantitative Analysis* (March 1972):1563. Thus, reserve growth and the balance of payments are negatively related to the rate of domestic credit expansion. (Ibid., p. 1564.)

103. See, for example, Hume, "Of the Balance of Trade," op. cit., pp. 62–63; see also Girton and Roper, op. cit., pp. 609–12.

104. Hume, "Of the Balance of Trade," op. cit., p. 64 [emphasis added].

105. Hume, "Hume to Montesquieu," op. cit., p. 189 [emphasis added].

106. Joseph Schumpeter, *History of Economic Analysis* (New York: Oxford University Press, 1954), p. 316.

107. See, for example, W. L. Taylor, *Francis Hutcheson and David Hume as Predecessors of Adam Smith* (Durham: Duke University Press, 1965), p. 35.

108. See Taylor, op. cit., p. 39.

109. See Taylor, op. cit., pp. 38 (footnote), 50–51.

110. Angell, op. cit., p. 38; Jacob Hollander, "The Development of the Theory of Money from Adam Smith to David Ricardo," *Quarterly Journal of Economics* (1911):435; and O'Brien, op. cit., p. 151. Hollander, for example, indicated that Smith's views on money always related to convertible currency. He stated, moreover, that "Adam Smith probably never conceived it possible that the Bank of England . . . should suspend specie payments." (Hollander, op. cit., p. 435.)

111. Adam Smith, *An Inquiry into the Nature and Cause of the Wealth of Nations* (New York: Random House, 1937), pp. 323–24. See also ibid., p. 188. (In the 1976 edition of the *Wealth of Nations* published by the University of Chicago Press, the passage appears on pp. 361–62; see also ibid., p. 209.) Smith goes on to say that "No commodities regulate themselves more easily or more exactly according to this effectual demand than gold or silver; because, on account of the small bulk and great value of those metals, no commodities can be more easily transported from one place to another, from places where they are cheap, to where they fall short of this effectual demand. . . . When the quantity of gold and silver imported into any country exceeds the effectual demand, no vigilance of government can prevent their exportation." In Smith, *Wealth of Nations* (Chicago: University of Chicago Press, 1976), pp. 456–57; 1937 edition, p. 404.

112. See Hegeland, op. cit., pp. 48, 50, 160.

113. Smith (1976 edition), op. cit., pp. 311, 318. (In the 1937 edition, these passages appear on pp. 284, 277–78.)

114. Douglas Vickers, "Adam Smith and the Status of the Theory of Money," In *Essays on Adam Smith*, ed. A. Skinner and T. Wilson (Oxford: Clarendon Press, 1975), p. 498.

115. Smith (1937 edition), op. cit., pp. 308–9. See also ibid., pp. 277–78, 284. (The above passage appears on p. 345 in the 1976 edition; see also ibid., pp. 311, 318.)

116. Smith (1976 edition), op. cit., p. 318. (In the 1937 edition, this passage appears on p. 284.)

117. See, for example, Robert V. Eagly, "Adam Smith and the Specie Flow Doctrine," *Scottish Journal of Political Economy* (February 1970):64.

118. Angell, op. cit., p. 34. Laughlin also explicitly interpreted Smith in this manner. See, for example, J. Laurence Laughlin, *The Principles of Money* (New York: Scribners, 1903), p. 238.

119. See, for example, Arthur I. Bloomfield, "Adam Smith and the Theory of International Trade," in *Essays on Adam Smith*, ed. Andrew Skinner and Thomas Wilson (Oxford: Clarendon Press, 1975), p. 480; O'Brien, op. cit., p. 146; and Vickers, op. cit., p. 484. This led some writers, like Viner, to contend that Smith's views on the balance of payments adjustment mechanism were a mystery. (See Viner, *Studies*, p. 84.) Although Smith mentioned prices in an earlier description of the adjustment mechanism, he indicated in that description that prices in different countries would always stay in line with one another. He stated, for example, that Hume "proves very ingenuously that money must *always* bear a certain proportion to the quantity of commodities in every country. . . . Thus, money and goods will keep near about a certain level in every country." In Smith, *Lectures on Justice, Police, Revenue and Arms* (New York: Kelley and Millman, 1956), p. 197, emphasis added.

120. See, for example, Smith, *An Inquiry into the Nature and Causes of the Wealth of Nations* (1976 edition), p. 311 (in the 1937 edition, this passage appears on pp. 277–78), and Bloomfield, op. cit., p. 480.

121. Angell, op. cit., p. 34. See also, for example, Laughlin, op. cit., p. 238.

122. See Chapter 3 above for explicit documentation of this assertion. See also, for example, Smith, *Wealth of Nations* (1976 edition), pp. 377, 451 (1937 edition, pp. 337, 399).

123. Smith, *Wealth of Nations* (1976 edition), p. 209; in the 1937 edition, see p. 188. See also Frank Petrella, "Adam Smith's Rejection of Hume's Price-Specie-Flow Mechanism: A Minor Mystery Resolved," *Southern Economic Journal* 34 (January 1968):372.

124. See, for example, the many references to Smith and Hume in the works of Thornton, Wheatley, and Ricardo.

125. Other bullionist writers, for example, included Blake, Boyd, and Horner.

126. Viner, for example, emphasized that "the bullionists were united in assigning responsibility for the excess, as between the Bank of England and the country banks, wholly or predominantly to the former." (Viner, *Studies*, p. 154.) Writers who took this position were, for example, Thornton, Boyd, King, and Ricardo.

127. See, for example, O'Brien, op. cit., p. 146.

128. For a lucid explanation of this mechanism, see Edwin Cannan, *The Paper Pound of 1797–1821* (New York: Augustus M. Kelley, 1969) (preface to the second edition). Cannan, for example, explains that when a paper "currency is convertible on demand into gold which the holder may freely use for any purpose or export, the whole currency, whether a large or small proportion of it consists of paper, cannot except for a moment be appreciably in excess of the amount which can circulate at par with gold. If the whole currency exceeds

this amount, its purchasing power over gold bullion must fall, and it becomes profitable to melt down or export gold coin or gold bars if these bars can be obtained at the mint price. In order to get gold coin or bars at that price people begin to present paper currency for redemption: The paper so redeemed is cancelled, while the coin or bars issued to redeem it do not take its place, because they are melted or exported. The whole currency is reduced in amount until its value is restored to par with gold bullion. Convertibility thus keeps the paper at par with bullion by limiting its amount—limiting it 'automatically' no doubt, but still limiting it." (Cannan, ibid., preface to the second edition, no page number.)

129. See, for example, Karl H. Niebyl, *Studies in the Classical Theories of Money* (New York: Columbia University Press, 1946), p. 74, and Norman J. Silberling, "Financial and Monetary Policy of Great Britain During the Napoleonic Wars: Ricardo and the Bullion Report," *Quarterly Journal of Economics* 38 (1924):405. Silberling, for example, stated that Boyd recognized: ". . . that the country banks were not legally enjoined from cash payment, and that they were in any case powerless to create credit 'in excess of local demands.' Should they attempt to do so, the local excess would be speedily and automatically reduced by demands for cash or Bank of England notes for use in other localities, such as London. 'It may be therefore inferred,' Boyd stated, 'that no part of their issues can possibly remain in circulation beyond what the increasing prosperity and industry of the country where they circulate can fairly absorb or digest.'"

130. Frank Fetter, *Development of British Monetary Orthodoxy*, p. 36.

131. Walter Boyd, *A Letter to the Right Honourable William Pitt*, London 1801, as quoted in Wu, op. cit., p. 88.

132. See, for example, Wu, op. cit., p. 88.

133. Rist, *History of Monetary and Credit Theory*, p. 136.

134. See, for example, Henry Thornton, *An Enquiry into the Nature and Effects of the Paper Credit of Great Britain*, 1802 (Fairfield: Augustus M. Kelley, 1978), p. 208.

135. Thornton, op. cit., p. 208 [emphasis added].

136. See, for example, Angell, op. cit., p. 46, where Angell states that Thornton "held that a country bank expansion will simply lead to increased country purchases in London, a drain of notes and drafts to meet the London debts, and a contraction in country reserves and note issues."

137. Silberling, op. cit., p. 407. See also Viner, *Studies*, p. 155.

138. Thornton, op. cit., pp. 210, 211, 260.

139. Thornton, op. cit., pp. 210, 260.

140. See, for example, Angell, op. cit., p. 47; Silberling, op. cit., p. 407; and Viner, *Studies*, p. 155.

141. Cannan, op. cit., p. 61.

142. See, for example, David Ricardo, in *The Works and Correspondence*, ed. Piero Sraffa, Volume III (Cambridge: Harvard University Press, 1951), p. 87.

143. See, ibid., p. 88. Here Ricardo states that "The Bank of England is the great regulator of the country paper. When they increase or decrease the amount of their notes, the country banks do the same; and in no case can country banks add to the general circulation, unless the Bank of England shall have previously increased the amount of their notes."

144. Thornton, op. cit., p. 260. See also Angell, op. cit., p. 47.

145. John Wheatley, *An Essay on the Theory of Money* (London: W. Bulmer, 1807), p. 48. See also Jacob H. Hollander, "The Development of

the Theory of Money from Adam Smith to David Ricardo," *Quarterly Journal of Economics* (1911):464.

146. See, for example, *History of Monetary and Credit Theory*, p. 119.

147. On reading the bullionist writings, it is evident that Ricardo contributed little originality to this literature. This is emphasized by Rist, who states: "It cannot be said that [Ricardo] made an original major contribution to currency theory. . . . His theory of the distribution of the precious metals is no more than a simple repetition of Hume's theory. What is peculiar to Ricardo is the talent of the polemist." (Rist, *History of Monetary and Credit Theory*, p. 140.) In concluding his classic essay, "The High Price of Bullion." Ricardo himself explicitly indicated that he was well aware that he had "not added to the stock of information with which the public has been enlightened by many able writers on the same important subject." (Ricardo, op. cit., Volume III, p. 99.)

148. Ricardo, op. cit., Volume III, p. 52. See also O'Brien, op. cit., p. 145, as well as Ricardo, op. cit., Volume I, p. 137, where Ricardo reemphasizes this point: "Gold and Silver, having been chosen for the general medium of circulation, they are, by the competition of commerce, distributed in such proportions amongst the different countries of the world as to accommodate themselves to the natural traffic which would take place if no such metals existed and the trade between countries were purely a trade of barter."

149. See, for example, Samuel Hollander, *The Economics of David Ricardo* (Toronto: University of Toronto Press, 1979), p. 476, where, when discussing Ricardo, Hollander indicates that: "Where a fully operative gold standard is presumed the equilibrium [domestic] level of prices is frequently taken as given and the question posed relates to the corresponding money supply required to assure such a level. In this sense it is the money supply that is taken as the 'dependent' variable." (See also Viner, op. cit., p. 376.)

150. Wheatley, *An Essay*, p. 39.

151. Ricardo, op. cit., Volume III, p. 53.

152. Ricardo, op. cit., Volume III, p. 105.

153. See, for example, Samuel Hollander, op. cit., p. 476.

154. Angell, op. cit., pp. 51-52.

155. See, for example, Wu, op. cit., pp. 106-07.

156. Wheatley, *An Essay*, p. 59.

157. Wheatley, *An Essay*, p. 42-44.

158. Wheatley, *An Essay*, p. 44.

159. Wheatley, *An Essay*, p. 45.

160. Wheatley, *An Essay*, p . 45-46.

161. Wheatley, quoted in Wu, op. cit., pp. 106-7.

162. See, for example, Wheatley, *An Essay*, p. 48.

163. After examining the data, Wheatley stated that "these facts sufficiently manifest a general coincidence of prices." (Wheatley, *An Essay*, p. 49.) Moreover, adjusting them for quality differences (such as ingredients of the bread, leanness of the meat, etc.) "reduces them in reality to a perfect identity." (Wheatley, *An Essay*, p. 49.) Wheatley also compared the prices of land, rent, and labor and came to similar conclusions. (See Wheatley, *An Essay*, pp. 49-59).

164. Wheatley, *An Essay*, pp. 52, 59.

165. See, for example, Thornton, op. cit., pp. 198, 262.

166. Thornton, op. cit., p. 262. See also Robert V. Eagly (ed.), "The Swedish and English Bullionist Controversies," in *Events, Ideology, and Economic Theory* (Detroit: Wayne State University Press, 1968), p. 26.

167. Thornton, op. cit., p. 119 footnote.

168. See, for example, Ricardo, op. cit., Volume III, pp. 52, 54, 57. See also Rist, *History of Monetary and Credit Theory,* p. 160, as well as Wu, op. cit., p. 114.

169. Ricardo, op. cit., Volume III, p. 56. See also ibid., pp. 52, 54.

170. In passages in his *Principles*, for example, Ricardo indicated that "at any given time the general value of money will typically differ between any two countries, the difference reflecting a differential purchasing power of money relative to non-traded 'home commodities.'" (Samuel Hollander, *The Economics of David Ricardo*, p. 471.) See also Ricardo, op. cit., Volume I, pp. 142, 146–47. When discussing goods whose prices were not equalized internationally, the context implies that Ricardo emphasized that these goods were nontraded goods. (See, for example, Viner, *Studies*, pp. 315, 323.)

171. Viner, *Studies*, p. 316.

172. Viner, *Studies*, p. 205.

173. See, for example, Samuel Hollander, op. cit., p. 466, where Hollander indicates that: "Viner . . . maintained that the prices of common tradable goods remain identical between countries under all circumstances including disequilibrium situations, such as, for example, that which exists immediately after an exogenous rise in the money supply in one country."

174. Wheatley, *An Essay*, pp. 30, 42, 48.

175. Wheatley, *An Essay*, pp. 286–87.

176. See, for example, Thornton, op. cit., p. 247; Ricardo, op. cit., Volume III, pp. 53–54, 57, 90–92, 64 footnote; Hegeland, op. cit., p. 57; Samuel Hollander, op. cit., p. 450; and Wu, op. cit., p. 113.

177. Wheatley, *An Essay*, p. 211.

178. See, for example, Viner, *Studies*, p. 316; Jacob Hollander, op. cit., p. 465; and Wu, op. cit., p. 109.

179. Wu, op. cit., p. 109.

180. See Thornton, op. cit., pp. 248–49.

181. See Thornton, op. cit., p. 238, footnote.

182. This is illustrated in Thornton's claim that "equality between private expenditures and private incomes tends ultimately to produce equality between commercial exports and imports." (Thornton, op. cit., p. 143.)

183. See, for example, Ricardo, op. cit., Volume III, pp. 57, 64, footnote, 90–92. See also Gottfried Haberler, *A Survey of International Trade Theory*, Special Papers in International Economics, No. 1 (Princeton: International Finance Section, Princeton University Press, 1961), p. 7.

184. See, for example, Rist, *History of Monetary and Credit Theory*, p. 147; Angell, op. cit., p. 56; and Wu, op. cit., pp. 112–13.

185. Jacob Viner, *Canada's Balance of International Indebtedness, 1900–1913* (Cambridge: Harvard University Press, 1924), pp. 195, 196 [emphasis added].

186. Viner, *Studies*, p. 316.

187. See, for example, Ricardo, op. cit., Volume III, pp. 53, 57.

188. Hegeland, op. cit., p. 59.

6

THE HISTORICAL DEVELOPMENT OF THE MONETARY MODEL OF THE SMALL OPEN ECONOMY UNDER FIXED EXCHANGE RATES: PART TWO

INTRODUCTION

The contributions of Hume, Smith, and the bullionist writers laid the foundations for monetary writers such as participants of both the currency and banking schools, as well as for virtually all important monetary writers of the nineteenth century. In this chapter, the currency/banking school controversy will be discussed. It will be demonstrated that an understanding is necessary of the monetary models of both the closed and the small open economy with a convertible currency, as well as the differences between these two models, in order for the issues of this controversy to be clarified. If these matters are not recognized, the controversy leads to confusion and misinterpretation. The chapter will then indicate that, in addition to being endorsed by banking school writers, the convertible currency model continued to be reaffirmed and used by nearly every major monetary writer during the remainder of the nineteenth century as well as by many writers in the early twentieth century. These endorsements—by important writers, such as J. S. Mill, Cairnes, Wicksell, Laughlin, Fisher, and others—will, in general, be documented chronologically in the chapter. The model continued to be acknowledged by writers in the early 1900s, until about World War I; after that, it fell into disuse. Reasons for this demise of the model, as well as its subsequent reemergence, will be briefly suggested.

THE CURRENCY/BANKING SCHOOL CONTROVERSY

The writings of Thornton, Wheatley, Ricardo, and other bullionists served as the foundation from which the positions of both the so-called currency school and the banking school developed. These three groups of monetary writers had much in common. Their analyses, for example, "took place within the common assumption of the desirability of metallic convertibility."[1] They also held that a convertible (paper) currency ought to conform to the principles of a purely metallic currency.[2] Moreover, as indicated above in Chapter 3, writers of all three of these schools endorsed the monetary model of the closed economy; that is, they were in full agreement with respect to their monetary views on the workings of the closed economy.

Major differences between the currency school and the banking school involved the means of securing the convertibility that both desired. This, in turn, related to their judgments as to whether or not the mixed currency of their day actually did conform to the laws of a metallic currency.[3] Whereas the currency school denied that it did, writers of the banking school contended that this mixed currency did indeed conform to these laws. Thus, the currency/banking school controversy (sometimes referred to as the bank charter debate) related to alternative interpretations of the functioning of the small open economy under fixed exchange rates, particularly in the short run. More specifically, the two schools posited alternative views as to the balance of payments adjustment mechanism as well as to the appropriate operating procedures for the central bank of an open economy under a convertible currency regime.

Several important differences between the two schools arose from misunderstandings as to the implicit underlying frameworks upon which their respective analyses were based. Banking school writers, for example, premised their discussion of the individual economy or region (or individual bank) on the assumption that the activities of all other economies or regions (or banks) remained unchanged. The writers of the currency school, on the other hand, assumed that the activities of all individual entities changed together; that is, they wrote as if all units of a closed system acted in unison. Thus, although both the currency and the banking schools evolved from the same source and had much in common, they were led to support many positions that were diametrically opposed to one another.[4] Hence, the controversy illustrates the importance of carefully delineating the assumptions of an analysis as well as the confusion that can result as a consequence of not doing so.

An important reason for these contrary positions evolving from the same source relates to the fact that these views were based on bullionist (or Ricardian) doctrine applicable, albeit implicitly, to differing contexts. An understanding of the currency/banking controversy, then, requires a thorough familiarity with the alternative frameworks employed in bullionist (and especially Ricardian) analysis.

One contention of the bullionists was, for example, that convertibility in and of itself was sufficient to prevent any substantial overissuance of bank notes by a single country and, therefore, sufficient to prevent single country inflation.[5] Convertibility, then, served as a mechanism for monetary (and inflation) control for the individual small open economy. This bullionist position was endorsed by banking school writers, such as Tooke, Fullarton, Wilson, and Gilbart.[6] However, as has been described in Chapter 3, Ricardo and the bullionists also demonstrated that if all countries expanded their note issue simultaneously (and in proportion), overexpansion and inflation would occur, despite convertibility. (See the section on the bullionists in Chapter 3 and the citations therein.) All countries acting in this manner would, of course, bring the principles of the closed economy back into effect. Convertibility, then, was not necessarily a guaranteed safeguard against monetary overexpansion and inflation, once it was recognized that there is less check to monetary overexpansion by all countries or all banks when they act in unison than when they act alone.[7] Bullionist writers had demonstrated, then, that different principles may apply when an analyst shifts emphasis from the context of an individual unit acting alone to the context of an aggregation of these units acting in unison.[8] Different contexts, therefore, require different analytical frameworks.[9] Viewed from the perspective of an aggregate of countries or banks as opposed to a single unit, therefore, currency school writers argued that even a convertible currency could be overissued, not permanently but long enough to endanger the maintenance of convertibility and possibly to cause financial crises.[10] More specifically, currency school writers held that "The Bank of England and the country banks, acting together could issue to excess even under convertibility."[11] Consequently, some form of control over banking and monetary policy, in addition to convertibility, was seen as necessary by the currency school writers, such as Torrens, Overstone, and Norman.[12]

The currency school writers, then, reached their conclusions by carrying out their analysis, albeit implicitly, within the context of a larger, more aggregative framework, whereas the banking school writers were always concerned with the actions of an individual unit, be it an individual country or an individual bank. Both schools, nonetheless, evolved from the Ricardian bullionist framework.[13]

It will be demonstrated here that banking school writers clearly recognized both the closed and the open monetary frameworks spelled out in Chapter 2 above.[14] Moreover, it will be shown that an understanding of these frameworks easily clarifies various issues of the currency/banking school controversy. Although comparisons between the two positions will be made, emphasis will be given to banking school writers, since these authors not only have been misunderstood but had a broader comprehension of the essentials of the two monetary frameworks.[15] In addition, attention will be focused on the most well-known contributor to banking school doctrine, Thomas Tooke.

Banking school writers, and particularly Tooke, clearly recognized the fixed exchange rate monetary model of the small open economy, as well as its important corollaries and implications. In addition, these writers were, in general, careful to emphasize the context to which their doctrines applied. Normally, their analysis pertained to an individual small country (or to the individual small bank).[16] They were very familiar with, and influenced by, the views of the practical banker.[17] These writers emphasized that in a small open environment, the quantity of a convertible currency was determined by (and passively adapted to) the demands or needs of the public; that is, the quantity of money was seen as a dependent, endogenous variable.[18] Any amount in excess of these demands would be immediately traded for other goods or securities. Accordingly, following not only Hume, Smith, and the bullionists, but the views of the country bankers as well, the banking school writers contended that overissuance of a convertible currency was impossible because of offsetting flows of specie (or, in the case of the country banks, the offsetting flows of Bank of England notes).[19,20] Tooke, for example, indicated that:

> . . . in the case both of the Bank of England and of the country banks, if it were conceivable, which it hardly is, that any addition, beyond the amount of notes required for specific purposes, could be forced into the hands of the public, there is an operation constantly going on which would almost *instantaneously* reduce the amount within the limits of these purposes. . . . The advance by a bank issuing only convertible paper does not . . . cause, necessarily, any increase in the circulation. . . . [An] increase of the outstanding circulation would be the effect of increased transactions and prices and not the cause of them. . . .[21]

Secondly, banking school writers—and especially Tooke—recognized, albeit implicitly, the law of one price (and, consequently, the workings of arbitrage). Tooke, being an empiricist, was familiar with price data for at least the period 1792–1856. Most of the data used by Tooke pertained to tradable goods.[22] He analyzed these data and, on the basis of his empirical studies, indicated that commodity prices were apparently independently determined in external international commodity markets and not related to changes in the domestic money supply, even in the short run. This interpretation of the banking school has been endorsed by several writers.[23] Viner, for example, indicated that under convertibility, the banking school held that "the national price level . . . was even in the short run internationally determined."[24] According to Tooke and the banking school, then, the balance of payments adjustment mechanism did not involve divergent movements in general price levels but, rather, was carried out by commodity and money flows. Tooke, for example, in his *Inquiry into the Currency Principle* indicates that:

> Transmissions of the precious metals might and would take place occasionally between this and other countries to a considerable amount . . . without affecting the . . . value of the currency of the country from which or to which the transmissions were made; and without being a cause or a consequence of alteration in general prices . . . consequently the doctrine by which it is maintained that every export or import of bullion in a metallic circulation must . . . cause a fall or rise of general prices, is essentially incorrect and unsound.[25]

This view of Tooke and the banking school writers was in accordance with the opinion of commercial bankers (with which Tooke and his colleagues were familiar) as to the international adjustment mechanism.[26]

An important implication of this, of course, was that the quantity theory of money—in the sense of causality running from changes in money to changes in prices—was not applicable to the individual small open economy under a convertible currency regime. Rather, changes in the circulation were the result of changes in factors such as real income or world prices. Fullarton and Tooke, for example, rejected the view that bank-created money would affect prices as long as the currency remained convertible.[27] The contention that the quantity theory did not apply to this case was explicitly and repeatedly noted by Tooke:

> . . . in point of fact and historically, as far as my researches have

> gone, in every single instance of a rise or fall in prices, the rise or fall has preceded and, therefore, could not be the effect of an enlargement or contraction of the bank circulation.[28]
>
> I believe that the amount of the circulating medium is the effect and not the cause of variations in prices.[29]
>
> The prices of commodities do not depend upon the quantity of money indicated by the amount of bank notes, nor upon the amount of the whole of the circulating medium, but that, on the contrary, the amount of the circulating medium is the consequence of prices.[30]

In testimony before the Parliamentary Committee on Banks of Issue in 1840 (which he later published in *History of Prices*), Tooke voiced this opinion repeatedly in responses to questions by the Committee. This is illustrated by Tooke's answers to the following two questions by the Committee:

> *Question 3303 [by Committee]:* "Suppose . . . the quantity of the precious metals in the world to remain constant, and that the number of deposits in bankers' hands available to the purchase and sale of commodities is doubled, trebled, and so on, will the prices of commodities vary in proportion to that increase of deposits in bankers' hands?"
>
> *Tooke's Response:* "Not in the slightest degree."
>
> *Question 3621 [by Committee]:* "Are the Committee, then, to understand, that so long as the paper is convertible into specie, you cannot attribute any effect whatever upon prices to the variations in the amount of the bank notes in circulation?"
>
> *Tooke's Response:* "I am perfectly satisfied that no alteration in the prices can be traced in any way to the amount of the circulation."[31]

Instead of supporting the quantity theory in the case of the small open economy, then, Tooke and other banking school writers endorsed a reverse causation hypothesis. That is, in accordance with their demand-determined view, they inverted the chain of cause and effect of the quantity theorists and argued that increases in the quantity of money were determined by increases in prices and incomes, rather than the reverse.[32] Moreover, "they were extremely careful to confine this proposition to the case of money convertible into specie and, hence, to a case where the arbitrage necessary to preserve the relevant price structure was possible."[33] Furthermore, it is evident in numerous passages that Tooke and other banking school writers emphasized this view as especially pertinent to individual small open economic units.[34] Being particularly relevant to such units, the theory was wholeheartedly accepted by bankers who, by their very nature, deal with money in an open economic environment.[35]

This banking school view was vigorously criticized by writers of the currency school who supported the quantity theory, even in the context of the small open economy with a convertible currency. That is, currency school writers contended that monetary over-expansion was possible in the small open economy under fixed exchange rates and, in describing adjustments to such an over-expansion, placed emphasis on divergent movements in general price levels rather than on commodity and money flows.[36] In criticizing writers of the banking school on this issue, currency school writers frequently tried to demonstrate the supposed fallacy of the banking school position by referring to examples of the quantity theory in very large or closed economies. That is, they essentially assumed that an increase in the money supply in a single small open economy had an inflationary effect that was analogous to a monetary increase in a large closed economy.[37] For example, Torrens, in his criticism of Tooke, essentially argued that large increases in the world gold stock and subsequent European inflation demonstrated the fallacy of the banking school position.[38]

The banking school authors, however, had been careful to indicate that their views were applicable to the small open economy under a convertible currency but not necessarily to the large or closed economy. They clearly recognized the distinction between these two types of economies. Tooke, Fullarton, and Wilson, for example, carefully distinguished between changes in a country's money supply resulting from domestic sources and those due to, for example, increases in the world gold stock and, hence, world money supply.[39] These authors clearly indicated that increases in the domestic money supply that reflected increases in the world money supply were inflationary, whereas increases in the domestic money supply arising from redistribution of the existing world supply (due, for example, to a favorable exchange) would not be inflationary.[40,41] That is, domestic (one country) inflation was impossible as long as the currency remained convertible.

That banking school writers clearly recognized this distinction is demonstrated by the following example. Wilson, after showing that Torrens equated an increase in the domestic money supply (due to domestic sources) to an increase in the world money supply, responded in the following manner:

> That this ingenious and accomplished economist should have stated these as two "analogous propositions" is the most striking evidence with which we have yet met of the utter confusion which prevails in men's minds of the real nature of currency and capital . . . some have an idea that in every case of an influx of bullion, a similar effect should be experienced locally that is produced generally by an increase of metals from the mines. The difference is very essential. In the case of an ordinary influx of gold into this country, caused by a favourable state of the exchanges, the general quantity of gold [in the world] is not changed, nor its relation in value to other commodities: A new distribution of it is all that takes place. [On the other hand], to those who received larger quantities of metal from South America . . . in consequence of the increased productiveness of the mines, the additional quantity [of world supplies] . . . would soon increase prices generally in proportion to the new supplies of the metals. But in the case of an influx of bullion, owing to a favourable exchange, the case is widely different. . . . We find that in practice, neither circulation nor prices increase under such circumstances. . . .[42]

Tooke explicitly quoted these comments of Wilson in his *A History of Prices* and clearly voiced his agreement with Wilson's view:

> I quite agree with Mr. Wilson in his opinion . . . of the difference of the effects on prices between an influx of gold caused by an increase of metals from the mines, and the influx caused by a favourable exchange. . . .[43]

Moreover, Tooke demonstrated his recognition of the distinction between domestic and world monetary expansion in numerous other passages. In his testimony before the Parliamentary Committee on Banks of Issue in 1840, for example, Tooke made it clear that when referring to the case of the small open economy, he was assuming that the world money supply was held constant. That is, he made note of the differences between the effects of world monetary variations on prices and the price level effects of variations in the domestic currency, world money held constant.[44] Subsequent questions by the Committee were explicitly prefaced by assuming that world money supplies be held constant.[45] Banking school writers, then, recognized the distinction between the small open economy and the large closed economy and the important implications of this distinction for analyzing such issues as the causal relationship between money and prices. Moreover, they presented empirical evidence to substantiate their contentions relating to the small open economy, whereas the divergent price level adjustment mechanism endorsed by currency school writers never received empirical support.[46] These currency school writers premised their analysis, albeit implicitly, in the context of a larger, more aggregative framework and, consequently, failed to distinguish carefully between the open and closed frameworks of analysis. Because they failed to make this distinction, they confused the issue by misrepresenting the banking school position. This confusion is evident in their discussion not only of the relationship between money and prices but, as pointed out above, in their discussion of the balance of payments adjustment mechanism as well as in their description of the possibility of convertible note overissuance.[47]

In sum, banking school writers clearly recognized both the closed and open models discussed above and their important corollaries. These authors were, in general, practical men who were not only familiar with a good deal of microoriented empirical data but well understood the views and opinions of bankers. Accordingly, their analysis emphasized the operation of the single small economic unit in an open environment and indicated among other things that the quantity theory, although valid in other contexts, did not apply in such circumstances. When these alternative theoretical frameworks were not clearly distinguished from one another, a good deal of confusion and misrepresentation resulted.[48] This confusion has led many subsequent economists to denigrate the writings of the banking school.

This section has indicated that the position of the banking school writers was a good deal more coherent and consistent than is frequently contended by various historical interpreters. Indeed, the banking school position came to be endorsed by many later prominent monetary theorists, such as J. S. Mill, Wicksell, Laughlin, and others. It is to these important monetary writers of the nineteenth century that we now turn.

IMPORTANT MONETARY WRITERS OF THE NINETEENTH CENTURY

Since most nineteenth-century monetary writers were well acquainted with the arguments of Hume, Smith, and the bullionists, as well as participants of the currency-banking school controversy, they were familiar with the essentials of the monetary model of the small open economy under a convertible currency. Since many of these essentials were well recognized and commonly accepted, rigorous reformulations of the view were often deemed unnecessary. Nonetheless, the lucid restatements and reaffirmations that were made of these principles further enhanced their credibility. Many writers who analyzed and endorsed this view were considered eminent monetary economists of their day. Although many of them are not typically associated with any particular monetary school of thought, their endorsements and refinements of the model served to enhance and propagate the reputation of the theory.

Nassau Senior

One writer who recognized many important elements of the model was Nassau Senior. One of these, which he clearly described, was the view that, for the most part, the world as a whole was a single integrated economy. He stated, for example, that "In fact the portableness of the precious metals and the universality of the demand for them *render the whole commercial world one country*, in which bullion is the money and the inhabitants of each nation form a distinct class of laborers."[49] This view of an integrated world economy was further acknowledged in another passage:

> The communication between the eastern and southern coasts of Great Britain, and the western coast of Europe, and that between the western coasts of England, Ireland, and Scotland, and the eastern coast of North America, is more easy than that between most of our countries which are not absolutely contiguous. The freight of a cask of wine from Oporto to London is rather less than the cost of carriage from London to Oxford.[50]

As a subscript to this observation, Senior indicated that Britain (in about 1830) would have been an even more open economy had it not been for the various government restrictions and regulations that had obstructed trade with other nations.[51]

As a consequence of recognizing the world as a single, integrated economy, Senior made reference to the "natural proportion" of money or, in his own words, that stock of money which "is requisite to enable [a country's] prices to bear their natural proportion to those of the rest of the commercial world."[52] Senior, like all classical economists, indicated that in equilibrium, "the value of money everywhere would be the same."[53] He asserted that it was an important attribute of the precious metals that, when used as money, "their value is almost entirely independent of locality."[54] Moreover, in what amounted to an endorsement of the efficacy of arbitrage and consequently the law of one price, Senior contended that any differences in the prices of homogeneous products in different localities were entirely due to costs of transport.[55] Elsewhere, he indicated that the prices of a country's traded goods were determined in (or highly constrained by prices in) world markets.[56]

In discussing the balance of payments adjustment mechanism, Senior, "for the sake of illustration," supposed a sharp and exogenous transfer of money from England to France.[57] He indicated that the resultant balance of payments adjustment occurred *immediately* and suggested that price levels remain unaffected at world-determined levels. Implicit in his analysis of the adjustment process is the natural distribution hypothesis and its important corollary, that money in any individual small open economy is a dependent variable determined, in part, by exogenously given world prices. His description of this adjustment process is illustrated in the following passage:

> It is impossible that, under such circumstances, [France] could retain for a month the five million [sterling] which I have supposed to have been paid to her. [Money] would flow from her in every direction . . . [as to England], the five millions would come back as rapidly as they went out. To suppose that the level of the precious metals in the commercial world can be permanently disturbed by taking money from one country to another, is as absurd as to suppose that the level of a pond can be altered by taking a bucket-full from one place, and pouring it in at another. The water *instantly* rushes to the place from which the bucket-full has been drawn, just as it rushes from the place into which it has been poured. Every country to which France exported any of the money she received from England would, to that extent, have more money than her *habitual state of prices would allow*. It would flow from her either directly to England, or to those countries which were in want of money in consequence of having previously exported it to England. It appears, therefore, that even in *the extravagant case which I have supposed* of an export of five millions of money, the loss, if it can be called one, would be *immediately* repaired."[58]

Still another aspect of the model recognized by Senior was the significance of the size of an economy relative to the rest of the world. Given his acknowledgment of an integrated world economy, Senior contended that virtually every individual national economy of the day was small relative to the rest of the commercial world. Consequently, should any individual national economy dramatically expand its paper issuance and, hence, export specie (even if this involved the exportation of its entire specie stock), there would result virtually no measurable effect on the world money stock and, hence, upon world prices.[59] Senior explicitly stated that this was true even of the relatively developed British economy of this period (about 1830).[60] World prices, then, were viewed as given exogenously to any single open national economy of this period.

James and John Stuart Mill

Another well-known economist who recognized important elements of the monetary model of the small open economy under fixed exchange rates was James Mill. Mill, being familiar with the writings of earlier economists such as Smith and the bullionists, acknowledged this model as well as the monetary model of the closed economy (as described in Chapter 3). In describing the open economy with a convertible currency, Mill indicated that the quantity of money was determined by its value and that money was distributed "through the whole connected chain of the commercial world" according to its relative demand.[61] The quantity of money, then, was treated as a dependent variable.

In endorsing this view, Mill indicated that the value of money was everywhere the same:

> No proposition seems to be more certainly established than this,—that the precious metals, in all countries which are not exceedingly distant from one another, approach very nearly to an equality of price. . . . The price of gold and silver must remain the same, or very nearly the same, in this country, for example, and all other countries in the world. . . . A gold and silver currency can never fall below the level of the price of those metals in surrounding countries. . . ."[62]

Moreover, Mill restated the law of one price. That is, he indicated that whereas the prices of homogeneous commodities may differ geographically, "the whole of such difference . . . resolves itself into cost of carriage."[63] In discussing the topic of regional and international price differences, Mill describes these as being due to transport costs and the existence of nontraded goods. He emphasizes that the moment these price differences exceed costs of transport, arbitrage quickly comes into play.[64]

Mill also recognized the significance of the size of an economy. Specifically, he indicated that should any individual economy increase the quantity of its convertible paper, the resultant specie outflow would have virtually no effect on world money and, hence, world prices.[65]

Given James Mill's endorsement of the model, it is not surprising that his son, John Stuart Mill, also gave it his support. (James Mill, it will be recalled, had a strong influence on the economic and monetary opinions of his son.) In discussing the evolution of the monetary model of the small open economy with a convertible currency, J. S. Mill looms as an important figure, if for no other reason than because he was so widely read. It has been established, for example, that during the latter half of the nineteenth century, Mill's *Principles of Political Economy* was "the undisputed bible of economists . . . as late as 1900, Mill's work was still the basic textbook in elementary courses in both British and American universities."[66] This observation, together with the fact that Mill endorsed a good many of the banking school propositions, makes him important in describing the evolution of these monetary principles.

Mill was familiar with and influenced by the writings of banking school authors such as Tooke and Fullarton and, in fact, supported the banking school position against the Act of 1844.[67] He explicitly reaffirmed various positions that had been supported by banking school writers.[68] For example, he often restated the natural distribution of specie hypothesis. In one passage, for example, he contended that "The currencies of all countries . . . come to a level; by which I do not mean . . . money became of the same value everywhere, but . . . the differences were only those . . . which correspond to permanent differences in the cost of obtaining it."[69] Moreover, Mill pointed out, in the normal "quiescent state," the overissue of a convertible currency was impossible, since it would lead to the outflow of specie via the balance of payments.[70] Specifically, he notes that in normal circumstances, alterations in convertible note issue can have no impact on prices: "There can be no addition, at the discretion of bankers, to the general circulating medium: Any increase of their issues either comes back to them, or remains idle in the hands of the public, and *no rise takes place in prices*."[71] Mill explicitly quoted passages both from Tooke and from Fullarton wherein they forcefully stated that because the volume of convertible note issue was determined by demand, it could not possibly increase prices in the small open economy.[72] Mill also took note that the unanimous opinion of country bankers examined before various parliamentary committees was in accord with this view.[73] After presenting these views of the banking school, Mill stated that this doctrine appeared to him to be "inconvertible." He went on to say that:

> I give complete credence to the assertion of the country bankers very clearly and correctly condensed . . . [by] Mr. Fullarton. I am

> convinced that they cannot possibly increase their issue of notes in any other circumstances than those which are there stated. I believe, also, that the theory, grounded by Mr. Fullarton upon this fact, contains a large portion of truth, and is far nearer to being the expression of the whole truth than any form whatever of the currency theory.[74]

In endorsing the view that any expansion of convertible note issue could not affect prices in the small open economy, Mill supported, albeit implicitly, the concept of integrated world commodity markets and the law of one price. Explicit endorsements of these concepts, however, were indeed made by Mill. In a letter to Cairnes, for example, he stated that: "Shortly before the gold discoveries (of the mid Nineteenth Century), there had begun to take place, and has been taking place ever since, a great increase of facilities of communication and a great enfranchisement of trade; having for their necessary effect to bring the price of many commodities in different parts of the world, far nearer to equality than they had ever been before."[75] Moreover, in one passage, Mill clearly acknowledges the law of one price: "As soon as the price of cloth is lower in England than in Germany, it will begin to be exported, and the price of cloth in Germany will fall to what it is in England. . . . By the fall, however, of cloth in England, cloth will fall in Germany also. . . . By the rise in linen in Germany, linen must rise in England also."[76]

In addition to integrated commodity markets, Mill suggested that capital markets were unified world markets as well. Capital, maintained Mill, "is becoming more and more cosmopolitan."[77] Accordingly, Mill presented in one passage an example whereby a money supply increase led to an immediate outflow of money via the capital account. In this case, the balance of payments adjustment took place via money and security flows but without divergent movements in general price levels, or in Mill's own words, "while the prices of commodities would have shown no trace of [money's] temporary presence."[78] Mill went on to say that "This is a case highly deserving of attention: and it is a fact now beginning to be recognized, that the passage of the precious metals from country to country is determined much more than was formerly supposed by the state of the loan market in different countries, and much less by the state of prices."[79]

According to Mill, then, balance of payments adjustments could certainly occur without divergent movements in general prices. In view of these considerations, he must be viewed as endorsing the position that, in the case of the small open economy with a convertible currency, the quantity theory (in the sense of causality running from money to prices) does not hold. Yet he clearly recognized the validity of that theory in the case of both the large closed economy (as described in Chapter 3) and the small open economy under an inconvertible currency.[80] In short, Mill clearly recognized all the fundamental frameworks outlined above in Chapter 2. Despite his support of the banking school version of the convertible currency model, however, in certain passages he appeared to lend some support to contrary views of the currency school.[81] Mill, being somewhat of an eclectic, to some extent had attempted to reconcile the differences between the banking and currency principles. This attempted reconciliation, however, was largely unsuccessful.[82] Consequently, Mill's views with respect to the currency and banking schools were not fully consistent. Overall, however, his views tended to support the position of the banking school.[83] Despite these apparent inconsistencies, Mill's support of the banking school principles had some very important implications. Since Mill's works were so widely read, his endorsement of the banking school served to propagate important elements of that view so as to make them known to later generations of economists.

MONETARY WRITERS AND THE GOLD DISCOVERIES OF THE MID-NINETEENTH CENTURY

In the period after about 1848, the development of the theory of international price relationships was stimulated by the gold discoveries of California and Australia.[84] In particular, these drew attention to the problem of the effect of the increased quantity of gold (or world money) on prices both in gold-producing countries and in non-gold-producing countries; in short, they stimulated the discussion of the problem of domestic and international price adjustments as well as the question of balance of payments adjustments.[85] Several monetary writers who investigated the price effects of these gold discoveries and their implications for international price relationships and balance of payments adjustments recognized important elements of the monetary model of the small open economy with a convertible currency. Among the authors of this period was John E. Cairnes.

Cairnes, like J. S. Mill, was familiar with and endorsed many of the arguments of banking school writers. He supported, for example, the banking school position against the Act of 1844.[86] Consequently, Cairnes was familiar with the important elements of the monetary approach to the balance of payments and often restated them in his writings.

In analyzing the gold discoveries and the subsequent transmission of world inflation, Cairnes was led to examine the relationships between the prices of various groups of commodities. This enabled him to distinguish between two basic categories of goods—traded goods and nontraded (home) goods. This distinction permitted Cairnes to better describe and analyze various aspects of the adjustment mechanism associated with the transmission of world inflation.

In describing the adjustment process to a gold discovery (that is, increase in world money), for example, Cairnes indicated that markets for traded goods were highly integrated world markets. Traded good markets, suggested Cairnes, were more important than nontraded good markets in executing balance of payments adjustments and transmitting world inflation. In traded good markets, arbitrage—or flows of commodities and money—worked rapidly to equalize prices over space. If prices increased in a gold-producing country (because of an increased demand for commodities), for example, arbitrage would immediately come into play; that is, traded commodities would quickly flow in from abroad in exchange for gold. Hence, the prices of traded goods would be rapidly equalized internationally: their prices could not differ geographically by more than the costs of transport.[87] Thus, Cairnes emphasized that any differences in the prices of homogeneous traded goods would be eliminated "at once" by the workings of the "most powerful corrective force," that is, the competition of producers of the same commodities in different countries.[88] In describing the transmission of world inflation resulting from the American and Australian gold discoveries, then, Cairnes contended that:

> It is evident that prices in England and the U. S. could not proceed very much in advance of prices on the continent of Europe, since the certain effect of such an occurrence would be to send consumers from the dearer to the cheaper markets, and thus to divert the tide of gold from the currencies of England and America to the currencies of France, Germany, and other continental states—a process which would be continued until prices were restored to nearly the same relative level as before. But it is only amongst nations which are competitors in the same description of commodities that this equalizing process comes into operation.[89]

For traded commodities, then, Cairnes—as well as others such as Jevons—endorsed the law of one price. Cairnes stated, for example, that:

> Among countries commercially connected there is a large class of commodities—all those, namely, which constitute the great staples of commerce, such as corn, flour, tea, sugar, metals, and most raw materials of industry—of which the prices can not vary much in different localities. As a rule the difference of prices will not be greater than the cost of carriage between the countries of production and consumption, always, of course, excepting the case where such articles come under the operation of local fiscal laws. In the exchange for commodities of this description, the value of gold . . . does not greatly vary within the range of general commerce.[90]

The principles underlying the law of one price were restated as the "law of indifference" by another well-known monetary writer of the period, W. Stanley Jevons. Specifically, Jevons indicated that:

> When a commodity is perfectly uniform or homogeneous in quality . . . in the same market, and at the same moment, all portions [of it] must be exchanged at the same ratio. . . . Hence [it] follows . . . that in the same open market, at any one moment, there cannot be two prices for the same kind of article. . . . I propose to call [this principle] the Law of Indifference, meaning that, when two objects or commodities are subject to no important differences as regards their purpose in view, they will either of them be taken instead of the other with perfect indifference by a purchaser.[91]

The law of one price implied, then, that (traded good) prices in gold-producing countries were constrained by and limited to the levels of prices in world markets.[92] Hence, increases in the quantity of money (or gold) in such a country would not affect its price level relative to the price level elsewhere. For the individual small open economy, then, causality did not run from changes in money to changes in prices. In addition, the law implied that, for the individual non-gold-producing small open economy, commodity prices were exogenously determined in world markets. This led Jevons to contend that for such an individual small open economy "inflation can only be imported, it can not be produced at home without resort to devaluation."[93] Similarly, Nicholson, in discussing the deflation after 1873, stated that:

> The question [of deflation] is constantly regarded from the point of view of this country alone; and the answer is, that in the close intercommunication of markets in these days, this limited view is entirely insufficient. . . . It is quite clear that if for any reason prices had fallen in other countries with which this country has commercial relations, the fall must have been reflected to our home markets.

> It would plainly be impossible—to take an example of a particular commodity—to explain the fall in the price of wheat, without considering the rates ruling in foreign markets—from America in the West to India in the East. And in precisely the same way, if general prices have fallen in other countries owing to the comparative pressure on gold, there will be a corresponding fall in this country. . . . It thus becomes clear that the *general level of prices in any one country depends on causes beyond the power of that country to control*, and a fall in prices cannot be explained without a wide survey. . . . Movements in general prices can only be explained by taking into account . . . the demand for and the supply of gold [world money].[94]

This recognition of the efficacy of arbitrage, the law of one price, and, hence, the exogeneous determination of prices for the small open economy had important implications in analyzing the balance of payments adjustment mechanism of such an economy. In particular, it implied that large divergent movements in general prices could not play an important role in this adjustment mechanism. This view was acknowledged by Cairnes. In discussing this adjustment mechanism, for example, Cairnes contended that balance of payments adjustments could occur without either changes in commodity prices or divergent movements in general prices.[95] Commodity and money flows, Cairnes indicated, were much more important elements of the balance of payments adjustment process than were divergent movements in price levels.[96,97] The balance of payments adjustment mechanism supported by Cairnes, then, was that of the monetary model of the small open economy described above and endorsed by the various monetary writers whose work has been outlined in this study.

In sum, important monetary writers of the postclassical period recognized and endorsed important components of the convertible currency model described above. They reaffirmed, for example, the integration of world commodity markets, the law of one price, and the exogenous determination of prices for the individual small open economy as well as the balance of payments adjustment mechanism of this model. The essence of the model, then, continued to be supported by the important monetary writers of this period.

Knut Wicksell

Although Wicksell was not an English economist, he was very familiar with most of the English authors discussed above. As a consequence, his ideas relating to monetary theory were, in large part, an extension and propagation of these views. Moreover, Wicksell's writings were available to English readers in the twentieth century and have been said to have greatly influenced subsequent British and American economists. He is of importance, therefore, in any discussion of the evolution of these monetary principles.

In any examination of Wicksell's writings, it is evident that he fully recognized the important contributions to monetary theory made by the authors discussed above, particularly those of Ricardo, banking school writers (such as Tooke and Fullarton), Senior, and J. S. Mill. These authors are quoted extensively throughout Wicksell's discussions of monetary theory, and he drew heavily from their work.[98] It is evident, moreover, that from his studies of these earlier writers Wicksell acquired a thorough comprehension of the fundamental frameworks outlined in Chapter 2, as well as an understanding of how the development of these frameworks evolved over time.[99] As a consequence, he supported the propositions related to the small open economy under a convertible currency presented by the above-cited authors. His interpretation of these propositions is entirely consistent with the explanations presented in the present chapter. Moreover, Wicksell stressed that these considerations pertained specifically to the small open economy under a convertible currency and could not be applied to other contexts.[100] Of the various elements of this theory, there is no doubt that Wicksell recognized that world commodity markets were well integrated. He repeatedly emphasized, for example, that under a gold standard, prices in different countries are closely related to one another. Moreover, in one passage, Wicksell stated that "It is now clear—and it has frequently been pointed out—that the continual improvement in transport that has taken place throughout the greater part of the nineteenth century, and the disappearance of many tariff barriers, must have brought about a gradual *equalisation* of price levels in different countries and districts."[101] In addition, it is evident that Wicksell "always took a high degree of international capital mobility for granted."[102] In one passage, for example, he stated that neither a single bank nor even all the banks of a single country united could (for long) alter the rate of interest. Rather, this rate was determined in world markets, or in Wicksell's own words "by the state of the universal money market."[103]

In accordance with his belief in integrated commodity and capital markets, Wicksell endorsed the law of one price and its important implications. Lucid and forceful restatements of this law are repeatedly presented in Wicksell's writings. He asserted, for example, that:

> No matter how eagerly the products of one country may be demanded by another country . . . no appreciable difference of prices can persist when there is a free interchange of goods. . . . The magnitude of [any] deviation [of prices] is determined by the general level of costs of transport.[104]

> The price of the same commodity cannot vary in two different countries by much more than the import duty and the freight.[105]

> If [the obligation to redeem bank notes in metal] exists, . . . then naturally a powerful brake is applied to the banks, simply because commodity prices in such a country can no longer rise materially above the price level in all other countries having the same metal as a measure of value.[106]

Elsewhere, Wicksell contended that if two countries exist which conduct free trade and are divided only by a land boundary, then:

> If these countries were both living under a specie regime, there could not possibly exist different prices of the same commodity on both sides of the frontier; and if we suppose, which of course is not exactly true, that the level of prices in the interior of each country is materially the same as in the boundary districts, there could be no difference of prices at all between them . . . difference[s] of prices in the two countries . . . would be theoretically impossible and practically confined between very narrow limits.[107]

In emphasizing the validity of the law of one price, Wicksell explicitly recognized its implication that divergent general price levels could *not* serve as an international adjustment mechanism under a convertible currency regime. He indicated that for the individual small open economy, prices were determined exogenously in world markets by direct and rapid arbitrage links, which were independent of specie movements.[108] Wicksell argued that although the alternative divergent price level adjustment mechanism was fine on paper, it did not work in practice.

Instead, he indicated, "it is . . . clear that international equilibrium of prices is usually restored far more rapidly and far more directly" by commodity flows without divergent movements in general prices.[109] Hence, in practice, price level movements were not part of the balance of payments adjustment mechanism. In order to support his position, Wicksell presented examples of balance of payments adjustments that occurred without movements in prices.[110] Moreover, he stated in several passages that, in fact, prices in various countries tend to move together rather than diverging.[111] Thus, "there is no suggestion in his work that prices in individual countries would ever move in anything but close harmony."[112]

These observations relating to the law of one price had several important implications. First, they implied that overissuance was not possible for a single country under convertibility.[113] Wicksell strongly supported the banking school position on this issue. Specifically, he argued that "never, if they are acting alone, would it be possible for [banks] . . . to expand their own circulation."[114] Secondly, these observations implied that the quantity theory of money (in the sense of causality) did not apply to the single small open economy under a convertible currency regime. Wicksell well recognized this contention in demonstrating not only that international balance of payments adjustments could take place without divergent price level movements, but also that domestic prices were determined by international forces independent of domestic monetary considerations.[115]

In addition to these considerations, Wicksell always understood the importance of recognizing the open vis-à-vis the closed economic framework. This is amply illustrated in his discussion of convertibility. For example, although he recognized that convertibility ensured the impossibility of single-country inflation, Wicksell restated the Ricardian position that if all countries pursued monetary expansion simultaneously (and therefore increased the world money supply), inflation could result despite convertibility.[116] The quantity theory, then, although not applicable to the individual small open economy, was still relevant to the closed economy.

J. Laurence Laughlin

Another important figure in discussions of the evolution of these monetary principles was J. L. Laughlin. Laughlin, who founded the *Journal of Political Economy* and was the first chairman of the Department of Political Economy at the University of Chicago, established a monetary workshop at Chicago, where he and his students conducted theoretical and empirical studies relating to a number of the monetary questions discussed in this chapter. Since many of these studies were widely read and because Laughlin emerged as a leading defender of many of the monetary principles outlined here, a brief discussion of his view is appropriate.

Although Laughlin understood well the essentials of all three of the frameworks described in Chapter 2, his understanding of the model of the small open economy under a convertible currency was especially thorough and comprehensive.[117] His discussion of that model and its important implications was among the most forceful and lucid of all the authors discussed in this study. This is not so surprising, however, since Laughlin was familiar with works of and quoted extensively from many of the authors discussed above.[118] In discussing this model, Laughlin endorsed the natural distribution of specie hypothesis. He repeatedly contended, for example, that:

> each country has that part of the money metal of the world which is in proportion of its transactions to those of other countries. . . . The quantity of its media of exchange . . . will automatically adjust itself, without any interference by the state, to the amount of exchanging to be done. . . . Any one country through its international trade will automatically receive as much gold as the proportion of its needs to those of other countries' demands. If it requires gold, it will instantly be imported.[119]

> Gold is distributed throughout the commercial world to each country in the proportion of its needs of all kinds. . . .The movement of gold follows and does not precede the events which determine the course of international trade. . . .[120]

Laughlin, then, indicated that the volume of money in a small open economy with a convertible currency was demand-determined (endogenous) and noted that a convertible note issue could not be overissued.[121] For such an economy, therefore, changes in prices could precede changes in the quantity of domestic money, and, hence, the money stock could not be treated as an exogenous, controllable variable.[122] Any discussion beginning with the assumption of an exogenous change in the money stock (*ceteris paribus*) in such an economy was, therefore, viewed by Laughlin as a fallacious argument.[123]

Laughlin also explicitly and repeatedly endorsed the law of one price. For example, in one passage, he noted that: "The action of the international markets, with telegraphic quotations from every part of the world, precludes the supposition that gold prices could in general remain on a higher level in one country than in another (cost of carriage apart) even for a brief time, because, in order to gain the profit, merchants would seize the opportunity to send goods to the markets where prices were high."[124] Moreover, Laughlin explained important implications of the law of one price. In particular, he explicitly recognized that for the individual small open economy with a convertible currency, prices are determined exogenously in world markets via the rapid workings of arbitrage and not by the domestic money stock:

> The whole business world . . . is always and actively at work to prevent any appreciable difference in the level of gold prices between nations. A rise in the price of any commodity due to local causes (such as deficient harvests, war, etc.) is *instantly* met by importations from other countries; indeed the actual event is more often discounted by shipments of goods. . . . The competition between trading countries, as between different parts of the same country, being exceedingly keen, merchants in the leading centres would send the goods themselves to the spot where high prices existed, and by a quick increase of the supply of goods they would reduce prices in the country whose level was artificially high . . . prices would *at once* fall by competition of goods with goods to a normal international level [allowing for differences due to costs of carriage]. . . . In fact, it has become clear, by the logic of events, that the shipment of gold between commercial countries has little or nothing to do with the level of prices of merchandise in any one country."[125]

Accordingly, Laughlin noted that, for the small open economy, divergent price levels could not be part of the international monetary adjustment mechanism, since such a mechanism would contradict the law of one price.[126] Thus, he rejected any adjustment mechanism that relied on the existence of differential price levels, and instead, viewed arbitrage as the equilibrating force. In so doing, he contended that no statistical evidence existed that supported the divergent price level adjustment mechanism.[127] Evidence was provided by Laughlin, however, that tended to support his view. Specifically, he presented data that indicated that instead of diverging from one another, U.S., English, and German prices moved in the same direction and very closely together for nearly fifty years (except for the United States during the Civil War period).[128] In stating this position, Laughlin repeated that he was essentially endorsing the view of Smith as well as the banking school writers and opposing that of the currency school.[129]

Movements in the domestic quantity of money, according to Laughlin's view, would not affect prices but rather resulted in gold flows via the balance of payments.[130] Accordingly, and unlike some other authors holding similar views, Laughlin very explicitly recognized the implications of this position for the quantity theory of money. In particular—following the views of the banking school—he stated repeatedly and forcefully that the quantity theory did not apply to the small open economy under a convertible monetary regime.[131]

In delineating his position, Laughlin spelled out the distinction between the closed and the open economy and the important implications of this distinction related to money and prices. He noted, for example, that for an individual country, an inflow of gold reflecting an increase in the world gold stock (and, hence, world money supply) would cause an increase in prices, whereas, a gold inflow reflecting a single country's favorable balance of payments and, hence, manifesting a redistribution of the existing world stock of gold would not affect the level of prices in that country.[132] Moreover, he noted that, under a convertible monetary regime, an increase in the domestic money supply could affect the domestic price level only if it were large enough to affect world prices.[133] Hence, the quantity theory was valid in the closed world economy and not applicable to the small open economy with a convertible currency.

In short, Laughlin well recognized the frameworks described above in Chapter 2. This contention is epitomized in the following noteworthy passage, where Laughlin refers to all of those frameworks:

> If my previous reasoning has been correct, prices would not rise merely from an increase in the media of exchange [of the small, open economy]; . . . prices would not rise unless there were a serious fall throughout the world in the value of gold—which, owing to its great stock, is quite unlikely to occur in any ordinary period of time. But it is as plain as a pikestaff that a rise of general prices may be brought about by a device that would lower the value of the standard, such as a debasement of the coinage, or any legislative operations which might transfer the standard to a cheaper metal, or which might establish an inconvertible paper as a standard on a depreciating level.[134]

OTHER IMPORTANT MONETARY WRITERS OF THE EARLY TWENTIETH CENTURY

As indicated by the discussion above, the important monetary writers of the nineteenth century recognized and endorsed the monetary model of the small open economy under a convertible currency regime as described in Chapter 2. This view continued to be supported by important monetary writers of the early twentieth century—at least until the interwar period. The following section documents this claim. During the early years of the twentieth century, such important monetary writers included Irving Fisher, Ludwig Mises, as well as writers associated with two important schools: Frank Taussig's Harvard School and students of Alfred Marshall associated with Cambridge.

Irving Fisher

Although Irving Fisher is probably best known for his monetary work pertaining to the closed economy (as discussed in preceding chapters), he did recognize alternative monetary models. In particular, he clearly demonstrated an awareness of the monetary model of the small open economy under a convertible currency regime, as well as many of its important implications. After discussing the workings of the closed economy, for example, Fisher indicated that an entirely different framework was essential in analyzing the open economy. His awareness of these differences is illustrated by the following remarks quoted from *The Purchasing Power of Money*:

> . . . where two or more nations trading with each other use the same standard, there is a tendency for the price levels of each to influence profoundly the price levels of the other.
>
> The price level in a small country like Switzerland depends largely upon the price level in other countries. . . . *When a single small country is under consideration, it is therefore preferable to say that the quantity of money in that country is determined by the universal price level, rather than to say that its level of prices is determined by the quantity of money within its borders*. An individual country bears the same relation to the world that a lagoon bears to the ocean. The level of the ocean depends, of course, upon the quantity of water in it. But when we speak of the lagoon, we reverse the statement, and say that the quantity of water in it depends upon the level of the ocean. As the tide in the outside ocean rises and falls, the quantity of water in the lagoon will adjust itself accordingly. . . .
>
> Let us, then, consider the causes that determine the quantity of money in a state like Connecticut. If the level of prices in Connecticut temporarily falls belcw that of the surrounding states, Rhode Island, Massachusetts, and New York, the effect is to cause an export of money from these states to Connecticut, because people will buy goods wherever they are cheapest and sell them wherever they are dearest. With its low prices, Connecticut becomes a good place to buy from, but a poor place to sell in. But if outsiders buy of Connecticut, they will have to bring money to buy with. There will, therefore, be a tendency for money to flow to Connecticut until the level of prices there rise to a level which will arrest the influx. . . . It follows that nowadays international and interlocal trade is constantly

> regulating price levels throughout the world . . . whatever may be the source of the difference in price levels, equilibrium will eventually be restored through an international or interlocal redistribution of money and goods brought about by international and interlocal trade.[135]

It is apparent that in this passage Fisher recognizes several important elements of the convertible currency model of the small open economy. He clearly indicates, for example, that in the individual small open economy, the price level is ultimately determined by the world price level rather than by the domestic quantity of money. Commodity arbitrage is certainly alluded to. Moreover, it is apparent that Fisher realizes that the money supply of such a small open economy is endogenous. Implicit in the passage is an endorsement of the natural distribution of specie hypothesis, whereby money is distributed such that it bears the same proportion to goods in various countries in order that price levels are equalized. As a consequence, Fisher was aware that comparative static exercises assuming an exogenous money supply were not applicable to a country with a convertible currency.[136] According to Fisher, then, substantial single-country inflation was not possible under such a regime:

> . . . no great increase of money *in any one country or locality can occur without spreading to other countries or localities*. As soon as local prices have risen enough to make it profitable to sell at the high prices in that place and buy at the low prices elsewhere, money will be exported. The production of gold in Colorado and Alaska first results in higher prices in Colorado and Alaska, then in sending gold to other sections of the United States, then in higher prices throughout the United States, then in export abroad, and finally in higher prices throughout the gold-using world. . . . An increase in the quantity of money in one country tends to spread to others using the same money metal . . . as soon as the price levels or the relative value of money and bullion differ enough to make export . . . profitable and to raise slightly world prices.[137]

Similarly, he indicated that the choice of parity rather than the domestic money supply in large part determined the price level in the small open economy maintaining a convertible currency.[138] Fisher, then, acknowledged and restated many important elements of the convertible currency model of the small open economy.

Fisher's thinking, however, was not *fully* in accord with this view. In discussion of the adjustment mechanism, for example, he was a little inconsistent. Despite the fact that he recognized commodity arbitrage, he indicated in one passage that world prices influenced domestic prices not directly, but only indirectly by affecting its domestic money supply: "The price level in an outside community is an influence . . . and operates by affecting [the] money in circulation and not by directly affecting its price level. The price level outside of New York City, for instance, affects the price level in New York City only via changes in the money in New York City. Within New York City it is the money which influences the price level, and not the price level which influences the money. The price level is the effect and not cause."[139] According to the monetary model of the small open economy under a convertible currency as presented above, however, domestic prices in such an economy are *directly* determined by commodity arbitrage. As indicated by Girton and Roper, "when the logic of Fisher's position is carried out for smaller economic units, certainly for a neighborhood or a family, his position becomes clearly untenable."[140] Although Fisher supported many elements of the above-stated convertible currency model, therefore, his discussion of the balance of payments adjustment mechanism was somewhat inconsistent.

Ludwig von Mises

Another well-known monetary writer of the period who supported various elements of the model was Ludwig von Mises. For example, Mises restated the natural distribution of specie hypothesis. He contended that money is distributed among different trading countries "according to the extent and intensity of the demand of each for money."[141] According to Mises, while money was so distributed, it maintained—assuming free trade—the same value in all countries.[142] In contending that money had the same value over space, Mises provided a forceful statement of the law of one price. He stated, for example, that "The money price of any commodity in any place, under the assumption of completely unrestricted exchange and disregarding the differences arising from the time taken in transit, must be the same as the price at any other place, augmented or diminished by the money cost of transport."[143] In expressing this view, Mises recognized that, with a convertible currency, single-country monetary expansion and inflation were not possible; that is, as long as a currency remained convertible, its value could not be changed unilaterally. Hence, for such a single small open economy, money was endogenous.[144]

Mises indicated that, whereas monetary expansion was constrained for the individual small open economy, such expansion could occur if all economies acted in unison. He outlined the important distinction between the individual small open economy acting alone and the aggregation of all economies acting together (that is, he delineated the distinction between the open and the closed economy).[145] In short, several key elements of the convertible currency model of the small open economy were recognized and restated by Mises.

MONETARY WRITERS ASSOCIATED WITH CAMBRIDGE

Key elements of this monetary model were also restated during this period by monetary writers associated with the University of Cambridge. These writers, who were influenced by Alfred Marshall, included such luminaries as Ralph Hawtrey, John Maynard Keynes, and Arthur Pigou. Indeed, Marshall himself subscribed to the natural distribution of specie hypothesis as well as to the law of one price. In examining two countries under a gold standard, for example, Marshall indicated that "trade tends so to adjust the supplies of gold relatively to the demands for gold in the two countries as to bring gold prices at the sea boards of the two countries to equality, allowance being made for carriage."[146] Similarly, he stated that "so long as national currencies are effectively based on gold, the wholesale price of each commodity tends to equality everywhere."[147]

Other writers associated with Marshall and Cambridge also reaffirmed key elements of this model. Since several of these monetary writers were well known and their writings were influential, a brief review of their endorsement of various elements of the model will be made.

One element that was repeatedly supported by these writers was the law of one price. This law was reaffirmed, for example, in the writings of John Maynard Keynes. Passages supporting it can be found both in *The Tract on Monetary Reform* and in *The Treatise on Money*:

> The prices of cotton in New York, Liverpool, Havre, Hamburg, Genoa, and Prague, expressed in dollars, sterling, francs, marks, lire, and krone, respectively, are never for any length of time much divergent from one another on the basis of the exchange rates actually obtaining in the market, due allowance being made for tariffs and the cost of moving cotton from one center to another; and the same is true of other articles of international trade, though with an increasing time-lag as we pass to articles which are not standardized or are not handled in organized markets. In fact, the theory, stated thus, is a truism, and as nearly as possible jejune.[148]

> Now, after allowances for tariffs and costs of transport, the price of every constituent of an international index must be the same for all countries, if they are reduced to terms of the same currency.[149]

Hawtrey also acknowledged the validity of the law of one price. For the individual small open economy, he contended, certain prices are determined in world markets: "The prices of foreign trade products have to preserve a certain relation to world prices. So long as markets work effectively, the wholesale price of any foreign trade product cannot differ from the price of the same product in a foreign country expressed in the same currency by more than the cost of transport to or from the foreign country."[150] In discussing the equalization of prices over space, Hawtrey emphasized that world commodity markets were well integrated. He stated, for example, that "the revolutionary changes in the means of communication . . . have unified markets to such a degree that . . . there is practically, a single world market and a single world price. . . . Local divergences of prices . . . are small and casual, and are speedily eliminated so long as markets work freely. . . . [In Ricardo's time] it was fallacious to explain the balance of payments adjustment wholly in terms of the price level. There was even at that time, an approximation to a world price."[151] Important implications of this view were also recognized and restated by these writers. Hawtrey, for example, noted that given a convertible currency, an increase in the domestic money supply of a single small open economy would not lead to an increase in prices for tradable goods, since the prices of these goods were governed by world prices. Rather, the increase in the money supply would lead to balance of payments deficits, that is, to increases in foreign imports and a division of exportable goods to the home market. These deficits, the gold outflows associated with them, and the subsequent monetary contraction would work to equilibrate the system. As long as the currency remained convertible, then, the domestic money supply could not increase faster (or slower) than the world money supply. Thus, Hawtrey realized that currency convertibility for the small open economy implied that its domestic money supply was endogenous and could not be arbitrarily controlled by the monetary authorities. Hawtrey implicitly, then, supported the natural distribution of specie hypothesis.[152]

A. C. Pigou was another monetary writer associated with Cambridge who subscribed to this view and delineated some of its important implications. Pigou, for example, emphasized that as long as the currency of a small open economy remained convertible, inflation was a world phenomenon—that is, single country inflation was not possible, and prices were determined in world markets and given exogenously to the small open economy. In discussing this view, Pigou explained why the size of an economy relative to the rest of the world was important. The following remarks made by Pigou in 1917 illustrate his views on this matter:

> If for any reason the value of gold falls relatively to commodities [i.e., if gold prices rise] *in the rest of the world outside a particular country*, gold will flow from the rest of the world to that country and commodities in greater quantities than usual will flow in the opposite direction. In this way, a new equilibrium will be established. *Since the rest of the world is large relatively to any one country*, the adjustment will have been brought about principally by an upward movement in gold prices in the single country and only to a slight extent by a downward movement in the rest of the world. *A rise of gold prices initiated in the rest of the world will thus be maintained there and also transferred to the single country in nearly full force.*
>
> If for any reason the value of gold falls relatively to commodities [i.e., if gold prices rise] in a single country, gold will flow from that country to the rest of the world and commodities will flow in abnormal quantities in the reverse direction. . . . But since the single country is small relatively to the rest of the world, a rise of gold prices initiated there will only be maintained there and transferred to the rest of the world in a small degree. . . .
>
> *These two propositions in conjunction yield the important practical result that gold prices in any single country are much more liable to be affected in a large degree by world causes than by causes special to that country; so that, when any large change is experienced, the general presumption is that a world cause rather than a local cause is at work. A local cause cannot produce a large effect, and therefore no modification in local action could make any important difference to the level of gold prices in this [or any other] single country*. . . . Provided . . . that the current money is not depreciated in terms of gold, *local action cannot have any great effect on prices.*[153]

The impotency of an individual central bank, the significance of size, and the fact that prices are exogenously given to the individual small open economy maintaining a convertible currency was also recognized by Keynes in his *Treatise on Money*:

> One or two central banks acting alone would not, unless they were very preponderant in size, be able to change the weather or

> direct the storm—any more than a single member bank can control the behavior of a national system. If a single central bank lags behind in a boom it will be overwhelmed by excess reserve resources, and if it steps ahead in a depression it will have its reserve resources quickly drawn from it . . . each bank is necessarily governed by the *average* policy of the banks as a whole. . . . It is evident that the main effect of an international gold standard . . . is to secure *uniformity* of movement in different countries —everyone must conform to the average behavior of everyone else.[154]

Monetary writers of the Cambridge School, then, subscribed to many of the important elements of the small open economy convertible currency model that had been endorsed by so many earlier well-known monetary writers. Despite this widespread support, some of these writers expressed inconsistent views in describing the balance of payments adjustment mechanism. Specifically, in certain passages and despite their support of the law of one price, both Keynes and Pigou endorsed the currency school view that divergent movements in general price levels constituted the balance of payments adjustment mechanism of a convertible currency system—a position that directly contradicted the law of one price. Indeed, this view led these writers to suggest that fixed exchange rates and price stability were incompatible.[155] As will be discussed below, these writers were so prominent and influential that their views on this issue contributed to the disfavor in which the convertible currency model of the small open economy was held during the interwar period.

Frank Taussig

During the same period, another group of economists associated with Harvard University and led by Frank Taussig analyzed many of these same issues. Taussig became prominent not only because of his own research, but because he was able to inspire and influence a number of his students and colleagues, several of whom later became well known in their own right. They included, for example, Jacob Viner, James Angell, W. E. Beach, and John H. Williams. Bertil Ohlin also indicated that he had been much influenced by Taussig.

In general, Taussig became known, perhaps mistakenly, as a leading representative of the classical tradition in international trade. He supported many key elements of the convertible currency model of the small open economy described above. In several passages, for example, he reaffirmed the law of one price and contended that world markets were well integrated:

> Those commodities that enter international trade have a common price the world over. The extraordinary cheapening of transportation during the last half century, the easy transmission of news, the perfected organization of markets and exchanges, contribute to make this assumption a safe one for all the great staples.[156]
>
> Very few propositions in economics are literally and unfailingly true; they stand for great general tendencies; and among such is the one here stated,—that goods which are the subjects of a constant and considerable foreign trade are sold at nearly the same price in all the trading countries.[157]

These views were, in general, supported by many of Taussig's students.[158]

Instead of fully endorsing the above model and its implications, however, Taussig and his students tended to emphasize exceptions to it. For example, although earlier economists had long recognized the existence of nontraded goods, he repeatedly stressed that these nontraded goods introduced exceptions to the law of one price and to the balance of payment adjustment mechanism.[159] In particular, he and his followers emphasized that there was no direct mechanism to equalize prices for nontraded commodities. According to Taussig, for example: "[the] prices of domestic goods obey laws of their own."[160] And "The prices of all these [nontradable goods] are determined under domestic conditions. They do not enter into international trade, and have no world level of prices."[161] This view suggested that there was little connection between the prices of nontraded and internationally traded goods and, moreover, induced Taussig to emphasize that "wide differences in wages and prices persist[ed]" between various international trading partners.[162] Followers of Taussig, such as Viner, reaffirmed the same point: "If the general price levels of any two countries be considered, including the prices of services, there is . . . a considerable range within which the price levels may diverge from each other in response to factors which are not common or identical in both countries."[163] This emphasis lead Taussig to become sympathetic to the view that balance of payments adjustments occurred via divergent movements in general price levels. He indicated, for example, that "Wicksell's denial of the possibility that relative price changes could be an important equilibrating factor, since, transportation costs aside, commodities tend to have uniform prices everywhere, overlooked the existence of 'domestic' commodities not entering into international trade, whose price movements could diverge from the movements of the prices of international commodities and thus contribute to the establishment of a new international equilibrium."[164] That Taussig adopted a divergent general price level adjustment mechanism can be seen, for example, in the following remarks: "When specie leaves a country, prices tend to fall. Hence that country becomes one in which it is advantageous to buy. Lower prices stimulate exports. Conversely, the country to which specie flows tends to have rising prices. It becomes one in which it is advantageous to sell. Higher prices stimulate imports."[165] Thus, Taussig's emphasis on exceptions to the law of one price and consequently his contention that balance of payments adjustments took place via divergent movements in general price levels, together with his reputation as a leading representative of the classical position, led many—especially U.S.—economists to believe that the classical specie flow mechanism did indeed work via divergent movements in general price levels.[166] This interpretation is supported by Fetter, who, when considering how this divergent price level interpretation of the classical adjustment mechanism came to be accepted, stated that "The familiarity of American economists with the specie-flow price-adjustment analysis and the belief that this was the accepted classical analysis . . . owes much to Taussig's influence as a teacher, by which this analysis became part of the oral tradition in the United States."[166]

As indicated in this study, however, the view that the balance of payments adjustment mechanism functioned via divergent general price levels was not an accurate presentation of the classical view. The overemphasis on the existence and implications of nontraded goods both by Taussig and by his followers lead them to misleading conclusions.

Although there admittedly is no *direct* link between nontraded goods and world prices, this does not necessarily imply that nontraded goods are not constrained by, or ultimately determined by, world prices. In particular, nontraded goods may be—especially in a longer-run time frame—good substitutes for traded goods in both consumption and production. Many indirect links between the prices of nontraded goods and world prices may exist to permit a close correlation between them.

The theory of international trade, for example, indicates that given factor immobility or nontraded factors, free trade in commodities will work to equate factor prices. This is commonly referred to as the factor price equalization theorem.[167] This theorem indicates, then, that free commodity trade in effect substitutes for factor mobility so as to equate the prices of nontraded factors in separate countries or locations—that is, factor movements and trade in goods in later stages of production are substitutes for one another in equating the prices of nontraded inputs in earlier stages of production.[168] This equating of the prices of nontraded goods in different countries may be explained in other ways. Some factors, such as capital or raw materials, for example, may be freely traded goods employed as inputs to nontraded commodities. More generally, goods at various stages of production may be traded goods employed as inputs to nontraded goods. Free trade in these inputs, then, tends to equalize costs of production, and consequently, tends to equalize prices of nontraded goods in later stages of production. Consequently, the prices of nontraded goods are more nearly similar in different countries than would otherwise be the case.[169] Similarly, the same factors are often used in the production of both traded and nontraded goods. In the long run, these factors must command the same price for different uses. These factor prices will be equated across countries as a result of the factor price equalization theorem cited above. Consequently, they will tend to have an equal influence and hence work to make the prices of nontraded goods in different countries more nearly similar than would otherwise be the case.

In addition to substitution in production, the prices of nontraded goods may be equalized across countries as a result of substitution in consumption. Prices of nontraded goods naturally cannot differ much from the prices of import or export goods if the latter can be substituted for, or are joint products with, home market goods.[170]

Because of this substitutability for other goods in consumption and production, the prices of nontraded goods in different countries are more closely related to one another than might appear at first sight. To the extent of this substitutability (particularly in the long run), general prices in the small open economy are still ultimately determined (or kept within narrow limits) by world prices.[171] Moreover, changes in the relative prices of nontraded goods to traded goods cannot play a crucial role in the balance of payments adjustment mechanism if nontraded goods are highly substitutable for traded goods either in production or in consumption, or if the nontraded goods sector is very small, as in the case of a highly open and small economy. In this case, the balance of payments adjustment mechanism is accomplished neither by changes in the terms of trade nor by changes in the relative price of traded to nontraded goods. Instead, it is carried out by real balance effects as described in Chapter 2. The emphasis given to nontraded goods by Taussig and his school, then, served to mislead or sidetrack the profession for a time.

THE DEMISE AND REEMERGENCE OF THE MODEL

As suggested above, the writings of Fisher, monetary writers associated with the Cambridge School, and Frank Taussig's Harvard School all took positions that were to some extent inconsistent with the convertible currency model of the small open economy as described in Chapter 2. As a consequence, this model began to fall into disfavor in the early twentieth century. Specifically, by the time of World War I and during the interwar period, the model went into eclipse, giving way to an elasticity approach to the balance of payments.[172] Thus, after being endorsed by generations of monetary economists, this model and its companion principle—the law of one price—were abandoned, at least until their recent revival in the modern monetary approach to the balance of payments. While the reason for this lapse is somewhat enigmatic, some suggestions have been offered in the literature.

One reason for the temporary demise of this model was the (above-mentioned) emphasis given to exceptions to the law of one price by various Harvard neoclassicists such as Taussig, Viner, Beach, and Williams. This emphasis apparently went unchallenged at the time and, consequently, contributed to the disfavor of the model.[173]

Another reason for the model's demise was the endorsement of the currency school version of the international adjustment mechansim under a convertible currency regime by prominent economists such as, for example, Fisher, Keynes, Pigou, and Taussig. That is, in certain places, the writings of these authors supported the view that divergent movements in general price levels constituted the adjustment mechanism of a fixed exchange rate (or convertible currency) system—a position that directly contradicted the law of one price. Indeed, this view led some of these writers to argue that fixed exchange rates and price stability were incompatible.[174] Although understandably influenced by the world monetary instability of the interwar period, this argument was misleading since its companion principle—that the general price level could be stabilized under flexible exchange rates—"directed the attention of many governments toward nationalistic autarkic policies."[175]

Accordingly, a third reason for the model's temporary demise was the all-encompassing emphasis given during the interwar period to domestic, national problems at the expense of international problems. Specifically, with international monetary arrangements in disarray and with the breakdown of international trade, countries pursued nationalistic monetary policies and beggar-thy-neighbor trade policies designed to stabilize their individual economies and to ensure the survival of their political systems rather than adopting a global perspective. As a consequence, the view of the world as an integrated, closed economy, and the policies appropriate to this view, fell into disuse and were replaced by policies emphasizing the individual domestic economy. This emphasis led to emergence of and preoccupation by economists with the macroeconomic analysis of the closed economy. The development of closed models, such as the Keynesian and later monetarist models, for example, directed the attention of the profession away from the analysis of open economic models. As Sir Hubert Henderson indicated in 1949: "Nothing has done more in my opinion to lead modern economists astray than the practice which Lord Keynes brought into fashion in the 1930's of reasoning on the hypothesis of a 'closed economy.'"[176] The same view was expressed somewhat differently by Harry Johnson: "The development of monetary theory since the 1930's, and more specifically since the Keynesian revolution, has tended to focus professional and policy attention on the unique circumstances of individual countries, to the neglect of the international monetary system as an integrated unit."[177]

This preoccupation with the closed economy is surprising in that so much of the world has historically consisted of open economies with fixed exchange rates. It is only in the years immediately following World War II that a country (namely, the United States,) had become sufficiently large so that, as a first approximation, it could be treated as a closed economy.[178] Perhaps this preoccupation with the closed economy is in part related to the many contributions and strong influence of U.S. macroeconomists during this period. In any case, for these (and probably other) reasons, the convertible currency model of the small open economy and its companion principle—the law of one price—were disregarded after the early twentieth century.

The model has reemerged, however, under the label of the monetary approach to the balance of payments and/or the global monetarist position. This reemergence was, in part, associated with research conducted at the International Monetary Fund (I.M.F.) as well as at the University of Chicago. The development of the "modern" model has been discussed elsewhere and consequently will not be outlined in detail here.[179] Nonetheless, it should be noted that the reemergence of this view was related to several significant factors that became apparent in the 1960s and early 1970s. These included, for example, the following:

1. the failure of the elasticity approach to explain the effects of a number of devaluations—and revaluations—most notably the failure of the British devaluation of 1967;
2. a revival of the view that countries belong to a world economy that is becoming more-and-more integrated over time;
3. the realization that with capital mobility—or the integration of world capital markets—the domestic money supply ceases to be exogenously determined;
4. the rejection of nationalistic economic policies that do not take into account the international forces associated with economic integration.

SUMMARY AND CONCLUSION

This chapter and the preceding one have described the development of the convertible currency model of the small open economy, as well as its important corollaries. Repetition is unavoidable in such an outline, since these views were continually restated and reaffirmed. Nonetheless, in documenting the repeated reaffirmation of this model by generation after generation of monetary economists, there can be little doubt as to the model's robustness.

The preceding chapter indicated that the essentials of the model were well established by the early nineteenth century. In part because of the prominence of some of these early nineteenth-century monetary writers, subsequent economists were familiar with and influenced by their views. In addition, the model seemed consistent with the empirical data; consequently, it came to be repeatedly endorsed by most important monetary writers of the nineteenth century. Well-known post-Ricardian proponents of this model were the banking school writers, Nassau Senior, James Mill, John Stuart Mill, Cairnes, Wicksell, Laughlin, and others. These monetary writers very clearly reaffirmed the law of one price, the integration of world commodity markets, the exogenous determination of prices for the individual small open economy under a convertible currency regime, the natural distribution of specie hypothesis, as well as the balance of payments adjustment mechanism of the model. Moreover, many of these authors made clear and emphatic distinctions between the closed and open economies and very clearly described the differing relationships between money and prices under these different circumstances.

Thus, they clearly acknowledged and distinguished between the alternative frameworks described in Chapter 2.

Important monetary writers in the early twentieth century, such as Fisher, Pigou, Keynes, Taussig, and others, supported many of the same propositions. However, these writers emphasized various exceptions to the above model, which led to its temporary demise. It reemerged, however, in the form of the monetary approach to the balance of payments in the late 1960s and early 1970s. The monetary approach to the balance of payments, then, is not a novel theory. Rather, it constitutes a return to the classical monetary principles that have been endorsed by nearly every important monetary economist during the past 200 years.

NOTES

1. Lionel Robbins, *Robert Torrens and the Evolution of Classical Economics* (London: Macmillan, 1958), p. 122. See also Dennis P. O'Brien, *The Classical Economists* (Oxford: Clarendon Press, 1975), p. 153.

2. See, for example, Marion R. Daugherty, "The Currency-Banking Controversy: Part I and Part II," *Southern Economic Journal* 9 (1942):152.

3. Ibid., p. 152.

4. Various analyses of the controversies between the currency and banking schools are given elsewhere. See, for example, Jacob Viner, *Studies in the Theory of International Trade* (New York: Augustus M. Kelley, 1968) and Frank W. Fetter, *Development of British Monetary Orthodoxy, 1797-1875* (Cambridge: Harvard University Press, 1965).

5. See, for example, Robbins, op. cit., pp. 100, 123, and O'Brien, op. cit., p. 153.

6. See, for example, Robbins, op. cit., p. 123. Here Robbins quotes Thomas Tooke, who indicated that as long as convertibility was maintained, no further bank regulation was necessary. Tooke, for example, stated that: "It was held by most writers of any authority on the subject of currency, till within the last few years . . . that the purposes of a mixed circulation of coin and paper were sufficiently answered, as long as the coin was perfect, and the paper constantly convertible into coin. . . . This, in point of fact, is what is understood in general terms as the banking principle. . . ." (Tooke, *An Inquiry into the Currency Principle*, p. 1, quoted in Robbins, op. cit., p. 123.)

7. Viner, *Studies*, p. 240.

8. Different principles may also apply when an analyst shifts emphasis from the context of an individual unit acting alone to the context of an economy which is very large relative to the rest of the world. Bullionist writers also recognized the significance of size in their analysis. (See bullionist section in Chapter 3.)

9. Viner recognized the importance of this distinction. He indicated, for example, that it was important to draw a "distinction between what a single

bank acting alone could do and what a large group of banks, or an entire banking system, could do, acting simultaneously. . . . The important principle that there is less check to overexpansion by banks when they act in unison than when they act singly, and that it is an error to infer, from the limitations upon expansion to which a single bank acting alone is subject, that overexpansion for a time is impossible for an important group of banks, or a fortiori for a banking system as a whole, when acting in unison. After 1826, this principle was frequently stated, and it was adopted by the currency school as one of the elements in their reply to the banking school doctrine that overissue was impossible under convertibility." (Viner, *Studies*, pp. 239–40.)

10. Viner, *Studies*, p. 223.

11. Viner, *Studies*, p. 235.

12. See, for example, Viner, *Studies*, p. 223.

13. Further evidence to support this contention is provided by the controversy regarding the responsibility for the overissuance during the period of restriction. Specifically, Ricardo recognized that if *all* banks, including the Bank of England, expanded notes simultaneously, then convertibility would not serve as a constraint to country bank note issue. Hence, banking and monetary controls were necessary. The view that the Bank of England and the country banks acting together would issue to excess even under convertibility was "adopted by the currency school as one of the elements in their reply to the banking school doctrine that overissue was impossible under convertibility." (Viner, *Studies*, p. 240. See also ibid., p. 235.) Implicitly, then, the currency school was employing the entire banking system as a frame of reference, whereas the banking school was focusing on the individual bank.

14. Banking school writers also recognized the monetary model of the small open economy with an inconvertible currency. See, for example, Tooke, *An Inquiry Into the Currency Principle* (London: London School of Economics and Political Science, 1959), pp. 69, 70, 92; Tooke, *A History of Prices* Volume IV (New York: Adelphi, 1928), p. 463; and T. E. Gregory, "Introduction," *A History of Prices* Volume I (New York: Adelphi, 1928), p. 85.

15. Although the currency school, in general, came to dominate British monetary thought, it never achieved a dominant position on the continent, where the banking school received more support. See David E. W. Laidler and A. R. Nobay, "International Aspects of Inflation: A Survey," in *Recent Issues in International Monetary Economics*, ed. Emil Claassen and P. Salin (New York: North-Holland, 1976), p. 301, footnote.

16. See, for example, Marion Daugherty, "The Currency-Banking Controversy: Parts I and II," *Southern Economic Journal*, 9 (1942):151.

17. Ibid., p. 149.

18. See, for example, ibid., p. 150; David Laidler, "Thomas Cooke on Monetary Reform," *Essays on Money and Inflation*, ed. David Laidler (Chicago: University of Chicago Press, 1975), p. 214; and Hugo Hegeland, *The Quantity Theory of Money* (Goteborg: Elanders Boktryckeri Aktiebulag, 1951), p. 61.

19. See, for example, Laidler, op. cit., p. 214; Robbins, op. cit., p. 126; Wicksell, *Interest and Prices* (New York: Augustus M. Kelley, 1965), p. 83; and Elmer Wood, *English Theories of Central Banking Control, 1819–1858* (Cambridge: Harvard University Press, 1939), p. 180.

20. Currency school writers contended that overissuance under convertibility could occur at least in the short run and be of a magnitude large enough to threaten convertibility. It was implicit in their writings that to bring this about, all banks would act in unison. See Viner, *Studies*, p. 240.

21. Thomas Tooke, *A History of Prices* Volume IV, pp. 185, 192, 194 [emphasis added]. See also Robbins, op. cit., p. 126. Here Fullarton contends that: "What Mr. Tooke, and those who hold similar opinions, contend for is, that: by the very constitution of a convertible currency, it can never be issued in larger quantities than are required for use and, therefore, can never be redundant." In J. Fullarton, *On the Regulation of Currencies*, 1844, p. 58, as quoted in Robbins, op. cit., p. 126. See also Tooke, *An Inquiry into the Currency Principle*, pp. 65–66, 122, where Tooke states "That neither the country banks nor the Bank of England have a direct power . . . of enlarging their circulation. . . . It is not in the power of Banks of Issue, including the Bank of England, to make any direct addition to the amount of notes circulating in their respective districts, however disposed they may be to do so."

22. See, for example, T. E. Gregory, "Introduction," *A History of Prices*, Volume I, pp. 13–14. It should be noted that the prices employed by Tooke were individual commodity prices and not index numbers.

23. See, for example, Viner, *Studies*, p. 223, footnote; Fritz Machlup, "Summary of the Discussion on Frenkel," *Recent Issues in International Monetary Economics*, ed. Emil Claassen and P. Salin (Amsterdam: North-Holland, 1976), p. 50; Daugherty, op. cit., p. 151; O'Brien, op. cit., p. 158; and Wood, op. cit., p. 157, where Wood explicitly states that Tooke assumed "an externally determined set of domestic prices." More specifically, Wood (op. cit., p. 157) indicates that "When Tooke asserted that credit could not affect prices but only contribute toward temporary conditions of overtrading, he was assuming implicitly that the world level of prices could not be disturbed by mere expansion of credit in England. Maintaining convertibility of the Bank note gave an externally determined set of domestic prices, he reasoned."

24. Viner, *Studies*, p. 223, footnote.

25. Tooke, *An Inquiry into the Currency Principle*, p. 121. See also Chi-Yuen Wu, *An Outline of International Price Theories* (London: Routledge, 1939), p. 135, where he makes a similar statement.

26. See, for example, Fetter, op. cit., p. 228, and Charles Rist, *History of Monetary and Credit Theory* (New York: Augustus M. Kelley, 1966), p. 181.

27. See, for example, Fetter, op. cit., p. 190.

28. Tooke, *A History of Prices*, p. 652, from John Stuart Mill, *Principle of Political Economy* (London: Longmans, Green, 1926), p. 652. See also Gregory, op. cit., pp. 76, 81.

29. Tooke, *A History of Prices*, Volume IV, p. 462. See also ibid., Volume I, p. 149, and Gregory, op. cit., p. 81.

30. Tooke, *An Inquiry into the Currency Principle*, pp. 123–24. See also Tooke, ibid., p. 70; O'Brien, op. cit., p. 158; Daugherty, op. cit., p. 149; and Hegeland, op. cit., pp. 60, 62, 162.

31. Tooke, *A History of Prices*, Volume IV, pp. 463, 470.

32. See, for example, Gregory, op. cit., p. 81; O'Brien, op. cit., p. 158; and Tooke, *A History of Prices*, Volume IV, p. 462.

33. Laidler and Nobay, op. cit., p. 301.

34. See, for example, Tooke, *A History of Prices*, Volume III, p. 191.

35. The views of the banking school writers were supported by all of the bankers who testified before various parliamentary committees on the subject. These bankers indicated that (in the words of Fullarton): "The amount of their issues is exclusively regulated by the extent of local dealings and expenditures in their respective Districts, fluctuating with the fluctuations of production and price, and that they neither can increase their issues beyond the limits which

the range of such dealings and expenditures prescribe, without the certainty of having their notes immediately returned to them nor diminish them, but at an almost equal certainty of the vacancy being filled up from some other source." (Fullarton, *Regulation of Currencies*, p. 85, quoted by John Stuart Mill, op. cit., p. 653. See also Wicksell, *Interest and Prices*, p. 84; Tooke, *An Inquiry into the Currency Principle*, p. 38; and Tooke, *A History of Prices*, Volume IV, p. 232, where he indicates that these bankers also contended that they could not influence prices.) It is no coincidence, then, that bankers have traditionally been skeptical of the quantity theory of money; they have always operated in the context of an open environment (always constrained from expanding loans and deposits by leakages—as in an open economy).

36. See, for example, Fetter, op. cit., p. 226, and Daugherty, op. cit., p. 146. See also Hegeland, op. cit., p. 62, footnote, where he indicates that "according to Tooke, Mr. Norman was the first to use the names of the Banking and Currency Schools. He characterized the idea that the circulation adapts itself to changes in the quantity of gold as the currency principle, and the opposite view, namely that the circulation adapts itself to prices, as the Banking Principle." (See Tooke, *A History of Prices*, Volume IV, p. 166.)

37. See Tooke, *A History of Prices*, Volume IV, p. 207.

38. Robert Torrens, *Principles and Practical Operation of Sir Robert Peel's Act of 1844* (third edition), p. 190 (quoted in Robbins, op. cit., p. 124).

39. See Fetter, op. cit., pp. 190–91, and Gregory, op. cit., pp. 30, 82.

40. Fullarton, for example, "went out of his way to make it clear that he did not deny the broad effects on prices of changes in the supply of the precious metals" (Robbins, op. cit., p. 125). See also Daugherty, op. cit., p. 245, where he states that Fullarton explicitly made a distinction "between the effects of an influx of gold from the mines (which, it was contended, would raise prices) and the effects of an influx of gold, which was part of the previously existing supply (which, it was said, could not have a causal effect on prices)."

41. See Tooke, *An Inquiry into the Currency Principle*, pp. 121–22; see also Tooke, *A History of Prices*, Volume IV, pp. 206–07. In an appendix to Volume IV, Tooke published his testimony before the Committee on Banks of Issue in 1840. Tooke's answer to one of the questions of the committee illustrates the point: *Question 3301 (by Committee)*: "Supposing the quantity of the precious metals in the world remain constant, and that in any country you go on increasing the quantity of the notes payable on demand, will the prices of commodities estimated in these notes undergo a variation proportionate to the increase in the notes?" *Response by Tooke*: "Not if the notes are payable in gold on demand, unless in the degree in which it may be supposed that the value of gold is affected in the commercial world by an extensive substitution of paper for gold [i.e., a decrease in the world demand for gold], I consider that these points were distinctly understood as the only conditions by which the money prices of commodities were likely to be affected, independently of the circumstances affecting the articles themselves." (Tooke, *A History of Prices*, Volume IV, p. 462.)

42. J. Wilson, *On Capital, Currency, and Banking*, pp. 85, 87, quoted in Tooke, *A History of Prices*, Volume IV, p. 208. See also Robbins, op. cit., p. 125.

43. Tooke, *A History of Prices*, Volume IV, p. 209.

44. Tooke, *A History of Prices*, Volume IV, p. 462. See also Fetter, op. cit., p. 191.

45. At one point in the testimony, Tooke indicated that he recognized the importance of country size. That is, he indicated that if a country's note issue increased to the extent that the single country specie outflow was large enough to affect world specie values, then prices of commodities in that particular country might still be affected. This, however, could not occur if the relevant economy was small. (See Tooke, *A History of Prices*, Volume IV, pp. 462–63.)

46. See, for example, Tooke, *A History of Prices*, Volume III, p. 66; Wicksell, *Lectures on Political Economy*, Volume II (New York: Augustus M. Kelley, 1971), p. 173; and Fetter, op. cit., pp. 227–28. Here Fetter indicates that under questioning by the Committee on Bank Acts of 1857, Lloyd (the currency school writer) failed to give explicit answers to questions of how and where movements in the price level would work to equilibrate the balance of payments. Indeed, he later gave a description of the adjustment mechanism through capital flows and not changes in price levels.

47. See, for example, Viner, op. cit., p. 240, and Hegeland, op. cit., p. 62.

48. See, for example, Fetter, op. cit., p. 191, and Wicksell, *Interest and Prices*, p. 85.

49. Nassau Senior, "Three Lectures on the Cost of Obtaining Money," 1829, Lecture I, *Selected Writings in Economics* (New York: Augustus M. Kelley, 1966), p. 14 [emphasis added].

50. Senior, ibid., p. 31.

51. Senior, ibid., pp. 31–32, 35.

52. Nassau Senior, "Three Lectures on the Transmission of the Precious Metals from Country to Country," in *Selected Writings in Economics* (New York: Augustus M. Kelley, 1966), p. 18.

53. Wu, op. cit., p. 126. See also Marion Bowley, *Nassau Senior and Classical Economics* (London: Allen and Unwin, 1937), p. 207.

54. Wu, op. cit., p. 126. See also Senior, Lectures 1826–30, Course I, Lecture 5, "On the Nature of Money," quoted in Bowley, op. cit., p. 207.

55. See Bowley, op. cit., p. 206–07.

56. Senior, "Three Lectures on the Transmission of the Precious Metals from Country to Country," p. 7. See also Bowley, op. cit., p. 211, where Senior is quoted as indicating that "when commodities of the same quality, or which may be substitutes for one another, can be imported from different quarters, a slight variation in price will decide which will be preferred."

57. In Senior's own words, he supposes "a sudden and great transmission of money" from England to France. (Senior, "Three Lectures on the Transmission of the Precious Metals from Country to Country," p. 13.)

58. Senior, "Three Lectures on the Transmission of the Precious Metals from Country to Country," pp. 12–13 [emphasis added].

59. Senior, "Three Lectures on the Cost of Obtaining Money," p. 43.

60. Senior, "Three Lectures on the Cost of Obtaining Money," p. 44.

61. James Mill, *Elements of Political Economy* (New York: Augustus M. Kelley, 1965), pp. 177–78.

62. James Mill, "Smith on Money and Exchange," *Edinburgh Review*, October 1808, Volume 13, No. XXV, pp. 50–68, reprinted in Donald Winch, *James Mill: Selected Economic Writings* (Chicago: University of Chicago Press, 1966), pp. 63–65.

63. James Mill, *Elements*, p. 175.

64. James Mill, *Elements*, p. 176.

65. James Mill, "Smith on Money and Exchange," p. 164.

66. Mark Blaug, *Economic Theory in Retrospect* (Homewood: R. D. Irwin, 1968), p. 180.

67. See, for example, Fetter, op. cit., p. 226; Wu, op. cit., p. 146; and Phyllis Dean, *The Evolution of Economic Ideas* (Cambridge: Cambridge University Press, 1978), p. 54, footnote.

68. See, for example, Charles Rist, *History of Monetary and Credit Theory* (New York: Augustus M. Kelley, 1966), p. 181, and Elmer Wood, *English Theories of Central Banking Control, 1819–1858* (Cambridge: Harvard University Press, 1939), p. 58, where Wood states that: "Mill was obviously much influenced by Tooke. In his review of Torren's book in defense of the Currency Principle and of Tooke's book opposing it, he gives nearly all of his attention to Tooke's. For it he has only words of praise."

69. John Stuart Mill, *Principles of Political Economy* (London: Longmans, Green, 1926), p. 631. For another explicit restatement of this hypothesis, see John Stuart Mill, op. cit., p. 625. In this regard, Mill indicated that: ". . . a newly acquired stock of money would diffuse itself over all countries . . . through all parts of the commercial world. The money . . . would spread itself to an equal depth over all commercial countries. . . . It would go on flowing until . . . the money had diffused itself so equally that prices had risen in the same ratio in all countries." (John Stuart Mill, op. cit., p. 630.)

70. See, for example, John Stuart Mill, op. cit., Book III, Chapters XIII and XXII. See also Wu, op. cit., p. 146, and Mordechai Kreinin and Lawrence Officer, *The Monetary Approach to the Balance of Payments: A Survey* (Princeton: Princeton Studies in International Finance, 1978), p. 28.

71. John Stuart Mill, op. cit., p. 654 [emphasis added]. See also Wicksell, *Interest and Prices*, p. 86, and Wicksell, *Lectures on Political Economy*, Volume II, p. 174, where Wicksell notes that "Mill considered that Tooke's view of the innocuousness of the banks as regards price movements was quite correct in normal, tranquil times. . . ."

72. John Stuart Mill, op. cit., pp. 652–53. See also Wu, op. cit., p. 146.

73. John Stuart Mill, op. cit., pp. 652–53.

74. John Stuart Mill, op. cit., p. 653.

75. This letter was dated 26 December 1863. It was quoted from Michael Bordo, "John E. Cairnes and the Effect of the Australian Gold Discoveries, 1851–73," *History of Political Economy* 7 (1975):349, footnote.

76. John Stuart Mill, op. cit., p. 622, footnote. See also Kreinin and Officer, op. cit., p. 28.

77. John Stuart Mill, op. cit., p. 575.

78. John Stuart Mill, op. cit., p. 497.

79. John Stuart Mill, op. cit., p. 497.

80. Mill, for example, devoted an entire chapter to the case of the small open economy under an inconvertible currency. See, for example, John Stuart Mill, op. cit., Book III, Chapter XIII.

81. See, for example, Fetter, op. cit., p. 226. In particular, he mentions price level adjustment as the adjustment mechanism in some passages.

82. See, for example, Wu, op. cit., p. 146.

83. See, for example, Blaug, op. cit., p. 204, and Rist, op. cit., p. 181.

84. See Wu, op. cit., p. 9.

85. Ibid.

86. See, for example, Daugherty, op. cit., p. 245, and Cairnes, *An Exami-*

nation into the Principles of Currency Involved in the Bank Charter Act of 1844 (New York: Augustus M. Kelley, 1966).

87. See, for example, John E. Cairnes, *Essays in Political Economy* (London: Macmillan, 1873), p. 40.

88. Cairnes, *Essays*, p. 70. See also Cairnes, *Essays*, p. 86, where he states that any increase in the prices of traded goods in one country relative to others would be "immediately followed by a sudden and extraordinary influx of foreign goods."

89. Cairnes, *Essays*, p. 70. See also Cairnes, *Essays*, p. 86.

90. Cairnes, *Some Leading Principles of Political Economy Newly Expounded*, quoted in Jacob Viner, *Canada's Balance of International Indebtedness, 1900-1913* (Cambridge: Harvard University Press, 1924), p. 211. See also Cairnes, *Essays*, p. 18, where Cairnes states: ". . . of dry goods and articles of general manufacture—of all commodities, in a word, not quickly perishable and easily portable—the prices in different European countries, allowance being made for the effect of tariffs, will as a rule, not differ by more than the cost of carriage between the compared localities."

91. Stanley W. Jevons, *The Theory of Political Economy* (London: Macmillan, 1924), p. 91.

92. See, for example, Cairnes, *Essays*, p. 28.

93. Jevons, op. cit., p. 43.

94. J. Shield Nicholson, *Treatise on Money* (London: Blackwood, 1888), pp. 100-1 [emphasis added].

95. Cairnes stated, for example, that: "It is quite conceivable . . . without supposing any alteration in the prices of commodities . . . that the relation between our exports and imports may be altered." (Cairnes, *An Examination into the Principles*, pp. 33-36, 38.)

96. See, for example, Cairnes, *Essays*, pp. 70-71.

97. Movements in prices probably became more relevant to the adjustment mechanism the greater the proportion of an economy's nontraded goods. The prices of nontraded goods, for example, are not necessarily determined in world markets or tightly constrained by arbitrage. These prices will ultimately adjust, but the process may be much more indirect and time-consuming.

In discussing the transmission of world inflation, Cairnes explicitly discussed the case of nontraded goods. To illustrate this, he supposed that large quantities of gold were discovered in a single small open economy with a convertible currency. In this case, prices would—in the first instance—increase due to an increased demand for commodities. As pointed out above, however, the prices of traded goods would be *immediately* driven back down to world levels by the workings of arbitrage. Nontraded goods prices, however, would not be driven down, unless these goods were substitutes for traded goods or employed traded goods as inputs. Ultimately, however, these prices would return to normal levels as resources shifted into the nontraded sector and, hence, increased the supply of and decreased the price of nontraded goods.

The prices of nontraded goods in non-gold-producing countries would participate in the world inflation in the following ways: First, if nontraded goods were substitutes for traded goods, their prices would increase with world traded goods prices. Secondly, with an increase in the prices of traded goods, nontraded inputs (such as labor) would ultimately shift into the traded goods sector, thus decreasing the supply of and, hence, increasing the price of nontraded goods. (See, for example, Cairnes, *Essays*, p. 59.)

98. See, for example, Wicksell, *Interest and Prices*, and Wicksell, *Lectures on Political Economy*, especially Volume II, p. 127. See also Laidler, and Nobay, "International Aspects of Inflation: A Survey," in *Recent Issues in International Monetary Economics*, ed. Emil Claassen and P. Salin (New York: North-Holland, 1976), p. 301.

99. In addition to understanding the fundamental ideas presented by Ricardo, banking school writers, Senior, and John Stuart Mill, Wicksell also recognized various subtle arguments of these authors, for example, the distinction made by Ricardo between the behavior of an individual economic unit and that of a universel set of these units acting in unison. That is, Wicksell had a thorough understanding of the subtle distinctions between an open and a closed economy. See, for example, Wicksell, *Interest and Prices*, pp. 81, 82, 85, and Wicksell, *Lectures on Political Economy*, Volume II, p. 171.

100. See, for example, Wicksell, *Interest and Prices*, p. 85.

101. Wicksell, *Interest and Prices*, p. 162.

102. Laidler and Nobay, op. cit., p. 300.

103. Wicksell, "The Influence of the Rate of Interest on Prices," *Economic Journal* (1907):217.

104. Wicksell, "The Influence," pp. 159-61.

105. Wicksell, *Lectures on Political Economy*, Volume II, p. 158.

106. Wicksell, *Lectures on Political Economy*, p. 171. See also ibid., p. 177.

107. Wicksell, "International Freights and Prices," *Quarterly Journal of Economics*, 32 (1918):405. See also Laidler and Nobay, op. cit., p. 301.

108. Wicksell, *Interest and Prices*, pp. 157-58. See also Viner, *Canada's Balance*, p. 305.

109. Wicksell, *Interest and Prices*, p. 157.

110. Wicksell, *Lectures on Political Economy*, Volume II, p. 177.

111. Wicksell, *Interest and Prices*, pp. 171-73.

112. Laidler and Nobay, op. cit., p. 301.

113. Wicksell, *Lectures on Political Economy*, Volume II, p. 171.

114. Wicksell, *Interest and Prices*, p. 85; see also ibid., pp. 83-85.

115. Wicksell, *Lectures on Political Economy*, Volume II, p. 177, and Wicksell, *Interest and Prices*, pp. 157-58.

116. Wicksell, *Lectures on Political Economy*, Volume II, p. 171, and Wicksell, *Interest and Prices*, pp. 81-82.

117. An excellent analysis of Laughlin and his monetary writing was recently presented by Girton and Roper. See Lance Girton and Don Roper, "J. Laurence Laughlin and the Quantity Theory of Money," *Journal of Political Economy* 86 (August 1978).

118. Laughlin frequently quoted, for example, the writings of Hume, Smith, Thornton, Ricardo, Tooke, Jevons, and John Stuart Mill. Moreover, Laughlin was well familiar with the bullionist controversy as well as with the currency-banking school debate. See, for example, J. Laurence Laughlin, *The Principles of Money* (New York: Scribners, 1903), pp. 254-58, 263-65.

119. Ibid., pp. 368, 409, 417. See also Girton and Roper, op. cit., pp. 616-17.

120. J. Laurence Laughlin. "Prices and the International Movement of Specie," *Journal of Political Economy* 10 (September 1902):534.

121. Laughlin, *Principles*, pp. 263, 377, 409, and 417. See also Girton and Roper, op. cit., pp. 609, 617.

122. See Laughlin, "Prices," p. 518. See also Girton and Roper, op. cit., p. 615.

123. See, for example, Girton and Roper, op. cit., pp. 605–8, 614.

124. Laughlin, *Principles*, p. 369. See also Laughlin, "Prices," p. 517.

125. Laughlin, *Principles*, pp. 380–2. See also ibid., pp. 252–53, 371–72, 375, 377, 379–82, 388, 417; Laughlin, "Prices," pp. 526–27; Girton and Roper, op. cit., pp. 614–15.

126. See, for example, Laughlin, *Principles*, pp. 614–15.

127. Laughlin stated, for example, that "no statistical evidence can be adduced to show that prices are, or have been, raised or lowered by the importation or exportation of gold into or from a country." (Laughlin, *Principles*, p. 372.)

128. See Laughlin, *Principles*, pp. 220–21 (Diagram No. XVI).

129. See, for example, Laughlin, *Principles*, pp. 257, 264, 268–69.

130. See, for example, Laughlin, *Principles*, pp. 238, 263, 268, 375, and 377. See also Girton and Roper, op. cit., pp. 599, 609, 614.

131. See, for example, Laughlin, *Principles*, pp. 247, 263, 371. See also J. Laurence Laughlin, "The Quantity Theory of Money," *Journal of Political Economy* (June 1924):276; and Girton and Roper, op. cit., pp. 609, 614.

132. See, for example, Laughlin, *Principles*, pp. 103, 379, 388–89, 393, and 417.

133. See Laughlin, *Principles*, pp. 135–37, 388–89, and 418. See also Laughlin, "Prices," p. 535; and Girton and Roper, op. cit., p. 609.

134. Laughlin, *Principles*, p. 393.

135. Irving Fisher, *The Purchasing Power of Money*, pp. 91-93, 95 [emphasis added].

136. Girton and Roper, op. cit., p. 612.

137. Fisher, op. cit., pp. 159, 182.

138. Girton and Roper, op. cit., p. 614.

139. Fisher, op. cit., p. 172.

140. Girton and Roper, op. cit., p. 616.

141. Ludwig von Mises, *The Theory of Money and Credit* (New York: Foundation for Economic Education, 1971), p. 249.

142. See, for example, Mises, op. cit., pp. 176, 178. See also Wu, op. cit., p. 233.

143. Mises, op. cit., p. 171.

144. Mises, ibid., p. 249.

145. See, for example, Mises, ibid., p. 354.

146. Alfred Marshall, *Official Papers* (London: Macmillan, 1926) pp. 170, 191. Also quoted in Wu, op. cit., p. 220; and Eprime Eshag, *From Marshall to Keynes* (Oxford: Blackwell, 1963) p. 27.

147. Alfred Marshall, *Money, Credit, and Commerce* (New York: Augustus M. Kelley, 1965), p. 145.

148. John Maynard Keynes, *Monetary Reform* (New York: Harcourt Brace, 1924), pp. 100–1.

149. John Maynard Keynes, *A Treatise on Money*, Volume I (Cambridge: Macmillan, 1971), p. 62. See also pp. 63, 65.

150. Ralph Hawtrey, *Currency and Credit* (London: Longmans, Green, 1934), p. 69.

151. Ralph Hawtrey, *The Art of Central Banking* (New York: Augustus M. Kelley, 1962), p. 144.

152. See, for example, Ralph G. Hawtrey "The Gold Standard and the Balance of Payments," *Economic Journal*, 36 (March 1926); Ralph G. Hawtrey, *Trade and Credit* (New York: Longmans, Green, 1928), p. 22; and Ralph G. Hawtrey, *Currency and Credit*, pp. 73–75.

153. A. C. Pigou, "Inflation," *Economic Journal*, 27 (1917):491-92 [emphasis added].

154. John M. Keynes, *A Treatise on Money*, Volume II, pp. 251, 255–56.

155. See, for example, John M. Keynes, *Monetary Reform*, p. 173; and Arthur C. Pigou, *Industrial Fluctuations*, p. 303.

156. Frank Taussig, "Wages and Prices in Relation to International Trade," *Quarterly Journal of Economics* 20 (August 1906):499.

157. Frank Taussig, *Principles of Economics* (New York: Macmillan, 1911), p. 481.

158. See, for example, Jacob Viner, *Studies in the Theory of International Trade*, p. 384.

159. See, for example, ibid., pp. 323–26; and Jacob Viner, *Canada's Balance*, p. 211.

160. Frank Taussig, *International Trade* (New York: Macmillan, 1927), p. 37.

161. Frank Taussig, *Free Trade, the Tariff, and Reciprocity*, p. 74 (quoted from Viner, *Canada's Balance*, pp. 238–39).

162. Frank Taussig, *International Trade*, p. 154.

163. Viner, *Canada's Balance*, p. 210.

164. Viner, *Studies in the Theory of International Trade*, p. 305.

165. Taussig, *Principles*, p. 458.

166. Frank W. Fetter, *Development of British Monetary Orthodoxy* (Cambridge: Harvard University Press, 1965), p. 228, footnote.

167. See, for example, Charles P. Kindleberger, *International Economics* (Homewood: Richard D. Irwin, 1968), Appendix B, pp. 547–54; and Bertil Ohlin, *Interregional and International Trade* (Cambridge: Harvard University Press, 1968), p. 146.

168. See, for example, Ohlin, ibid. p. 105.

169. Ibid., p. 105.

170. Ibid., p. 106.

171. See, for example, in Donald N. McCloskey and J. Richard Zecher, "How the Gold Standard Worked, 1880–1913," in *The Monetary Approach to the Balance of Payments*, ed. Frenkel and Johnson (Toronto: University of Toronto Press, 1976), p. 375, where the authors state that "In long-run equilibrium, the distinction between direct and indirect is besides the point and the relationship of domestic to international prices is not even somewhat flexible."

172. There were, however, a few notable exceptions. These were Bertil Ohlin, *Interregional and International Trade*; and especially P. B. Whale, "The Working of the Pre-War Gold Standard," *Economica* (February 1937).

173. J. G. Witte and B. Henneberry, "A Monetary-Real Approach to Balance of Payments Theory: Old-New Synthesis for Old New Problems." Unpublished manuscript, Indiana University, November 1974, p. 2.

174. See, for example, Irving Fisher, *The Purchasing Power of Money*, p. 172; John M. Keynes, *Monetary Reform*, pp. 167–69, 173; and Arthur C. Pigou, *Industrial Fluctuations*, p. 303. See also John M. Letiche, *Balance of Payments and Economic Growth* (New York: Augustus M. Kelley, 1967), pp. 45–46.

175. Ibid., p. 46.

176. Hubert Henderson, "The Function of Exchange Rates," *Oxford Economic Papers*, 1 (1949):9–10.

177. Harry G. Johnson, *Inflation and the Monetarist Controversy* (Amsterdam: North-Holland, 1972), p. 76.

178. See, for example, Girton and Roper, op. cit., p. 614.

179. See, among others, the writings of Harry G. Johnson on the subject. They include, for example, the following: *Inflation and the Monetarist Controversy*; "The Monetary Approach to the Balance of Payments: A Nontechnical Guide," *Journal of International Economics* 7 (1977); "The Monetary Approach to the Balance of Payments Theory," *Journal of Financial and Quantitative Analysis* (March 1972); and "Elasticity, Absorption, Keynesian Multiplier, Keynesian Policy, and Monetary Approaches to Devaluation Theory: A Simple Geometric Exposition," *American Economic Review* (June 1976).

APPENDIX

A GLOBAL MONETARIST MODEL OF WORLD INFLATION AND THE BALANCE OF PAYMENTS

The inflation of the past 15 years has been a worldwide phenomenon. Accordingly, analysts have become increasingly aware that any satisfactory explanation of price level behavior must account for its international character. These analysts fall into three main schools. First are the *eclectics*, who attribute world inflation to a complex and ever-changing mixture of causes, e.g., the exercise of monopoly power by oil-producing nations; the international conjuncture of cyclical booms; and the occurrence of bad harvests, poor fish catches, and other autonomous reductions in the supplies of key commodities. Second are the members of the *cost-push school*, who blame inflation on worldwide labor militancy. Third are the *global monetarists*, who, in sharp contrast with the other schools, focus largely or exclusively on the monetary factor.

The theoretical basis of this third approach is the monetary theory of the balance of payments. As usually presented, this theory assumes that the countries of the world are linked together (as they actually were until 1973) by fixed exchange rates between freely convertible currencies. The sum total of these currencies converted into a common unit at the fixed exchange rate constitutes the world money stock. This stock, in conjunction with the demand for it, determines the world price level, which is then transmitted to individual countries by commodity arbitrage, the operation of which tends to equalize prices in all markets. Finally, by importing or exporting money in exchange for goods and securities, each nation uses the mechanism of the balance of payments to bring its domestic money stock into line with the exact quantity required to support the price level. When applied to the interpretation of recent inflationary experience—at least up to 1973 when fixed rates were widely abandoned for flexible ones—this theory implies that excessive world monetary expansion generated the inflation, that commodity arbitrage propagated it, and that the balance of payments mechanism distributed the world money supply as required to accommodate or validate it in each nation.

This appendix seeks to explain the foregoing theory and its public policy implications with the aid of a simple expository model of the international monetary mechanism. Although originally constructed for the specific purpose of analyzing the economic effects of a currency devaluation, the model is easily adaptable to the monetarist explanation of world inflation.[1] In fact, it constitutes an almost ideal framework within which to articulate the global monetarist view because it embodies most of the elements essential to that view. These elements are outlined in the following section, which serves as a necessary preliminary to the description of the model and its components.

MONETARIST PROPOSITIONS

Any analytical model that conveys the essence of the global monetarist explanation of world inflation must contain certain key ingredients that characterize that approach. These elements include the following:

1. THE VIEW OF THE WORLD AS THE RELEVANT CLOSED ECONOMY

The global monetarist views the world as a closed system of interdependent open national economies connected by fixed or imperfectly floating exchange rates. In this view, nations are interpreted as *regions* of the closed world economy, and problems of inflation in any particular nation are treated as purely regional manifestations of an aggregate world phenomenon, as are questions relating to an individual nation's distributive share of the world money stock.

2. THE QUANTITY THEORY OF MONEY

The quantity theory constitutes the second key component of the global monetarist view. The quantity theory states that the path of world prices in long-run equilibrium is completely determined by the path of the world money stock. This conclusion follows from the theory of the interaction between the demand for real (price-deflated) money balances and the nominal stock of money. The demand for real balances is interpreted as a stable mathematical function of a few macroeconomic variables, the most important being real income and an interest rate variable representing the opportunity cost of holding money. Given the values of these independent variables, the theory states that the price level will adjust to bring the real volume of any nominal stock of money into equality with the amount demanded. From this it follows that if the income and interest rate determinants of the demand for money are given, an exogenously given nominal stock of money completely determines the price level. More generally, in terms of a growing world economy, the long-run rate of world monetary expansion determines the steady-state rate of world inflation, given the trend growth rate of world output. Two important implications of the quantity theory should be noted at this point. The first is that money has no influence on real economic variables in the long run. The second is that in long-run equilibrium the price level will vary in exactly the same proportion as the money stock. Known as the neutrality and equiproportionality postulates, respectively, these two propositions must be embodied in any mathematical model that purports to represent the logical structure of the global monetarist view.

3. LAW OF ONE PRICE

From the universally accepted proposition that commodity arbitrage tends to equalize prices of identical traded goods across countries—due allowance of course being made for tariffs and transportation costs—monetarists move directly to the proposition that general price levels also tend to be equalized. Monetarists note that in a world of rigidly fixed exchange rates between freely convertible currencies money itself becomes a homogeneous traded good whose price, like that of any other traded good, will be equalized internationally. But since the domestic price of money in terms of goods is simply the inverse of the general price level, it follows that equalization of the price of money implies equalization of national price levels. This point, incidentally, distinguishes modern global monetarists from those who stress relative price level changes in the international adjustment mechanism. The latter group, unlike global monetarists, argues that the volume of imports and exports depends on domestic prices relative to foreign prices and that changes in these relative prices constitute a key link in the automatic specie-flow mechanism that operates to correct payments imbalances and to maintain the equilibrium international distribution of the precious metals. Global monetarists deemphasize such relative price effects on the grounds (1) that efficient arbitrage prevents price disparities from developing except for the briefest of intervals and (2) that the automatic adjustment process operates mainly through divergences between income and expenditure rather than through the classical relative price mechanism.

4. MONETARY INTERPRETATION OF THE BALANCE OF PAYMENTS

The fourth key component of the monetarist approach is the concept of the balance of payments as the means by which open economies adjust their existing stocks of money to the stocks they desire to hold. Suppose a country's actual money stock is smaller than the stock its residents desire to hold. Endeavoring to replenish their cash balances, these residents will cut their expenditure thereby releasing resources for the export trade. The country will run a trade balance surplus, exporting goods and importing money until the gap between actual and desired money stocks is eliminated. Conversely, if the existing stock of money is greater than that desired, national expenditure will exceed national output and the country will run a trade balance deficit, importing goods and exporting money until the excess money balances were worked off. In this manner, each nation will use its balance of payments to attain monetary equilibrium, and for the world as a whole, the balance of payments mechanism will distribute the world money stock across nations consistent with monetary equilibrium in each nation. The key assumption underlying the foregoing view is that, in the long run at least, national central banks do not use open market operations and other policy weapons to offset or neutralize ("sterilize") the impact of external money flows on the behavior of the domestic money stock. One justification for this assumption is that the effect of sterilization operations would be to create international interest rate differentials that would induce capital flows sufficient to undermine the sterilization policy. Finally, it should be noted that the nonsterilization assumption means that from the point of view of an individual country the money supply is an endogenous variable completely determined by the public's decisions to acquire or get rid of cash through the balance of payments. Here the traditional monetarist assumption of an exogenous money stock applies only to the closed world economy and not to individual open national economies.

Constituting the essential ingredients of the monetarist theory of world inflation, these four elements are incorporated in the analytical model presented below.

THE MODEL AND ITS COMPONENTS

The model itself consists of a hypothetical two-country world economy represented by a set of equations containing the following variables. Let D be the desired stock of national nominal money balances and M the actual stock composed of a domestic credit component C and an international reserve component R. Furthermore, let $\dot{M}$ and $\dot{R}$ be the rates of change (time derivatives) of the national money stock and its foreign exchange reserve component, respectively, and A be an adjustment coefficient representing the speed of adjustment of actual to desired money stocks. Also, let K be the desired ratio of nominal cash balances to nominal income, Y the level of real output, P the price level, and X the exchange rate (domestic currency price of a unit of foreign currency). The cash balance ratio K is treated as a numerical constant, and the output and exchange rate variables are taken as exogenously-determined givens. Finally, let E be nominal national expenditure and B the trade balance measured in domestic currency. For simplicity, the trade balance is identified with the overall balance of payments, i.e., the capital account and international capital flows are ignored. Unstarred variables refer to the home country, starred variables to the foreign country (i.e., rest of the world), and the subscript w to the closed world economy. Percentage rates of change of variables are represented by lower-case letters—for example, p is the percentage rate of change of the price level P.

PURCHASING POWER PARITY EQUATION

The first equation of the model is the goods arbitrage or purchasing power parity equation

$$(1) \quad P = XP^*,$$

which embodies the "law of one price" proposition that international arbitrage tends to equalize the money price of goods in terms of either currency. The equation states that the price level in the home country is equal to the product of the exchange rate and the price level in the foreign country, implying that the price levels in the two countries are the same when converted into a common unit at the fixed exchange rate. Note that this equation corresponds to the global monetarist view that national commodity markets are merely parts of a single unified world commodity market.

MONEY DEMAND EQUATIONS

The second part of the model consists of demand for money equations, one for each country. These equations express the stock of nominal money balances that the public desires to hold in the aggregate as a constant fraction K of the level of nominal national income (the product of the price level and the exogenously given level of real output). The equations are written as follows:

(2) $D = KPY$ and $D^* = K^*P^*Y^*$.

As written, these demand functions comply with the quantity theory of money in at least three respects. First, the exogeneity of the real output variable squares with the quantity theory's assumption that output is determined independently of the behavior of money in the long run. Second, the demand functions exhibit a one-to-one relationship between the quantity of money demanded and the price level. In the technical jargon of monetary theory, the functions are said to be homogeneous of degree one in prices. This homogeneity property implies both (1) absence of money illusion (the inability of economic agents to distinguish between real and nominal economic magnitudes) and (2) long-run neutrality of money as postulated by the quantity theory. It also ensures that the theory's equiproportionality postulate will be satisfied, i.e., that the price level will vary in exactly the same proportion as the money supply. Third, the demand functions exhibit the stability required by the theory, this stability being assured by the assumed constancy of the desired money/income ratios.

MONEY SUPPLY EQUATIONS

The foregoing demand equations represent only one side of the money market and must be matched by supply equations representing the other. These equations are derived from the consolidated balance sheet of the commercial banks and the central bank of each country. By a simple accounting identity, the monetary liabilities of those sectors can be shown to be backed by an equivalent amount of assets as indicated by the equations

$$(3)\quad M = C + R \text{ and } M^* = C^* + R^*.$$

Here M is the narrowly defined money supply (currency plus demand deposits), C is domestic credit defined as the banking system's holdings of net domestic assets, and R is the banking system's holdings of international reserves. The foregoing equations merely express national money stocks as the sum of their respective source components, domestic and foreign. Of these two components only the first is under the control of the monetary authority. By contrast, the foreign source component—and therefore the money stock itself—is determined by the public's demand for cash. If the public is just satisfied to hold the existing stock of money, any policy-engineered change in the domestic credit component will induce an equal but opposite change in the foreign source component, leaving the nation's money stock unchanged.

Corresponding to the national money supply equations is the equation

$$(4)\quad M_w = M + XM^*$$

that defines the world money stock M_w as the sum of national money stocks expressed in a common currency unit. The world money stock is treated as an exogenous variable. This follows from the assumption that the quantity of world reserves is given. Given the latter, all the components of the world money stock, namely the domestic source component of the national money stocks plus world reserves, are exogenous and therefore so is the world money stock itself. Note, however, that while total world reserves can be treated as a given, a single nation's reserve holdings cannot be so treated, which is the reason national money supplies are endogenous variables from the viewpoint of the national authorities. Despite their simplicity, equations 3 and 4 are taken as constituting an accurate specification of the supply side of the money market.

Money market equilibrium, of course, requires that money demand equal money supply in each nation, implying a zero excess demand for money. Although this condition must be satisfied in the long run, it may well be violated in the short run, in which case national money markets will exhibit temporary disequilibrium as manifested by excess demands for or supplies of money. When monetary disequilibrium occurs, however, an automatic self-corrective mechanism starts to function as people begin to adjust their cash holdings to bring actual liquidity back into line with desired liquidity.

MONEY STOCK ADJUSTMENT EQUATIONS

The adjustment mechanism mentioned in the preceding paragraph is represented by the model's fifth set of equations, which state that the rate at which each country augments or depletes its cash holdings is proportional to the excess demand for money. These money stock adjustment equations are written as follows:

$$(5)\quad \dot{M} = A(D - M) \text{ and } \dot{M}^* = A^*(D^* - M^*),$$

where $\dot{M}$ is the change in money holdings per unit of time, $D - M$ is excess demand for money (the difference between desired and actual stocks), and A is an adjustment coefficient expressing the speed at which money stocks are adjusted in response to excess demand. The closer the coefficient is to unity the faster the adjustment, and the closer it is to zero the slower the adjustment. In the extreme case where the coefficient has a numerical value of unity, adjustment is sufficiently rapid to eliminate excess stock demand within the same period it occurs. In the opposite case, i.e., a zero coefficient, adjustment never occurs and excess demand persists indefinitely. The model assumes that the coefficient is large enough to insure that full stock adjustment is eventually achieved. The channel or mechanism through which monetary adjustment is accomplished is, of course, the balance of payments.

BALANCE OF PAYMENTS EQUATION

The sixth component of the model is the balance of payments equation, which performs two important functions. First, it specifies the role of the external trade balance in the money stock adjustment process. Specifically, the equation states that the trade balance surplus (the excess of money receipts from sales abroad over monetary expenditures on purchases from abroad) is by definition equal to the country's net change in international reserves and therefore, given domestic credit, in the stock of money itself, i.e., $B = \dot{R} = \dot{M}$. This expression corresponds to the monetary theory of the balance of payments according to which a nation adds to its stock of money by running a trade balance surplus, exporting goods in exchange for money, and reduces its money stock by running a trade deficit, importing goods in exchange for exports of money. The expression also embodies the key monetarist assumption that the policy authorities do not offset or nullify ("sterilize") the impact of payments disequilibria and reserve flows on the domestic money supply.

The second purpose of the equation is to insure that the two-country model is internally consistent by imposing the condition that, for the world as a whole, the sum of the individual trade balances when measured in terms of a common monetary unit is identically equal to zero. This condition means that if the home country is running a trade balance surplus, the foreign country (rest of world) must be running a trade deficit of the same amount when measured in terms of home country currency. Symbolically, the balance of payments identity is $B = - XB^*$, where B is the home country's trade balance surplus and $-XB^*$ is the foreign country's trade deficit (a negative surplus) expressed in units of domestic currency at the fixed exchange rate. This expression, showing how the individual countries are unified via the balance of payments identity, constitutes a mathematical statement of the global monetarist view of the world as a closed system of interdependent open economies.

To summarize, the complete balance of payments equation, expressing both the zero world trade balance identity and the monetary view of the external accounts, is written as follows:

$$(6) \quad B = -XB^* = \dot{M} = \dot{R} = -X\dot{M}^* = -X\dot{R}^*.$$

Note that since by definition the foreign country's trade deficit measured in terms of domestic currency must equal the home country's surplus, it follows that the money outflow from the former country must also equal the money inflow into the latter. Here is the global monetarist view of the balance of payments as the allocation mechanism that distributes a given total of world money across nations.

EXPENDITURE EQUATIONS

Completing the model are the expenditure equations that describe the connection between the money market and the commodity market. These equations indicate that in a world in which the public can hold only money and/or goods, an excess demand for one implies a corresponding excess supply of the other and vice versa. Written as follows:

$$(7)\quad E = PY - \dot{M} \text{ and } E^* = P^*Y^* - \dot{M}^*,$$

the equations express a relationship between domestic expenditure E (i.e., spending by domestic residents on both home- and foreign-produced goods), nominal income PY, and the rate of accumulation or decumulation of cash balances $\dot{M}$.

According to the equations, spending equals income only when cash balances are not being augmented or depleted, i.e., when the public is just satisfied to hold the existing stock of money. An excess supply or demand for money, however, causes expenditure to deviate from income. For example, an excess demand for cash means that commodity expenditure falls short of income as the public endeavors to build up its cash balance. Conversely, an excess supply of money implies that expenditure exceeds income as the community tries to get rid of its excess cash holdings. Note also that the equations imply a relationship between spending, income, and the trade balance. This corresponds to the monetarist view that the international adjustment process operates primarily through divergences between expenditure and income rather than through changes in the relative prices of exports and imports. The equations imply that when domestic spending for goods exceeds domestic income (production), net commodity imports will fill the gap and the trade balance will be in deficit. Similarly, when domestic expenditure falls short of production, the unabsorbed output will be exported, thereby resulting in a trade surplus. Only if expenditure just equals production will the trade balance be zero.

THE EQUATIONS SUMMARIZED

Taken together, the foregoing equations embody the main elements of the global monetarist view of the world economy. The equations link the levels of prices, expenditures, and desired and actual money stocks in the two countries as well as the flows of money and goods between them. To summarize, the equations are written as follows:

$$(1)\quad P = XP^*$$

(2) $D = KPY$ $D^* = K^*P^*Y^*$

(3) $M = C + R$ $M^* = C^* + R^*$

(4) $M_w = M + XM^*$

(5) $\dot{M} = A(D - M)$ $\dot{M}^* = A^*(D^* - M^*)$

(6) $B = -XB^* = \dot{M} = \dot{R} = -X\dot{M}^* = -X\dot{R}^*$

(7) $E = PY - \dot{M}$ $E^* = P^*Y^* - \dot{M}^*$.

Equations 1–4 help determine the equilibrium (steady-state) values of the price and monetary variables, while equations 5–7 describe the adjustment mechanism by which equilibrium is restored following a monetary disturbance. Specifically, the equilibrium world price level is determined by equating the world money supply shown in equation 4 with the aggregate world real demand for money implicit in equation 2. Once determined, the world price level is then transmitted to the two countries via commodity arbitrage as described in equation 1. The resulting country price levels enter equation 2 to determine nominal national demands for money. If these latter variables differ from the existing national money stocks shown in equation 3, the discrepancy enters equation 5 to determine the rate of money stock adjustment, which enters equations 6 and 7 to determine national expenditures, trade balances, and the corresponding international redistribution of the world money stock.

Less formally, the model implies the following causal chain:

1. Given world money demand, the world stock of money determines the world price level.
2. International arbitrage brings national prices into equality with world prices.
3. Given real output, national price levels determine national nominal demands for money.
4. National money demands in conjunction with national money supplies determine the rate of money stock adjustment.
5. Money stock adjustment determines spending, trade balances, and the direction and volume of international money flows.

6. This process continues until the equilibrium international distribution of money is achieved, and money market equilibrium is restored in each country. At this point the system is said to be in steady-state equilibrium.

LONG-RUN STEADY-STATE SOLUTION OF THE SYSTEM

In any economic system, the long-run steady-state is characterized by full stock equilibrium, i.e., a situation in which existing asset stocks just equal desired asset stocks. In the hypothetical system described by the model, steady-state equilibrium occurs when the existing stock of money (the sole asset) equals the desired stock. As can be seen from equations 5 through 7, this in turn implies that money stock adjustment, trade balances, and the gap between expenditure and income are all zero. In long-run equilibrium, therefore, equations 5 through 7 are irrelevant, and one can analyze the determination of world prices and their rate of inflation from the first four equations alone.

WORLD PRICE LEVEL AND INFLATION RATE

A central proposition of global monetarism is that, under a regime of fixed exchange rates, the steady-state path of world prices is determined by the path of the world money stock. A version of the quantity theory of money, this proposition can be demonstrated with the aid of the four equations relevant to the analysis of long-run equilibrium.

The demonstration requires several steps. First, impose the condition of stock equilibrium and set the supplies of money equal to demands, e.g., $M = KPY$. Second, use the fixed exchange rate to express the money stock and price variables as world-level magnitudes. As defined in equation 4, the world money stock is the sum of the national money stocks measured in terms of a single currency, i.e., $M_w = M + XM^*$. Similarly, by virtue of the purchasing power parity assumption, each nation's price level expressed in terms of a common unit is equal to the world price level, i.e., $P_w = P = XP^*$. Note that the assumption of a fixed exchange rate is absolutely indispensable here since it provides the invariable common unit required to convert national variables into a single homogeneous world-level measure that has analytical significance.[2] The third step is to recognize that by choice of an appropriate unit of measurement for either currency the exchange rate can be set equal to unity, thus permitting the relationship between the world money stock and the world price level to be written simply as $M_w = M + M^* = (KY + K^*Y^*)P_w$. In long-run equilibrium, the variables enclosed by parentheses are regarded as exogenously determined by tastes, technology, and resource endowments, and consequently are taken as given. It follows, therefore, that, in terms of the model, the world price level is fully determined in the long run by the world money stock, with changes in the latter variable causing equiproportionate changes in the former.

Corresponding to the preceding equilibrium money-price relationship is the equilibrium distribution of the world money stock. The home country's natural proportional share or fraction S of world money can be expressed as $S = M/M_w = KY/(KY + K^*Y^*)$, and similarly for the other country (rest of world), whose share, of course, is $1 - S$. This important result states that, in steady-state equilibrium, the fraction of world money distributed to each nation depends upon the relative importance of the nation's demand for real cash balances as compared with the demands of the entire world. The demand for real balances, of course, is expressed as the product of the desired money/income ratio and real income. Assuming both countries have identical money/income ratios, the country with the greater real income will command the lion's share of the world money stock. As shown below, the distributive share parameters S and $1 - S$ appear in the expression for the world rate of inflation, the derivation of which constitutes the final step of the demonstration.

The expression for the world rate of inflation is derived by taking the time derivative of the logarithm of the world money-price level relationship and is written as $p_w = m_w - [Sy + (1 - S)y^*]$.[3] Here p_w is the percentage rate of world inflation, m_w is the percentage rate of growth of the world money stock, y and y^* are the exogenously given trend growth rates of real output in the two countries, and S and $1 - S$ are the shares of each country in the world money stock. This equation states that the rate of world inflation is equal to the difference between the world rate of monetary expansion and the growth rate of world output as measured by the sum of the weighted national output growth rates, the weights being the countries' shares in the world money supply. In short, the equation is an exact statement of the monetarist conclusion that inflation results when world monetary expansion out-paces world output growth.

THE DYNAMIC ADJUSTMENT PROCESS

So much for the determination of the path of world prices in steady-state equilibrium. The next stage of the analysis deals with the international adjustment mechanism as described in equations 5 through 7. Regarding the adjustment process, three questions are especially pertinent. First, what responses are provoked by an autonomous increase in the domestic money supply of a single open economy? Second, how do these responses raise the world price level? Third, how do individual countries subsequently adjust to the higher world price level?

To answer these questions, start from a hypothetical situation of worldwide monetary equilibrium, and let this equilibrium be disturbed by a monetary expansion in the home country. According to the model, this disturbance generates an excess supply of money leading to a trade balance deficit and an excess home demand for goods in the world commodity market, putting upward pressure on world prices. The resulting world price increase, disseminated abroad via the international arbitrage mechanism, induces corresponding changes of opposite sign in the demand-for-money, stock-adjustment, expenditure, and trade-balance equations of the foreign country.[4] Adjustment continues until both monetary redundancy in the one country and monetary deficiency in the other are eliminated. When equilibrium is restored, world and national price levels will have risen in proportion to the rise in the world money supply.

The preceding corresponds closely to the monetarist interpretation of the worldwide inflation of the late 1960s and early 1970s. According to this view, excessive monetary expansion in the U.S. generated a persistent excess demand for goods and consequently a series of balance of payments deficits that pumped dollars into the international monetary system in sufficient quantities to contribute significantly to global inflation. This view departs from the model only in one key respect. It contends that, because the dollar itself constituted the primary international reserve asset, the U.S. was able to engage in domestic credit expansion that led to the inflationary rise in world liquidity without suffering a loss of its own reserves. Lacking an external reserve constraint, the U.S., in this view, became a potentially potent source of world inflation.

POLICY IMPLICATIONS OF THE MODEL

The model described in the preceding paragraphs contains some radical implications for economic stabilization policy. These implications can be classified according to whether they pertain to small or to large open economies. Small economies are those whose domestic policy actions can be treated as having a negligible impact on the rest of the world. Large economies, by contrast, are those whose policies have a significant global influence. In some cases—e.g., the United States—an economy may be so large as to warrant interpretation as a closed economy. In what follows it is also well to remember that the often unconventional conclusions derived from the model reflect the particular assumptions underlying it, and that many of these assumptions are open to serious criticism. This is especially true of the assumptions of (1) full employment, (2) perfect international arbitrage, (3) exogeneity of real income, (4) nonsterilization of international money flows, and (5) the existence of an inherently stable self-regulating world economy. While these assumptions may hold in long-run equilibrium, empirical evidence suggests that they may not hold over any realistic current policy-making horizon nor over the transitional adjustment period following monetary shocks. Recognition of this fact would certainly modify—perhaps drastically—any policy prescriptions based on the model. Subject to these caveats, the policy implications of the model are summarized below.

SMALL COUNTRY IMPLICATIONS

The first and most radical implication stemming from the model is that, in the case of small open economies operating with fixed exchange rates, traditional macroeconomic monetary and balance of payments policies are both unnecessary and useless. They are unnecessary because the international adjustment mechanism works automatically to correct economic disequilibria and to provide each country with sufficient money to accommodate full capacity levels of output. They are useless because the domestic authorities cannot control the money supply or the balance of payments, both of which are endogenous variables determined by the public's demand for money.

Suppose, for example, the authorities try to improve the country's balance of payments by devaluing the currency, i.e., engineering a one-time increase in the pegged exchange rate. This devaluation has no permanent impact on the trade balance. There is, to be sure, a favorable *short-run* impact, but this impact is inherently transient as can be seen by tracing the sequence of events triggered by the policy action. First, the devaluation causes a step increase in the exchange rate. Given the foreign price level, however, the home price level must immediately rise in the same proportion as the exchange rate to preserve purchasing power parity. The domestic price increase raises the stock of cash balances demanded by the public. This generates an excess demand for money, leading to a reduction in expenditure and to a trade balance surplus. The surplus, however, is short-lived, since it is accompanied by an inflow of money that eventually eliminates the discrepancy between actual and desired cash balances. When this happens, the adjustment process ceases, domestic spending again equals production, and the trade balance surplus vanishes. The sole long-run effect of the devaluation is on the price level which, according to the demand for money equation, rises in exact proportion to the increase in the domestic money supply. Within the context of the example, the authorities are powerless to exercise permanent control over the balance of payments.

The only thing the monetary authorities can control in a small open economy is the *composition* of the money supply, i.e., the mix between domestic credit and international reserves. They cannot, however, govern the size or total quantity of the money supply. For according to the monetary theory of the balance of payments, an expansion in the controllable domestic credit component of the money stock will result in a balance of payments deficit and an outflow of the uncontrollable international reserve component until the money stock returns to its initial level. When equilibrium is restored, the mix of the money stock will be changed—domestic credit having displaced international reserves dollar for dollar—but the total will be unaltered. This conclusion follows directly from the model as can be seen by setting the money supply equation equal to the money demand equation to yield $C + R = KPY$. Given the long-run equilibrium values of the variables on the right-hand side of this equation, it follows that any change in the domestic credit component C must be offset by a change identical in size but opposite in sign in the international reserve component R to keep the total money stock equal to the unchanged steady-state demand for it. In short, the total stock of money is no more a controllable variable than is the balance of payments in a small open economy.

A second policy implication is that, assuming the absence of monetary contraction abroad, a nation's monetary authorities are solely to blame for its balance of payments deficits, since there can be no deficits unless there is an excess supply of money. It should be noted, however, that such deficits are inherently transitory phenomena. For the model predicts that they will vanish as soon as the redundant money is diffused throughout the world economy by the operation of the international adjustment mechanism.

A third policy implication is that, in a world of fixed exchange rates, a small open economy can control neither its price level nor its rate of inflation, since both are determined in world markets. This means that an individual country will find it impossible to avoid inflating at the world rate. It also means that in a fixed exchange rate system all national inflation rates must eventually converge. This latter conclusion can be demonstrated by taking the time derivative of the logarithm of the purchasing power parity equation. This operation yields the result $p = x + p^*$ where p and p^* are the percentage rates of price inflation in the home and foreign country, respectively, and x is the percentage rate of change of the exchange rate. This result states that rates of inflation in the home country and the rest of the world can differ only by the proportional rate of change of the exchange rate. In a system of fixed exchange rates, however, the latter variable is zero and therefore the two inflation rates must converge. In short, with fixed exchange rates, countries cannot continually inflate at different rates.

A fourth policy implication, therefore, is that if a country wishes to choose its own inflation rate independent of the rest of the world it must operate with a flexible exchange rate. By letting its currency float, a country can gain control over its money supply and hence its rate of inflation. The logic behind this conclusion is straightforward. Floating exchange rates operate to maintain continuous equilibrium in a country's external accounts, thereby obviating the need for international money flows. It follows, therefore, that increases in the domestic money stock, instead of being diffused abroad through the balance of payments, will remain at home to induce equiproportional rises in the domestic price level. Note that the adjustment mechanism in the floating rate case differs markedly from that of a fixed rate regime. In the latter, money market equilibrium is restored by *quantity* adjustments, namely, international flows of money. In the former case, however, stock equilibrium is restored by *price* adjustments, namely, changes in the domestic price levels. To summarize, with the exchange rate floating so as to equilibrate the balance of payments, a nation's money stock becomes an exogenous variable which the authorities can control to achieve any rate of inflation they desire.

If a floating exchange rate permits a country to determine its own rate of inflation, then it also insulates that country from inflation originating abroad. Thus when a foreign nation inflates its money supply while the home country holds its currency constant, the resulting rise in the foreign price level will be offset by an equiproportional fall in the exchange rate, leaving domestic prices unchanged. Note, however, that this conclusion has an important corollary, namely, that under a flexible exchange rate a country must suffer the full consequences of its inflationary policies since it cannot export its inflation abroad.

It would be wrong to conclude from the above arguments that monetarists believe that flexible exchange rates are inherently superior to fixed rates. On the contrary, many monetarists are opposed to floating rates for at least two reasons. First, floating rates eliminate the risk-pooling and efficiency advantages of international money associated with fixed rates. Second, volatile exchange rates between currencies would tend to reduce the effectiveness of money as a social institution for economizing on the use of scarce resources in the production and dissemination of economic information.

It is on the basis of such arguments that some monetarists—e.g., Robert A. Mundell and Arthur Laffer—urge the restoration of a system of fixed exchange rates, with the rate of world monetary expansion being regulated by a world central bank. By contrast, other monetarists such as Milton Friedman, Harry G. Johnson, and David Laidler, while agreeing that volatile exchange rates introduce risk and inefficiency into the international economy, do not believe that a regime of institutionally fixed exchange rates is necessarily the best solution. According to these latter monetarists, floating rate volatility stems from domestic monetary policies that are erratic, variable, and divergent as between countries. This volatility, it is claimed, would be eliminated if all countries abandoned discretionary countercyclical monetary management for fixed monetary rules. The adoption of rules calling for a constant rate of domestic monetary expansion equal to the trend growth rate of real output supposedly would make the flexible rate virtually as stable as a rigidly fixed rate. Moreover, flexible rates have the added advantage of being determined by market forces, thus freeing governments to use their policy instruments in pursuit of purely domestic objectives.

It is apparent from the above that while monetarists agree that exchange rate stability is necessary for an efficiently operating international economy, they disagree on the equation of the most appropriate exchange rate regime. This disagreement is not as important as it appears, however, since all monetarists acknowledge that the key to exchange rate stability lies less in the way the foreign exchange market is organized than in finding a means of coordinating national monetary policies. True, the policy coordination problem has not been solved, although many solutions have been proposed (including the above-mentioned proposals of rules and a world central bank). But if and when it is solved, the exchange rate—whether fixed or floating—will be stable. And once the exchange rate is stabilized, inflation will again be an international rather than a national problem. This is because a stable rate of exchange between national currencies makes the sum of those currencies an economically relevant aggregate and also implies that national inflation rates will converge on a common (world) level.

LARGE COUNTRY IMPLICATIONS

The policy implications discussed in the preceding paragraphs refer to small open economies. As pointed out earlier, however, the implications are substantially different when the individual country is large relative to the rest of the world. The main difference concerns the ability of a country to control its own inflation rate under a system of fixed exchange rates. As noted earlier, in a fixed rate regime an individual country's domestic monetary expansion will affect its price level only indirectly by influencing the world money supply and the world price level. The strength of this influence is in direct proportion to the relative economic size of the country as measured by its share of the world money supply. For an individual small country this share is negligible and therefore so is the country's ability to influence its own price level. In sharp contrast, a large country's money stock forms a substantial proportion of the world money stock such that an expansion in the former stock will result in a significant expansion in the latter and, therefore, in the world and national price levels. Because of its size, the large country is able to indirectly regulate its own money stock and price level even in a world of fixed exchange rates. In this sense, a large country's money stock becomes an exogenous variable and its price level an endogenous one, which is just the reverse of the case for small countries.

Apart from sheer size, there is a second reason why a large country may be able to control its money supply even in a fixed rate regime. The country may be a *reserve currency country*, i.e., one whose currency is held by other countries as a form of international reserves. As previously mentioned, in a fixed rate world with no reserve currency country, nations can control the composition but not the quantity of their individual money stocks. According to the monetary theory of the balance of payments, an expansion in the controllable domestic credit component of a nation's money stock will result in a balance of payments deficit and an outflow of the uncontrollable international reserve component until the money stock returns to its initial level.

In the case of a reserve currency country, however, an expansion in the domestic credit portion of the money supply need not lead to an offsetting contraction in the international reserve component if the rest of the world holds its increased reserves in the form of government securities issued by the reserve currency country. Although the country runs a balance of payments deficit as a result of its domestic monetary expansion, its status as a reserve currency country enables it to effectively neutralize the impact of the payments deficit on its money supply. Thus despite the deficit, the authority is able to achieve an expansion of the money supply. Apparently such was the case in the last 1960s and early 1970s when the reserve currency status of the dollar enabled the U.S. to expand its money stock in the face of large external deficits. This latter experience indicates that the reserve currency case constitutes an important exception to the monetarist prediction that payments deficits tend to be accompanied by reductions in the nation's money stock.

SUMMARY

This appendix has expounded the global monetarist explanation of inflation within the framework of a simple two-country model that links national price levels, money stocks, money flows, spending, and the balance of payments. The model can account for the generation of world inflation under fixed exchange rates, for the transmission of that inflation to individual national economies, and for the distribution of world money necessary to support it in each nation. Typically monetarist, the model stresses the role of the demand for money in determining both the steady-state path of world prices and the dynamic adjustment to that path. The model also yields the standard predictions of the quantity theory, namely equiproportionality of money and prices, long-run neutrality of money, and the equilibrium international distribution of money. Moreover, it embodies the global monetarist conception of the international economy as a stable self-regulating mechanism in which monetary and payments disequilibria are inherently transitory phenomena. Finally, the model provides a framework for stating clearly the macroeconomic policy problems confronting small open economies.

NOTES

1. The model is presented by Dornbusch in [3]. See Mundell [4, Chapter 8; 5, Chapters 9, 10, 11, 12, 15] for an earlier and somewhat different treatment of the main elements of the model. The most complete description of the Dornbusch model appears in Whitman [7], who uses it to explain the global monetarist approach to the balance of payments. Swoboda [6] and Claassen [2] employ the Dornbusch model to analyze world inflation under fixed and flexible exchange rates, respectively. Also see Branson [1] for a similar approach. The present version follows Whitman and Swoboda closely.

2. A flexible exchange rate implies two distinct national money stocks and price levels separated by a variable exchange rate relationship between them, and therefore precludes any meaningful concept of a single world money stock and world price level.

3. Note that the derivation of this formula requires that the model be reinterpreted to allow for steady-state growth of the relevant variables. Accordingly, the equilibrium magnitudes of the variables are expressed not as absolute dollar levels but rather as constant percentage rates of change.

4. The rise in world prices also affects the home country, reducing but not eliminating the excess supply of money there. This latter result follows from the fact that world prices rise in proportion to the world, not the national, money stock. Since the home country's stock is but a fraction of the world stock, a given percentage change in the former corresponds to a smaller percentage change in the latter, and therefore in the world price level. In short, world prices will not rise sufficiently to eliminate the initial excess supply of money in the home country. The redundant money must be gotten rid of through the balance of payments.

REFERENCES

1. Branson, William H. "Monetarist and Keynesian Models of the Transmission of Inflation." *American Economic Review* 65 (May 1975), 115-19.

2. Claassen, Emil M. "World Inflation Under Flexible Exchange Rates." *Scandinavian Journal of Economics* 78, No. 2 (1976), 346-65.

3. Dornbusch, Rudiger. "Devaluation, Money, and Nontraded Goods." *American Economic Review* 63 (December 1973), 871-80.

4. Mundell, Robert A. *International Economics*. New York: Macmillan, 1968.

5. ——. *Monetary Theory: Inflation, Interest, and Growth in the World Economy*. Pacific Palisades: Goodyear, 1971.

6. Swoboda, Alexander K. "Monetary Approaches to the Transmission and Generation of Worldwide Inflation." Geneva: Graduate Institute of International Studies, 1975. (Mimeographed.)

7. Whitman, Marina v.N. "Global Monetarism and the Monetary Approach to the Balance of Payments." *Brookings Papers on Economic Activity* 6, No. 3 (1975), 491-536.

III

OPEN ECONOMY UNDER FLOATING EXCHANGE RATES

7

FROM FIXED TO FLOATING EXCHANGE RATES IN THE MONETARY APPROACH

THE COMMON ANALYTICAL FRAMEWORK

The preceding chapters have dealt with the monetary approach to the balance of payments under fixed exchange rates. By contrast, the chapters that follow extend the monetary approach to the case of freely floating exchange rate regimes. As pointed out by Bilson,[1] Mussa,[2] and Parkin,[3] this extension is easily accomplished, since both the fixed and floating exchange rate versions of the monetary approach stem from the same analytical framework. That framework identifies excess money supplies and demands as the proximate cause of international balance of payments and exchange rate adjustment and specifies such adjustment as the means by which monetary equilibrium is restored. The framework distinguishes between two channels of adjustment, namely reserve flows through the balance of payments and exchange rate changes, respectively. Each adjustment channel or combination of channels corresponds to a different exchange rate regime. For example, under fixed exchange rates adjustment occurs through reserve flows through the balance of payments, whereas under freely floating exchange rates it occurs through exchange rate movements. Finally, in a regime of managed or "dirty" floating, adjustment occurs both through the balance of payments *and* through exchange rate channels.

The purpose of this chapter is to outline the common analytical framework underlying the monetary approach and to indicate how it can be adapted to explain international monetary adjustment under floating as well as fixed exchange rates. In so doing, the chapter introduces the third and final section of the book, namely the section dealing with the monetary approach to the small open economy operating under freely floating exchange rates. Before proceeding to the floating rate case, however, it is useful to review the fixed rate version of the basic monetary framework.

ADJUSTMENT IN A FIXED EXCHANGE RATE REGIME

Under a system of fixed exchange rates, in which the government is obligated to buy and sell foreign exchange with its own currency in order to maintain the exchange rate at the fixed parity, adjustment occurs through the balance of payments. Thus a rise in money demand and/or fall in money supply such that actual cash balances fall short of desired cash balances induces a balance of payments surplus as cashholders seek to obtain money from abroad in exchange for exports of goods and securities. The balance of payments surplus puts downward pressure on the price of foreign exchange, contrary to the commitment to maintain fixed exchange rates. To prevent the exchange rate from appreciating, the monetary authority purchases foreign exchange, thereby expanding the foreign reserve component of the money supply. Via the balance of payments surplus and the associated inflow of foreign reserves, the money stock expands until actual cash balances equal desired cash balances and monetary equilibrium is restored. In this manner, the initial deficiency of money is eliminated by an induced inflow of foreign exchange reserves through the balance of payments.

Conversely, under fixed exchange rates an initial excess supply of money would induce a balance of payments deficit as domestic cashholders attempt to get rid of the excess money by spending it for foreign goods and securities. To prevent the external deficit from depreciating the exchange rate (that is, to maintain the fixed parity in the face of the deficit), the authorities would sell foreign exchange, thereby reducing the foreign source component of the money stock. Via the balance of payments deficit and the associated outflow of foreign exchange reserves, the money stock would contract until the excess supply of money is eliminated and monetary equilibrium is restored. In both cases, monetary adjustment occurs via reserve flows through the balance of payments.

ADJUSTMENT IN A FLOATING EXCHANGE RATE REGIME

In the case of floating exchange rates, adjustment occurs through exchange rate changes and not through foreign exchange reserve flows through the balance of payments. Adjustment cannot occur through the latter channel since exchange rate changes maintain continuous equilibrium in the balance of payments, thereby precluding changes in foreign reserves. More precisely, by continuously clearing the market for foreign exchange, exchange rate variations prevent balance of payments disequilibria and thereby forestall international reserve flows. With reserve flows ruled out, actual cash balances are adjusted to desired cash balances by exchange rate changes that alter the valuation of the money stock. That is, exchange rate variations equilibrate money supply and demand by adjusting the real value of the money stock to the level that people desire to hold. Thus a rise in money demand and/or fall in money supply such that actual cash balances fall short of desired cash balances induces a decrease in spending and an incipient balance of payments surplus that is eliminated by an immediate appreciation of the exchange rate. The resulting fall in the exchange rate restores monetary equilibrium by increasing the real value of the domestic money stock to the level people desire to hold. In short, an initial excess demand for money is eliminated by an induced appreciation of the exchange rate.

Conversely, an initial excess supply of money would induce an exchange rate depreciation that would eliminate the monetary excess by reducing the real value of the nominal money stock to the level desired by cashholders. Adjustment occurs through exchange depreciation, because with floating rates money cannot leak out into foreign trade. Instead, the increased spending induced by the initial excess supply of money stays at home to put upward pressure on all prices, including the price of foreign exchange. The resulting rise in the exchange rate restores monetary equilibrium by reducing the real value of the nominal money stock to the level people desire to hold. To summarize, in a floating rate regime exchange rate changes themselves provide the mechanism through which the demand for money is adjusted to the given money supply.

ADJUSTMENT IN A REGIME OF MANAGED FLOATING

Finally, under a regime of controlled (managed) floating, adjustment occurs both through the balance of payments *and* through exchange rates. In such a regime, the authorities intervene in the foreign exchange market to control exchange rate fluctuations without attempting to maintain absolutely fixed exchange rates. As before, shifts in money supply and demand such that actual cash balances differ from desired cash balances will put pressure on the exchange rate. The authorities must decide how much of this pressure is to be relieved through exchange rate movements and how much through reserve flows. Assuming the authorities assign part of the adjustment to exchange rates and part to reserves, both variables will change and both will contribute to the restoration of monetary equilibrium.

In sum, the common analytical framework underlying the monetary approach applies equally to all exchange rate regimes and specifies the particular adjustment mechanism used by each regime. To see this, a formal algebraic statement of the common monetary model may be of use.

COMMON ANALYTICAL MODEL

The common monetary model that underlies the fixed, floating, and managed exchange rate versions of the monetary approach can be summarized succinctly. The model assumes a single small open economy producing a composite good which it trades with the rest of the world. In its simplest form the model consists of four components, namely

1. a money demand function linking the demand for money to real income and the interest rate;
2. a money supply identity defining the money stock in terms of its domestic and foreign source components;
3. a purchasing power parity relationship linking domestic prices to world prices via the exchange rate; and
4. a monetary equilibrium condition expressing equality between money supply and demand.

The model is written as follows:

(1) $D = D(Y, i)$

(2) $M = R + C$

(3) $P = EP_w$

(4) $M/P = D$ or $M = DP$

where

D = real money demand (i.e., desired quantity of real cash balances),

Y = real income (assumed to be exogenously given at the full capacity level of output),

i = nominal interest rate,

M = nominal money stock,

R = foreign exchange reserves (i.e., the foreign source component of the money stock),

C = domestic credit component of the money stock,

P = domestic price level,

E = exchange rate, and

P_w = world price level.

Equation (1) expresses the public's demand for real cash balances D as a function of the level of real income Y (a proxy for the transaction demand for money) and interest rates i (the opportunity cost of holding money instead of earning assets). Equation (2) defines the nominal money stock M as the sum of its foreign reserve R and domestic credit C components, this definition resulting from a consolidation of the balance sheets of the central bank and the commercial banking system. More precisely, equation (2) states the basic balance sheet accounting identity that the banking sector's monetary liabilities M must by definition equal the sum of its foreign and domestic assets, denoted by R and C, respectively. Equation (3) is the purchasing power parity equation linking domestic prices P to world prices P_w via the exchange rate E. This equation expresses the purchasing power parity condition or law of one price, according to which commodity arbitrage renders the real price of goods everywhere the same stated in terms of a common currency so that there exists no advantage to purchasing in one market over the other. Finally, equation (4) states the monetary equilibrium condition according to which the real (price deflated) value of the given nominal money stock equals the real demand for it, thereby clearing the market for real cash balances. Note that the monetary equilibrium condition also implies that actual nominal cash balances M equal desired nominal cash balances (that is, desired real balances D times the price level P) such that all money is willingly held.

Substituting equations (1) through (3) into (4) yields

$$(5) \quad R + C = D(Y, i)EP_w$$

which expresses equality between nominal money supply (in terms of its foreign and domestic source components) and nominal money demand (measured in terms of world prices converted into domestic prices at the equilibrium rate of exchange). Depending upon the exchange rate regime, this equality is maintained by changes in two variables, namely foreign exchange reserves R, the exchange rate E, or a combination of both. To see this, consider what would happen in the equation if there occurred a shift in money supply or demand due to exogenous changes in domestic credit C, real income Y, nominal interest rates i, and world prices P_w.

Under fixed exchange rates, the exchange rate E is a fixed constant, and variations in reserves R operate to maintain monetary equilibrium. Thus, changes in money supply or demand resulting from exogenous shifts in the underlying variables C, Y, i, and P_w would induce offsetting changes in R through the balance of payments. As predicted by the monetary model, these reserve flows would operate to maintain equality between both sides of equation (5). By contrast, under floating exchange rates, reserves R are a fixed constant, and the exchange rate E varies to maintain monetary equilibrium. In the floating rate case, changes in money supply and demand owing to autonomous shifts in the underlying variables C, Y, i, and P_w induce compensating changes in the exchange rate, and these changes work to keep both sides of equation (5) in balance. Finally, under a regime of controlled (managed) floating, the monetary authority chooses a combination of exchange rate changes and reserve flows to keep equation (5) in balance. In this manner, exogenous shifts in the underlying determinants of money supply and demand induce compensating changes in the variables R and E, and these latter changes act to restore monetary equilibrium as required by equation (5). As summarized in equation (5), the common monetary model holds for all exchange rate regimes.

ELABORATION OF THE FLOATING RATE VERSION OF THE MONETARY APPROACH

The general analytical framework underlying the monetary approach having been covered, the remainder of this volume concentrates on the freely floating rate version of the framework, examining its constituent components, its economic content, its policy implications, its alleged deficiencies, and especially its evolution over time in the history of monetary controversy.

More precisely, the plan for the rest of the book is as follows: Chapter 8 refines and extends the simple floating exchange rate monetary model presented above to include supply and demand equations for foreign as well as domestic money stocks. The chapter also incorporates exchange rate expectations into the model and shows how those expectations are formulated consistent with the exchange rate to three groups of factors, namely (1) relative national money stocks, (2) relative real incomes, and (3) relative nominal interest rates reflecting relative expected future rates of money growth per unit of real money demand, respectively. Chapter 9 then empirically tests this equation by fitting it to the statistical data on selected exchange rates under the assumption that exchange rate expectations are proxied by nominal interest rate differentials.

Chapter 10 traces the origin and historical evolution of the floating rate version of the monetary approach through three famous policy debates. The chapter demonstrates that the monetary approach has a long history, that it played a key role in eighteenth-, nineteenth-, and twentieth-century exchange rate controversies, and that virtually all of its components had been fully recognized and integrated into a coherent monetary framework by the early 1920s. One of these components, of course, is the purchasing power parity doctrine. Chapter 11 focuses specifically on this doctrine, spelling out its logic, content, and policy implications, as well as identifying the contributions of H. Thornton, J. Wheatley, G. Cassel, and C. Bresciani-Turroni to the development of the doctrine.

In addition to the purchasing power parity doctrine, other components of the modern monetary approach include (1) the asset market view of short-run exchange rate behavior, (2) the role of expectations in exchange rate determination, and (3) the rational expectations hypothesis concerning the way people formulate exchange rate expectations consistent with the predictions of the monetary model itself. Chapter 12 discusses these elements and shows that they were well recognized and clearly described by such earlier twentieth-century monetary theorists as G. Cassel, D. H. Robertson, and L. von Mises. In particular, with respect to the asset market and rational expectations components, Chapter 12 demonstrates that Robertson contributed insights remarkably suggestive of recent work. His contributions, although virtually ignored in recent accounts of the monetary approach, mark him as an important early proponent of that approach.

A basic criticism of the monetary approach is that it ignores the influence of real relative price changes on the exchange rate. In particular, it allegedly ignores the effects of changes in the real terms of trade and internal relative prices, respectively, and therefore cannot account for real shocks affecting the exchange rate through these nonmonetary channels. Chapter 13 evaluates this criticism and shows that it can be forestalled by incorporating a real exchange rate component into the monetary approach. The result is an augmented monetary model that captures all factors, real as well as monetary, affecting exchange rates. Chapter 13 constructs such a model and uses it to interpret certain characteristic features and policy implications of observed exchange rate behavior in the post-1973 period of generalized floating.

Finally, Chapter 14 summarizes the succession of exchange rate models employed in the historical development of the monetary approach. The chapter shows how each successive model augmented and enriched the monetary approach, reinforcing its basic conclusion that exchange rates are largely determined by factors affecting money supplies and demands.

NOTES

1. John F. O. Bilson, "Recent Developments in Monetary Models of Exchange Rate Determination," *IMF Staff Papers* 26 (June 1979):201–23.

2. Michael Mussa, "The Exchange Rate, the Balance of Payments and Monetary and Fiscal Policy under a Regime of Controlled Floating," *Scandinavian Journal of Economics* 78 (May 1976):229–48.

3. Michael Parkin, "Comment on M. Mussa, 'The Exchange Rate, the Balance of Payments and Monetary and Fiscal Policy under a Regime of Controlled Floating," *Scandinavian Journal of Economics* 78 (May 1976):249–54.

8

THE MONETARY APPROACH TO EXCHANGE RATE DETERMINATION

Historically, interest in the monetary approach to exchange rates tends to revive when countries switch from fixed to floating exchange rate regimes. This pattern is evident in the most recent revival of the monetary approach, a revival dating from early 1973, when the major nations of the world decided to let their currencies float, jointly or individually. These actions marked the end of the old Bretton Woods system of pegged exchange rates and inaugurated the post-Bretton Woods era of generalized floating. Since then, exchange rates have exhibited sharp fluctuations both on a short-run (weekly, monthly, quarterly) and a longer-run (yearly) basis.

Among the explanations advanced to account for these fluctuations is the monetary approach, which views national monetary policies as the primary factor directly or indirectly influencing exchange rates. As usually presented, the monetary approach emphasizes:

- that the exchange rate (by definition the relative price of two national monies) is determined by demands for and supplies of those national money stocks;
- that it reaches its equilibrium level when both money stocks are willingly held;
- that as an asset price it is subject to the same influences as other asset prices (such as stock prices);
- that it is particularly sensitive to expectations about future exchange rates,

expectations that are heavily conditioned by current monetary policy and other indicators of the likely course of future monetary policy;

- that it reflects all available information about the two currencies and therefore alters in response to new information about changed circumstances.

In accord with this view, proponents of the monetary approach contend that the observed short-run volatility of exchange rates stems largely from monetary policies that are variable and erratic. Unexpected policy changes, so the argument goes, have induced asset holders to alter their expectations of future monetary policies and hence future exchange rates, thereby resulting in large movements in current observed exchange rates. Over the longer run, however, the main factor allegedly contributing to exchange rate movements is lack of policy coordination among nations, as manifested by divergent rates of monetary growth. Proponents of the monetary approach contend that this factor produces international differential inflation rates that constitute the primary source of persistent exchange rate movements. The implication is that the best way to achieve exchange rate stability is for countries to abandon monetary fine-tuning for policy rules calling for uniform constant rates of monetary growth per unit of trend real output.

The foregoing views derive from a specific analytical framework underlying the monetary approach. This chapter presents one version of this framework and discusses its public policy implications. The framework itself is represented in the form of a simple two-country, seven-equation expository model of exchange rate determination.[1] This model has a long history dating back at least 175 years. A rudimentary version of it was first used by David Ricardo, John Wheatley, and other classical economists to explain the fall of the paper pound following Britain's shift from fixed to floating exchange rates during the Napoleonic wars. Later it was employed by the Swedish economist Gustav Cassel to explain the fall of the German mark during World War I and afterward in the famous hyperinflation of the early 1920s. In fact, the model, in one form or another, has been at the center of monetarist policy discussion and analysis whenever flexible exchange rates have been in operation.[2] Applied to recent experience, the model is potentially capable of explaining both long- and short-term movements in exchange rates. In particular, it is capable of explaining why exchange rates have been so volatile and why expectational influences have caused them to deviate from levels suggested by underlying rates of monetary and real output growth alone.

KEY PROPOSITIONS

Central to the model are six ingredients that should be identified at the outset. These include (1) the quantity theory of money, (2) the purchasing power parity doctrine, (3) the real interest rate parity concept, (4) the Fisher relationship (named for the American economist Irving Fisher who first formulated it) between nominal and real interest rates, (5) a monetarist rational expectations hypothesis, and (6) the efficient markets hypothesis.

The quantity theory states that the price level clears the market for money balances by deflating the real value of the nominal money stock to the level people desire to hold. Given the real demand for money, this means that the price level varies equiproportionally with the money stock such that a doubling, say, of the quantity of money produces a corresponding doubling of the price level.

The purchasing power parity doctrine states that the equilibrium exchange rate must equal the ratio of domestic to foreign general price levels. This condition ensures that the real price of goods expressed in terms of a common currency unit is everywhere the same, so that there exists no advantage to buying in one market over another. Likewise, the doctrine also implies that the real value (purchasing power) of money is everywhere the same—that is, that a unit of either currency commands the same quantity of real goods and services abroad after conversion into the other currency at the equilibrium exchange rate as it commands at home. Such equalization of the real value or purchasing power of money is a necessary prerequisite for international monetary equilibrium. By eliminating profitable opportunities for commodity arbitrage and the associated incentive to switch from low- to high-value currencies, it ensures that existing stocks of both currencies will be willingly held and that the markets for real cash balances in both countries will clear simultaneously. Similar reasoning underlies the real interest rate parity concept, which states that the real rate of return on capital assets tends to be the same everywhere and independent of the currency denomination of the asset.

The Fisher relationship states that the nominal interest rate equals the given real rate of interest plus the expected rate of inflation. Taken together, the Fisher relationship and the real interest rate parity concept imply that international nominal interest rate differentials reflect differential anticipated rates of inflation in the two countries.

The monetarist rational expectations hypothesis states that the public forms its expectations of future inflation consistent with the way inflation is actually generated in the economy. Thus, if inflation is actually generated by excessive monetary growth per unit of real money demand, then inflationary expectations will be generated by predictions of future demand-adjusted monetary growth based on predictions of the likely future course of monetary policy. Finally, the efficient markets hypothesis asserts that these predictions will embody all available information about prospective events likely to affect future monetary growth and that the predictions will be revised instantaneously to incorporate new information. Constituting the central analytical core of the monetary approach to exchange rate determination, the foregoing propositions are embodied in the model presented below.

THE MODEL AND ITS COMPONENTS

The model itself consists of two hypothetical national economies represented by a set of equations containing the following variables: Let M be the nominal money stock (assumed to be exogenously determined by the central bank) and m the demand-adjusted rate of growth of that stock, that is, the difference between the respective growth rates of the nominal money supply and real money demand, this difference by definition being equal to the rate of price inflation. Furthermore, let D be the real demand for money, that is, the stock of real (price-deflated) cash balances that the public desires to hold, Y the exogenously-determined level of real income, and i and r the nominal and real rates of interest, respectively. Also let E be the exchange rate (defined as the domestic currency price of a unit of foreign currency), P be the price level, p^e and m^e the expected future rates of price inflation and demand-adjusted money growth, respectively, and I the information used in formulating those expectations. Asterisks are used to distinguish foreign-country variables from home-country variables, and the subscript w refers to the entire world economy. The foregoing variables are linked together via the relationships described below.

MONETARY EQUILIBRIUM EQUATIONS

The first part of the model consists of monetary equilibrium equations, one for each country

(1) $P = M/D$ and $P^* = M^*/D^*$.

These equations, which can also be written in the form $M/P = D$, state that the price level in each country adjusts to bring the real (price-deflated) value of the nominal money stock into equality with the real demand for it, thereby clearing the market for real cash balances. This market-clearing price-adjustment process relies chiefly on equilibrating changes in aggregate expenditure induced by discrepancies between actual and desired real balances. For example, if actual balances exceed the desired level, cashholders will attempt to get rid of the excess via spending for goods. The increased spending for an exogenously given level of real output exerts upward pressure on prices, however, thereby reducing the real value of the money stock to the level the public wishes to hold. Conversely, a shortfall between actual and desired real balances will induce a cut in expenditures leading to a fall in prices and a corresponding rise in the real value of the money stock. This process will continue until actual real balances are brought into equality with desired real balances. Note that the equations also imply that, given the real demand for money, the price level is determined by and varies equiproportionally with the nominal money supply. This latter result, of course, is the essence of the quantity theory of money. For that reason, the equations could also be called quantity theory equations.

REAL CASH BALANCE EQUATIONS

Aggregate real demand-for-money functions constitute the second part of the model. Written as follows

(2) $D = KYi^{-a}$ and $D^* = K^*Y^*i^{*-a}$

these equations express the public's demand for real cash balances as the product of a fixed constant K and two variables, namely real income and the nominal interest rate. The income variable is a proxy for the volume of real transactions effected with the aid of money and thus represents the transactions demand for money. By contrast, the interest rate variable measures the opportunity cost of holding money instead of earning assets. The parameter $-a$, which appears as the exponent on the interest rate variable, is the interest elasticity of demand for money. It measures the sensitivity or responsiveness of money demand to changes in the interest rate and is assumed to be a negative number indicating that the quantity of real balances that people desire to hold varies inversely with the cost of holding them. For expositional simplicity, the numerical magnitude of the interest elasticity parameter is assumed to be the same for both countries. For the same reason, the income elasticity of demand for money, as represented by the exponential power to which the income variable is raised, is assumed to possess a numerical value of unity.

PURCHASING POWER PARITY EQUATION

The third equation of the model is the purchasing power parity relationship

(3) $P = EP^*$

showing how national general price levels are linked together via the exchange rate. As indicated by the equation, prices in both countries are identical when converted into a common currency unit at the equilibrium exchange rate. This means that the exchange rate equalizes such common-currency price levels and, by implication, the buying power of both moneys expressed in terms of a common unit. In other words, exchange rate adjustment ensures that a unit of a given currency commands the same quantity of goods and services abroad when converted into the other currency at the equilibrium exchange rate as it commands at home. This condition of equalized purchasing power is of course necessary if the two national money stocks are to be willingly held and monetary equilibrium is to prevail in both countries. For if the purchasing powers were unequal, people would demand more of the high- and less of the low-purchasing power currency on the foreign exchanges. The resulting excess demand for the former currency and the corresponding excess supply of the latter would force the exchange rate between the two currencies to adjust until purchasing power was equalized and no advantage existed to converting from one currency into the other. Only then would monetary equilibrium prevail across countries, ensuring that both money stocks are willingly held. Note also that the purchasing power parity equation can be rearranged to read $E = P/P^*$, thus corresponding to the economic interpretation of the exchange rate as the relative price of the two currencies, that is, as the ratio of the foreign currency's internal value in terms of goods to the domestic country's internal value in terms of goods. Since the internal value of a unit of currency in terms of a composite market basket of commodities is the inverse of the general price level 1/P, it follows that the relative price of the two moneys is simply the ratio of national price levels as indicated by the equation.

NOMINAL INTEREST RATE EQUATIONS

The fourth group of relationships in the model are the nominal interest rate equations, one for each country

(4) $i = r + p^e$ and $i^* = r^* + p^{e*}$.

Following Irving Fisher, these equations define the nominal interest rate as the sum of the real rate of interest and the expected future rate of inflation, the latter variable being the premium added to real yields to prevent their erosion by inflation.

REAL INTEREST RATE PARITY CONDITION

The fifth equation expresses the real interest rate parity condition

(5) $r = r^* = r_w$

according to which the real rate of return on capital assets tends to be the same everywhere and independent of the currency denomination of the assets. This equation reflects the global monetarist assumption of a highly integrated efficient world capital market. In such a world, capital is mobile internationally, that is, foreigners can purchase domestic securities and domestic citizens can purchase foreign securities. Given these conditions, it follows that real yield equalization is necessary if all asset stocks are to be willingly held. Accordingly, the equation states that real interest rates in both countries are the same and are equal to a given constant world rate. Taken together, equations (4) and (5) imply that international nominal interest rate differentials reflect differences in expected future national rates of inflation. For example, if the market expects the future rate of inflation to be 12 percent in the United Kingdom and 5 percent in the United States, then the U.K. nominal interest rate will be 7 percentage points above the corresponding U.S. interest rate.

PRICE EXPECTATIONS EQUATIONS

Completing the model are the sixth and seventh equations, which together explain how the public forms its anticipations of the future rate of inflation. These inflationary expectations constitute the anticipated future rates of depreciation of money holdings. As such, they enter the foreign and domestic demand for money functions via the nominal interest rate variables and thereby play an important role in exchange rate determination. Regarding the formation of price anticipations, equation (6) states that inflationary expectations are based on what the public believes the future rate of demand-adjusted money growth will be. Written as follows

$$(6)\quad p^e = m^e \text{ and } p^{e*} = m^{e*}$$

where p^e and m^e denote inflationary price expectations and anticipated future money growth per unit of real money demand, respectively, these equations embody the so-called *rational expectations hypothesis*, according to which the public's predictions of future inflation are the same as those yielded by the actual inflation-generating mechanism represented in the model. This rational expectations assumption ensures that the model is internally consistent, that is, that the equations describing the formation of inflationary anticipations are consistent with equations describing how price inflation is actually generated. Such consistency is characteristic of the forecasting behavior of rational agents who use knowledge of the actual inflation-generating process in forming expectations of future inflation. Since the model asserts that the actual rate of price inflation is produced by demand-adjusted money growth—see equation (1)—it follows that expected inflation is generated by the anticipated future value of that same variable as shown in equation (6).

ANTICIPATED MONEY GROWTH EQUATION

Equation (6) says that prospective inflation depends on prospective future money growth per unit of money demand. This, of course, means that the public must forecast the future rate of demand-adjusted monetary growth in order to forecast the future rate of inflation. Equation (7) suggests how money growth forecasts are formulated. Written as follows

$$(7)\quad m^e = m^e(m, I) \text{ and } m^{e*} = m^{e*}(m*, I*)$$

where m^e and m are expected and actual money growth rates per unit of real money demand and I is other information used in forming expectations, these equations embody the assumption that people formulate expectations rationally, using all available information in predicting future monetary growth and revising those predictions as new information appears. Relevant information might include new policy pronouncements, imminent political and economic changes expected to have a bearing on future money growth, recent and current behavior of the monetary aggregates, past observations on the policymaker's response to changes in the economy, and the like. In equation (7), the information input is represented by two variables, namely current demand-adjusted monetary growth m and all other information I. The model does not attempt to explain precisely how money growth forecasts are derived from this information. It simply assumes that the forecasts are somehow made, that they constitute the most accurate predictions possible given the state of the public's knowledge and the availability of information regarding likely future monetary growth, and that they form the basis for future price anticipations. In this regard, note that the substitution of equation (7) into equation (6) yields the efficient markets hypothesis that the price expectations embodied in the exchange rate reflect all available information concerning it.

LINKAGES AND CAUSATION

Taken together, the foregoing relationships constitute a simple seven-equation system that embodies the modern monetary approach to exchange rate determination. The equations imply two unidirectional channels of influence—one direct, the other indirect—running from money and real income (both exogenous variables) to prices and the exchange rate. Regarding the former channel, the model implies that money and income affect the exchange rate directly through the monetary equilibrium and purchasing power parity equations. Reverse causation is ruled out by the assumed exogeneity of money and real income. As for the indirect channel, the model implies that the anticipated future growth rates of money and real income influence the exchange rate through the price-expectations component of the nominal interest rate variable in the demand for money function. More specifically, the model postulates the following causal chain:

1. currently observed demand-adjusted monetary growth and other exogenous information influences predictions of future demand-adjusted monetary growth;
2. predictions of future demand-adjusted monetary growth determine the expected rate of inflation;
3. given the exogenously-determined real rate of interest, the expected rate of inflation determines the nominal rate of interest;
4. the latter variable, together with the given level of real income, determines the demand for money;
5. given the demand for money, the nominal money stock determines the price level;
6. finally, the two price levels, foreign and domestic, together determine the exchange rate.

In brief, when the expected future demand-adjusted money growth rate rises, price expectations also rise, and so too does the nominal interest rate (the cost of holding money). This reduces the quantity of real cash balances that people desire to hold, that is, cash-holders will want to get out of money and into goods. The resulting increased spending for goods puts upward pressure on domestic prices, causing them to rise relative to foreign prices. With domestic prices getting out of line with foreign prices, however, the exchange rate must rise to restore purchasing power parity. The exchange rate will be bidded up by an excess demand for foreign exchange as people seek to convert domestic into foreign currency for the purpose of making cheaper purchases abroad. The same would happen if cash-holders initially sought to spend their excess cash balances on foreign instead of domestic goods. The resulting rush to convert domestic into foreign currency would quickly drive up the exchange rate and with it the domestic currency price of foreign goods. Either way prices and the exchange rate will continue to rise until the real (price-corrected) value of the nominal money stock is deflated to the level people desire to hold and the discrepancy between actual and desired real cash balances is eliminated.

Clearly, in the model presented here, the linkages run from actual and expected money stocks and real incomes to prices and the exchange rate. Moreover, all variables determining the exchange rate do so through monetary channels, that is, through the demand for and supply of money. In this sense, money demand and supply may be said to constitute the *proximate* determinants of the exchange rate. The *ultimate* determinants, however, are the variables that underlie and determine the monetary factors themselves.

DETERMINANTS OF THE EXCHANGE RATE

To show the relationship between the exchange rate and its ultimate determinants, simply substitute equations (1) to (2) and (4) to (7) into equation (3) and solve for the exchange rate. The resulting reduced form expression is

$$(8)\quad E = (K/K^*)\,(M/M^*)\,(Y^*/Y)\,(i/i^*)^a$$

or, since the nominal interest rate i is the sum of the real interest rate r and the expected rate of inflation p^e—the latter variable being equal to the anticipated future growth rate of money per unit of money demand m^e—the equation can be alternatively expressed as

$$(8')\quad E = \left[\frac{K^*}{K}\right]\left[\frac{M}{M^*}\right]\left[\frac{Y^*}{Y}\right]\left[\frac{r + m^e(m, I)}{r^* + m^{e*}(m^*, I^*)}\right]^a$$

Disregarding the fixed constants (the Ks), equation (8)—or (8′)—collects the determinants of the exchange rate into three groups, namely relative money supplies, relative real incomes, and relative nominal interest rates comprised of a fixed real rate component and a variable price expectations component. Of these three groups, the first captures the direct monetary influences on the exchange rate, while the second and third capture real and expectational influences, respectively.

Regarding direct monetary influences, the equation predicts that, all else being equal, the country with the faster monetary growth will find its currency depreciating on the foreign exchanges. As for the second group of determinants, the equation predicts that, everything else being equal, the country with the faster growth of real income and hence real demand for money will experience an appreciating exchange rate. Note that the conclusion that rapid real growth results in currency appreciation contradicts the conventional trade balance view of exchange rate determination. According to this latter view, income growth tends to depreciate a country's currency by inducing a rise in imports and a consequent trade balance deficit. By contrast, the monetary approach depicts real growth as stimulating the demand for the country's money (and thereby generating a capital account surplus that more than offsets the trade balance deficit). Given the nominal money stock, this increased real money demand necessitates a fall in the price level to clear the market for money balances. With foreign prices given, the fall in domestic prices requires an equivalent appreciation of the exchange rate to maintain purchasing power parity. In short, the model predicts that real growth-induced rises in the real demand for money will raise the internal, and therefore also the external, value of a currency.

As for expectational influences, the equation predicts that the country with the poorer inflationary prospects will have a depreciating exchange rate. That is, a rise in the expected rate of inflation in one country (as reflected in its interest rate) relative to the other will cause the former's currency to depreciate on the foreign exchanges. There are two reasons for this. First, people will desire to hold relatively less of the currency whose value is expected to fall the most. Therefore the relative asset demand for that currency will fall and the exchange rate will depreciate—assuming, of course, that no compensating changes occur in relative money supplies. Second, contracts will tend to be written in terms of the currency that is expected to depreciate the least, that is, the stronger currency will be preferred to the weaker as an international unit of account, standard of value, and medium of exchange. The resulting fall in the relative transactions demand for the weaker currency will reduce its value on the foreign exchanges. In short, an anticipated depreciation of a currency will reduce both the asset and transactions demand for it, thereby helping to bring about the very depreciation that is anticipated. Note, however, that such anticipations are not independent of currently observable monetary policies—(represented by the variables m and m* in equation (8′)—but are strongly conditioned by them. Thus, within the context of the model, at least, observations of unrestrained monetary expansion will produce expectations of more of the same, thereby contributing to the weakness of the currency on the foreign exchanges. Conversely, observed monetary stability will help create the favorable expectations that contribute to a currency's strength.

The preceding discussion gives some indication of the importance that modern monetarists attach to the role of expectations in determining exchange rates. Corresponding to this emphasis on expectations, equation (8′) specifies divergent inflationary prospects as the reason why exchange rates often deviate from levels suggested by relative money stocks and relative real incomes alone. According to the equation, the exchange rate will conform to the level suggested by these variables only when inflationary expectations are the same in both countries. In this special case, expected future rates of return on both currency holdings are identical and cancel out, and the exchange rate is determined solely by relative money stocks and real incomes. In all other cases, however, differential expected inflation rates influence the exchange rate and cause it to deviate from the level predicted by the money and income determinants.

Finally, it should be noted that the model's prediction of a direct relationship between interest rate movements and exchange rate movements runs counter to the conventional balance of payments view. According to this latter approach, a rising interest rate should lower the exchange rate either by attracting capital from abroad (thereby improving the capital account of the balance of payments) or by reducing domestic expenditure for imports and potential exports (thereby improving the current account). This cannot happen in the present model where, instead of improving the balance of payments, a rising interest rate induces a shift from cash to goods resulting in domestic inflation and exchange rate depreciation. In short, equation (8′) predicts that a country will experience exchange rate depreciation when its relative money stock rises, its relative income falls, and its relative inflationary expectations rise.

SOURCES OF EXCHANGE RATE VOLATILITY

Equation (8′) would be of little interest to analysts and policymakers were it incapable of explaining other characteristic of recent floating rate experience, namely exchange rate volatility. Fortunately, however, the equation can account for such behavior and does so by identifying two main sources of exchange rate movements. The first is shifts in relative money supplies (M/M^*) owing to monetary policies that are variable and divergent as between countries. For example, oscillatory movements in the exchange rate could be produced by two countries engaging in discretionary countercyclical monetary policy but always in opposite directions. A's money stock expanding when B's contracts, and vice versa.

The second source of exchange rate volatility identified by equation (8′) is expectational shifts occasioned by the appearance of new information—such as announced changes in policy targets—about future monetary policies affecting the future prospects for various currencies. The new information leads the market to revise its opinion about the future costs and returns from holding the different currencies. Reflecting these expectational shifts, exchange rates alter until the existing stocks of the various currencies are again willingly held. Note that exchange rates are no different than stock or equity prices in this respect. Just as the price of a firm's stock at any moment reflects all available information about the future profitability of the firm, so also does an exchange rate embody all known information about the future values of two currencies. New information that alters the market's perception of these future values will result in sudden changes in exchange rates, just as new information about future firm profitability causes sharp shifts in a stock's price. Both are special cases of the general rule that, given new information about changed circumstances, the market price of any asset—whether bond, equity share, or foreign exchange—must change until the outstanding stock of the asset is willingly held.

A third possible source of exchange rate instability is variations in relative real incomes (Y^*/Y). This factor is deemphasized, however, by monetarists who believe it to be dominated by shifts in relative money stocks and relative inflationary expectations.

POLICY IMPLICATIONS

This chapter has presented a monetarist model that specifies relative money stocks and relative inflationary expectations as key determinants of exchange rates and stresses the role of monetary policy in influencing these determinants. Specifically, the model postulates that money stocks are exogenously controlled by national central banks and that the public's expectations about the future purchasing power of various currencies are strongly influenced by current policy actions and announcements. Several policy implications follow from the model. Before discussing these implications, however, it is well to remember that they reflect the particular assumptions underlying the model and that some of these assumptions are disputable. This is especially true of the assumptions of purchasing power parity, real interest rate parity, rational expectations, and real income exogeneity. While these conditions may hold in long-run equilibrium, empirical evidence suggests that they may not hold over any realistic short-run policy horizon nor over the transitional adjustment period following economic shocks. Moreover, as shown in Chapter 13, the model also abstracts from changes in the *terms of trade* and *internal relative prices*, both of which may produce persistant deviations from purchasing power parity. Recognition of this fact would probably modify any policy prescriptions based upon the model. Subject to these caveats, the policy implications of the model are summarized below.

The first implication is that, given the rate of foreign money growth, the most effective means of halting and reversing a depreciation of the exchange rate is a preannounced permanent reduction in the rate of growth of the domestic money stock. As new information, the announcement itself will have an immediate impact on the exchange rate through the price expectations channel. For this impact to be anything more than temporary, however, the public must be convinced that the announced target is a reliable indicator of the future rate of monetary expansion. To convince the public of this, the authorities must make the actual rate of monetary growth conform to the announced target rate, since the public forms its expectations of future money growth at least partly on the basis of observed current money growth. Assuming this is done and the stable money growth rate target is thereafter permanently adhered to, the exchange rate will continue to be strengthened through the direct money stock and price anticipation channels.

A second policy implication is that exchange rate movements will occur when monetary policies are divergent and inconsistent between countries. This can be demonstrated by rewriting equation (8) as

$$E = \left[\frac{K^*}{K}\right] \left[\frac{M/Y}{M^*/Y^*}\right] \left[\frac{i}{i^*}\right]^a .$$

Disregarding the constants (the Ks), this expression shows the relationship between the exchange rate, its underlying relative national money/output ratios, and relative interest rates, respectively. Dissimilar monetary policies (international differences in rates of money growth per unit of real output) cause the money/output ratios to diverge. When this happens, relative inflationary expectations are also affected, thereby producing changes in the ratio of interest rates. These changes augment and reinforce the impact of the divergent money/output ratios on the exchange rate. Because of these influences, the exchange rate will vary when monetary policies differ between countries.

The exchange rate will be stable only if both countries agree to keep their money/output ratios constant or at least growing at the same rate. This in turn requires that both countries abandon divergent monetary policies for a uniform rule tying the money growth rate to the growth rate of real income. Note in particular that within the context of the model it is impossible for a single country to stabilize the exchange rate by adhering to a monetary rule if the other country persists in monetary fine-tuning. In short, exchange rate stability is virtually impossible when countries pursue incompatible monetary policies.

A third policy implication, therefore, is that policy coordination or harmonization is the key to exchange rate stability. If two countries agree to adopt the same monetary expansion rate—for example, a rule calling for a constant rate of monetary growth fixed in relation to the trend growth rate of real output—then both will experience the same long-run stable inflation rate, and the floating exchange rate between their currencies will be virtually as constant as an institutionally fixed rate. In this case, policy coordination would allow the countries to enjoy the advantages of a fixed exchange rate while retaining some degree of national monetary autonomy.

The preceding discussion raises two questions. First, why is exchange rate constancy so important? Second, is the type of exchange rate regime per se crucial to the attainment of that objective? Regarding the first question, many advocates of the monetary approach hold that exchange rate constancy is a necessary prerequisite for an efficiently operating international monetary system. This is so because money, in its role as a social device for economizing on the use of scarce resources in the generation and transmission of economic information, performs most effectively when its value across countries is stable, certain, and predictable. These qualities are, however, lacking when exchange rates fluctuate and money therefore functions poorly as a resource economizer. In such situations, traders themselves must forecast shifts in the value of currencies, bear the risks of such shifts, or hire someone else to bear the risks. Either way, real resources—effort, time, knowledge—are diverted from productive pursuits into forecasting and risk-taking activities that would be totally unnecessary if exchange rates were constant. This wasteful and inefficient use of resources means that the international economic system will not operate at peak efficiency as long as exchange rates fluctuate. On efficiency grounds alone, therefore, proponents of the monetary approach argue that exchange rate constancy is a desirable objective.

As for the question of whether a specific exchange rate regime —fixed or floating—is crucial to the attainment of that objective, the answer appears to be in the negative. The preceding analysis suggests that the key to achieving exchange rate constancy lies less in the way the foreign exchange market is organized than in finding a means of coordinating national monetary policies. As previously mentioned, policy coordination in the form of adoption of uniform rules is required if exchange rates are going to be constant in a floating rate regime. Similarly, some sort of coordination is necessary in a fixed rate regime, otherwise countries might inflate their domestic money stocks at different rates, forcing a breakdown of the system. To summarize, policy coordination, not the exchange rate regime per se, is the *sine qua non* for exchange rate stability.

SUMMARY

This chapter has presented a simple expository model of exchange rate determination incorporating key elements of the monetary approach. These elements lead to the conclusion that the exchange rate is determined by relative money stocks, relative real incomes, and relative inflationary expectations, with the last variable being strongly conditioned by observed rates of monetary growth and other current information about prospective events likely to affect future growth rates of money supply and demand. The model is useful in explaining long-run exchange rate movements as well as short-run exchange rate volatility. Finally, the model provides a useful framework for specifying the conditions necessary for the attainment of exchange rate stability.

NOTES

1. Similar models can be found in the recent literature. For example, see J. Bilson, "Recent Developments in Monetary Models of Exchange Rate Determination," *IMF Staff Papers* 26 (June 1979), pp 201–21; J. Bilson, "The Monetary Approach to the Exchange Rate: Some Empirical Evidence," *IMF Staff Papers* 25 (March 1978), pp. 48–75; J. Bilson, "Rational Expectations and the Exchange Rate," Ch. 5 in *The Economics of Exchange Rates: Selected Studies*, ed. J. Frenkel and H. Johnson (Reading, Mass.: Addison-Wesley, 1978), pp. 75–96; J. Frenkel and K. Clements, "Exchange Rates in the 1920's: A Monetary Approach." Working Paper 290, National Bureau of Economic Research, October 1978; R. Dornbusch, "Monetary Policy under Exchange Rate Flexibility," in *Managed Exchange Rate-Flexibility: The Recent Experience*, Federal Reserve Bank of Boston, October 1978, pp. 92–94; and M. Mussa, "The Exchange Rate,

the Balance of Payments and Monetary and Fiscal Policy Under a Regime of Controlled Floating," *Scandinavian Journal of Economics* 78, No 2 (1976), pp. 229-48. Much of the relevant empirical work on the model is summarized in S. Magee, "The Empirical Evidence on the Monetary Approach to the Balance of Payments and Exchange Rates," *American Economic Review* 66 (May 1976), pp. 163-70; and M. Kreinen and L. Officer, *The Monetary Approach to the Balance of Payments: A Survey*, Studies in International Finance, No. 43 (Princeton, N. J.: Princeton University, International Finance Section, 1978), pp. 20-27, 39-40, 47-50.

2. For discussions of the role of the monetary approach in earlier exchange rate debates see J. Frenkel, "A Monetary Approach to the Exchange Rate: Doctrinal Aspects and Empirical Evidence," *Scandinavian Journal of Economics* 78, No. 2 (1976), pp. 200-24; and J. Myhrman, "Experiences of Flexible Exchange Rates in Earlier Periods: Theories, Evidence, and a New View," *Scandinavian Journal of Economics* 78, No. 2 (1976), pp. 166-96.

9

FACTORS DETERMINING EXCHANGE RATES: A SIMPLE MODEL AND EMPIRICAL TESTS

This chapter constructs and tests a simple static equilibrium model of exchange rate determination.[1] The model assumes a regime of freely floating currencies and posits that the exchange rate, by definition the relative price of two national moneys, is determined by the basic factors underlying the demands for and supplies of those national money stocks. Besides the money supply itself, these factors include real income and interest rates—the latter reflecting expectational influences that enter into exchange rate determination.

The chapter proceeds as follows. First, it discusses the logic and economic content of the individual equations that constitute the major building blocks of the model. Second, it condenses the model to one reduced-form equation that expresses a functional relationship between the exchange rate and its ultimate determinants. Third, it fits the foregoing equation to the statistical data on several foreign exchange rates, assesses the accuracy of the fit, and discusses some problems involved in testing the model.

THE MODEL AND ITS ELEMENTS

The model itself consists of two hypothetical national economies represented by a set of equations containing the following variables. Let M be the nominal money stock (assumed to be exogenously determined by the central bank) and m the demand-adjusted rate of growth of that stock, i.e., the difference between the respective growth rates of the nominal money supply and real money demand, this difference by definition being equal to the rate of price inflation. Furthermore, let D be the real demand for money, i.e., the stock of real (price-deflated) cash balances that the public desires to hold, Y the exogenously-determined level of real income, and i and r the nominal and real rates of interest, respectively. Also let X be the exchange rate (defined as the domestic currency price of a unit of foreign currency), P be the price level, and E and m^e be the expected future rates of price inflation and money growth, respectively. Asterisks are used to distinguish foreign- from home-country variables, and the subscript w denotes the entire world economy. The foregoing elements are linked together via the relationships described below.

MONETARY EQUILIBRIUM EQUATIONS

The first part of the model consists of monetary equilibrium equations, one for each country

(1) $P = M/D$ and $P^* = M^*/D^*$.

These equations, which can also be written in the form $M/P = D$, state that the price level in each country adjusts to bring the real (price-deflated) value of the nominal money stock into equality with the real demand for it, thereby clearing the market for real cash balances. This market-clearing price-adjustment process relies chiefly on equilibrating changes in aggregate expenditure induced by discrepancies between actual and desired real balances. For example, if actual balances exceed desired, cash-holders will attempt to get rid of the excess via spending for goods. Given the exogenously-determined level of real output, however, the increased spending will exert upward pressure on prices thereby reducing the real (price-deflated) value of the nominal money stock. Prices will continue to rise until actual real balances are brought down to the desired level. Conversely, a shortfall between actual and desired real balances will induce a cut in expenditure leading to a fall in prices and a corresponding rise in the real value of the money stock. This process will continue until actual real balances are brought into equality with desired balances. To summarize, disequilibrium between actual and desired real balances generates the changes in spending that cause prices to alter sufficiently to eliminate the disequilibrium.

Note that the equations also imply that, given the real demand for money, the price level is determined by and varies equiproportionally with the nominal money supply. This latter result, of course, is the essence of the quantity theory of money. For that reason, the equations could also be called quantity theory equations.

REAL CASH BALANCE EQUATIONS

National demand for money functions constitute the second part of the model. Written as follows

(2) $D = KYi^{-a}$ and $D^* = K^*Y^*i^{*-a}$

these equations express the public's demand for real cash balances as the product of a constant K and two variables, namely real income and the nominal interest rate. The income variable is a proxy for the volume of real transactions effected with the aid of money and thus represents the transaction demand for money. By contrast, the interest rate variable measures the opportunity cost of holding money instead of earning assets. The parameter $-a$, which appears as the exponent of the interest rate variable, is the interest elasticity of demand for money. It measures the sensitivity or responsiveness of money demand to changes in the interest rate and is assumed to be a negative number indicating that the quantity of real balances demanded varies inversely with the cost of holding them. For simplicity the numerical magnitude of the interest elasticity parameter is assumed to be the same for both countries. For the same reason the income elasticity of demand for money, as represented by the exponential power to which the income variable is raised, is assumed to possess a numerical value of unity.

THE PURCHASING POWER PARITY EQUATION

The third equation of the model is the purchasing power parity relationship

(3) $P = XP^*$

showing how national price levels are linked together via the exchange rate. As indicated by the equation, prices in both countries are identical when converted into a common currency unit at the equilibrium rate of exchange. This means that the exchange rate equalizes such common-currency price levels and, by implication, the buying power of both moneys expressed in terms of a common unit. In other words, exchange-rate adjustment insures that a unit of a given currency commands the same quantity of goods and services abroad when converted into the other currency as it commands at home. This condition of equalized purchasing power is of course necessary if the two national money stocks are to be willingly held and monetary equilibrium is to prevail in both countries. For if the purchasing powers were unequal, people would demand more of the high- and less of the low-purchasing power currency on the market for foreign exchange. The resulting excess demand for the former and the corresponding excess supply of the latter would cause the exchange rate between the two currencies to adjust until purchasing power was equalized and both money stocks were willingly held. Note also that the purchasing power parity equation can be rearranged to read $X = P/P^*$, thus corresponding to the economic interpretation of the exchange rate as the relative price of the two currencies, i.e., as the ratio of the foreign currency's internal value in terms of goods to the domestic currency's internal value in terms of goods. Since the internal value of a unit of currency in terms of a composite market basket of commodities is the inverse of the general price level $1/P$, it follows that the relative price of the two moneys is simply the ratio of the national price levels as indicated by the equation.

NOMINAL INTEREST RATE EQUATIONS

The fourth group of relationships in the model are the nominal interest rate equations, one for each country. Written as follows

(4) $i = r + E$ and $i^* = r^* + E^*$

they define the nominal interest rate as the sum of the real rate of interest and the expected future rate of inflation, the latter variable being the premium added to real yields to prevent their erosion by inflation.

REAL INTEREST RATE PARITY CONDITION

The fifth equation expresses the interest-parity condition

$$(5) \quad r = r^* = r_w$$

according to which the real rate of return on capital assets tends to be everywhere the same and independent of the currency denomination of the asset. This equation reflects the model's assumption of a highly-integrated efficient world capital market. In such a world, capital is mobile internationally, i.e., foreigners can purchase domestic securities and domestic citizens can purchase foreign securities. Given these conditions it follows that real yield equalization is necessary if all asset stocks are to be willingly held. Accordingly, the equation states that real interest rates in both countries are the same and are equal to a given constant world rate r_w. Note that equations 4 and 5 taken together imply that international nominal interest rate differentials reflect differences in expected future national rates of inflation. For example, if the market expects the future rate of inflation to be 12 percent in the UK and 5 percent in the US, then the UK nominal interest rate will be 7 percentage points above the corresponding US interest rate.

PRICE EXPECTATIONS EQUATIONS

Completing the model are price expectations equations that describe how the public forms its anticipations of the future rate of inflation. These inflationary expectations constitute the anticipated future rates of depreciation of money holdings. As such, they enter the foreign and domestic demand for money functions via the nominal interest rate variables and thereby play an important role in exchange rate determination. Written as follows

$$(6) \quad E = m^e \text{ and } E^* = m^{e*}$$

the equations state that the expected rate of inflation E is given by the expected future rate of demand-adjusted money growth m^e.

These equations embody the *rational expectations hypothesis* according to which the public's predictions of future inflation are the same as those yielded by the actual inflation-generating mechanism represented in the model. This feature insures that the equations describing the formation of inflationary expectations are consistent with equations describing how inflation is actually generated. Such consistency is characteristic of the forecasting behavior of rational agents who use knowledge about the actual inflation-generating mechanism in forming expectations of future inflation. Since the model asserts that the actual rate of inflation is produced by demand-adjusted money growth (see equation 1), it follows that expected inflation is determined by the anticipated future value of that same variable as shown in equation 6. These anticipations are based on current information about prospective events likely to affect the future growth rates of money supply and demand.

LINKAGES AND CAUSATION

Taken together, the foregoing relationships constitute a simple six-equation model of exchange rate determination. For convenience the model is summarized below.

(1) $P = M/D$ and $P^* = M^*/D^*$.

(2) $D = KYi^{-a}$ and $D^* = K^*Y^*i^{*-a}$.

(3) $P = XP^*$.

(4) $i = r + E$ and $i^* = r^* + E^*$.

(5) $r = r^* = r_w$.

(6) $E = m^e$ and $E^* = m^{e*}$.

The foregoing equations imply two unidirectional channels of influence—one direct, the other indirect—running from money and income (both exogenous variables) to prices to the exchange rate. Regarding the former channel, the model implies that both exogenous variables affect prices and the exchange rate directly through the monetary equilibrium and purchasing power parity equations. As for the indirect channel, the model implies that the expected future rates of growth of the exogenous variables influence the exchange rate indirectly via the price expectations component of the nominal interest rate variable that enters the demand for money function. More specifically, the model postulates the following causal chain:

1. Predictions of future demand-adjusted money growth determine the expected rate of inflation.
2. Given the real rate of interest, the expected rate of inflation determines the nominal rate of interest.
3. The latter variable, together with the given level of real income, determines the demand for money.
4. Given the demand for money, the nominal money stock determines the price level.
5. Finally, the two price levels, foreign and domestic, together determine the exchange rate.

In brief, when the expected future demand-adjusted money growth rate rises, price expectations also rise and so too does the nominal interest rate (the cost of holding money). This reduces the quantity of real cash balances that people desire to hold, i.e., cash-holders will want to get out of money and into goods. The resulting increased spending for goods puts upward pressure on the price level and, via the purchasing power parity nexus, also on the exchange rate. Clearly the linkages run from money stocks and real incomes to prices to the exchange rate.[2] Moreover, all variables affecting the exchange rate do so through monetary channels, i.e., through the demand for and supply of money. In this sense, money demand and supply may be said to constitute the *proximate* determinants of the exchange rate. The *ultimate* determinants, however, are the variables that underlie and determine the monetary factors themselves.

DETERMINANTS OF THE EXCHANGE RATE

To show the relationship between the exchange rate and its ultimate determinants, simply substitute equations 1–2 and 4–6 into equation 3 and solve for the exchange rate. The resulting "reduced form" expression is

$$(7) \quad X = [K^*/K]\,[M/M^*]\,[Y^*/Y]\,[i/i^*]^a$$

or, since the nominal interest rate i is the sum of the real interest rate r and the expected rate of inflation E—the latter variable itself being equal to the anticipated future growth rate of money per unit of money demand m^e—the equation can be expressed as

$$(7') \quad X = \left[\frac{K^*}{K}\right]\left[\frac{M}{M^*}\right]\left[\frac{Y^*}{Y}\right]\left[\frac{r + m^e}{r^* + m^{e*}}\right]^a.$$

Disregarding the fixed constants (the K's), equation 7 (or 7′) collects the determinants of the exchange rate into three groups, namely relative money supplies, relative real incomes, and relative nominal interest rates comprised of a fixed real rate component and a variable price expectations component. Of these three groups, the first captures purely monetary influences on the exchange rate while the second and third capture real and expectational influences, respectively.

Regarding monetary and real influences, the equation predicts that a country's exchange rate will depreciate (i.e., rise) if its demand-adjusted money stock is growing faster than in the other country. Conversely, a nation will find its currency appreciating on the foreign exchanges when its money stock grows slower and its real income faster than in the other country. Note that the model's conclusion that rapid real growth results in currency appreciation contradicts the conventional balance of payments view of exchange rate determination. According to this latter approach, income growth tends to depreciate a country's currency by inducing a rise in imports and a consequent trade balance deficit. By contrast, the present model depicts real growth as stimulating not imports but rather the demand for money. Given the nominal money stock, this increased real money demand necessitates a fall in the price level to clear the market for money balances. With foreign prices given, the fall in domestic prices requires an equivalent appreciation of the exchange rate to maintain purchasing power parity. In short, the model predicts that growth-induced rises in the real demand for money will raise the internal and therefore also the external value of a currency.

As for expectational influences, the equation predicts that a rise in the expected rate of inflation in one country (as reflected in its interest rate) relative to the other will cause the former's currency to depreciate on the foreign exchanges. The reason, of course, is that when interest rates rise, desired real cash balances fall. Cashholders attempt to get rid of unwanted balances via expenditure for goods thereby putting upward pressure on prices. According to the model, the rise in prices will be relatively greater in the country experiencing the larger rise in interest rates. In this way increasing relative interest rates cause corresponding increases in relative national price levels that must be offset by exchange rate depreciation to preserve purchasing power parity. Note again that the model's prediction of a direct relation between interest rate movements and exchange rate movements runs counter to the conventional balance of payments view. According to this latter approach, a rising interest rate should lower the exchange rate either by attracting capital from abroad (thereby improving the capital account of the balance of payments) or by reducing domestic expenditure for imports and potential exports (thereby improving the trade balance). This cannot happen in the present model where, instead of strengthening the balance of payments, a rising interest rate induces a shift from cash to goods resulting in domestic inflation and exchange rate depreciation. In short, equation 7 predicts that a country will experience currency depreciation when its relative money stock rises, its relative real income falls, and its relative inflationary expectations rise.

EMPIRICAL APPLICATION

This chapter has constructed a simple economic model that states that the bilateral exchange rate between any two national currencies is determined by relative money stocks, relative real incomes, and relative nominal interest rates—the last variable reflecting relative expectations regarding national inflationary prospects. All that remains is to illustrate how the model can be applied in empirical studies of exchange rate determination. With this objective in mind, an attempt is made below to estimate the model's reduced-form exchange rate equation (equation 7) and to use it to explain the behavior of the US/UK and US/Italy exchange rates, respectively, over the post-1972 period of generalized floating. To do this, it is necessary to transform equation 7 into linear form by expressing the variables as logarithms. This step is required because equation 7 is nonlinear, and nonlinear equations are difficult to estimate directly. The resulting log-linear version of equation 7 is written as

$$(8)\quad \ln X = a_0 + a_1(\ln M - \ln M^*) + a_2(\ln Y^* - \ln Y) + a_3(\ln i - \ln i^*)$$

where ln stands for the logarithm of the attached variable and the a's are coefficients to be estimated from the statistical data. Note that according to equation 7 the a priori expected values of the coefficients attached to the money and income variables are unity whereas the coefficient attached to the interest rate variables should lie between zero and unity, consistent with previous empirical estimates of the interest elasticity of demand for money.

Equation 8 was estimated for quarterly US/UK and US/Italy data for the period 1973 I through 1976 II. The money supply variable used for each country was M1. The income variables used were real gross national product for the US and real gross domestic product for the UK and Italy, respectively. As for the interest rate variables, the treasury bill rate was used for each country in the US/UK equation and the rate on medium-term government bonds was used for each country in the US/Italy equation. All data were taken from the IMF's *International Financial Statistics* with the exception of the figures for UK real gross domestic product, which were taken from the OECD's *Main Economic Indicators*.

The results are shown in Table 1 below.

In general the empirical results are consistent with the theoretical model. According to the estimated equations, fully 87 percent of the variation of both the dollar/pound and dollar/lira exchange rates are explained by variations in the money stock, real income, and interest rate variables. In both cases the coefficients on the explanatory variables have the expected positive signs. All coefficients are statistically significant at the 0.05 level except for those on the US/Italy income and interest rate variables. Moreover, the coefficient on the US/Italy money stock variable is close to its expected (theoretical) value of unity, as is the coefficient on the US/UK income variable. The interest rate coefficients in both equations are also consistent with previous empirical estimates of the interest elasticity of demand for money.[3] These results are perhaps better than one might expect considering the extreme simplicity of the model, the degree to which floating rates are managed instead of free, the limited number of observations (14), and the fact that short-run data are used to test a long-run equilibrium model.

In sum, the equations reported above provide at least modest empirical support for the theoretical model developed earlier in the

TABLE 1. Regression Results for US/UK and US/Italy Exchange Rates

Quarterly Data: 1973 I–1976 II

I. Dollar/pound exchange rate

$$\ln X = 5.87 + \underset{(2.79)^*}{0.49}(\ln M_{US} - \ln M_{UK}) + \underset{(2.78)^*}{0.96}(\ln Y_{UK} - \ln Y_{US}) + \underset{(2.34)^*}{0.24}(\ln i_{US} - \ln i_{UK})$$

$R^2 = 0.87 \qquad DW = 1.17$[1]

II. Dollar/lira exchange rate

$$\ln X = -4.44 + \underset{(3.93)^*}{0.92}(\ln M_{US} - \ln M_{IT}) + \underset{(1.32)}{0.70}(\ln Y_{IT} - \ln Y_{US}) + \underset{(1.62)}{0.17}(\ln i_{US} - \ln i_{IT})$$

$R^2 = 0.87 \qquad DW = 1.24$[1]

*Indicates statistical significance at the 5 percent level of confidence. t-statistics are given in parentheses beneath the estimated coefficients.

[1] The reported Durbin-Watson statistics are in the inconclusive region in testing for serial correlation. Correcting for serial correlation using the Cochrane-Orcutt method did not significantly alter the results.

article. One should not make too much of these results, however. Just as one swallow does not make a summer, two regression equations do not prove a theory. In particular, equation 8 may not fit the data well for other countries and other time periods. In fact, an attempt was made to test the equation against recent data for Canada, Japan, and Germany, as well as for data pertaining to the UK during the early 1920s when that country was off the gold standard. For the first three countries, the equation performed poorly. For the UK from 1920–1924, however, it was at least partially successful. As shown in Table 2, the equation performed adequately except for the coefficient on the income variable, which bears the wrong sign. This of course may be due to the unreliability of UK income data for that

TABLE 2: Regression Results for US/UK Exchange Rates

Quarterly Data: 1920 I–1924 IV

Dollar/pound exchange rate

$$\ln X = -0.17 + \underset{(4.48)^*}{0.55}(\ln M_{US} - \ln M_{UK}) - \underset{(-1.55)}{0.16}(\ln Y_{UK} - \ln Y_{US}) + \underset{(2.77)^*}{0.10}(\ln i_{US} - \ln i_{UK})$$

$R^2 = 0.76$ DW = 1.31

*Indicates statistical significance at the 5 percent level of confidence. t-statistics are given in parentheses beneath the estimated coefficients.

period rather than to short-comings inherent in the model.[4] Nevertheless, the fact that the equation does not work well for all countries is reason to interpret the results reported here with caution.

PROBLEMS IN TESTING THE MODEL

In closing this article, it may be appropriate to consider why the data did not exactly fit the model like a glove. Regarding this question, at least three likely explanations come to mind. First, the model assumes that exchange rates are permitted to float freely while in fact governments still intervene in foreign exchange markets from time to time in order to achieve a managed float. This suggests that there may be some reverse causality running from exchange rates to money, at least in the short run. In brief, the model may not be a completely accurate description of existing exchange rate regimes.

Second, quarterly data may not be suitable for testing what is essentially a model of long-run equilibrium. Quarterly data are short-run data. As such they may be dominated by transitory dynamic adjustment phenomena that are absent in long-run static equilibrium. Annual (or longer) data are more appropriate for testing an equation that is based on assumptions of purchasing power parity, interest rate parity, monetary equilibrium, real income exogeneity, and unidirectional causality between money and exchange rates—all propositions about long-run equilibrium. Unfortunately, the post-Bretton Woods era of floating rates is only four years old, and the number of annual observations is insufficient to test these proportions. Even the number of quarterly observations is distressingly low.

An alternative solution would be to augment the model with additional equations and variables to represent dynamic adjustment processes. While this might permit the specification of short-run influences affecting the exchange rate, it would unduly complicate the model, contrary to the objective of keeping it simple. Note, however, that this latter feature may constitute a third reason for the model's failure to conform exactly to the data, i.e., the model may be far too simple to capture all the influences on the exchange rate. This does not necessarily mean that the model is conceptually unsound. The underlying theory may be correct even though its empirical form is inadequate to fit the facts. Thus the model can be faulted on the grounds that its empirical money demand equations are too simple, that it lacks dynamic adjustment mechanisms, and that it arbitrarily constrains the elasticity coefficients to be the same for each country. These considerations should be kept in mind when interpreting the results of the regression analysis.

SUMMARY

This chapter has developed and estimated a simple model of exchange rate determination. The model states that exchange rate movements are determined by shifts in relative money stocks, relative real incomes, and relative inflationary expectations as manifested in relative interest rate movements. Although the model receives some empirical support from post-1972 data for the dollar/pound and dollar/lira exchange rates, it does not perform well when applied to data for other countries and other time periods. One is therefore advised to take an agnostic attitude regarding the validity of the model until all returns are in. In short, additional experience with floating exchange rates, together with the application of empirical techniques of greater sophistication than those employed here, will be necessary to establish conclusively the validity or invalidity of the model.

NOTES

1. Variants of the model have been employed by a number of analysts to explain recent exchange rate movements. See in particular the papers by Bilson [1, 2], Frenkel [4], and Putnam and Woodbury [7] cited in the list of references at the end of the chapter. Much of the relevant empirical work on the model is summarized in the surveys by Isard [5] and Magee [6].

2. Note that reverse causality is effectively ruled out by the assumed exogeneity of the money stock and income variables. Therefore, while these variables can affect the exchange rate, the exchange rate cannot influence them —at least not within the context of the model.

3. Boorman [3] reports that recent empirical studies of the demand for money suggest an interest elasticity of about -0.2 for short-term rates, quite close to the estimates appearing in Table 1.

4. Since quarterly national income figures are not available for this period, the Federal Reserve's Index of Industrial Production was used as a proxy for US real income. No such official index is available for the UK. Therefore a quarterly industrial production index constructed in 1927 by Rowe [8] was used as a proxy for UK real income. However, the reliability of this index is open to question.

REFERENCES

1. Bilson, John F. O. "The Monetary Approach to the Exchange Rate: Some Empirical Evidence." Unpublished manuscript, Northwestern University, October 1976.

2. ——. "Rational Expectations and the Exchange Rate." Unpublished manuscript, Northwestern University, August 1976.

3. Boorman, John T. "The Evidence on the Demand for Money: Theoretical Formulations and Empirical Results." *Current Issues in Monetary Theory and Policy*. Edited by Thomas M. Havrilesky and John T. Boorman. Arlington Heights, Illinois; AHM Publishing Corp., 1976.

4. Frenkel, Jacob A. "A Monetary Approach to the Exchange Rate: Doctrinal Aspects and Empirical Evidence." *Scandinavian Journal of Economics*, 78, No. 2 (1976), 200-24.

5. Isard, Peter. "The Process of Exchange Rate Determination: A Survey of Important Models and Major Issues." Federal Reserve Board, International Finance Division Discussion Paper No. 101 (January 1977), pp. 56-60.

6. Magee, Stephen P. "The Empirical Evidence on the Monetary Approach to

the Balance of Payments and Exchange Rates." *American Economic Review: Papers and Proceedings* 66 (May 1976), 167–68.

7. Putnam, Bluford H. and John R. Woodbury. "Exchange Rate Stability and Monetary Policy: A Case Study." Unpublished manuscript, Federal Reserve Bank of New York, August 1976.

8. Rowe, J. W. F. "An Index of Industrial Production." *Economic Journal* 37 (June 1927), 186.

10

THE MONETARY APPROACH TO EXCHANGE RATES: ITS HISTORICAL EVOLUTION AND ROLE IN POLICY DEBATES

The noted British economist and Nobel Laureate Sir John R. Hicks once remarked that advances in monetary theory are stimulated by particular historical episodes and events involving severe monetary disturbances. Hick's observation would seem to apply in the case of the monetary approach to floating exchange rates. Conforming to his dictum, the monetary approach to exchange rates has evolved in response to events provoked by major changes in monetary arrangements, notably shifts from fixed to floating exchange rate regimes. More precisely, the monetary approach has evolved through a succession of policy debates triggered by episodes of price inflation and currency depreciation following the suspension of the gold convertibility of paper currencies and the attendent move from fixed to floating exchange rates. At issue in these debates was the cause of exchange rate movements. In each debate two explanations were advanced, namely the monetary view and the rival nonmonetary balance of payments view.

A legacy of mercantilism, the balance of payments view attributes exchange rate movements to autonomous real (that is, nonmonetary) disturbances to particular components of the balance of payments. It stresses a channel of causation running from real shocks through the balance of payments to the exchange rate and thence to domestic prices and sometimes further to the money supply. It prescribes nonmonetary (and mercantilistic) remedies in the form of export promotion and import restriction measures as correctives for exchange rate depreciation and appreciation. The monetary approach, by contrast, attributes exchange rate movements largely to actual and anticipated changes in relative money supplies and demands. It stresses a channel of causation running from money supply and demand to spending to prices to the exchange rate. With respect to policies, it prescribes monetary restriction as the proper remedy for exchange rate depreciation, and monetary expansion as the corresponding cure for exchange rate appreciation. It eschews all non-monetary export promotion and import restriction schemes; such mercantilistic policy prescriptions are antithetical to the monetary view. These two rival views have been pitted in a succession of policy debates going back more than 200 years.

The most important of these debates contributing to the evolution of the monetary approach were the Swedish bullionist controversy of the 1750s, the English bullionist controversy of the early nineteenth century, and the German inflation controversy during and immediately following World War I. Each debate was provoked by episodes of price inflation and currency depreciation that occurred when countries had left the gold standard for a regime of floating exchange rates. The sequence of events in each episode was the same. First came the move to floating exchange rates. Then followed sharp rises in the prices of commodities and foreign exchange. The reigning balance of payments view was then advanced to explain these phenomena, and it was, in turn, opposed by the rival monetary explanation.[1]

These debates contributed heavily to the evolution of the monetary approach to floating exchange rates. Each successive debate added a new stage to that evolutionary process, consolidating and building upon the contributions of earlier stages and laying the groundwork for subsequent developments. Each debate saw essential elements or components incorporated into the monetary approach. Consisting chiefly of a quantity theory relationship linking money to prices, a purchasing power parity relationship linking prices to the exchange rate, and an expectations theory specifying how anticipations of future money supplies and demands are formed and how they influence observed exchange rates, these elements constitute the analytical foundations of the floating rate version of the monetary approach. This chapter traces the evolution of that approach through the Swedish, English, and German debates and outlines the contributions of each debate to the development of the monetary theory of floating exchange rates.

THE SWEDISH BULLIONIST CONTROVERSY (1755-65)

One of the earliest historical episodes contributing to the development of the monetary approach was the Swedish bullionist controversy of the mid-1700s, a period during which many elements of mercantilist views prevailed.[2] The events precipitating the debate were as follows: In 1745, Sweden shifted from a metallic monetary system with fixed exchange rates to an inconvertible paper system with flexible exchange rates. The suspension of convertibility was followed more than ten years later by sharp increases in the banknote issue accompanied by rapid rises in the prices of commodities and foreign exchange. A debate then arose between the two main political parties of the time—the so-called Hats and Caps, respectively—over the cause of these price increases.

The Hat Political Party

The Hats advanced the nonmonetary balance of payments theory, blaming both the external and internal depreciation of the Swedish mark on Sweden's adverse trade balance. In particular, they held that the adverse trade balance had produced a depreciating exchange rate, that exchange rate depreciation had rendered imported goods more expensive, and that the rise in import prices had spread to the rest of the economy, thereby raising the general level of prices. Here is an early example of the tendency of nonmonetary balance of payments theorists (1) to attribute both domestic inflation and exchange depreciation to external nonmonetary shocks and (2) to assert a chain of causation running from autonomous real shocks to the balance of payments to the exchange rate to prices, rather than from money to prices to the exchange rate as in the monetary approach. Consistent with their balance of payments view, the Hats prescribed export promotion and import restriction schemes as remedies for inflation and exchange rate depreciation. Nothing was said about money or monetary remedies. The connection between banknote expansion and exchange rate depreciation was totally ignored, as was the possibility of halting that depreciation by stopping monetary growth. The Hats' position was that exchange rate depreciation stemmed solely from real nonmonetary causes and therefore required real nonmonetary remedies. Curbing monetary growth, they felt, was useless for correcting a depreciation caused by external real shocks. In such situations only real remedies would suffice. Accordingly, the Hats advocated a variety of nonmonetary measures, including export loans and subsidies, high protective tariffs, direct controls on imports, and the like—all designed to correct the trade deficit by encouraging exports and discouraging imports.

Contributing to the Hats' refusal to acknowledge a connection between money growth and exchange rate depreciation was their mercantilistic money-stimulates-trade doctrine. A monetary theory of real output, this doctrine holds that money growth strengthens rather than weakens the currency on the foreign exchanges. More precisely, as explained by the Hats, the doctrine states that monetary expansion promotes production, that increased production supplies more goods for export, and that, provided imports are constrained by direct controls, increased exports improve the trade balance and thereby strengthen the currency on the foreign exchanges.[3] In this manner, an increase in the money supply would cause the exchange rate to appreciate rather than depreciate. The predictions of this theory, however, were refuted by the actual behavior of the exchange rate. Because of this the Hats emphasized the alternative balance of payments explanation of the fall of the Swedish mark.

The Cap Political Party

The opposition Cap party emphatically rejected the Hats' balance of payments theory and pointed instead to the importance of the monetary factor. They blamed both domestic inflation and the external depreciation of the Swedish mark largely on the Riksbank's overissue of banknotes following the suspension of convertibility. Postulating a channel of causation running from money to prices and the exchange rate, they stated that the price of foreign exchange and the price of goods in general had risen in Sweden because of the increases in the note issue of the national Bank.[4] In so doing, they laid down two fundamental building blocks of the monetary approach to floating exchange rates. Consisting of (1) the notion that money is the dominant determinant of exchange rates, and (2) the corresponding concept of a monetary transmission mechanism connecting money with the exchange rate, these building blocks formed the basis of the Caps' policy prescriptions. They favored a policy of monetary contraction to roll back prices and the exchange rate to pre-inflation levels. Their position can be summarized by the relationship

$$(1) \quad E = E(M)$$

expressing the exchange rate E (defined as the domestic currency price of a unit of foreign currency) as a function of the domestic money stock M.

The preceding was not the only explanation offered by the Caps. They also adhered to an evil-speculator theory of exchange rate movements, arguing that a small group of rapacious speculators had employed excessive banknote issues to drive up the price of foreign exchange. That is, in their analysis of exchange rate depreciation they stressed the actions of greedy and evil men.[5] Such a conspiracy theory, however, is antithetical to the monetary approach. For that reason, although the Caps laid some foundations of the monetary approach, they cannot be considered as full-fledged consistent advocates of that approach.

Pehr Niclas Christiernin

One participant who did articulate a view fully consistent with the monetary approach was Pehr Niclas Christiernin, an academic economist at the University of Uppsala, who advanced a quantity theory explanation of the transmission mechanism linking money with the exchange rate.[6] In his *Lectures on the High Price of Foreign Exchange in Sweden* (1761), Christiernin maintained that the chief cause of currency depreciation was an overissue of banknotes by the Riksbank and that causation flowed from money to spending to all prices, including the prices of commodities and foreign exchange. He saw monetary expansion as stimulating demand. Part of the demand pressure falls on domestic commodity markets raising prices there. The rest spills over into the current account of the balance of payments in the form of increased demand for imports. The resulting import deficit then puts upward pressure on the exchange rate, which consequently rises to restore equilibrium in the current account. Clearly, money-induced changes in total spending constitute the driving force in Christiernin's version of the transmission mechanism running from money to the exchange rate. This component has been a hallmark of the monetary approach ever since.

The only thing missing from Christiernin's analysis is the recognition of a *real balance effect* whereby the exchange rate equates money supply and demand by deflating the former to the level people desire to hold. Except for this, his analysis embodies all the standard ingredients of the monetary approach. He asserted, for example, that an excess supply of money must be matched by an excess demand for goods, an incipient balance of payments deficit, and a corresponding excess demand for foreign exchange, all of which put upward pressure on the exchange rate. Moreover, he realized that the resulting rise in the exchange rate would simultaneously tend (1) to clear the market for foreign exchange, (2) to eliminate the incipient balance of payments deficit, and (3) to raise the domestic price level, which is linked to the given world price level through the exchange rate. Finally, he realized that the exchange rate attains its equilibrium level when the real value or purchasing power of either currency is the same whether spent at home or converted into foreign currency at the equilibrium exchange rate and spent abroad. That is, he enunciated the purchasing power parity doctrine, albeit in rudimentary form.[7] What he neglected to make explicit, however, was that the exchange rate restores equilibrium by deflating the real value of the actual money stock to the level people desire to hold. In so doing, it eliminates the excess supply of money that is the root cause of excessive spending and the resulting incipient balance of payments deficit that puts upward pressure on the exchange rate. It should be noted, however, that his explanation of the transmission mechanism linking money with the exchange rate is fully consistent with the operation of the real balance effect. Thus, while not stated in explicit form, a real balance effect is nevertheless implicit in his work.

As for policy recommendations, Christiernin advocated cessation of money growth as the only way to stop currency depreciation and to stabilize the exchange rate. In his view, a stable exchange rate required a stable (constant) money stock. While favoring a policy of stabilizing money and the exchange rate at fixed levels, however, he strongly opposed the Caps' plan to restore the exchange rate to its original preinflation level via contraction of the note issue. His opposition stemmed from his belief that prices adjusted sluggishly in response to deflationary pressure, so that the monetary contraction required to restore the exchanges to parity would bring painful declines in output and employment rather than the desired price decreases. For this reason, he recommended stabilizing the exchange rate at the level established during the inflation rather than restoring it to the preinflation level.[8] Unfortunately, his advice was ignored, and the Caps enacted a deflationary policy that resulted in the very drop in output and employment that he had predicted.

Contributions to the Evolution of the Monetary Approach to Exchange Rates

To summarize, the Swedish bullionist controversy saw the emergence of rudiments of the monetary approach to exchange rates. These rudiments included the notion of the money stock as the dominant determinant of exchange rates and the concept of a monetary transmission mechanism connecting money with the exchange rate. The Caps supplied these elements, and Christiernin contributed two more when he identified and analyzed the workings of the quantity theory and purchasing power parity components of the transmission mechanism. In so doing, these writers laid the groundwork for later developments of the monetary approach.

THE ENGLISH BULLIONIST CONTROVERSY (1797-1819)

The monetary and balance of payments theories clashed again in the famous early-nineteenth-century Bank Restriction Controversy over the cause of the fall of the British pound and the rise in the price of gold following the Bank of England's suspension of the convertibility of banknotes into gold during the Napoleonic wars.[9] As in the earlier Swedish controversy, one side blamed currency depreciation on the central bank's overissue of notes while the other blamed it on an adverse balance of payments. This time, however, the proponents of the monetary and balance of payments views were known as the bullionists and the antibullionists, respectively.

The bullionists did more than any group before or since to develop and clarify the monetary view. Their position was not as homogenous, however, as some interpretations would lead one to believe. In particular, with respect to their monetary views they can be subdivided into two distinct groups labeled *strict* and *moderate*, respectively. The so-called strict bullionists crystallized the monetary theory of exchange rates in rigorous form, and the moderate bullionists modified, elaborated, refined, and extended it. The strict bullionists included Walter Boyd, Lord King, David Ricardo, and John Wheatley, while the moderate bullionists included William Blake, Francis Horner, William Huskisson, Thomas Malthus, and, above all, Henry Thornton. These writers contributed heavily to the development of the monetary approach, adding new elements or improvements to the groundwork laid before. Their contributions are outlined in the following sections, which deal first with the strict bullionists, second with the moderate bullionists and their policy conclusions, third with the nonmonetary doctrines of the so-called antibullionist writers, and last with the bullionists' critique of those nonmonetary antibullionist doctrines.

The Strict Bullionists: Ricardo and Wheatley

The strict bullionists made several major contributions to the monetary approach. They were the first economists writing in the English language to specify and explain the workings both of the quantity theory and of purchasing power parity links in the transmission mechanism connecting money and the exchange rate. For clarity, rigor, and precision, their lucid exposition of these concepts far surpassed Christiernin's, whose work was unknown to them. In addition, they stated the monetary approach in its most rigid and uncompromising form, asserting that, under conditions of inconvertibility where money cannot drain out into foreign trade, the exchange rate varies in exact proportion with changes in the money supply and is therefore neutral in its impact on real economic variables. They arrived at this conclusion via the following route.

First, they assumed that under inconvertibility domestic prices P vary in strict proportion with the quantity of money in circulation, M. Implying the strict neutrality of money, this is, of course, the rigid version of the quantity theory of money, which had been formulated earlier by various closed economy writers and then extended to the open economy by Christiernin. Consistent with these earlier writers, the strict bullionists recognized that whereas the quantity theory of money might not apply in the case of the small open economy under fixed exchange rates, it did apply to the small open economy under floating exchange rates. In this context, the quantity theory may be expressed as

$$(2) \quad P = kM$$

where P is the price level, M is the money stock, and k is a constant coefficient equal to the ratio of the circulation velocity of money to real output, with these last two variables treated as fixed constants by the strict bullionists.

Second, they maintained that under inconvertibility the exchange rate E moves in proportion to the ratio of domestic to foreign general price levels (including the prices of all goods, traded and nontraded). Enunciated by Wheatley in his 1803 discussion of the "par of exchange" and endorsed by Ricardo in his *Principles of Political Economy and Taxation* (1817), this proposition is the famous purchasing power parity doctrine, so christened by Gustav Cassel who rediscovered it more than 100 years later in 1918. The

Wheatley-Ricardo-Cassel purchasing power parity condition may be written as

(3) $E = P/P^*$

implying that external currency valuations derive from their real internal values and that the general price level and its counterpart, the purchasing power of money, are everywhere the same when converted into a common unit at the equilibrium rate of exchange.

Third, they assumed that the foreign price component P^* of the purchasing power parity ratio was a constant equal to the given world bullion price of commodities, so that exchange rate movements reflected corresponding movements in domestic paper money prices only. Given this assumption, the exchange rate is a good proxy for domestic prices and may be expressed as

(4) $E = P$

assuming the constant foreign price level is "normalized" and set equal to unity.[10]

Finally they substituted the exchange rate proxy for the price variable in the quantity theory relationship, thereby obtaining the result

(5) $E = kM$

which states that, consistent with the neutrality postulate, the nominal exchange rate varies in exact proportion with the nominal money supply. On this basis they were able to conclude that a rise in the exchange rate above its gold parity constituted both proof and measure of overissue of inconvertible currency. In other words, if the exchange rate stood 5 percent above its gold parity, then this was prima facie evidence that the note issue was 5 percent above what it would have been under convertibility. This was most clearly stated by Ricardo who wrote

> If a country used paper money not exchangeable for specie, and, therefore, not regulated by any fixed standard, the exchanges in that country might deviate from par *in the same proportion* as its money might be multiplied beyond that quantity which would have been allotted to it by general commerce, if . . . the precious metals had been used.[11]

Wheatley extended the analysis to the case where both countries are on an inconvertible paper standard. He simply substituted quantity theory relationships for both the domestic and foreign price variables in equation 3. This gave him the result that the exchange rate varies in proportion with relative money supplies, i.e.,

$$(6) \quad E = kM/k^*M^* = K(M/M^*)$$

where K is the ratio of the constants k and k*. Wheatley stated this result when he declared that "the course of exchange is the exclusive criterion of how far the currency of one country is increased beyond the currency of another."[12]

Another contribution of the strict bullionists was their assertion that exchange rate movements are purely a monetary phenomenon. They rejected the antibullionist argument that real disturbances to the balance of payments—such as harvest failures, wartime disruption of trade, military expenditures abroad, remittances to foreign governments and the like—were responsible for the fall of the paper pound during the Napoleonic wars. Regarding supply shocks and foreign remittances, they denied that such factors could influence exchange rates even in the short run. Ricardo's position was that the slightest upward pressure on the exchange rate exerted by real shocks would, by making British goods cheaper to foreigners, result in an instantaneous expansion of exports sufficient to eliminate the pressure. Wheatley advanced the slightly more ingenious argument that domestic crop failures, by reducing domestic real income and hence the capacity to purchase, would also reduce the demand for nonfood imports sufficiently to offset food imports occasioned by the crop failure itself and thus leave the exchange rate undisturbed. As seen by Ricardo and Wheatley, the exchange rate was immune to real shocks. In their view, an adverse exchange was solely and completely the result of an excess issue of currency. Ricardo even went so far as to argue that even if foreign transfers and domestic crop failures *did* affect the exchanges by reducing real income and hence the demand for money, the cause of exchange depreciation is still an excess stock of money, albeit one arising from a reduction of money demand rather than an expansion of money supply. Ricardo's point was simply that real factors could only affect the exchange rate through shifts in money demand not offset by corresponding shifts in money supply. In such cases the inappropriate money supply was to blame for exchange rate movements. The notion that all factors affecting the exchange rate must do so through monetary channels, that is, through the demand for or supply of money, is of course central to the modern monetary approach to exchange rate determination.

Finally, with respect to policy, the strict bullionists prescribed monetary restraint as the *only* cure for a depreciating currency. They held that a rise in the price of foreign exchange constituted an infallible sign that the currency was in excess and *must* be contracted. Ricardo even defined an excess issue in terms of exchange depreciation, thus implying a single unique correct money stock, namely one associated with the exchange being at its former gold standard parity.[13]

The Moderate Bullionists: Thornton and Blake

As previously noted, the bullionists fell into two distinct groups with regard to their views on money and exchange rate movements. In addition to the hard-line or strict bullionist group, there was the so-called moderate bullionist group that included Francis Horner, William Huskisson, Thomas Malthus, and, above all, William Blake and Henry Thornton. The moderate bullionists modified the strict bullionists' analysis in three respects. First, they pointed out that it applies to long-run equilibrium situations but not necessarily to the short run. Second, they advanced an analysis of the money-price-exchange rate nexus that was far more subtle and sophisticated than that offered by the strict bullionists. Henry Thornton, in particular, argued that interest rates and the circulation velocity of money enter the nexus, that velocity is extremely variable in the short run owing to shifts in business confidence, and that this variability modifies the rigid money-price-exchange rate linkage postulated by the extreme bullionists.[14] In terms of equation 5 he argued that the velocity/output ratio k is a variable determined by the interest rate i and the state of business confidence, c, namely,

$$(7) \quad k = k(i, c)$$

Since k varies in the short run, the exchange rate and money do not exhibit exactly equiproportional movements. A given change in the money stock affects k as well as the exchange rate. In the long run, however, k is a constant, and the equiproportionality postulate holds (that is, neutrality holds).

The third modification made by the moderate bullionists involved the incorporation of real disturbances into the monetary model of exchange rate determination. While acknowledging that long-run (persistent) exchange rate depreciation stemmed solely from note overissue, they were willing to admit that real shocks could affect the exchanges in the short run. Their position is best exemplified by William Blake's distinction between the *Real* and the *Nominal* exchange rates, or what modern economists refer to as the terms of trade and the purchasing power parity, respectively.[15] Together, these two variables constitute the components of actual observed exchange rates.

According to Blake, the real exchange rate or real barter terms of trade expresses the relative real price of goods at home and abroad. That is, assuming that all goods are traded, it expresses the relative price of one country's output in terms of the other country's output. Being a real economic variable, it is determined by real (that is, nonmonetary) factors. Also, as the relative real price of goods, it influences the demands for exports and imports, adjusting to bring the two into balance. That is, it operates to equilibrate the balance of payments. It possesses a long-run natural equilibrium value of unity determined by the arbitrage condition that the real price of goods must be the same everywhere, so that there exists no advantage to buying in one market over another. Because commodity arbitrage is not instantaneous, however, transitory departures from real exchange rate equilibrium may occur from time to time. In particular, exogenous real disturbances to the balance of payments—crop failures, unilateral transfers, military expenditures abroad, and the like—may cause the real exchange rate to deviate temporarily from its long-run normal level. But such deviations will be automatically self-correcting through the feedback effect of the real exchange rate on exports and imports. Thus a shock to the balance of payments that temporarily depreciates the real exchange rate will, by raising the relative real price of goods abroad and lowering it at home, act to stimulate exports and check imports, thereby reequilibrating the balance of payments and restoring the real exchange rate to its equilibrium level.

In sharp contrast to the real exchange rate is Blake's concept of the nominal exchange rate or purchasing power parity. A purely nominal variable that has no effect on real economic variables, the nominal exchange rate consists of the ratio of nominal general price levels expressing the relative purchasing power of the two currencies as determined by relative demand-adjusted money stocks. Given the foreign price level and the domestic demand for money, the nominal exchange rate varies solely with changes in the domestic money stock. Unlike the real exchange rate, which is self-correcting, the nominal exchange can remain permanently depreciated as long as the domestic money stock is excessive. Therefore persistent exchange rate depreciation is a sure sign of an excess issue of currency. In Blake's own words,

> the *real* exchange depends on the proportion between the foreign payments which a country has to make, and the payments it has to receive. The *nominal* exchange depends on the comparative value of the currencies. The *real* exchange has an immediate effect on exports and imports. The *nominal* exchange, whether favorable or unfavorable, has no effect whatever upon exports and imports. The *real* exchange cannot be permanently favorable or unfavorable, whatever be the state of the currency. The *nominal* exchange may continue for any length of time favorable or unfavorable provided the value of the currency continues to be depreciated. Now the *computed* exchange depends upon the combined operation of the *real* and *nominal* exchange.[16]

Blake's analysis can be summarized by the equation

$$(8) \quad E = RN$$

that expresses the actual observed exchange rate E as the product of its real (R) and nominal (N) components, both of which contribute to exchange rate movements in the short run. In the long run, however, the real exchange rate is self-correcting (that is, it returns to its equilibrium level) and cannot be the source of persistent exchange rate depreciation. Only the nominal exchange rate can remain permanently depreciated. And, since the nominal exchange rate is determined by the money stock in conjunction with the demand for that stock, it follows that persistent exchange depreciation is a sure sign of an excess issue of currency.

Moderate Bullionist's Policy Analysis

Having developed the real/nominal exchange rate framework, the moderate bullionists employed it in their policy analysis. Two versions of the framework were utilized. The strict version fixed the real exchange at its equilibrium level, so that only the nominal component contributed to exchange rate movements. By contrast, the moderate version permitted temporary movements in the real component of the exchange rate. On the basis of these frameworks the moderate bullionists reached at least six conclusions regarding the post-1797 depreciation of the paper pound.

First, the fall of the paper pound following the move to floating exchange rates was due entirely to excessive note issues by the Bank of England. Real disturbances to the balance of payments played at best a temporary role, producing transitory deviations of the exchange rate from its purchasing power parity path dictated by the nominal exchange rate. Referring to such real shocks as (1) extraordinary food imports occasioned by domestic crop failures, (2) overseas military expenditures, and (3) remittances to foreign governments, the moderate bullionists argued that, in the long run at least, these real shocks wash out and the exchange rate returns to its nominal path. They further pointed out that only the nominal component of the exchange rate can be continually depreciated. And since that component itself is determined by the money stock, it follows that the persistent depreciation of the pound in the early 1800s was due to excessive monetary growth. In so concluding, the moderate bullionists rejected the central bank's contention that the fall of the pound was a real phenomenon that had nothing to do with money. That is, they dismissed the Bank of England's contention that the depreciation of the pound was due to special factors beyond its control, namely autonomous real disturbances to the balance of payments. Instead, they blamed the fall of the pound on the inflationary policies of the Bank of England itself. They contended that the Bank had taken advantage of the suspension of the gold standard to expand its note issue recklessly. This overissue of money, they thought, was largely, if not solely, responsible for the rise in prices of goods, gold, and foreign exchange experienced by Britain in the first two decades of the nineteenth century.

The moderate bullionists' second policy conclusion was that monetary contraction was the only way to strengthen the pound. Accordingly, they advocated monetary restriction roughly in proportion to the depreciation of the exchange rate. If the pound was depreciated five percent relative to its pre-Napoleonic war level, this was a sure sign that the money stock was five percent in excess of what it would have been under the gold standard and should be contracted. Monetary contraction was all that was needed to restore the pound to its prewar level. Mercantilist-type nonmonetary policies aimed at improving the real exchange rate by encouraging exports and discouraging imports are useless, they thought. The real exchange rate is automatically self-correcting and cannot be the source of persistent exchange rate depreciation. Only the nominal exchange rate can remain depreciated. Therefore, only the nominal exchange requires correction by the policy authorities. And this can be accomplished by reducing the money stock to a level consistent with a zero rate of inflation.

The moderate bullionists' third conclusion was that exchange rate depreciation has no lasting effect on the trade balance. Only deviations of the real exchange rate from its equilibrium level can influence the trade balance, and these deviations are bound to be temporary. The self-correcting real exchange rate invariably returns to equilibrium. And when it does, actual observed exchange rate movements merely reflect changes in the nominal price level and have no effect on the real trade balance. In short, while deviations from purchasing power parity can affect the trade balance, movements along the purchasing power parity path itself have no such effects. The nominal exchange rate (that is, the purchasing power parity) is neutral in its impact on real economic variables.

The fourth conclusion reached by the moderate bullionists was that persistent undervaluation or overvaluation of the currency is impossible. This conclusion involved direct application of the concept of the self-correcting real exchange rate. When the real exchange returns to its equilibrium value of unity, the actual observed exchange rate accurately reflects the domestic purchasing power of the currency, that is, the external and internal values of the currency coincide. Because the currency tends to conform to the purchasing power parity path dictated by economic fundamentals—namely, the underlying monetary conditions in each country—there is little need for policy intervention aimed at preventing under- or overvaluation. As previously mentioned, the strict bullionist writers (David Ricardo, John Wheatley) pushed this argument to the extreme, denying that the currency could *ever* be over- or undervalued, even in the short run. According to these writers, the real component of the exchange rate is always in equilibrium. Therefore the exchange rate itself is always at the purchasing power parity, and no corrective intervention is ever warranted. The moderate bullionists strongly endorsed the last part of this conclusion.

The moderate bullionists' fifth conclusion referred to the rising price of gold that accompanied the depreciation of the pound following Britain's 1797 move to floating exchange rates. They concluded that the cause of the rise in the sterling price of gold was the Bank of England's inflationary overissue of notes, the same factor responsible for the rise in the paper pound price of all goods and foreign currencies. They pointed out that under floating exchange rates the price of gold is determined by the quantity of paper money bidding for that precious metal. Thus the rise in the paper pound price of gold meant that a larger quantity of pound notes was bidding for the fixed world stock of gold. They were careful to note, however, that gold was not selling at a premium abroad. In particular, they pointed out that while the sterling price of gold had advanced sharply, its price in terms of stable (noninflated) Dutch guilders had remained relatively flat. They used this argument to refute the Bank of England's contention that the rising sterling price of gold had nothing to do with overissue of notes but reflected instead a shortage of gold caused by an increasing world gold demand for a fixed world gold supply. The Bank's contention, which implied a universal rise in the price of gold, was effectively refuted by the moderate bullionists who presented evidence of an unchanged foreign currency price of gold. Thus the rise in the domestic- but not the foreign-currency price of gold reflected an overissue of paper pounds rather than a world shortage of gold. From this, the moderate bullionists concluded that money growth in Britain had been excessive relative to money growth abroad.

Finally, the moderate bullionists concluded that the state of the exchanges and the price of gold together constituted the best existing indicators of the ease or tightness of monetary policy. Exchange depreciation and a rise in the price of gold signified that money was excessive and should be contracted. Conversely, exchange appreciation and a falling price of gold signified tight money. Although the bullionists considered other potential indicators of monetary policy, they rejected them as inferior to the exchange rate and the price of gold. They rejected, for example, the general price level as an indicator on the grounds that it was not readily measurable (price index numbers being little known at the time). Similarly, they rejected the money stock as an indicator on the grounds that it fails to capture the money demand factor influencing inflation and therefore is an inadequate measure of monetary policy. By contrast, the exchange rate and the price of gold are both readily measurable and embody all the monetary conditions producing inflation. As such, they were accepted as the best existing indicators of how well the monetary authorities are doing.

The preceding has examined the exchange rate doctrines of the early nineteenth-century bullionist writers. Their principal conclusion was that persistent exchange rate depreciation is primarily a monetary phenomenon. In their view, temporary real shocks have at best a transitory impact on the exchange rate, while permanent real shocks are likely to be dominated by monetary disturbances. Persistent exchange rate movements are for the most part dictated by monetary factors determining the nominal exchange rate rather than by real factors determining the real exchange rate. According to the bullionists, it followed that the post-1797 fall of the pound stemmed primarily from monetary causes and required a monetary cure, namely, putting the domestic money stock on a permanent noninflationary path. On this point the bullionists were in perfect agreement with modern advocates of the monetary approach.

The Antibullionists

Except for an expectations mechanism, the bullionists had assembled and integrated all the elements of the monetary theory of exchange rate determination. Compared to this accomplishment, the contributions of the antibullionists appear pretty meager indeed. They attributed exchange depreciation and domestic inflation solely to real factors—crop failures, overseas military expenditures, and the like—operating through the balance of payments. They correctly asserted that the exchange rate is determined by the supply of and demand for foreign exchange arising from external transactions. But they failed to see that an important factor influencing supply and demand might be relative national general price levels determined by relative money stocks. In fact, they rejected all monetary explanations, claiming that banknote expansion could not affect the exchanges in the slightest. They thought that the price of foreign exchange could rise indefinitely without indicating the existence of an excess note issue. As for policy recommendations, they urged mercantilist remedies, such as curtailment of imports and overseas military expenditures, to improve the balance of payments and to strengthen the pound. They doubted that any conceivable reduction in the banknote issue could restore the exchanges to prewar parity.

Their main analytical tool was the *real bills doctrine*, which they employed in an unsuccessful attempt to refute the bullionists' charge that the Bank of England had overissued the currency. The real bills doctrine states that money can never be issued to excess as long as it is advanced against commercial paper arising from real transactions in goods and services. In other words, the doctrine asserts the impossibility of overissue provided the money stock is tied to loans made strictly for productive purposes. Henry Thornton exposed the fallacy of this doctrine, however, when he pointed out that rising prices would require an ever-growing volume of loans just to finance the same level of real transactions. Under the real bills criterion, these loans would be granted and the money stock would therefore expand. In this manner, price inflation would generate the very monetary expansion necessary to sustain it, and the real bills criterion would not effectively limit the quantity of money in existence. In short, the real bills criterion virtually ensures that *any* rate of inflation, no matter how high, will be underwritten (validated) by accommodating monetary growth. Moreover, Thornton argued persuasively that an insatiable demand for loans (and, hence, a limitless supply of real bills) results when the loan rate of interest is arbitrarily pegged below the expected rate of profit on capital. In such cases the real bills criterion provides no bar to overissue. Thornton's demonstration of the invalidity of the real bills doctrine constituted a victory for the bullionists and for the monetary approach to the exchange rate. The victory was, however, not definitive; for when nations abandoned gold convertibility for floating exchange rates in World War I, the balance of payments approach had reemerged as the dominant view in government circles, thus setting the stage for the third great policy debate involving the monetary approach.

THE GERMAN INFLATION CONTROVERSY (1916-23)

The debate began in 1916, when Gustav Cassell used his purchasing power parity doctrine together with the quantity theory of money to attack the official balance of payments explanation of the wartime fall of the German mark. Whereas the policymakers blamed the currency depreciation on real disturbances to the balance of payments—such as obstructions to German shipping, wartime disruption of trade, external supply shocks, and the like—Cassel blamed it on excessive monetary expansion in Germany relative to that of her trading partners.

Cassel's Critique of the Balance of Payments Approach

Cassel's criticism of the balance of payments theory was virtually the same as that of his British bullionist counterparts more than 100 years earlier. Like them, he argued that the real exchange rate is automatically self-correcting in response to real shocks to the balance of payments. Such disturbances he regarded as having at best a transitory impact on the exchange rate. That is, he saw the latter as tending to return quickly to its equilibrium path dictated by purchasing power parity. Since real disturbances have no lasting effect on the exchange rate, they cannot be the source of sustained exchange rate movements. Therefore the balance of payments theory, which highlights the role of external real shocks, is incapable of accounting for persistent exchange rate depreciation such as that experienced by the German mark during World War I. In voicing these views, Cassel in essence endorsed the bullionists' contributions to the floating rate version of the monetary approach.

Regarding the operation of the self-correcting exchange rate mechanism, he noted that when balance of payments disturbances push the external value of a currency below its internal value, the currency becomes undervalued on the foreign exchanges, that is, its domestic purchasing power is greater than indicated by the exchange rate. Such undervaluation, he held, will immediately invoke forces returning the exchange rate to its purchasing power parity equilibrium where the external and internal values of the currency coincide. For as soon as a country's currency becomes undervalued relative to its purchasing power parity, foreigners will find it profitable to purchase the currency for use in procuring goods from that country. The resulting increased demand for the currency will bid its price back to the level of purchasing power parity. In short, deviations of the exchange rate from purchasing power parity generate corrective alterations in the trade balance, which eliminate the deviations. Both the balance of payments and the exchange rate return swiftly to equilibrium. Thus, contrary to the balance of payments view, external nonmonetary shocks have no lasting impact on the exchange rate.[17] It follows that any persistent depreciation must be due to excessive monetary growth that raises domestic prices and thereby alters the purchasing power parity or equilibrium exchange rate itself. In this connection he repeated Ricardo's dictum that an excess supply of money, whether stemming from a rise in money supply or a fall in money demand, is always and everywhere the cause of exchange rate movements.[18]

Cassel also criticized the proposition that exchange rate depreciation causes domestic inflation rather than vice-versa. In his view, exchange rate depreciation is a consequence, not a cause, of domestic price inflation. A rise in the equilibrium exchange rate, he said, merely reflects a rise in the purchasing power parity stemming from a rise in domestic prices and/or a fall in foreign prices. In this case the exchange rate adjusts to offset nominal price level changes in order to maintain the real (exchange-rate corrected) price of goods the same everywhere. He did, however, acknowledge that currency depreciation relative to purchasing power parity (that is, currency undervaluation) could produce import price increases. But he denied that these import price increases could be transmitted to general prices provided the money stock and hence total spending were held in check. He maintained that, given monetary stability, the rise in the particular prices of imported commodities would be offset by compensating reductions in other prices, leaving the general price level unchanged. In short, he denied that causation ran from the exchange rate to domestic prices as contended by the balance of payments approach.[19]

Hyperinflation and the Reverse Causality Argument

Despite Cassel's forceful and vigorous attack on the balance of payments doctrine, the debate did not go into high gear until the postwar German hyperinflation episode of the early 1920s,[20] when the price of foreign exchange rose to fantastic multiples of its prewar level, and everybody wanted to know why. Advocates of the monetary approach, including Cassel and his followers, pointed to the explosive growth of the money supply as the obvious answer. But proponents of the balance of payments approach dismissed the monetary factor and attributed exchange depreciation instead to the adverse balance of payments caused by the burden of reparations payments combined with Germany's alleged "fixed need for imports" and "absolute inability to export." In their view, money had nothing to do with the fall of the mark. On the contrary, they blamed that fall on external nonmonetary shocks operating through the balance of payments and claimed that causation ran from the exchange rate to money rather than vice-versa. More precisely, they identified a transmission mechanism running from reparations burdens and structural changes in trade, to balance of payments deficits, to exchange rate depreciation, to rising import prices and thence to general price inflation, to rising money demand, and, finally, to the money stock itself. That is, they specified the following causal chain: external real shocks, balance of payments deficits, depreciating exchanges, rising import prices, rising domestic prices, consequent budget deficits and increased demand for money requiring an accommodative increase in the money supply.[21]

Regarding the increase in the money supply, they contended that the exchange-induced rise in prices created a need for more money on the part of business and government to carry on the same level of real transactions, and that it was the Reichsbank's duty to accommodate this need, a duty that it could accomplish without affecting prices.[22] Here is the familiar argument that the central bank must accommodate supply-shock inflation in order to prevent a disastrous contraction of the real (price-deflated) money stock. German proponents of the balance of payments view, however, pushed this argument to ridiculous extremes. In 1923, when the Reichsbank was already issuing currency in denominations as high as 100 trillion marks and 30 paper mills were working around the clock just to keep the Reichsbank supplied with paper for its banknotes, Rudolph Havenstein, the President of the Reichsbank, expressed hope that the installation of new high-speed currency printing presses would help overcome the money shortage. Citing the real bills doctrine, he refused to believe that the Reichsbank had overissued the currency. He also flatly denied that that Reichsbank's discount rate of 90 percent was too low although the market rate of interest on short-term loans was an astronomical 7,300 percent per annum.[23]

Characteristics of the Balance of Payments School

It is instructive at this point to identify the chief characteristics of the German balance of payments school, if only because some of these characteristics persist in popular discussions of exchange rate movements. First, members of the school adhered to nonmonetary theories of the exchange rate. Some relied on superficial supply and demand explanations, asserting that the exchange rate is determined by supply and demand without saying what factors influence supply and demand. Others specified autonomous real factors operating through the balance of payments as the underlying determinants of foreign exchange supply and demand. None recognized that relative price levels and/or relative money stocks might also play a role. These variables were effectively excluded from the balance of payments school's list of exchange rate determinants.

The school's second characteristic was its tendency to identify exchange depreciation with specific items in the balance of payments. In particular, members singled out vital raw material imports as the culprit, just as some modern analysts currently blame petroleum imports. Still other members of the balance of payments school cited capital account disturbances, namely, reparations burdens. Third, members tended to treat the items in the balance of payments as predetermined fixed quantities that are independent of each other and of prices, when in fact they are interdependent variables determined by prices and the exchange rate. Imputing zero price elasticities to the demand for German exports and imports, they asserted that Germany's import requirements were irreducible regardless of price and that her exports were likewise fixed. They then extended this reasoning to the capital accounts of the balance of payments. Fourth, they denied the operation of a balance of payments adjustment mechanism. This denial followed from their assumption that the balance of payments is exogenously determined by factors that are independent of money, prices, and the exchange rate. Implying zero price elasticities of demand, this assumption permitted no equilibrating feedback effects from the exchange rate to the balance of payments. M. J. Bonn, a prominent balance of payments theorist, expressed the point as follows:[24] Suppose, he said, that import contraction is impossible, given Germany's urgent relief and reconstruction needs for imported raw materials and foodstuffs. Likewise, export expansion is impossible even at lower prices because of tariff barriers and economic depression abroad, both of which limit the foreign demand for German goods. Now assume a random real disturbance that produces a deficit in Germany's trade balance, thereby causing a depreciation of the real exchange rate or undervaluation of the mark relative to its purchasing power parity equilibrium. According to Cassel and his school, the undervaluation should, by lowering the foreign price of German exports and raising the domestic price of her imports, spur the former and check the latter, thereby restoring equilibrium in the trade balance. But these price-induced readjustments in trade are impossible when imports and exports are invariant with respect to real price and exchange rate changes. In such cases, real exchange rate depreciation will fail to correct the current account deficit, and even with zero money growth an adverse trade balance may persist in the face of an undervalued currency, contrary to the conclusions of the monetary school. Finally, the fifth characteristic of the German balance of payments school was its categorical rejection of the proposition that money influences prices and the exchange rate. As previously mentioned, this anti-monetarist view was implicit in the school's reverse causation, money shortage, and real bills doctrines, as well as in its strong endorsement of accommodating monetary policy.

The Monetary School's Critique

Members of the monetary school had little trouble exposing the fallacies in these views. They noted that supply and demand constitute only the *proximate* determinants of the exchange rate, that the *ultimate* determinants are the factors underlying supply and demand themselves, and that these factors include relative national price levels determined by relative national money stocks. They pointed out that the components of the balance of payments are variables rather than constants, that they are determined simultaneously by prices and the exchange rate, and that exchange rate movements primarily reflect monetary pressure on the entire balance of payments rather than nonmonetary disturbances to particular subsets or accounts. Regarding the reparations account, they contended that the depreciation of the mark was not caused by these reparations payments per se but rather by the inflationary way they were financed, namely, by fresh issues of paper money. As for Germany's alleged need for a fixed physical quantity of imports regardless of price, they argued that needs are not incompressible and independent of prices. In particular, they argued that even the import demand for absolute necessities possesses some price elasticity. Moreover, they pointed out that exports, too, are responsive to changes in relative prices and that the exchange rate mechanism would therefore tend to equilibrate exports and imports, were it not continually frustrated by inflationary money growth.[25] They maintained that had domestic prices stopped rising, a further depreciation of the mark would, by making German goods cheaper to foreigners and foreign goods dearer to Germans, have stimulated exports and restrained imports until a new equilibrium was reached. In their view, it was only the rise in domestic prices consequent upon the increase in the money supply that prevented the expansion of exports and the contraction of imports. Otherwise balance of payments equilibrium would have been restored by the exchange-induced shift in the relative price of exports and imports.

Most important, advocates of the monetary approach argued convincingly that exchange depreciation originated in excessive money growth and that the monetary authorities could have stopped the depreciation, had they been willing to exercise control over the money stock. In short, they insisted that the price of foreign exchange could not have risen indefinitely unless sustained by inflationary money growth. Had the latter ceased, the exchange rate would have stabilized.

The Expectations Element

The German inflationary controversy produced more than the definitive critique of the balance of payments approach to exchange rates. It also contributed the last of the three major elements to the monetary approach. The English bullionist writers had, of course, established the quantity theory and purchasing power parity elements and had lucidly enunciated their policy implications. All that remained was the statement and development of the expectations theory linking anticipations of future money supplies and demands with the current exchange rate. This step was taken during the hyperinflation debate, when the monetary school sought to explain why the dollar/mark exchange rate actually rose faster than the German money supply. According to the strict quantity theory and purchasing power parity hypotheses, the two variables should rise at roughly the same rate. Their failure to do so was taken by the balance of payments school as constituting evidence of the invalidity of the monetary approach. Advocates of the monetary approach rescued it, however, from this criticism by explaining the exchange rate/money growth disparity in terms of market expectations. In a nutshell, they contended that during periods of rapid inflation expectations of future inflationary money growth are discounted into the current exchange rate, causing it to rise faster than the current money stock.

To reach this conclusion they argued (1) that exchange rates are determined by relative money supplies and demands, (2) that relative money demands depend upon the expected future rate of change of the exchange rate (the anticipated depreciation cost of holding domestic rather than foreign money), and (3) that the expected rate of exchange rate depreciation depends, in turn, upon expected future inflationary money growth based on predictions of future monetary policies. From these considerations they concluded that an expected future depreciation of the exchange rate, by raising the anticipated cost of holding domestic rather than foreign currency, would shift demand from the former to the latter, thereby causing the exchange rate to rise faster than the money stock. In other words, assuming stable noninflationary policies abroad, expectations of inflationary domestic monetary policies would induce a drop in the demand for domestic relative to foreign currency, thereby putting additional upward pressure on the exchange rate. In this way exchange rate depreciation stems not only from a rise in money supply but also from an expectations-induced fall in money demand. This drop in money demand magnifies and reinforces the impact of current monetary growth on the exchange rate, causing the latter to rise faster than the money stock. Ludwig von Mises enunciated this view, arguing that inflationary money growth, by generating expectations of future inflation and hence future currency depreciation, would induce a flight from marks to foreign currencies, thereby bidding up the exchange rate relative to the money stock.[26] In so stating, he anticipated the modern rational expectations hypothesis, according to which exchange rate expectations are formed consistent with the way exchange rates are actually determined in the economy (that is, by money supply and demand).

Similarly, other members of the German monetary school insisted that the exchange rate reflects not only current monetary conditions but also expectations of future monetary conditions. Thus Howard Ellis, in his *German Monetary Theory 1905–1933* (1934), cites several economists, notably Gustav Cassel, Walter Eucken, Fritz Machlup, Melchior Palyi, Ludwig von Mises, A. C. Pigou, and

Dennis Robertson, who claimed that the exchange rate reflects anticipated increases in the money stock and that the external value of the mark varied in proportion to the expected future quantity of money rather than to the actual current quantity. In other words, observers watching the money supply accelerate month after month naturally came to expect future money growth to exceed present money growth, and these expectations, by inducing a flight from the mark, caused the exchange rate to outpace the money supply.

Similar explanations were advanced to account for disparities between the rate of domestic price inflation and the rate of currency depreciation in Germany. Eucken, Machlup, and von Mises argued that the exchange rate embodies inflationary expectations and that exchange rate movements parallel movements in expected future prices, not actual current prices. To explain why exchange rates adjust faster to changes in expectations than do national price levels (that is, why prices lag behind exchange rates), these analysts contended that asset markets such as the foreign exchanges are more efficient than commodity markets in exploiting new information about future prospects. For this reason, they claimed, expectations are discounted into exchange rates prior to being discounted into commodity prices, and the exchange rate therefore deviates from the purchasing power parity computed from current price levels. As Ludwig von Mises expressed it: "Foreign exchange quotations . . . are speculative rates of exchange—that is, they . . . consider not only the present but also potential future developments. Thus, the depreciation of the money becomes apparent relatively soon in the foreign exchange quotations . . . long before the prices of other goods and services are affected. . . ."[27] Cassel, however, perhaps put the matter most clearly when he wrote that

> A depreciation of currency is often merely an expression for discounting an expected fall in the currency's internal purchasing power. The world sees that the process of inflation is continually going on, and that the condition of State finances, for instance, is rendering a continuance of the depreciation of money probable. The international valuation of the currency will, then, generally show a tendency to anticipate events, so to speak, and becomes more an expression of the internal value the currency is expected to possess in a few months, or perhaps in a year's time.[28]

As this passage suggests, members of the monetary school not only explained how expectations affect the exchange rate, but also how expectations themselves are determined. In essence, they said that people form their exchange rate expectations from predictions of future monetary conditions resulting from future monetary policies. These predictions, they contended, are derived from all available information, including the observed behavior of the policy authorities, and especially the latter's monetary and fiscal response to large budgetary commitments such as reparations payments. These observations yield information about the authorities' policy strategy, which people use in predicting future policy actions affecting money supplies and the exchange rate. As Dennis Robertson put it in his famous textbook *Money* (1922), ". . . the actual rate of exchange is largely governed by the *expected* behavior of the country's monetary authority . . ."[29] Similarly, von Mises declared that the exchange rate "is affected only by changes in the relation between the demand for, and quantity of, money and the prevailing opinion with respect to expected changes in that relationship, including those produced by governmental monetary policies."[30] In the case of Germany, the policy authorities were already demonstrating a pronounced tendency to finance reparations payments with budget deficits and excessive monetary growth. People expected this policy to continue in the future, and these expectations were embodied in the exchange rate.[31]

To summarize, in addition to the German monetary school's definitive critique of the rival balance of payments approach, the hyperinflation episode produced a monetarist rational expectations analysis of exchange rate expectations. In so doing, it added the last of the major elements to the monetary approach and thus constituted a crucial stage in the historical evolution of that approach.

CONCLUSION

This chapter has surveyed the development of the monetary approach to floating exchange rates in three historical controversies with the rival balance of payments approach. The chapter offers some support for Sir J. R. Hicks's argument that monetary theory, unlike other branches of economic theory, tends to develop in response to particular historical events and episodes, notably severe monetary disturbances and institutional changes that alter the character of the monetary system.[32] In the case of the monetary theory of the exchange rate, at least, Hicks's argument seems valid. For, as discussed above, the main elements of the monetary approach emerged from controversies triggered by currency, price, and exchange rate upheavals following the suspension of the gold convertibility of paper currencies and the attendant move to floating exchange rates. Specifically, the chapter argues that elements of the monetary approach originated in the Swedish bullionist controversy of the 1750s, that its quantity theory and purchasing power parity components were thoroughly established and lucidly spelled out during the English bullionist controversy of the early 1800s, and that an expectations component was added during the German inflation debate of the early 1920s.

This is, of course, not to say that all of the implications of the evolving monetary approach were explicitly recognized and fully articulated in these debates. Missing, for example, was a rigorous and systematic statement of the *real balance effect*, through which exchange rate and price level adjustments remove discrepancies between actual and desired cash balances by deflating the real value of the nominal money stock to the level people desire to hold. Nevertheless, these early debates clearly established the essential analytical foundations of the modern monetary approach to exchange rates. Consisting of the quantity theory of money, the purchasing power parity doctrine, and the monetarist rational expectations analysis of exchange rate expectations, these essentials provide a powerful conceptual framework capable of explaining a large part of exchange rate movements.

NOTES

1. For another treatment of the role of the monetary and the balance of payments approaches in these debates see Johan Myhrman, "Experiences of Flexible Exchange Rates in Earlier Periods: Theories, Evidence, and a New View," *Scandanavian Journal of Economics,* 78, No. 2 (1976), 169–96.
2. On what follows, see Robert V. Eagly, *The Swedish Bullionist Controversy* (Philadelphia: American Philosophical Society, 1971).
3. Ibid., p. 14.
4. Ibid., p. 19.
5. Ibid., p. 19.
6. On Christiernin, see Eagly, ibid., pp. 23–99.
7. Ibid., pp. 49–50.
8. Ibid., pp. 27–29, 34.
9. On the English bullionist controversy see Denis P. O'Brien, *The Classical Economists* (London: Oxford University Press, 1975), pp. 147–53 and Jacob Viner, *Studies in the Theory of International Trade* (New York: Augustus Kelley, 1965), pp. 119–70.

10. Due to the unavailability of reliable general price indexes, the Classical economists also used the paper money price of bullion as an empirical proxy for the commodity price level. They reasoned that since the paper price of goods by definition is the paper price of gold times the gold price of goods, rises in the paper price of gold measure the degree of inflation of the paper price of goods when the gold price of goods is a given constant. In much of their policy analysis the classical economists assumed that the gold price of goods was indeed a constant determined on the world market and given exogenously to the small open (British) economy. Accordingly, they interpreted a rise in the paper pound price of gold as both a sign and measure of general price inflation and therefore the need for monetary contraction.

11. David Ricardo, *The Principles of Political Economy and Taxation* (London: J. M. Dent and Sons, 1917), p. 151, quoted in James W. Angell, *The Theory of International Prices* (New York: Augustus Kelley, 1965), p. 69, No. 3. [Emphasis added.]

12. John Wheatley, *Remarks on Currency and Commerce* (London: Burton, 1803), p. 207, quoted in Angell, op. cit., p. 52.

13. Regarding the policy implications of the Ricardian definition of monetary excess, see O'Brien, op. cit., p. 148.

14. Thornton's contribution is discussed in O'Brien, op. cit., pp. 149-150.

15. On Blake, see O'Brien, op. cit., pp. 150-51.

16. William Blake, *Observations on the Principles Which Regulate the Course of Exchange and on the Present Depreciated State of the Currency* (1810) (New York: Burt Franklin, 1969), pp. 86-88.

17. Gustav Cassel, *Money and Foreign Exchange After 1914* (New York: Macmillan, 1922), pp. 149, 164-65.

18. Cassel held that drops in output and the demand for money could not affect the exchange rate if offset by corresponding equiproportional reductions in the money supply. Therefore an inappropriate money supply was to blame for exchange rate movements. Ibid., pp. 61-62, 168-69.

19. Ibid., pp. 145, 167-68.

20. What follows relies heavily on Ellis's classic survey of the German inflation controversy. See Howard S. Ellis, *German Monetary Theory, 1905-1933* (Cambridge: Harvard University Press, 1934), Chapters 12-16.

21. Balance of payments theorists placed the blame for budget deficits on externally-generated inflation rather than on the actions of the fiscal authorities. Inflation, they said, automatically boosted government outlays, which were fixed in real terms and thus rose in step with prices. By contrast, taxes were fixed in nominal terms in the short run and thus adjusted sluggishly to inflation. The result was a succession of inflation-induced fiscal deficits that had to be financed by money growth. The fiscal authorities were viewed as having nothing to do with these deficits. The monetary school rejected this argument on the grounds that the government possessed the power to reduce its real expenditures, and moreover, that the authorities had deliberately engaged in massive deficit spending for several years prior to the hyperinflation thus establishing the fiscal and monetary preconditions essential to that episode.

22. Far from seeing currency expansion as the source of inflation, they argued that it was the solution to the acute shortage of money caused by skyrocketing prices. In this connection they advanced the peculiar theory that monetary excess could not possibly be the source of German inflation since the real or price-deflated value of the German money stock was smaller than it had

been before the inflation started. They failed to realize that excessive nominal money growth itself was responsible for the shrinkage in the real money stock. They did not see that inflationary monetary growth, by generating expectations of future inflation (expectations that constitute the anticipated depreciation cost of holding money) had greatly reduced the demand for money and had stimulated a corresponding rise in velocity. This inflation-induced rise in velocity had caused prices to rise faster than the nominal money stock thus producing the observed shrinkage in the real money stock. This sequence of events, however, was beyond their comprehension. Hence even though the nominal money stock was several trillion times larger than at the beginning of the inflation, they argued that it was still not large enough because prices had actually risen faster than the money stock. They thought that they could prevent further shrinkage of the real money stock by increasing the nominal money stock. In so doing they succumbed to the fallacy that the policymakers can systematically control real economic variables (e.g., the real money stock) by controlling nominal economic variables (e.g., the nominal money stock).

23. Leland Yeager, *International Monetary Relations: Theory, History, and Policy*, 2nd edition, (New York: Harper & Row, 1976), p. 314.

24. Bonn's views are discussed in Paul Einzig, *The History of Foreign Exchange* (London: Macmillan, 1962), pp. 271–72, and Ellis, op. cit., pp. 248-52.

25. In Howard Ellis's words, the monetary school denied that Germany could "experience a continuous depreciation of exchange by reason of 'inability to export' even if this is combined with an 'inflexible demand for necessities'. A heavy demand for these imports forces up foreign rates; but the rising rates make certain other goods produced within the country cheaper for foreigners, so that the resulting export pays for the imported necessities. [Only] *continuous* inflation may result in a persistently unfavorable balance, because the new income continuously advances the prices of imports," Ellis, op. cit., pp. 230–31.

26. See his remarkable 1923 monograph *Stabilization of the Monetary Unit—from the Viewpoint of Theory* reprinted in *On the Manipulation of Money and Credit*, translated by Bettina Bien Greaves and edited by Percy L. Greaves, Jr. (Dobbs Ferry, New York: Free Market Books, 1978). In that work he asserts that "in the final analysis, the foreign exchange rates are determined by nothing more than the anticipated future purchasing power attributed to a unit of each currency" (p. 28) such that "the configuration of foreign exchange rates on the Bourse forecasts anticipated future changes in commodity prices" (p. 31). To explain how expectations are incorporated (i.e., discounted) into exchange rates, he states that "if the future prospects for money are considered poor, its value in speculations, which anticipate its future purchasing power" will fall (p. 8). Given the anticipated future depreciation of the currency, the prospective "loss a person suffers becomes greater the longer he holds on to money" (p. 7). As a consequence, "the demand for money throughout the entire economy . . . goes down" (p. 8) and people "start to accumulate other moneys . . . which are valued more highly because their quantity cannot be increased by the government" (p. 11). The resulting shift from domestic to foreign money brings about the very depreciation that is anticipated. In short, when "people mistrust the reliability of the value of notes, they will seek to invest a portion of their cash holdings in foreign money" (p. 34) and the resulting exchange rate will "more nearly correspond to anticipated future conditions than to the present . . . quantity of money in circulation" (p. 8).

27. L. von Mises, "Balance of Payments and Foreign Exchange Rates" (1919) in *On The Manipulation of Money and Credit*, op. cit., p. 51.

28. Cassel, op. cit., pp. 149–50.

29. Dennis Robertson, *Money* (London: Cambridge University Press, 1922), p. 133.

30. L. von Mises, *Stabilization of the Monetary Unit—from the Viewpoint of Theory*, op. cit., p. 25. Note that von Mises here argues that since actual exchange rates are determined by money stocks per unit of real money demands, it follows that expected future exchange rates are determined by expected future values of those same monetary variables. These expectations in turn depend primarily on predictions of future monetary policies. Here is an early statement of the rational expectations hypothesis according to which exchange rate expectations are formulated consistent with the way exchange rates are determined in the monetarist model.

31. Expectations were not the only factor cited by the monetary school as causing the exchange rate to lead prices and money. Another was *currency substitution*, i.e., the substitution of stable dollars for unstable marks in German residents' transactions and asset money balances. Ludwig von Mises (ibid., pp. 5–7, 11, 13) provided one of the best descriptions of this phenomenon, pointing out how the expected capital loss from holding a weak domestic currency lowers its relative attractiveness as a medium of exchange and a store of value thereby encouraging its replacement by strong foreign currencies. He noted that such currency substitution, besides intensifying depreciation, tends to increase with the expected rate of depreciation itself, becoming especially pronounced in hyperinflations. In this connection he predicted in early 1923 that strong foreign currencies would increasingly supplant depreciated marks and that usage of the latter would shrink. This pattern was indeed evident in the later stages of the hyperinflation when Germans increasingly employed the U.S. dollar as a unit of account, standard of value, and medium of exchange.

32. Sir John Hicks, *Critical Essays in Monetary Theory* (London: Oxford University Press, 1967), pp. 156–58.

11

THE PURCHASING POWER PARITY DOCTRINE

INTRODUCTION

This chapter expounds the purchasing power parity (PPP) theory of exchange rates. In so doing it completes the discussion begun in Chapters 8 and 9. Those chapters identified the theory as an essential component of the monetary approach and located its position in the analytical framework underlying that approach. They showed how the PPP doctrine, together with the quantity theory of money, comprises the key linkage in the money-price-exchange rate nexus or transmission mechanism postulated by the monetary approach. Whereas the quantity theory links money supply and demand to prices, the purchasing power parity relationship links prices with the exchange rate. In so doing, it provides the vehicle through which relative money supplies and demands affect the exchange rate, that is, those monetary variables influence the exchange rate through the PPP ratio of domestic to foreign price levels. Seen in this perspective, the PPP doctrine is simply an extension of the quantity theory of money to the open economy under floating exchange rates. Accordingly, Chapters 8 and 9 demonstrated that all of the standard quantity theory propositions regarding proportionality, neutrality, money-to-price causality, and exogenity apply in the case of the monetary approach to floating exchange rates. What those chapters did not do, however, was to spell out fully the logical structure or analytical core of the PPP doctrine that produces these results. That task is left for the present chapter.

As expounded in this chapter, the purchasing power parity doctrine holds that currencies are valued for what they will buy. Therefore, the relative external value of two currencies, that is, the exchange rate between them, is determined by their relative internal purchasing powers as measured by the ratio of the general price levels in the two countries concerned. From this it follows that exchange rate changes reflect underlying changes in relative national price levels. In particular, the purchasing power parity theory predicts that the percentage rate of change of the exchange rate will tend to equal the differential between the relative rates of price inflation at home and abroad. Thus, if the domestic rate of inflation in the United States is, say, five percentage points higher than the comparable rate of inflation in Switzerland, the theory maintains that the dollar will tend to depreciate on the foreign exchanges at a rate of five percent relative to the Swiss franc. It follows from the theory that the way to strengthen a currency's external value on the foreign exchanges is to strengthen its internal value by reducing the domestic rate of inflation. In terms of the preceding example, the way to arrest the fall of the dollar relative to the Swiss franc is to bring the U.S. rate of inflation down to the lower Swiss rate. With both currencies experiencing the same rate of inflation (or fall in internal purchasing power), their relative purchasing power will remain unchanged, and the exchange rate will stabilize.

The foregoing view is hardly new. Rather, it is the product of at least 175 years of past theorizing about the connection between money, prices, and exchange rates. It is no exaggeration to say that the PPP doctrine, like the monetary approach itself, has attracted the attention of some of the leading monetary theorists of all time, including Thornton, Wheatley, Ricardo, Marshall, Cassel, von Mises, Keynes, and Viner. As proponents or critics, these economists helped formulate, develop, modify, and refine the central analytical propositions of the PPP doctrine. The purpose of this chapter is to identify and explain these propositions, to trace their development within the context of the monetary approach to exchange rates, and to indicate the extent of their survival in modern versions of the PPP theory. As a preliminary, however, it may be useful to begin with a rigorous brief statement of the PPP concept itself.

WHAT IS THE PPP DOCTRINE?

In essence, the PPP doctrine is a theory of the determination of the nominal exchange rate and its movements in long-run equilibrium when the trade balance is zero and the so-called real exchange rate or real barter terms of trade and its underlying real determinants are presumed to be constant. Given these conditions and assuming that all goods are exportable, the equilibrium exchange rate can be expressed as the multiplicative product of the terms of trade and relative general price levels, respectively. In symbols,

$$(1) \quad E = T\, P/P^*$$

where E is the exchange rate (defined as the domestic currency price of a unit of foreign currency), T the real exchange rate or real commodity terms of trade (that is, the quantity of exports given up to obtain a unit of imports), P the home country price level, and P^* the foreign price level. The derivation of this equation is particularly simple in the case where each country produces only one good, part of which it exports to the other. Trade balance equilibrium requires that the total value of each country's exports must exactly equal the total value of its imports measured in terms of a common currency unit. For the home country, this condition can be expressed as $QP = Q^*P^*E$, where Q is the physical quantity of exports of the home country, Q^* is the physical quantity of its imports (that is, the quantity of the foreign country's exports), P the home currency price of home country product, P^* the foreign currency price of foreign country product, and E the exchange rate defined as the home currency price of a unit of foreign currency. This expression says that the values (quantity times price) of exports and imports are the same denominated in terms of the home country's money. Solving this expression for the exchange rate yields $E = (Q/Q^*)(P/P^*)$, where the first term on the right-hand side is the real terms of trade, that is, the quantity of exports given up to obtain a unit of imports. Denoting the terms of trade variable as T, the foregoing expression reduces to $E = TP/P^*$, or equation 1 above. Since the terms of trade T is presumed to be at its constant long-run equilibrium value, it can be normalized via an appropriate choice of commodity units and set equal to unity. This step permits the PPP theory to be stated conventionally in its so-called absolute and relative versions.

The *absolute* version of the doctrine states that the equilibrium exchange rate equals the ratio of domestic to foreign general price levels, that is,

$$(2) \quad E = P/P^*.$$

As documented below, original formulators of the doctrine tended to state it this way, arguing that since currencies are valued for what they will buy, the exchange rate between them must equal their relative internal purchasing powers measured by the ratio of general price levels.

The *relative* version of the doctrine states that changes in the equilibrium exchange rate will equal changes in the ratio of general price levels, or, more generally, that the percentage rate of change of the exchange rate will equal the differential between the percentage rates of price inflation at home and abroad. In symbols, the relative version of the PPP doctrine is

$$(3) \quad e = p - p^*$$

where the lower-case letters denote percentage rates of change of the variables in equation 2.

The foregoing brief statement of the doctrine is, however, hardly sufficient. More than just the bare conclusion that the exchange rate and its movements tend to equal relative national price levels and their movements, the doctrine also consists of a number of interrelated propositions that underlie and support that conclusion. The most important of these propositions refer to (1) the international equalization of general price levels measured in terms of a common currency, (2) the corresponding international equalization of the real value of money, (3) the stability of PPP equilibrium, (4) the neutrality of equilibrium exchange rate changes, and (5) the causal role of money. Taken together, these propositions constitute the central analytical core of the PPP doctrine.

PRICE LEVEL EQUALIZATION

The first proposition states that the equilibrium floating exchange rate must equalize foreign and home country general price levels measured in terms of a common currency unit at the rate of exchange. General prices must be equalized across countries, because if they were not, goods would be a bargain in one country compared to the other. Everybody would want to buy in the low-price country and sell in the high-price one. The resulting excess demand for the currency of the former country and the corresponding excess supply of the currency of the latter would force the exchange rate into PPP equilibrium, thereby eliminating the price disparity.

That the condition of price equalization is implied by PPP can be seen by rearranging equation 2 to read $P = EP^*$, which says that home and foreign price levels are the same when expressed in terms of home currency units at the equilibrium rate of exchange. Likewise, price levels are also the same when expressed in foreign currency units, as can be seen by arranging the equation to read $P/E = P^*$. This condition ensures that the real (exchange rate-adjusted) price of goods is the same everywhere so that there exists no arbitrage advantage to buying in one country over the other. In short, the PPP doctrine implies that a representative bundle of goods will cost the same everywhere measured in terms of either money. Neither country will enjoy a price advantage over the other at the PPP exchange rate. Nor will residents of either country be able to purchase goods more cheaply at home with local currency than abroad after converting local into foreign currency. Neglecting transport costs, Londoners will find goods to be as cheap in New York as in London, and vice versa for New Yorkers.

EQUALIZATION OF THE VALUE OF MONEY

A second PPP proposition refers to the international equalization of the real value (purchasing power) of money. According to the PPP doctrine, the equilibrium value of money must be the same everywhere. For if it were not, people would demand more of the high- and less of the low-purchasing power money on the market for foreign exchange. The resulting excess demand for the former money and the corresponding excess supply of the latter would cause the exchange rate between the two moneys to adjust, until purchasing power was equalized and both money stocks were willingly held. Equalization of the real value of money across countries is therefore a necessary prerequisite of international monetary equilibrium. For only if such equalization prevails would there be no inducement to switch from one currency to the other. Only then will both money stocks be willingly held and the markets for money balances in both countries be cleared simultaneously.

Note that equalization of the real value of money is the exact counterpart of price level equalization. By definition, the value of money is nothing other than its purchasing power over goods. And since the purchasing power of money in terms of a representative market basket of goods is simply the inverse of the general price level $1/P$, it follows that equalization of price levels automatically implies equalization of the value of money. That is, when PPP prevails, any currency tends to command roughly the same amount of goods and services, whether spent at home or converted into foreign currency at the equilibrium rate of exchange and then spent abroad. Thus a dollar will purchase no more in the United States than it will buy in the United Kingdom after conversion into pounds sterling at the equilibrium rate of exchange, and vice versa for sterling.

STABILITY OF EQUILIBRIUM

A third proposition refers to the stability of PPP equilibrium. Regarding stability, the PPP doctrine contends that when the actual rate of exchange deviates from the PPP equilibrium, automatic responses tend to eliminate the deviation and restore the exchange rate to parity. With respect to disturbances to equilibrium, the PPP theory readily admits a host of factors—real shocks, expectations, sluggish commodity price adjustment, speculation, capital flows, and the like—that may cause the exchange rate to deviate temporarily from PPP. But it also describes strong stabilizing pressures that work to correct such deviations and push the exchange rate back toward equilibrium.

More specifically, the doctrine postulates an automatic self-correcting mechanism that keeps the actual exchange rate hovering close to its purchasing power parity equilibrium level. This mechanism relies on the corrective influence of price-induced shifts in international trade and the associated shifts in the demand for and supply of foreign exchange. For example, suppose the dollar price of the pound falls below its PPP equilibrium. On the market for foreign exchange, the pound is now undervalued and the dollar overvalued relative to their actual internal purchasing powers (that is, their values in domestic commodity markets). The undervalued pound makes British goods seem underpriced to Americans, whose eagerness to purchase them deluges the foreign exchanges with dollars seeking to buy pounds. Conversely, the overvalued dollar makes American goods appear overpriced to Britons, whose reluctance to buy them dries up the supply of pounds seeking to buy dollars. The resulting surplus of dollars and the corresponding shortage of pounds would quickly bid the exchange rate back to PPP where the external and internal values of the currencies correspond. Via this self-adjusting mechanism, the actual exchange rate would tend toward its equilibrium level, that is, the exchange rate would tend to hover about the PPP.

NEUTRALITY OF EXCHANGE RATE CHANGES

A fourth tenet of the PPP doctrine is that equilibrium nominal exchange rate movements that merely reflect differential inflation rates have no effect on real economic variables such as exports, imports, the trade balance, or the terms of trade. These real variables are determined by real (exchange rate-adjusted) relative prices. More precisely, they are determined by the so-called real or price-deflated exchange rate, that is, the nominal exchange rate deflated by the purchasing power parity ratio of national nominal price levels. According to equation 2, however, the real exchange rate of real relative price term EP^*/P is a fixed constant equal to one. This means that movements in the equilibrium exchange rate exactly offset changes in the nominal price ratio P/P^*, thereby preserving the real terms of trade between foreign and domestic goods.

For example, equation 2 says that a doubling of domestic prices relative to foreign prices will be accompanied by a corresponding doubling of the exchange rate, leaving real (exchange rate-deflated) relative prices unaltered. Since the real relative price of domestic goods compared with foreign goods is the same after inflation as before, the general rise in domestic prices will not affect imports or exports. The physical quantities of those variables will be the same as originally, and only the monetary units in which they are measured will have changed. In short, the PPP doctrine holds that exchange rate movements serve to offset differential rates of inflation and thus leave real relative prices and all real variables undisturbed. Provided the exchange rate corresponds to PPP, its changes will not affect real economic magnitudes. Being perfectly synchronized with price movements, such exchange rate changes are entirely neutral in their impact on the real economy. Within the context of the monetary approach, this proposition extends the neutrality postulate of the quantity theory of money to the open economy under floating exchange rates.

CAUSAL ROLE OF MONEY

The fifth proposition refers to the direction of causality between price levels and the equilibrium exchange rate. Strictly speaking, the

PPP price/exchange rate relationship is an equilibrium condition between two endogenous variables jointly determined by exogenous monetary conditions. However, it is often interpreted in the PPP literature as part of a simple unidirectional cause-and-effect relationship. Causation is typically viewed as running from price levels to the exchange rate, rather than vice versa. That is, monetary impulses are thought to be transmitted to the exchange rate through prices rather than to prices via the exchange rate. In particular, many PPP theorists argue that in the long run, when the determinants of the demand for money have stabilized at their steady-state equilibrium values, national money stocks determine national price levels, which, in turn, determine the equilibrium exchange rate. If true, this means that the ultimate determinant of the equilibrium exchange rate is relative national money stocks per unit of real money demands, and that the exchange rate moves over time as the differential in the growth rates of the money stocks. It also means that depreciation of the equilibrium exchange rate is a consequence rather than a cause of domestic inflation.

EMERGENCE OF THE PPP DOCTRINE

The foregoing propositions are hardly new. They originated more than 400 years ago in the rudimentary version of the purchasing power parity doctrine formulated by sixteenth-century Spanish scholastic writers to explain fluctuations in the Spanish currency price of foreign money.[1] They also underlie the view, expressed by John Locke and others in the seventeenth century, that "raising the money would raise the prices of all things accordingly and force up the rates of foreign exchange to the same extent."[2] Pehr Niclas Christiernin expounded them, albeit briefly and somewhat obscurely, in his 1761 *Lectures on the High Price of Foreign Exchange in Sweden*.[3] Their most lucid, rigorous, and systematic formulation, however, dates from the celebrated Bank Restriction Controversy of the early nineteenth century, when British bullionist writers enunciated them to explain the fall in the external value of the floating paper pound following Britain's 1797 suspension of the gold convertibility of its currency. Among the bullionist writers, four in particular—namely Henry Thornton, John Wheatley, David Ricardo, and William Blake—were instrumental in formulating, developing, and establishing the PPP doctrine and in integrating it into a monetary approach to exchange rates. Their contributions are discussed below.

HENRY THORNTON

Henry Thornton (1760–1815) was one of the first economists writing in the English language to explain clearly the operation of the self-adjusting mechanism that keeps the exchange rate close to its purchasing power parity equilibrium. In his classic *The Paper Credit of Great Britain* (1802) he argued that a rise in the price level in a country with an excess stock of paper money would automatically produce a roughly equivalent rise (that is, depreciation) in the exchange rate. He explained how a rise in British prices relative to foreign prices would, at the preexisting exchange rate, make foreign goods seem relatively cheap to Britons, whose desire to acquire those goods would increase the supply of pounds seeking to buy foreign exchange. At the same time, British goods would become relatively expensive to foreigners whose unwillingness to purchase them would reduce the supply of foreign currency seeking to buy pounds. The resulting excess supply of pounds and the corresponding excess demand for foreign money on the foreign exchanges would immediately bid the exchange rate up to the new PPP equilibrium consistent with the higher level of British prices.[4] Here is the clearest early explanation of the stability of PPP equilibrium.

Thornton was also one of the first British economists to advance the notion of the neutrality of purchasing power parity exchange rate changes. He noted that the rise in British prices would not act as an obstacle to British exports, because the corresponding change in the equilibrium exchange rate would "obviate the dearness of our articles" and "serve as a compensation to the foreigner" for the higher price of British goods. In this manner, he said, the offsetting rise in the exchange rate would "prevent the high price of goods in Great Britain from producing that unfavorable balance of trade, which, for the sake of illustrating the subject was supposed to exist."[5] Here is one of the clearest and most succinct early expositions of the proposition that PPP exchange rate changes cannot affect real economic variables such as the balance of trade since they merely offset divergent nominal inflation rates and thus leave real (exchange rate-adjusted) relative prices unaltered.

JOHN WHEATLEY

Thornton's discussion of PPP took the foreign money stock and price level as given constants. On this basis he concluded that the equilibrium or PPP exchange rate moves with the domestic price level alone. His contemporary John Wheatley (1772–1830), however, extended his analysis by considering variations in money and prices abroad as well as at home. Wheatley concluded that the relative quantity of money operating through relative national general price levels is the sole determinant of the exchange rate, so that the latter varies in strict proportion to relative money stocks. He reached this conclusion via the following route.

First, he asserted that "the course of exchange is exclusively governed by the relative state of prices, or the relative value of money, in the various countries between whom it is negotiated."[6] This, of course, is the absolute version of the PPP theory stating that the equilibrium exchange rate equals the ratio of domestic to foreign price levels according to the relationship

$$(4)\quad E = P/P^*.$$

Second, he argued that under purely paper monetary standards where money cannot drain out into foreign trade, the level of prices in each country varies in strict proportion to the quantity of money. This is, of course, the rigid version of the quantity theory of money, which may be expressed as

$$(5)\quad P = kM \text{ and } P^* = k^*M^*$$

where M is the money stock, k is a constant coefficient equal to the ratio of the circulation velocity of money to real output (both variables treated as fixed constants by Wheatley), and the asterisks denote foreign country variables.

Third, he substituted equation 5 into equation 4. This gave him the result that the exchange rate varies in strict proportion with relative money supplies, that is,

$$(6)\quad E = kM/k^*M^* = K(M/M^*)$$

where K is the ratio of the constants k and k*. He stated this result when he declared that "the course of exchange is the exclusive criterion of how far the currency of one country is increased beyond the currency of another."[7]

Wheatley commented at length on the key propositions of the PPP doctrine. Regarding the direction of causation between price levels and exchange rates, he asserts that "variation in the state of the exchange . . . is the effect, not the cause," of variation in price levels.[8] With respect to equalization of price levels and the value of money, he asserted that "prices are everywhere the same" and that money serves "as a uniform measure of value over the whole world."[9] Two things, he said, operate to ensure price equalization across countries. The first is exchange rate adjustment, which equalizes the common currency value of any given local currency price levels. The second is commodity arbitrage, which equalizes the common currency prices of internationally traded goods at any given exchange rate. Regarding the equalization of prices by commodity arbitrage, he contended that the openness of modern national economies rendered the law of one price applicable to general price levels as well as to the specific prices of internationally traded goods. That is, he assumed that under modern conditions of rapid and cheap transportation and communication commodity markets are integrated to such a degree that most goods are actually or potentially tradeable in a unified world market. He also assumed that the prices of non-traded goods are kept in line with the prices of traded goods through high degrees of intercommodity substitution in consumption and production, as well as by interindustry competition for factors of production. Given these conditions, the law of one price would apply to general as well as to individual prices. As he put it, "The facility with which the reciprocal communications of nations is carried on has a necessary influence on the markets of all, and approximates the price of their produce to a general level."[10]

Nevertheless, he insisted that the essence of the PPP concept consists of more than just the law of one price. Specifically, he interpreted PPP as a condition of international monetary equilibrium in which the real value of money is equalized across countries, and exchange rate variations are the primary means by which this result is achieved. That this is indeed his view is evident from his statement that "the course of exchange constitutes the practical means, by which money is enabled to discharge its functions over the whole world as a uniform measure of value."[11] To Wheatley, the central role of the exchange rate is to clear all markets for money balances by equalizing the internal purchasing power of various currencies. It therefore follows that "fluctuations in the exchange exclusively arise from the efforts of the different individuals of different countries to reduce their respective currencies to the same relative amount for the purpose of maintaining the general equivalency [of purchasing power]."[12]

Wheatley also discussed the stability of PPP equilibrium and the neutrality of equilibrium exchange rate changes. His treatment of these issues is among the more rigid and uncompromising in the monetary literature. Regarding temporary deviations from PPP, he flatly denied they could occur. In his view, the exchange rate is always at its PPP equilibrium level and thus it is impossible for currencies to be temporarily over- or undervalued on the market for foreign exchange. In other words, the self-equilibrating mechanism works perfectly and instantaneously to maintain the exchange rate at its PPP equilibrium. Here is a supreme example of Wheatley's tendency to apply the PPP theory of long-run equilibrium to the short run as well. This tendency is also manifest in his treatment of the neutrality issue. Regarding neutrality, he argues that because the exchange rate is always in equilibrium, its fluctuations will not affect trade in the slightest.

To summarize, Wheatley's version of the PPP doctrine is among the more extreme in the history of monetary analysis. Not only did he argue that the exchange rate is determined solely by relative money supplies operating through relative price levels, he also emphatically denied that real shocks could ever affect the exchange rate. His position was that such shocks, by affecting real national incomes, would immediately alter each country's demand for the other's product sufficient to maintain equilibrium in the trade balance and the exchange rate. For example, he argued that a domestic crop failure requiring increased food imports would, by reducing British real income and capacity to purchase, tend to force a compensating contraction of nonfood imports, leaving total imports and thus the trade balance undisturbed. Conversely, if imports were not curtailed, the resulting rise in British purchases from abroad would itself increase the income of foreign exporters, and so their demand for British goods. Britain's exports would therefore rise to match her imports, thus leaving the trade balance and the exchange rate undisturbed. Either way, adjustment would occur frictionlessly through income changes without affecting the exchange rate.[13] By ruling out real exchange rate disturbances, Wheatley was able to assert that the exchange rate never deviates even momentarily from PPP and that causation runs in a strict unidirectional channel from money to prices to the exchange rate. In his view, exchange rate movements are always and everywhere solely a monetary phenomenon and the PPP doctrine is merely an extension of the strict quantity theory of money to the open economy under floating exchange rates.

DAVID RICARDO

Like Wheatley, David Ricardo (1772–1823) also adhered to an extreme monetarist version of the PPP doctrine. He, too, denied that real shocks could affect the exchange rate even temporarily. Such shocks he regarded as automatically and instantaneously self-correcting, having no impact on the exchange rate. That is, he simply assumed that the slightest real pressure on the exchange rate would, by making British goods cheaper to foreigners, result in an immediate expansion of exports sufficient to eliminate the pressure.[14] In his view (1) the exchange rate is always at the PPP equilibrium determined by relative money stocks and (2) rises in the exchange rate are solely and completely the result of an overissue of currency. Consequently, he regarded exchange rate depreciation, together with the premium on gold bullion, as constituting both proof and measure of excessive money creation. In other words, if the exchange rate is 5 percent above its old gold standard par, then this is prima facie evidence that the money stock is also 5 percent in excess of its nonflationary level and should be contracted. This policy conclusion embodies the standard quantity theory propositions of proportionality, neutrality, monetary exogenity, and money-to-price causality, respectively, and shows that Ricardo, like Wheatley, interpreted PPP as an extension of the quantity theory of money to the open economy under flexible exchange rates.

The PPP doctrine also appears in the famous *Bullion Report* (1810), where it is expressed in the following words:

> In the event of the prices of commodities being raised in one country by an augmentation of its circulating medium, while no similar augmentation in the circulating medium of a neighboring country has led to a similar rise in prices, the currencies of the two countries will no longer continue to bear the same relative value to each other as before. The intrinsic value of the one currency being lessened while that of the other remains unaltered, the exchange will be computed between these countries to the disadvantage of the former. In this manner, a general rise of all prices, . . . and a fall of the foreign exchanges, will be the effect of an excessive quantity of circulating medium in a country which has adopted [an inconvertible paper] currency. . . .[15]

Like Ricardo and Wheatley, the *Bullion Report* concludes that exchange rate movements, together with the premium on gold bullion, "form the best general criterion from which any inference can be drawn as to the sufficiency or excess of paper currency in circulation."[16]

WILLIAM BLAKE

Both Wheatley and Ricardo assumed (1) that real disturbances could not affect observed exchange rates even momentarily, (2) that deviations from purchasing power parity could never occur, and therefore (3) that there was no difference between short-run and long-run exchange rate equilibrium, as far as PPP was concerned. These assumptions were relaxed by the bullionist writer William Blake (1774–1852), who argued that real shocks operating through the balance of payments could indeed produce temporary deviations from purchasing power parity. He maintained, however, that such deviations would eventually be eliminated by the operation of the self-equilibrating PPP mechanism. In so doing, he distinguished between real and monetary disturbances, between the short run and the long run, and between disequilibrium and equilibrium exchange rates. He also specified more thoroughly than his contemporaries the process by which PPP equilibrium is restored following external real disturbances. His work stands out as the most complete, lucid, and sophisticated exposition of the PPP doctrine in the early 1800s.

Blake's contributions to the purchasing power parity doctrine are contained in his *Observations on the Principles Which Regulate the Course of Exchange* (1810). In that work he contributed at least five innovations to the purchasing power parity theory of exchange rates.

First, he distinguished between *nominal* and *real* exchange rates, pointing out that both are underlying components of actual observed exchange rates. In particular, he expressed the actual observed exchange rate as the multiplicative product of its constituent nominal and real exchange rate components. Of these two components, the former captures the influence of monetary factors on the exchange rate, while the latter captures the influence of real (that is, nonmonetary) factors. That is, monetary factors affect the nominal exchange, whereas real factors affect the real exchange.

Second, he identified the nominal exchange rate with the purchasing power parity, pointing out that the "nominal exchange rate depends on the comparative values [i.e., purchasing powers] of the currencies" produced by underlying monetary conditions in the countries concerned.[17] That is, he defined the nominal exchange rate as the ratio of domestic to foreign nominal general price levels expressing the relative purchasing power of the two currencies as determined by relative money stocks. Regarding the nominal exchange rate, he specified that it is always at its purchasing power parity equilibrium dictated by relative money stocks. Moreover, as a purely nominal variable, it has no effect on real economic variables such as commodity exports and imports. As he put it, "the *nominal* exchange produces no alteration in the imports or exports of ordinary produce."[18] In so stating, he reaffirmed the neutrality proposition, according to which purely monetary changes have no effect on real economic variables.

Third, he defined the real exchange rate essentially as the relative price of one country's output in terms of the other country's output. Given the absence of nontraded goods in his analysis, the real exchange rate is the same as the real terms of trade. Regarding the real exchange rate, he pointed out that, unlike its nominal or monetary counterpart, it exerts a nonneutral effect on real economic variables. In particular, he asserted that it influences the demands for exports and imports, adjusting to bring the two into balance. That is, he argued that it operates to equilibrate the balance of payments.

Fourth, consistent with the PPP doctrine he implied that the real exchange rate possesses a long-run equilibrium value of unity determined by the arbitrage condition that the real price of goods must be the same everywhere so that there exists no advantage to buying in one market over another. He pointed out, however, that commodity arbitrage is not instantaneous and, as a result, transitory departures from real exchange rate equilibrium may occur from time to time. In particular, he argued that exogenous real disturbances to the balance of payments—crop failures and the like—may cause the real exchange rate to deviate temporarily from its long run equilibrium level dictated by the purchasing power parity. But he noted that such deviations will be automatically self-correcting through the feedback effect of the real exchange rate on exports and imports. Thus, according to Blake, a shock to the balance of payments that depreciates the real exchange rate will, by raising the relative real price of goods abroad and lowering it at home, act to stimulate exports and check imports, thereby reequilibrating the balance of payments and restoring the real exchange rate to its equilibrium level. In his own words, "an unfavorable real exchange will operate" both as a "bounty on exportation" and "a duty on importation," thereby expanding exports, contracting imports, and improving the trade balance. In this way the depreciated real exchange rate will continue to correct itself "until the consequent bounty upon all exported, and the duty on all imported, commodities shall restore it to par."[19]

Blake's analysis of the self-correcting real exchange rate is illustrated in Figure 1, which depicts the balance of payments B as an increasing function of the discrepancy between the actual (R) and the equilibrium ($\bar{R}$) real exchange rates. Note that the balance of payments function intersects the horizontal axis at unity, indicating that the external accounts achieve a zero balance when the real exchange rate is at its equilibrium value of unity such that PPP prevails. Starting from this equilibrium point assume that a transitory real disturbance (such as a harvest failure necessitating increased food imports) temporarily shifts the balance of payments line to the right (not shown on the diagram), thereby producing

Figure 1. Blake's Theory of the Self-Correcting Real Exchange Rate

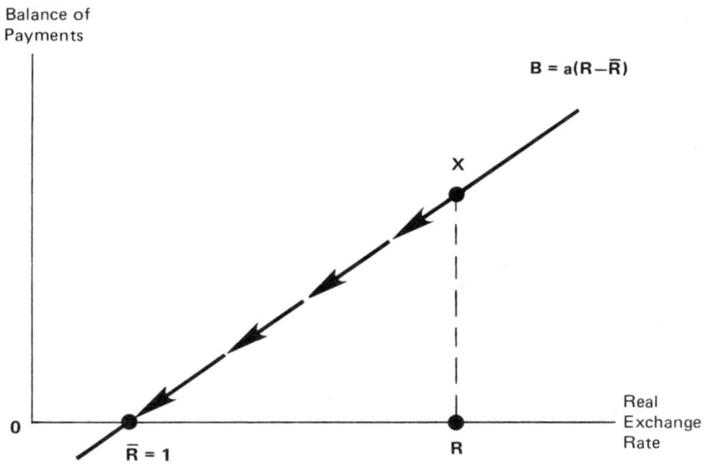

A shock to the balance of payments depreciates the real exchange rate, raising it to **R**. This depreciation, by raising the real relative price of goods abroad and lowering it at home, stimulates exports and discourages imports thereby producing a surplus in the balance of payments (point **X**) and a corresponding increased foreign demand for domestic currency. The increased demand to convert foreign into domestic money puts downward pressure on the real exchange rate which falls until it reaches its equilibrium level of unity. We go from **$\bar{R}$** to **R** to **X** and back to **$\bar{R}$**.

a trade deficit at the initial equilibrium exchange rate and bidding the actual real exchange rate up to R. Following the shock, the balance of payments line returns to its initial position, while the real exchange rate, reflecting time lags in the operation of commodity arbitrage, remains temporarily depreciated. This depreciation, however, by raising the real relative price of goods abroad and lowering it at home, stimulates exports and checks imports, thereby producing a surplus in the balance of payments (point X) and a corresponding excess foreign demand for domestic currency. This excess foreign demand for domestic money puts downward pressure on the real exchange rate, which continues to fall until the balance of payments is reequilibrated and purchasing power parity is restored.

Fifth, from the preceding analysis Blake concluded that, whereas real shocks can induce temporary deviations from purchasing power parity, in the long run purchasing power parity holds. Specifically, in the long run the self-correcting real exchange rate returns to its equilibrium value of unity. And when that happens, the observed exchange rate conforms to the purchasing power parity dictated by relative money stocks.

To summarize, the essentials of Blake's version of the PPP doctrine can be stated most succinctly in the form of the following simple seven-equation algebraic model:

(1) $E = NR$

(2) $N = P/P^* = K(M/M^*)$

(3) $R = EP^*/P$

(4) $\bar{R} = 1$

(5) $R = \bar{R} + S$

(6) $B = a(R - \bar{R})$

(7) $\dot{R} = -bB = -ab(R - \bar{R})$

The first equation defines the actual observed exchange rate E as the product of its nominal (N) and real (R) exchange rate components. The second equation identifies the nominal exchange rate as the purchasing power parity ratio of relative national price levels determined by relative national money stocks. The third equation defines the real exchange rate as the real (exchange rate-adjusted) price of foreign output relative to the price of domestic output. As previously mentioned, this real exchange rate is identical to the real commodity terms of trade when all goods are traded. The fourth equation fixes the equilibrium value of the real exchange rate $\bar{R}$ at unity consistent with the spatial arbitrage condition that the equilibrium real price of goods tends to be everywhere the same. The fifth equation specifies that, because of informational lags in the workings of commodity arbitrage, the real exchange rate R can deviate temporarily from its equilibrium value $\bar{R}$ by a factor S where S represents the real shock-induced disparity between the actual and equilibrium real exchange rates. Substituting equations 2–5 into 1 yields

$$(8) \quad E = (P/P^*)(1 + S) = K(M/M^*)(1 + S)$$

which says that real shocks operating through the balance of payments can cause the observed exchange rate to deviate temporarily from its purchasing power parity equilibrium dictated by underlying relative monetary conditions. Equation 6 explains how the real exchange rate affects the balance of payments. According to the equation, the balance of payments B is positive when the real exchange rate exceeds its equilibrium level, negative when the real exchange rate is below equilibrium, and zero when the real exchange rate is at equilibrium. Finally, equation 7 describes the self-equilibrating mechanism that restores purchasing power parity following an external real disturbance. That is, the equation specifies the determinants of the rate of change of the disequilibrium real exchange rate R where the dot over that variable denotes its rate of change (time derivative). In particular, equation 7 says that the real exchange rate adjusts to its equilibrium at a speed that is proportional to the balance of payments gap produced by the disparity between the actual and equilibrium real exchange rates. This equation ensures that the disparity will be eliminated and that the real exchange rate will converge on its equilibrium value consistent with the restoration of purchasing power parity. Constituting the most rigorous and complete analysis of the PPP doctrine in the nineteenth century, Blake's model presaged the work of Gustav Cassel more than 100 years later.

GUSTAV CASSEL

The preceding has specified the key propositions of the PPP theory and has traced their historical roots primarily to Thornton, Wheatley, and Blake in the early 1800s. For the classic statement of these propositions, however, it is necessary to turn to the writings of the

Swedish economist Gustav Cassel during and immediately following World War I. It was Cassel who introduced the phrase "purchasing power parity" into the literature. He did so when he resurrected the theory to explain the behavior of the dislocated European exchanges during the war and afterward in the hyperinflation episodes in the early 1920s. His forceful and systematic exposition of the theory was largely responsible for the popularity it enjoyed in the 1920s. His contributions to the doctrine include the following.

First, as previously mentioned, he gave the theory the name it bears today. Second, he clarified the concept of the PPP exchange rate, defining it in its absolute version as "the quotient between the general levels of prices in the two countries" and in its relative version as "the old rate multiplied by the quotient of the degree of inflation" in both countries.[20] Third, he redefined the somewhat vague notion of equalization of the value of money to mean that "a certain representative quantity of commodities must cost the same in both countries, if the exchange rate . . . stands at its equilibrium."[21] He pointed out, however, that this statement is strictly true only if the representative market basket of commodities is identical for both countries.

Fourth, he reformulated and refined the neutrality proposition in the following words.

> . . . the purchasing power parity represents an indifferent equilibrium of the exchanges in the sense that it does not affect international trade either way. Thus a country's export is not checked by low rates of exchange, provided only these rates correspond to a high price level abroad, or a low level at home; nor . . . is export particularly stimulated by high foreign exchange rates, so long as they only correspond to the relative purchasing power of the different currencies. Similarly, low prices of foreign currencies do not mean the encouragement of import from abroad or keener competition for the home producers, so long as these rates are merely a true expression for the purchasing power parity of the foreign currencies. On the same hypothesis high prices of foreign currencies do not in any way act as a check on import.[22]

Here is the classic statement of the proposition that PPP exchange rate changes leave the real (inflation-adjusted) exchange rate unaltered and so do not affect real exports and imports. From this Cassel drew the practical policy conclusion that no country could increase its competitiveness in foreign markets simply by deflating its price level. The deflation, he said, will be matched by an identical fall in the equilibrium exchange rate, leaving the real exchange rate and hence real exports unchanged.[23]

Cassel's fifth contribution was his identification of the sources of temporary deviations from PPP and his description of the self-correcting mechanism that operates to eliminate such deviations. Regarding causes of temporary deviations from PPP, he specified (1) differential speeds of adjustment of exchange rates and commodity prices in response to changes in expectations regarding future monetary conditions, (2) speculation against the currency, (3) forced sales of a country's currency abroad at arbitrarily low prices, (4) failure of export prices to move equiproportionally with general prices in response to monetary shocks, and (5) random real disturbances to the balance of payments. For all these reasons, he notes, a country's currency may be temporarily undervalued on the foreign exchanges. Regarding the operation of the self-correcting mechanism in such cases, he writes that "as soon as a country's currency is undervalued compared with its purchasing power parity, it will be of peculiar advantage to buy this currency, and to employ the money thus obtained in procuring commodities from that country. This stimulus thus applied to demand will necessarily very soon raise the price of the currency to the level of the purchasing power parity."[24]

Conversely, the corresponding overvaluation of the currency of the other country will, by making its goods seem overpriced on international markets, reduce the demand for its exports and thus for its currency. If country A's currency is overvalued and B's currency undervalued, then the "export from A to B must be largely checked. . . . At the same time the import from B to A would be artificially stimulated by such a valuation. Indeed, both these influences would tend to raise the value of B's currency in A, and to restore it to the purchasing power parity, which shows that this parity is the true equilibrium of the exchanges."[25] In short, deviations from PPP affect trade flows in a direction that counteracts the deviation and represents a corrective to it.

Finally, Cassel elaborated on the issue of price–exchange rate causality and its implications. Like Wheatley, he repeatedly states that causation runs from price levels to the equilibrium exchange rate, that is, that the latter variable is "determined by" or "dependent upon" the ratio of the price levels.[26] More precisely, he invokes the quantity theory of money to assert that money determines prices, which, in turn, determine the exchange rate. In short, he argues that the exchange rate is determined by relative national money stocks operating through relative price levels. This means that relative national money stocks are the ultimate determinant of exchange rates. In his words, the exchange rate between two countries "must vary as the quotient between the quantities of their respective circulating media."[27]

From the foregoing he drew two implications. The first is that in a regime of floating exchange rates, inflation is entirely homemade and cannot be imported from abroad. "An important consequence of the . . . dependence of the exchange on the purchasing power parity," he said, "is . . . that a rise in prices in a foreign country can never cause a rise in prices at home."[28] For, assuming, the exchange rate is at PPP, "a rise in prices in a foreign country should have no other effect than that of the country's currency being quoted so much lower that the prices on goods imported therefrom remain unaltered. If the influence of the rise in foreign prices is carried further, it is a sign that it has found support in an independent domestic inflation."[29] In sum, a rise in foreign prices will be offset by a corresponding drop in the equilibrium exchange rate, leaving the price of imports, and so the domestic price level, unchanged. If the domestic price level does indeed rise, it is because of domestic monetary expansion and not the rise of foreign prices.

The second implication is that exchange rate depreciation itself cannot cause domestic inflation. A rise in the equilibrium exchange rate, he said, is the result not the cause of domestic inflation. True, he did acknowledge that a rise in the exchange rate above the PPP could produce import price increases. But he denied that these import price increases could be transmitted to general prices, provided the money stock and total spending were held constant. He maintained that, given a fixed money stock, the rise in the particular prices of imported commodities would be offset by compensating reductions in other prices, leaving the general price level unchanged. As he put it, "Only if the B currency were quoted above the PPP . . . could the high price of this currency have any influence to raise the prices in country A. But even this influence would not be able to raise the general price level unless it had the support of a more plentiful supply of means of payment. . . ."[30]

LUDWIG VON MISES

Rivaling Cassel as the principal proponent of the PPP doctrine in the 1920s was the famous Austrian economist Ludwig von Mises. It is not necessary to give a lengthy summary of his writings on the subject. Three quotations will suffice. The first refers to equalization of the value of money, the second to the stability of PPP equilibrium, and the third to the causal role of money—all key propositions of the PPP doctrine. Regarding equalization of the value of money, he states that "exchange rates must eventually be established at a height at which it makes no difference whether one uses a piece of money directly to buy a commodity, or whether one first exchanges this money for units of a foreign currency and then spends that foreign currency for the desired commodity."[31]

The operation of the self-equilibrating mechanism is described by von Mises in the following words:

> Should the rate deviate from that determined by the purchasing power parity . . . an opportunity would emerge for undertaking profit-making ventures. It would then be profitable to buy commodities with the money which is legally *under*valued on the exchange, as compared with its purchasing power parity, and to sell those commodities for that money which is legally *over*valued on the exchange, as compared with its actual purchasing power. Whenever such opportunitues for profit exist, buyers would appear on the foreign exchange market with a demand for the undervalued money. This demand drives the exchange up until it reaches its "final rate" [i.e., the PPP].[32]

Finally, with respect to the causal role of money in the determination of the equilibrium exchange rate, he states that "exchange rates rise because the quantity of the domestic money has increased and commodity prices have risen."[33] That is, he traces a unidirectional chain of causation running from money to prices to the exchange rate and in so doing enunciates a strong version of the monetary approach. It should be noted, however, that his enthusiastic acceptance of the PPP doctrine was not universally endorsed by his contemporaries, many of whom were beginning to question the validity of the doctrine.

CRITICISMS OF THE PPP DOCTRINE

Even at the height of its popularity in the 1920s and early 1930s, the PPP doctrine was the target of severe criticism. Critics such as Frank Taussig, J. M. Keynes, A. C. Pigou, and Jacob Viner contended that the theory suffered from certain crippling defects. For one thing, it ignored factors other than relative national price levels that also determine exchange rates. Consisting of the terms of trade, various obstacles to trade (tariffs, transport costs, and the like), and the structure of prices in both countries, these factors may produce a permanent disparity between the equilibrium exchange rate and the calculated absolute PPP. Moreover, their movements over time tend to generate a persistent discrepancy between exchange rate movements and those of the PPP, thus invalidating the relative version of the doctrine. For example, changes in the terms of trade caused by shifts in international demand, capital movements, and changes in the relative productivity of labor would produce permanent changes in the equilibrium exchange rate even if the PPP ratio of general price levels remained unchanged. Likewise changes in tariffs and transport costs as well as alterations in the relationship between export prices and general prices in either country would prevent the equilibrium exchange rate from adhering to the path dictated by PPP. Discrepancies may also stem from the existence of nontraded (purely domestic) goods whose prices have no close connection with the exchange rate although they do enter the general price levels used to compute the PPP. For these reasons the critics argued that the doctrine is incorrect when applied to general price levels. They held that it was valid only when restricted to the prices of international traded goods, in which case, to use Keynes's expression, it becomes a "truism, and as nearly as possible jejune."[34]

BRESCIANI-TURRONI'S CRITIQUE

The foregoing criticisms were themselves evaluated in a famous 1934 paper by the Italian economist Costantino Bresciani-Turroni.[35] In what is perhaps the most rigorous and systematic analysis of the PPP doctrine to be found in the economic literature, Bresciani-Turroni concluded (1) that the absolute version of the doctrine is indeed generally incorrect, (2) that the relative version, however, is theoretically correct in the case of monetary but not real shocks, and (3) that, as an empirical matter, the relative verison may be approximately correct even in the latter case. In so doing, he provided a masterful defense of the relative version of the theory.

The foregoing conclusions are derived by Bresciani-Turroni on the basis of a simple analytical model, which he constructed via the following steps. First, he assumed that tariffs, transport costs, and other obstacles to trade tend to raise the supply price of each country's exports by a certain fraction. Thus if P_x and P_x^* are the domestic pretrade prices of a unit of home and foreign country exportables, respectively, and t and t* represent the fraction by which those prices are raised by obstacles to trade, then the total supply prices to buyers of the countries' exports will be $P_x(1 + t)$ and $P_x^*(1 + t^*)$, respectively. These expressions state that the price of goods in the buying market must exceed the price in the selling market by the cost of transport and tariffs.

Second, he argued that long-run equilibrium requires that the total value of each country's exports be exactly equal to the total value of its imports measured in terms of a common currency. For the home country, this zero trade balance equilibrium condition can be expressed as

$$(9) \quad QP_x(1 + t) = Q^*P_x^*(1 + t^*)E$$

where Q is the quantity of physical exports of the home country, Q^* the physical quantity of its imports (that is, the quantity of the foreign country's exports), $P_x(1 + t)$ the home currency supply price (including transport costs) of home-country exports, $P_x^*(1 + t^*)$ the foreign currency supply price of foreign country exports, and E the exchange rate defined as the home currency price of a unit of foreign currency.

Third, he assumed that the domestic price of each country's exportables can be linked to general price levels P and P^* via the following relationships:

$$(10) \quad P_x = RP \text{ and } P_x^* = R^*P^*$$

where R and R^* denote the equilibrium ratio of export prices to general prices in each country, as can be seen by expressing the equations in the form $R = P_x/P$ and $R^* = P_x^*/P^*$. Representing the equilibrium relative prices of exportables in terms of general price levels at home and abroad, these equations summarize the equilibrium *structure* of prices in the two countries concerned.

Finally, he substituted equation 10 into equation 9 and solved for the equilibrium exchange rate, thereby obtaining the expression

$$(11) \quad E = \left[\frac{Q}{Q^*}\right]\left[\frac{1 + t}{1 + t^*}\right]\left[\frac{R}{R^*}\right]\left[\frac{P}{P^*}\right]$$

which says that the equilibrium exchange rate is the product of four determinants, namely the unobstructed barter terms of trade, relative transport and tariff costs, relative price structures, and the PPP, respectively. Regarding these determinants, note that the terms of trade variable shows the quantity of exports the home country must give up in the absence of tariff and transport costs to obtain a unit of imports (the other country's exports) and thus represents the real cost of obtaining the latter in terms of the amount of the export good sacrificed. Determined by real factors such as tastes, technology, and resource endowments, the terms of trade variable captures nonmonetary influences affecting the exchange rate.

The relative tariff and transport cost variable shows the impact on the exchange rate of natural and artificial obstacles to trade. Note that when the obstacles are identical both for exports and for imports such that $t = t^*$, the ratio reduces to one and thus cannot distort the exchange rate from the PPP. Only if trade barriers are more severe in one direction than another—that is, exports and imports are hampered unequally—would such distortion exist.

The remaining determinants can be summarized briefly. The price structure variable compares the relationship between export prices and general price levels at home and abroad. Unless both countries possess identical price structures, this determinant will cause a persistent discrepancy between the equilibrium exchange rate and the PPP. Note also that the price structure variable is determined not by monetary but by real factors (such as tastes, technology, resource supplies), which means that it is largely invariant to monetary changes. By contrast, the PPP variable is, in Bresciani-Turroni's own words, determined by "the monetary conditions particular to each country" and thus varies with changes in relative money stocks.[36]

On the basis of equation 11, Bresciani-Turroni reached the following conclusions regarding the validity of the PPP theory. First, the absolute version of the theory is generally incorrect. Evidently the equilibrium condition is not "exchange rate equals PPP" but rather "exchange rate equals PPP multiplied by the terms of trade, relative obstacles to trade, and relative internal price structures." These other things may cause the equilibrium exchange rate to deviate permanently from the PPP.

Second, the relative version of the doctrine remains valid if these other factors are constant. That is, other things remaining the same, the exchange rate varies equiproportionally with relative price levels as predicted by the theory. This can be demonstrated by holding the other factors constant in equation (11) and letting the PPP double or quadruple. The changes in the PPP will be matched by a corresponding doubling or quadrupling of the exchange rate.

Third, whether other things remain the same depends upon whether disturbances emanate from the monetary or real sectors of the economy. Purely monetary disturbances will not affect the long-run equilibrium values of the non-PPP determinants of the exchange rate. These determinants are real variables. As such, they are largely invariant to monetary shocks. In long-run equilibrium the latter affect only price levels and the PPP. It therefore follows that the relative version of the theory holds in the case of monetary changes.

Fourth, in sharp contrast to purely monetary disturbances, real disturbances will indeed alter the non-PPP determinants of the exchange rate, thus producing systematic divergences between exchange rate variations and those of the PPP. This means that the relative version will not hold exactly in the case of real changes. Nevertheless, it may hold at least *approximately* if the real effects are small. And, according to Bresciani-Turroni, that is exactly what one would expect to find. He maintained that there are limits to how far away from the PPP real disturbances can distort the exchange rate. These limits are set by the price sensitivity (elasticity) of international demands. If this sensitivity is high, then even slight deviations from PPP will invoke large price-induced shifts in trade sufficient to check further deviations. It follows, he said, that "when international demands are very elastic, which happens in the case of modern industrial countries with a considerable resourcefulness of supply," the influence of real changes on exchange rates is "likely to be confined within narrow limits." If so, "there will be for exchange rate indexes a tendency to settle at a level approximately equal to the ratio of . . . price indexes."[37] In short, provided international demand elasticities are high, the relative version of the doctrine remains approximately valid even in the case of real disturbances and structural changes.

Finally, mention should be made of Bresciani-Turroni's views of the so-called commodity arbitrage interpretation of PPP. This interpretation sees PPP as an extension of the law of one price, according to which the operation of goods arbitrage equalizes the common currency price of goods across countries. There are two principal versions of this hypothesis. The strict version holds that the law of one price applies only to traded goods, because only those goods are directly subject to commodity arbitrage. An alternative version, favored by monetarists who regard PPP as a measure of the relative buying power of money over a comprehensive list of goods, extends the law of one price to general price levels. This view assumes either that all goods are traded (so that general prices are identical to traded goods prices), or that the prices of nontraded goods are kept in line with traded goods prices by high degrees of commodity substitution in production and consumption as well as by interindustry competition for factors of production.

Bresciani-Turroni adhered to this latter view, arguing that "domestic [that is, nontraded goods] prices and export prices will tend in the long run to move in the same direction."[38] He emphatically dismissed the strict traded goods version of the law of one price as a trivial truism devoid of economic content. He argued that because internationally traded goods have a single world price, their common currency prices by definition must be the same everywhere (transport costs aside). In other words, the ratio of their prices in domestic currencies must, shipping costs aside, move with exchange rates purely as a matter of arithmetic. Moreover, since arbitrage by definition equalizes prices of traded goods at *any* given exchange rate, it fails to explain how a unique equilibrium exchange rate is determined. He took it for granted, of course, that commodity arbitrage would occur, but he insisted that the essence of the PPP doctrine was not simply the law of one price but rather the notion that exchange rates accurately reflect the monetary conditions in the countries concerned. And if the purpose of the PPP is to indicate relative monetary conditions, then one should compare not the prices of traded goods alone but rather general price levels that measure the real value of money.

FRIEDMAN AND SCHWARTZ

The principal contribution to the PPP doctrine since Bresciani-Turroni's analysis has been Milton Friedman's and Anna Schwartz's 1963 generalization of the price-induced PPP self-equilibrating mechanism to apply to all items in the balance of payments. This was a new development. Prior to Friedman and Schwartz, stabilizing price pressures were viewed as operating solely or primarily through the trade accounts alone. Cassel, for example, argued that the exchange rate would be brought into conformity with PPP via price-induced changes in commodity trade. In his view, a doubling of U.S. prices relative to foreign prices at the existing exchange rate would, by making U.S. goods twice as expensive to foreigners and foreign goods half as expensive to U.S. residents, discourage U.S. exports and encourage U.S. imports, thereby resulting in an increased supply of dollars seeking to buy a reduced supply of foreign currency on the market for foreign exchange. The resulting excess demand for foreign currency and the corresponding excess supply of dollars would bid the exchange rate to double its original level. In this way, changes in exports and imports and the corresponding shifts in the supply and demand for foreign exchange would raise the exchange rate to the level dictated by PPP. Thus, in the traditional view, price-induced changes in commodity trade constitute the primary means by which the exchange rate is restored to the PPP equilibrium.[39]

Friedman and Schwartz argued, however, that such adjustment is not restricted to the trade accounts alone. In particular, price-induced changes in unilateral transfers and capital movements also play a role. Regarding unilateral transfers, they contended that a doubling of wages and prices in the United States relative to those abroad "would mean that a given number of dollars transferred by immigrants, for example, to their families abroad would constitute only half as large a fraction of the immigrants' wages and so would tend to increase the amount sent."[40] On the market for foreign exchange, this increased desire to make unilateral transfers would translate into an increased supply of dollars seeking to buy foreign currencies, thereby putting upward pressure on the exchange rate.

The same holds true for capital flows. Regarding such flows, Friedman and Schwartz state that, given the U.K. price level and the dollar/pound exchange rate, a doubling of U.S. prices "would mean that a given number of pounds sterling intended for capital investment in the United States would buy only half as much physical capital while still commanding an unchanged amount at home and so would discourage capital investment in the U.S."[41] On the market for foreign exchange, this reluctance to invest in the United States would be reflected in a reduced supply of pounds seeking to buy dollars. Likewise, the corresponding increased desire of Americans to invest in Britain would be manifested in an increased supply of dollars seeking to buy pounds. The resulting excess demand for pounds and the corresponding excess supply of dollars would help bid the exchange rate up toward its PPP equilibrium. In this manner the self-equilibrating mechanism operates through the capital account as well as the current account of the balance of payments. More generally, since all items in the balance of payments are critically dependent on relative national price levels, all contribute to the stability of PPP equilibrium.

CONCLUDING COMMENTS

This chapter has traced the evolution of the PPP theory of floating exchange rates from its initial rigorous formulation by Thornton,

Wheatley, and Blake in the early 1800s to its definitive critique and restatement by Bresciani-Turroni in the mid-1930s. It is now time to summarize the views of current proponents of the doctrine.

With the exception of Friedman and Schwartz, modern proponents have added little beyond Bresciani-Turroni's analysis. Like him, they hold that the long-run behavior of the equilibrium exchange rate is chiefly, but not solely, determined by the behavior of relative demand-adjusted money stocks (that is, nominal money supplies per unit of real money demands) operating through relative national price levels.[42] Like him, they readily acknowledge that a variety of factors—tariff changes, productivity growth differentials, shifts in international commodity demands, capital movements, and the like—impinge on the equilibrium rate and force it to deviate from the path dictated by the PPP. And, like him, they argue that price parities operate to limit these deviations and hold them in check. In particular, they contend that divergences from PPP will trigger the restraining force of price-induced trade and capital flows that arrest further deviations. For example, they argue that real factors that push the external value of a currency below its PPP will inevitably generate price incentives tending to spur exports and check imports. The resulting trade balance improvement and the associated strengthening of demand for the currency on the foreign exchanges will halt further deviations from price parity. In this manner, the PPP mechanism tends to confine systematic distortions between the equilibrium exchange rate and PPP within relatively narrow limits.

The same mechanism, proponents note, also works to correct random exchange rate variations and to keep the actual rate tending toward the equilibrium rate, whether or not the latter differs from PPP. That is, suppose the equilibrium rate is permanently distorted from purchasing power parity, as indicated by the expression $E = K(P/P^*)$ where K is the divergence between the two variables. Notwithstanding this distortion, the self-corrective mechanism will tend to eliminate all deviations from PPP up to the factor K, and the equilibrium exchange rate will remain powerfully related to the PPP.

Finally, proponents note that the PPP theory completely explains equilibrium exchange rate movements stemming from purely monetary changes. Moreover, they contend that it applies, albeit approximately, when monetary disturbances dominate real disturbances. They point out that a money-induced rise in the PPP tends to be reflected to its full extent, without modification, in the exchange rate. By contrast, a real shock operating through the balance of payments provokes compensating changes in exports and imports that limit its long-run effect on the exchange rate.

In the long run, therefore, exchange rate movements will largely reflect changes in relative money stocks as predicted by the theory. For these reasons, proponents hold that the PPP theory remains a sound and useful concept and a valid component of the monetary approach to exchange rates.

NOTES

1. On the Spanish origins of the PPP doctrine see Marjorie Grice-Hutchison, *The School of Salamanca: Readings in Spanish Monetary Theory, 1544–1605* (Oxford: Clarendon Press, 1952), pp. 55–58, 96–103, 113–14. See also Paul Einzig, *The History of Foreign Exchange* (London: Macmillan, 1979), pp. 146–47 and Murray N. Rothbard, "New Light on the Prehistory of the Austrian School," in *The Foundations of Modern Austrian Economics*, ed. Edwin G. Dolan (Kansas City: Sheed and Ward, 1976), pp. 57–58.

2. John Locke, quoted in Chi-Yuen Wu, *An Outline of International Price Theories* (London: Routledge, 1939), p. 74.

3. For a translation and summary of Christiernin's *Lectures* see Robert V. Eagly, *The Swedish Bullionist Controversy* (Philadelphia: American Philosophical Society, 1971), pp. 41–99. Eagly points out that, consistent with the PPP doctrine, Christiernin presumed that both the real value of money and its counterpart, the real (i.e., gold) price of goods, tend to be equalized across nations. Regarding such international equalization of the value of money, Christiernin wrote that "The exchange rate is at parity" when the real value or gold content of a unit of domestic money is the same abroad after conversion into foreign currency at the going exchange rate as it is at home (Eagly, pp. 49–50). Christiernin also commented on other propositions of the PPP doctrine. For example, with respect to the neutrality proposition, he wrote that a depreciation of the nominal (i.e., PPP) exchange rate cannot affect real economic variables as "the absolute level of the exchange rate is in itself of no consequence for commerce and industry" because "mere nominal changes [in the exchange rate] cannot constitute real dearness" (Eagly, pp. 87, 76). He recognized, however, that real (as opposed to nominal) exchange rate changes caused by deviations from PPP could, indeed, affect real economic variables. But he thought that such deviations would be short-lived and inherently self-correcting. In this connection, he indicated how departures from PPP are corrected by trade-induced shifts from overvalued to undervalued currencies. These shifts, he noted, bid the exchange rate back to PPP equilibrium at which both money stocks are willingly held (Eagly, p. 85).

4. Henry Thornton, *An Enquiry into the Nature and Effects of the Paper Credit of Great Britain* (1802) (Fairfield: Augustus Kelley, 1978), pp. 198–99.

5. Thornton, p. 199.

6. John Wheatley, *An Essay on the Theory of Money and Principles of Commerce* (London: T. Cadell and W. Davies, 1807), p. 85.

7. John Wheatley, *Remarks on Currency and Commerce* (London: Burton, 1803), p. 207.

8. Wheatley, *Essay*, p. 88.

9. Ibid., p. 59.

10. Ibid., p. 45.

11. Ibid., p. 25.

12. Ibid., p. 25.

13. Regarding Wheatley's notion of the frictionless income adjustment mechanism see Frank W. Fetter, *Development of British Monetary Orthodoxy 1797-1875* (Cambridge, Mass.: Harvard University Press, 1965), p. 47; Lloyd A. Metzler, "The Theory of International Trade" in *A Survey of Contemporary Economics*, ed. Howard S. Ellis (Philadelphia: Blakiston, 1948), p. 217; and Denis P. O'Brien, *The Classical Economists* (Oxford: Clarendon Press, 1975), p. 149.

14. On this point see Fetter, p. 47; Metzler, p. 217; and O'Brien, p. 149.

15. "Report from the Select Committee on the High Price of Gold Bullion" (*Bullion Report*) (No. 349) III, 1810, quoted in Constantino Bresciani-Turroni, "The 'Purchasing Power Parity' Doctrine," *L'Egypte Contemporaine* 25 (May, 1934), 433–64; reprinted in his *Saggi di Economia* (Milan: Giuffre, 1961), p. 91.

16. Quoted in Bresciani-Turroni, p. 91.

17. William Blake, *Observations on the Principles Which Regulate the Course of Exchange and on the Present Depreciated State of the Currency* (1810) (New York: Franklin, 1969), pp. 86, 43.

18. Ibid., p. 51.

19. Ibid., pp. 20, 19, 96.

20. Gustav Cassel, "The Present Situation of the Foreign Exchanges," *Economic Journal* 26 (March 1916), p. 62; and *Money and Foreign Exchange after 1914* (New York: Macmillan, 1922), p. 140.

21. Ibid., p. 175.

22. Ibid., p. 157.

23. Ibid., p. 143.

24. Ibid., p. 149.

25. Ibid., p. 158.

26. Ibid., pp. 141, 185, 186.

27. Cassel, "The Present Situation of the Foreign Exchanges," p. 62.

28. Cassel, *Money and Foreign Exchange*, p. 145.

29. Ibid., p. 167.

30. Ibid., p. 168.

31. Ludwig von Mises, *Stabilization of the Monetary Unit—from the Viewpoint of Theory* (1923), in *On the Manipulation of Money and Credit*, tr. Bettina Bien Greaves, ed. Percy L. Greaves, Jr. (Dobbs Ferry, N.Y.: Free Market Books, 1978), p. 30.

32. Ibid., pp. 30–31.

33. Ibid., p. 31.

34. John Maynard Keynes, *A Tract on Monetary Reform* (1923), volume 4 of the *Collected Writings of John Maynard Keynes* (London: Macmillan for The Royal Economic Society, 1971), p. 75.

35. Bresciani-Turroni, "The 'Purchasing Power Parity' Doctrine," *Saggi di Economia* (Milan: Giuffre, 1961).

36. Ibid., p. 93.

37. Ibid., p. 122.

38. Ibid., p. 121.

39. Recall, however, that in Wheatley's view income adjustments also play a role.

40. Milton Friedman, and Anna Jacobson Schwartz, *A Monetary History of the United States, 1867–1960* (Princeton, N.J.: Princeton University Press, 1963), p. 61.

41. Ibid., p. 61.

42. What follows draws heavily from Leland Yeager, *International Monetary Relations: Theory, History, and Policy*, second ed. (New York: Harper & Row, 1976), pp. 210, 214–23.

ADDITIONAL REFERENCE

1. Viner, J. *Studies in the Theory of International Trade*. New York: Augustus Kelley, 1965.

12

DENNIS H. ROBERTSON AND THE MONETARY APPROACH TO EXCHANGE RATES

Prominent among competing explanations of exchange rate determination in a regime of floating exchange rates is the so-called *monetary approach*, which holds that the exchange rate between two national currencies is determined by current and prospective relative supplies of and demands for those national money stocks. This theory has a long tradition going back more than 300 years. As an integral part of pre-Keynesian international monetary theory, it formed the central analytical core of classical and neoclassical explanations of exchange rate behavior. Although it was temporarily eclipsed by the rival elasticities and foreign trade multiplier or income–expenditure approaches that gained popularity with the domination of the Keynesian revolution, it has recently made a comeback and today is widely employed by academic and business economists to explain the behavior of exchange rates in the post-Bretton Woods era of generalized floating. For example, such well-known economists as Robert Barro, John Bilson, Jacob Frenkel, and Michael Mussa have successfully employed the monetary approach to account for recent exchange rate experience, as have analysts at Citibank, Chase Manhattan, and other financial institutions. Finally, it is worth noting that certain segments of the financial press, notably the editorial pages of *The Wall Street Journal*, regularly espouse the monetary approach.

Corresponding to the growing popularity of the monetary approach has been an accompanying interest in its historical antecedents. Accordingly, in the past few years Jacob Frenkel, Johan

Myhrman, and Mordechai Kreinin and Lawrence Officer, respectively, have published papers dealing with the doctrinal development of that approach.[1] These papers, however, suffer from one serious omission. For while they cite several prominent economists writing in the 1920s—notably Cassel, Gregory, Hawtrey, and Keynes—as important early proponents of the monetary approach, they say nothing about the great British economist Dennis Robertson. The result is to foster the erroneous impression that Robertson, generally recognized as one of the leading monetary theorists of the twentieth century, had virtually nothing to say about the monetary approach when in fact he was one of its principal proponents. Not only did he endorse and utilize the established components of the monetary approach, he also presaged recent developments in the theory of exchange rate expectations. For these reasons his work merits consideration.

The purpose of this chapter is twofold. First, it identifies and explains the essentials of the monetary approach to exchange rates. Second, it documents Robertson's views on that approach. This is a fairly easy task, since the bulk of Robertson's work on floating exchange rates is contained in one volume, namely the 1929 edition of his famous Cambridge Economic Handbook *Money*.[2] In that book he divides his discussion of exchange rate determination into two sections, one dealing with conditions of monetary stability and the other dealing with episodes of violent and rapid inflation. His views on the monetary approach are to be found in these two sections. What particular elements identifying the monetary approach should one look for in his views?

BASIC INGREDIENTS OF THE MONETARY APPROACH

To demonstrate that Robertson was a proponent of the monetary approach, it is necessary to spell out the key ingredients or propositions that characterize that approach.[3] These elements include the following:

1. MONETARY VIEW OF LONG-RUN EXCHANGE RATE DETERMINATION

The monetary approach holds that the long-run equilibrium exchange rate between two national currencies is determined chiefly by relative national money supplies and demands operating through relative national price levels. This proposition implies a particular monetary transmission mechanism or channel of causation linking money to exchange rates. Accordingly, the monetary approach specifies such a mechanism and identifies quantity theory of money and purchasing power parity relationships as the key links in that mechanism. The quantity theory says that the general price level is determined by the demand-adjusted money stock, i.e., by the nominal quantity of money per unit of real money demand. In other words, the price level equates money supply and demand by deflating the real value of the nominal money stock to the level people desire to hold. By contrast, the purchasing power parity doctrine states that the long-run equilibrium exchange rate tends to equal the ratio of the price levels in the two countries concerned. This condition ensures that the real (exchange rate-adjusted) price of goods is everywhere the same so that there exists no arbitrage advantage to buying in one country over the other. It also ensures that both moneys have the same real (exchange rate-adjusted) purchasing power such that there exists no incentive to switch from one currency to the other. Taken together, the quantity theory and purchasing power parity components imply that relative money supplies and demands operating through relative national price levels determine the long-run equilibrium exchange rate. And according to the monetary approach, the stability of that equilibrium is ensured by the self-correcting characteristic of the purchasing power parity mechanism itself. Thus, should random deviations from purchasing power parity occur, they would be quickly eliminated. For by overvaluing one currency and undervaluing the other on the foreign exchanges, such deviations would shift demand from the former currency to the latter and in so doing bid the exchange rate back to purchasing power parity equilibrium.

2. ASSET MARKET VIEW OF SHORT-RUN EXCHANGE RATE BEHAVIOR

The foregoing proposition refers to exchange rate determination in the long run when purchasing power parity holds. With respect to exchange rate determination in the short run when purchasing power parity may not hold, the monetary approach advances the so-called *asset market* view. According to that view the exchange rate between two national currencies behaves like an asset price in an efficient market, adjusting instantly to a level at which both asset (i.e., money) stocks are willingly held. As an efficient asset price, the current spot exchange rate is particularly sensitive to expectations of future exchange rates, expectations that are heavily conditioned by recent and current monetary policy and other indicators of the future course of monetary policy. More generally, as an efficient asset price the current exchange rate embodies all available information about current and prospective events likely to affect the future external values of the two currencies and adjusts instantaneously to incorporate new information about changed conditions. In this manner new information about future exchange rates is discounted into the current exchange rate analogously to the way that news about the future profitability of a corporation is discounted into the current market price of its equity shares.

3. ROLE OF EXPECTATIONS

As noted above, one implication of the asset market view is that the current spot exchange rate is strongly influenced by current expectations of future exchange rates. This is so because the expected rate of change of the exchange rate is the same as the anticipated rate of return from holding foreign rather than domestic money. As such, expectations affect the relative demand for the two currencies and thereby influence the exchange rate. Thus a rise in the expected rate of depreciation of the exchange rate will, by raising the expected yield from holding foreign rather than domestic currency, shift demand from the latter to the former thereby depreciating the current spot exchange rate. In short, the spot exchange rate is determined by exchange rate expectations operating through relative money demands.

4. RATIONAL EXPECTATIONS HYPOTHESIS

Besides explaining how expectations affect exchange rates, the monetary approach also explains how expectations themselves are determined. According to the monetary approach, people formulate exchange rate expectations consistent with the way that exchange rates are actually determined in the economy. Thus, if actual observed exchange rates are determined by money supply and demand, it follows that expected future exchange rates are determined by forecasts of future values of those same monetary variables. In particular, the monetary approach maintains that exchange rate expectations are governed by expectations of future money supplies per unit of real money demands. These latter expectations, the monetary approach asserts, are formed from all available information about prospective events likely to influence future money supplies and demands. In so arguing, the monetary approach advances the *rational expectations hypothesis* according to which the market's predictions of future exchange rates are the same as those generated by the actual mechanism that determines exchange rates. This assumption ensures that the monetary approach is internally consistent, i.e., that its explanation of expectations formation is consistent with its explanation of exchange rate determination. Such consistency is thought to be characteristic of the forecasting behavior of rational agents who use knowledge of the actual exchange rate-generating mechanism in formulating expectations of future exchange rates.

> Knowing that money supplies and demands determine actual exchange rates, rational agents will predict future exchange rates from forecasts of future money supplies and demands.

Constituting the central analytical core of the modern monetary approach to floating exchange rates, the foregoing ingredients must be found in Robertson's work if he is to be judged a proponent of that approach. Accordingly, the following paragraphs show what he had to say on each of the propositions listed above.

Before discussing Robertson's views, however, it should be pointed out that the long-run quantity theory version of the monetary approach (i.e., proposition one above) long predates him. That version dates back at least to the mid-sixteenth century when Spanish scholastic writers of the Salamanca School used it to explain fluctuations in the Spanish currency price of Flemish money.[4] And in the famous Bank Restriction Controversy of the early 1800s, David Ricardo, John Wheatley, and other bullionist writers employed it to explain the fall of the paper pound on the foreign exchanges following Britain's switch from fixed to floating exchange rates during the Napoleonic wars.[5] The theory was endorsed by A. Marshall in the late 1880s and revived by Gustav Cassel in 1916 to explain exchange rate movements during World War I.[6] After the war the theory was widely used to explain the fall of the German mark in the famous hyperinflation episode of the early 1920s.[7] Robertson of course was well aware of this and goes out of his way to disclaim any originality in his presentation of the theory. His views on this long established or "customary" (as he called it) doctrine are presented immediately below [14, p. 58].

LONG-RUN EQUILIBRIUM EXCHANGE RATE

The first proposition of the monetary approach states that the long-run equilibrium exchange rate between two national currencies is determined by the relative supplies of and demands for those national money stocks. That Robertson was in basic agreement with this proposition is evident from his discussion of the determination of the "normal level of the rate of exchange" between two inconvertible paper currencies (or "arbitrary independent standards" as he called them) [14, pp. 57, 58]. In his discussion he attributes the state of the exchanges largely to the underlying monetary conditions in the two countries concerned. Although he denies that these monetary factors are the sole determinants of exchange rates, he repeatedly refers to them as the dominant determinants. For example, in various places he specifically identifies "the monetary situation" or "the supply of money in the two countries" or "the state of a country's monetary glands" as "the essential condition for the maintenance of a given rate of exchange" [14, pp. 60, 103]. Elsewhere, when discussing the stability of exchange rate equilibrium, he reiterates his belief in the importance of the monetary factor when he notes that the exchange rate must always gravitate to that particular equilibrium level "which the existing money supply of the country as compared with that of other countries renders permanently maintainable" [14, p. 101].

Embodied in the monetary approach is a particular model of the monetary transmission mechanism connecting money with exchange rates. As usually presented, that model contains quantity theory of money and purchasing power parity relationships, the former linking money supplies and demands to prices and the latter linking prices to the exchange rate. These same elements can be found in Robertson's work. Consistent with the monetary approach, he combines them to arrive at the conclusion that exchange rates are determined largely by relative money supplies and demands operating through price levels, particularly the prices of internationally-traded goods. He reaches this conclusion via the following route.

First, he argues that "the value of money . . . depends on the conditions of demand for it and the quantity of it available" [14, p. 32]. This of course is the quantity theory of money which may be written as

$$(1) \quad P = M/D$$

where P is the general price level (the inverse of the value of money), M the nominal money stock, and D the real demand for money. This equation, which says that the price level is determined by and varies equiproportionally with the stock of money per unit of real money demand, is expressed by Robertson in the following words: "given the conditions of demand for money . . . the general level of prices varies directly as the quantity of money available" [14, p. 26]. Note that equation 1, which may be written as $M/P = D$, also says that the price level adjusts to equate the real (price-deflated) value of the nominal money stock with the public's real demand for it, thereby clearing the market for real cash balances. Consistent with his adherence to the quantity theory, Robertson employs this alternative interpretation when he declares that, given the public's real demand for money, a ten percent rise in the nominal money stock will produce a corresponding ten percent rise in the price level such that the price-deflated or "aggregate real value of the public's money supply is no greater than it was before" [14, p. 76].

Second, he presents the purchasing power parity relationship, stating that "the normal level of the rate of exchange depends on the relative price levels, in the moneys of the two countries, of the things which enter into trade between them" [14, p. 58]. This of course is the traded-goods or commodity arbitrage version of purchasing power parity, which holds that the equilibrium exchange rate is equal to the ratio of the domestic and foreign price levels of internationally traded goods. In symbols

$$(2)\quad E = P_T/P_T^*$$

where E is the exchange rate (defined as the domestic currency price of a unit of foreign currency), and P_T and P_T^* are the domestic- and foreign currency prices of traded goods, respectively.

Third, he assumes that in long-run equilibrium the price of traded goods bears a certain equilibrium relationship to the general price level. This relationship can be expressed as

$$(3)\quad P_T = RP$$

where R denotes the equilibrium ratio of traded-goods prices to general prices in the home country, as can be seen by rewriting the equation in the form $R = P_T/P$. Representing the relative price of traded goods in terms of the general price level, this equation summarizes the equilibrium *structure* of prices in the home country. This notion of a stable equilibrium price structure can be inferred from Robertson's statement that he is assuming conditions of "comparative stability" characterized by the absence of "violent and continuous monetary dislocation" [14, p. 58]. It can also be inferred from his willingness to substitute traded-goods prices interchangeably for general prices as a measure of the value of money.[8]

Fourth, he substitutes equations 1 and 3 into equation 2 to obtain the following result

$$(4)\quad E = (1/P_T^*)R\frac{M}{D}$$

which says that given foreign prices and the domestic price structure the exchange rate depends on the domestic money supply per unit of real money demand. Robertson states this result when he declares that "given the price level of traded goods in terms of utopes [Robertson's hypothetical foreign currency] . . . the monetary situation in England turns out to be the essential condition for the maintenance of a given rate of exchange" [14, p. 60].

Finally, he assumes that prices in the foreign country are determined analogously to their domestic counterparts. Specifically, the foreign price of traded goods is linked through a price structure variable to the foreign general price level which is determined by foreign money supply and demand. Substituting this assumption into equation 4 yields the following expression

$$(5) \quad E = \frac{R}{R^*} \frac{D^*}{D} \frac{M}{M^*}$$

which says that the long-run equilibrium exchange rate is determined by the product of three groups of factors, namely relative price structures, relative real money demands, and relative nominal money supplies, respectively.[9] Of these three groups, the first two capture the effect of real (nonmonetary) influences on the exchange rate while the third captures purely monetary influences.

Equation 5, which summarizes Robertson's theory of long-run exchange rate determination, puts him squarely in the ranks of the monetary approach. To be sure, the equation does contain a relative price structure variable (and hence an extra channel through which real factors can affect exchange rates) not usually found in the monetary approach. Apart from this, however, the equation is exactly the same as that advanced by the monetary approach. It embodies the latter's assumption of quantity theory and purchasing power parity linkages running from money to the exchange rate, and therefore, in Robertson's words, "serves to remind us that the exchange rates are . . . connected with the supply of money in the two countries" [14, p. 60]. Moreover, like the monetary approach, it identifies relative money demands and supplies as key determinants of the exchange rate. Finally, it yields the standard monetarist homogeneity postulate that a ceteris paribus rise in the relative money supply produces an equiproportional rise in the nominal exchange rate. That Robertson accepts this homogeneity postulate is evident from his statement that if "the supply of Utopian money had become double . . . while neither the supply of English money nor any other conditions of the problem had changed, we should not be surprised to learn that the rate of exchange had become 10 utopes to the pound instead of 5" [14, p. 60]. In short, to the extent he accepts these features, Robertson is a proponent of the monetary approach.

Before concluding this section it is necessary to compare Robertson's views of the purchasing power parity relationship with those of the monetary approach. Regarding purchasing power parity there are at least three main issues, the first referring to the relevant price levels to use in calculating the parity. On this issue Robertson disagrees with the monetary approach. For whereas the latter holds that general prices should be employed in computing the purchasing power parity, Robertson argues that only the prices of internationally traded goods should be used. Thus in stating that the equilibrium exchange rate tends to equal the ratio of domestic to foreign prices, he makes it emphatically clear that he is referring to the prices of "traded goods" or "those goods which are the subject of trade" [14, pp. 60-61]. He apparently believes that purchasing power parity logically holds only for prices subject to international equalization by commodity arbitrage, for he states that it is only the movement of such prices "which we should expect to correspond closely to the movements of the exchanges" [13, p. 141]. Not mentioned by him is a point stressed by the monetary approach, namely that, with intercommodity substitution in production and consumption and interindustry competition for factors of production, the prices of traded and nontraded goods tend to be sufficiently closely related such that general prices can be used to approximate the purchasing power parity. Nevertheless, on at least one occasion he apparently accepts this proposition. For he uses a general price index to proxy the purchasing power parity claiming that, as a practical matter, the index is "good enough . . . to illustrate the general normal relation between price levels and exchanges" [13, p. 141].

The second issue relating to purchasing power parity concerns the purpose or role of the exchange rate. On this issue the monetary approach contends that the chief function of the exchange rate is to clear the market for money balances by equating the real purchasing power of both currencies such that both money stocks are willingly held. That Robertson is in substantial agreement with this point can be inferred from such comments of his as "the normal rate of exchange between [two countries] depends on the relative values of their moneys in terms of traded goods," and "the normal rate . . . reflects the condition of the country's money supply as compared with that of the other countries" [14, pp. 61, 102]. The first comment implies that the purchasing power parity exchange rate embodies the relative price deflator that, when applied to relative nominal national money supplies, serves to equalize the real (price-deflated) value of money across nations. Robertson's second comment implies that exchange rates, like prices, also summarize the underlying monetary conditions in each country. Both implications are consistent with the notion that the exchange rate functions to clear the market for national money balances by equating the real purchasing power of both currencies such that there exists no incentive to switch from one currency to the other.

Robertson recognizes, as do proponents of the monetary approach, that the exchange rate also plays a commodity arbitrage role, adjusting to equalize the real price of traded goods across nations so that there exists no advantage to buying in one market over another. In this connection he points out that if the real price of goods were to differ between countries such that it became advantageous to buy in the cheaper country and sell in the dearer one, the resulting excess demand for the currency of the former country would quickly bid the exchange rate up to the purchasing power parity level at which the common currency prices of goods are everywhere the same. While recognizing the arbitrage function of the exchange rate, however, he nevertheless apparently places greater emphasis on its money market clearing role. For whereas he mentions the commodity arbitrage role but once, he repeatedly contends that the equilibrium exchange rate must be consistent with the underlying monetary conditions in the countries concerned [14, pp. 59, 60, 61, 101, 103]. In so doing, he implicitly endorses the proposition that the chief function of the exchange rate is to achieve international monetary equilibrium by clearing the markets for national money balances.

As for the third issue, namely whether the purchasing power parity is an equilibrium condition or a cause-and-effect relationship between prices and exchange rate, Robertson obviously holds it to be the former. In so doing, he agrees with the monetary approach. Like proponents of that approach, he maintains that prices and the exchange rate are both endogenous variables simultaneously determined by underlying monetary conditions. As he puts it, both variables are "rendered possible by the monetary situation," i.e., both are established at levels "which the existing money supply of the country, as compared with that of other countries, renders permanently maintainable" [14, pp. 60, 101]. In short, on this issue as with most of the others, Robertson adheres to the monetary approach.

ASSET MARKET VIEW

The second component of the monetary approach is the asset market view according to which the exchange rate behaves like an efficient asset price, embodying all available information about the future values of the currencies and adjusting instantaneously to incorporate new information about changed circumstances. Robertson possessed a sophisticated understanding of the asset market view, which he used in explaining "the misbehavior of the foreign exchanges" during the post-World War I hyperinflation episodes of the early 1920s. For example, regarding the proposition that the current exchange rate registers the market's perceptions about the future exchange rate—i.e., market participants discount the expected future value of the currencies into the current spot exchange rate—he says that exchange rates tend "to reflect the degree of confidence felt in the future of a country's money by the nimble-witted dealers in exchange" [14, p. 101]. These dealers he describes as being especially "well-informed and impressionable" implying that, consistent with the concept of an efficient market, they utilize all available information in predicting future exchange rates [14, p. 99].

As for the speed of adjustment of exchange rates in response to new information, Robertson implies that adjustment is virtually instantaneous. For "if a country is rapidly increasing its supply of money," he says, a "lack of confidence in the future of the money . . . strikes like a flash upon the consciousness of the well-informed and impressionable gentlemen whose business it is to carry on dealings in foreign money" [14, p. 99]. As a result, these dealers "become highly willing to buy foreign money and to sell the money of their own country" and in so doing immediately bid up the exchange rate [14, p. 99]. In this manner new information about the likely future value of the currencies is immediately impounded in the current spot exchange rate, which adjusts instantly to its new equilibrium level consistent with anticipated future monetary conditions.

Having developed the asset market view, Robertson used it to explain why the *external* value of a currency (i.e., its value on the foreign exchanges) could temporarily depreciate faster than its *internal* value (i.e., its value in domestic commodity markets) during periods of rapid inflation. In so doing he presents the rudiments of a theory of differential speeds of price adjustment in asset and commodity markets, respectively. According to him, whereas the exchange rate adjusts instantaneously to changes in expectations of future monetary conditions, the prices of "home produced goods and services" adjust slowly, i.e., they "come lumbering after" the exchange rate with a lag [14, p. 101]. In other words, the market for foreign exchange is more efficient than domestic commodity markets in exploiting new information about future prospects. For this reason, expectations are discounted into exchange rates prior to being discounted into domestic commodity prices and "the external value of a country's money falls faster than the internal" [14, pp. 101, 108].

Robertson's views on asset and commodity price adjustment sound remarkably like those of the monetary approach. The same conclusions, namely that differential speeds of price response cause the exchange rate to adjust faster than commodity prices and thereby produce temporary disparities between the external and internal values of the currency, continue to be voiced by modern proponents of the monetary approach. Here, for example, is what one of those proponents, M. Mussa, has to say on the subject.

> Relative adjustment speeds of prices . . . in different markets are of vital importance in understanding fluctuations in exchange rates. . . . In the asset market approach to exchange rate theory, it is asserted that the exchange rate is a relative asset price that is determined primarily by conditions of equilibrium in the market for asset stocks. What this means is that the exchange rate . . . responds essentially instantaneously to changes in economic conditions, in particular, to new information that is received by market participants. Of course, exchange rates are also related to general price levels. . . . But, if price levels adjust relatively slowly in comparison with exchange rates, then . . . exchange rate movements should frequently anticipate, rather than follow, movements in national price levels [11, pp. 196–97].

In short, because the exchange rate responds more rapidly to news about future events than do commodity prices, the external value of the currency deviates temporarily from its internal value. On this point Robertson and Mussa agree.

Prior to ending this section it should be pointed out that Robertson was not alone in endorsing the asset market view of exchange rates in the 1920s. Gustav Cassel, for example, also enunciated it. Perhaps its strongest proponent, however, was Ludwig von Mises, whose contributions to the monetary approach, like those of

Robertson, have been largely overlooked. As early as 1919 von Mises wrote that exchange rates, like the prices of other assets traded on organized markets, "are speculative rates of exchange," that they reflect "not only the present but also potential future developments," and that they respond to news of excessive monetary growth "relatively soon . . . long before the prices of other goods and services" [8, p. 51]. Again, in 1923, he wrote that the current spot exchange rate "forecasts anticipated future changes in commodity prices," that it is "determined by nothing more than the anticipated future purchasing power attributed to a unit of each currency," and that it adjusts faster than commodity prices to news about future events [8, pp. 28, 31]. Any notion that the asset market view is a recent development is quickly dispelled by a reading of Robertson and von Mises.

ROLE OF EXPECTATIONS

The third proposition of the monetary approach deals with exchange rate expectations. Consistent with the monetary approach, Robertson recognized that expectations play a central role in short-run exchange rate determination. In so doing he implicitly accepted the proposition that the expected future rate of change of the exchange rate constitutes the expected cost of holding one currency rather than the other and therefore affects the current spot exchange rate through relative money demands. To be sure, he did not state this proposition explicitly. That is, he did not specify the expected rate of change of the exchange rate as a cost or rate of return variable in the money demand function. He did, however, assume that the demand for money in each country is affected by the expected rate of inflation in that country [14, pp. 97–98]. By implication, however, this means that relative money demands are affected by expected inflation differentials. And since the expected inflation differential is closely related to the expected future rate of depreciation of the exchange rate, he implicitly reached the conclusion that expectations of exchange rate depreciation affect the current exchange rate through the channel of relative money demands. In particular, he argued that if everybody expects the currency to depreciate, they will attempt to get out of that currency into other assets, including foreign exchange. The resulting reduction in the demand for the currency will produce the very depreciation that is anticipated. In his own words, if the public expects a depreciation of the currency, "every individual passes it on as quickly as he is able, knowing that if he keeps it it will lose value still further in his hands, and seeks with ingenuity and persistence to embody his resources in any other form" [14, p. 98]. One of these forms is foreign exchange. Consequently, people "become highly willing to buy foreign money and to sell the money of their own country" and "this involves their coming on to the exchange market as purchasers of foreign money" [14, p. 99]. The resulting reduction in the demand for domestic relative to foreign money causes the exchange rate to depreciate. On this point Robertson is in perfect agreement with the monetary approach.

RATIONAL EXPECTATIONS HYPOTHESIS

Finally, Robertson endorsed the last ingredient of the monetary approach, namely the rational expectations hypothesis. The latter states that people formulate exchange rate expectations from information about prospective policy actions and other events believed to have a bearing on the future values of the monetary variables that actually determine exchange rates. Knowing that monetary policies are a basic determinant of long-run equilibrium exchange rates, rational agents will predict future equilibrium exchange rates from forecasts of future monetary policies and these forecasts will be immediately discounted into the current spot exchange rate. That this was indeed Robertson's view is evident from his statement that "the actual rate of exchange is largely governed by the *expected* behavior of the country's monetary authority" [14, p. 102]. The same idea was expressed by von Mises, who declared that the exchange rate "is affected only by changes in the relation between the demand for, and quantity of, money and the prevailing opinion with respect to expected changes in that relationship, including those produced by governmental monetary policies" [8, p. 25].

Robertson also stressed that exchange rate changes largely stem from *unexpected* policy actions. In his words, if the monetary "authority behaves in a way which is not expected, the rate will ultimately alter" [14, p. 102]. In stating this point Robertson presaged the monetary approach's distinction between the effects of expected versus unexpected policies, respectively. According to this distinction, expected policy actions should have little or no impact on the exchange rate since those policies have already been fully anticipated and discounted into the exchange rate. Having been foreseen in advance, such policies entail no disappointed expectations, no surprises, no new information to discount into the exchange rate. By contrast, unexpected policies should indeed affect the exchange rate. Not having been foreseen in advance, they produce forecasting errors that constitute new information that the market discounts into the exchange rate. In this manner they alter the exchange rate, which adjusts to incorporate the new information represented by the policy surprises. In recognizing this point Robertson foreshadowed much of the recent research on rational expectations.

CONCLUSION

The preceding has identified four basic essentials of the monetary approach to exchange rates and has documented Robertson's views on each. His writings indicate that he largely accepted these essentials and that he incorporated them into his own analysis of the foreign exchanges. Moreover, with respect to the asset market and rational expectations components, he contributed insights that are remarkably suggestive of recent work. All in all, his position is consistent with the monetary approach. This is not to say, however, that everything he wrote conformed to the monetary approach. On the contrary, at one point he used the rival elasticities approach to deny the existence of a stable equilibrium exchange rate [14, p. 100]. At another point he suggested, contrary to the monetary approach, that national money stocks may be endogenous rather than exogenous variables [14, p. 102]. Nor is it to claim that he was the only economist in the 1920s to recognize and discuss all the ingredients of the monetary approach. Ludwig von Mises, for one, enunciated them even more emphatically and lucidly than Robertson. Nevertheless, Robertson did endorse and utilize these ingredients and for that reason deserves to be recognized along with Cassel, Hawtrey, Keynes, and von Mises as one of the important early proponents of the monetary approach.

NOTES

1. See Frenkel [2], Myhrman [12], and Kreinin and Officer [7, pp. 28–31].

2. Unless otherwise noted, all references are to the 1963 reprint of the 1947 edition, which is virtually the same as the 1929 edition as far as the discussion of floating exchange rates is concerned.

3. The essentials of the modern monetary approach are expounded more fully in Bilson [1], Frenkel [2], Frenkel and Clements [3], and Mussa [9, 10].

4. See Grice-Hutchinson [6, p. 55].

5. See Myhrman [12, pp. 170–73].

6. On Marshall, see Eshag [5, pp. 26–34]. On Cassel, see Myhrman [12, pp. 177–78].

7. See Ellis [4, pp. 209–36].

8. See Robertson [14, p. 61] where he refers to the value of money measured "in terms of traded goods."

9. Asterisks refer to foreign country variables.

REFERENCES

1. Bilson, J. "Recent Developments in Monetary Models of Exchange Rate Determination." *IMF Staff Papers* 26, No. 2 (June 1979):201–23.

2. Frenkel, J. "A Monetary Approach to the Exchange Rate: Doctrinal Aspects and Empirical Evidence." *Scandinavian Journal of Economics* 78, No. 2 (May 1976):200–24.

3. Frenkel, J., and Clements, K. "Exchange Rates in the 1920's: A Monetary Approach," Working paper No. 290. NBER Working Paper Series. Cambridge: National Bureau of Economic Research, October 1978.

4. Ellis, H. *German Monetary Theory, 1905–1933.* Cambridge: Harvard University Press, 1934.

5. Eshag, E. *From Marshall to Keynes: An Essay on The Monetary Theory of the Cambridge School.* Oxford: Basil Blackwell, 1963.

6. Grice-Hutchinson, M. *The School of Salamanca: Readings in Spanish Monetary Theory, 1544–1605.* Oxford: Clarendon Press, 1952.

7. Kreinin, M., and Officer, L. *The Monetary Approach to the Balance of Payments: A Survey.* Princeton Studies in International Finance, No. 43, Princeton: Princeton University, International Finance Section, 1978.

8. Mises, L. v. "Balance of Payments and Foreign Exchange Rates" (1919), and *Stabilization of the Monetary Unit—from the Viewpoint of Theory* (1923). In *On the Manipulation of Money and Credit.* Translated by Bettina Bien Greaves and edited by Percy L. Greaves, Jr. Dobbs Ferry, New York: Free Market Books, 1978.

9. Mussa, M. "The Exchange Rate, the Balance of Payments and Monetary and Fiscal Policy under a Regime of Controlled Floating." *Scandinavian Journal of Economics* 78, No. 2 (May 1976):229–48.

10. ——. "Empirical Regularities in the Behavior of Exchange Rates and Theories of the Foreign Exchange Market." In vol. 11 of the Carnegie-Rochester Conference Series on Public Policy, a supplementary series to the *Journal of Monetary Economics*, 1979, pp. 9-57.

11. ——. "Macroeconomic Interdependence and the Exchange Rate." *International Economic Policy: Theory and Evidence.* Edited by R. Dornbusch and J. Frenkel. Baltimore: Johns Hopkins University Press, 1979.

12. Myhrman, J. "Experiences of Flexible Exchange Rates in Earlier Periods: Theories. Evidence and a New View." *Scandinavian Journal of Economics* 78, No. 2 (May 1976):169--96.

13. Robertson, D. H. *Money.* New York: Harcourt Brace and Co., 1922.

14. ——. *Money.* Fourth edition. Chicago: University of Chicago Press, 1963.

13

EXPLAINING EXCHANGE RATE BEHAVIOR: AN AUGMENTED VERSION OF THE MONETARY APPROACH

Prominent among competing theories of exchange rate determination in a regime of floating exchange rates is the monetary approach. This approach rests on the view that the exchange rate between two national currencies is determined by the respective national money supplies and demands in the two countries and the resulting effects on their general price levels.[1] To reach this conclusion the monetary approach combines the quantity theory of money with the purchasing power parity theory of exchange rates. The quantity theory says that the general price level is determined by the demand-adjusted money stock, i.e., by the nominal stock of money per unit of real money demand.[2] And the purchasing power parity doctrine holds that the exchange rate tends to equal the ratio of the price levels in the two countries concerned.[3] Taken together, the quantity theory and the purchasing power parity doctrine imply that the exchange rate is determined by relative demand-adjusted money stocks operating through relative national price levels.

The monetary approach has a long history dating back at least to the early 1800s when David Ricardo, John Wheatley, and other British bullionist writers used it to explain the fall of the paper pound on the foreign exchanges following Britain's switch from fixed to floating exchange rates during the Napoleonic wars. Later it was employed by the Swedish economist Gustav Cassel to explain the fall of the external value of the German mark during the famous hyperinflation episode of the early 1920s. Most recently, however, it has been employed, albeit with mixed results,[4] to explain the behavior of floating exchange rates in the post-1973 era of generalized floating.

The main shortcoming of the monetary approach is that it ignores the effect of real relative price changes on the exchange rate. In particular, it ignores the influence of changes in the *real terms of trade* (i.e., the relative price of imports and exports) and *internal relative prices* (i.e., the relative price of exports and domestic non-tradeable goods), both of which function to clear national and international markets for real goods and services by equating commodity demand and supply. Determined by underlying shifts in consumer preferences, technology, and resource supplies, these real relative price changes necessitate equilibrium changes in exchange rates relative to the purchasing power parity ratio of nominal national price levels. Because the monetary approach assumes that purchasing power parity always holds, however, it cannot account for the influence of these real relative price changes on exchange rates. The result is that it ignores a key source of exchange rate disturbance, namely real shocks impinging on the exchange rate through the channels of the terms of trade and internal relative prices.[5] Far from recognizing these real channels, the monetary approach asserts that all factors affecting exchange rates must do so through monetary channels alone, i.e., through money supplies and demands. While this assumption may be warranted during periods of hyperinflation when exchange rate disturbances are of a predominantly monetary origin, it is clearly invalid in turbulent periods, such as the 1970s, when real shocks abound.

The foregoing shortcoming can be remedied by incorporating a real exchange rate component into the analytical framework of the monetary approach. The result is an augmented monetary model that captures all factors, real and monetary, affecting exchange rates. This chapter constructs such a model, discusses its constituent components, and uses it to explain certain characteristic features and policy implications of observed exchange rate behavior in recent years.

THE MODEL AND ITS COMPONENTS

The model itself assumes two hypothetical open national economies each with its own currency and each producing two goods, namely

(1) a purely domestic (nontradeable) good and (2) a unique exportable good, part of which is consumed domestically and part of which is exported to the other country. The basic building blocks of the model include (1) a terms of trade identity that links the exchange rate with export prices, (2) a price structure identity that links export prices to general prices via a term containing the relative price of exportables and nontradeables, (3) a quantity theory equation that links general prices to money supply and demand, and finally (4) a money demand equation that links the demands for foreign and domestic currencies to the expected rate of change of the exchange rate. Taken together, these components imply that the exchange rate is determined by the multiplicative product of the terms of trade, relative price structures, relative nominal money stocks, and relative real money demands, respectively. Of these four determinants, the first two constitute the so-called real or price-deflated exchange rate that captures the effect of real disturbances operating through nonmonetary channels. By contrast, the last two determinants constitute the nominal or monetary element of the exchange rate. As such they capture the effect of monetary, real, and expectational disturbances operating through monetary channels, i.e., through money supply and demand.

The foregoing variables are denoted by the following symbols: let E be the observed market exchange rate (defined as the domestic currency price of a unit of foreign currency), R the real or price-deflated value of that exchange rate (i.e., the exchange rate divided by the purchasing power parity ratio of national price levels), and e the expected future rate of change of the exchange rate. Furthermore, let M be the nominal money stock (assumed to be exogenously determined by the central bank) and D the real demand for money, i.e., the stock of real (price-deflated) cash balances that the public desires to hold. Also let T be the real terms of trade (defined as the quantity of exports given up per unit of imports obtained) and S be the structure of prices in each country as represented by the relative price of exportable goods in terms of the general price level. Finally, let P_x be the price of exportable goods, P_n the price of nontradeable goods, and P the general price level defined as the weighted average of the prices of exportable goods and nontradeable goods, respectively (i.e., the aggregate price of gross domestic product). Asterisks distinguish foreign-country variables from home-country variables. The foregoing variables are linked together via the model's basic building blocks described below.

TERMS OF TRADE

The first building block of the model is the concept of the real terms of trade. Representing the quantity of exports that must be sacrificed to obtain a unit of imports, the terms of trade T is defined as the relative price of imports and exports (i.e., the ratio of import prices to export prices). Since the domestic currency price of goods imported from abroad is the same as their foreign currency export price multiplied by the market exchange rate between domestic and foreign currency, the terms of trade may be defined as

$$(1)\quad T = E\,P_x^*/P_x\,,$$

where T is the terms of trade, E the exchange rate, P_x^* the foreign currency price of foreign country exportables, and P_x the domestic currency price of domestic exportables. Via this identity the terms of trade variable links the exchange rate to export prices in both countries as can be seen by rewriting the identity as $E = T\,P_x/P_x^*$.

Being a real relative price, the terms of trade is affected by real economic variables such as productivity, consumer preferences, resource supplies, and the structure of particular markets in both countries. For example, if productivity is increasing faster in A's export-producing sector than in B's, the consequent rise in A's export supply relative to B's means that A must give up more exports per unit of imports obtained from B. As a result, A's export price will fall relative to B's and the terms of trade will turn against A. Likewise a shift in world demand from A's exports to B's exports will raise the relative price of the latter and worsen A's terms of trade. Finally, suppose B's export sector becomes monopolized while A's remains competitive. B's exporters could exploit their newly acquired market power by restricting output and raising prices, thereby turning the terms of trade against A. In general, the greater the relative productivity and the lower the degree of market power in A's export sector compared with B's, and the lower the intensity of demand for A's exportables relative to B's, the worse the terms of trade for A and vice versa for B.

INTERNAL PRICE STRUCTURE

The second building block of the model is the concept of the internal price structure that links export prices to general prices via a term that summarizes the composition of relative prices in each country. Written as follows

(2) $P_x = SP$ and $P_x^* = S^*P^*$

the internal price structure S is the ratio of export prices to general prices as can be seen by rewriting the identities as $S = P_x/P$ and $S^* = P_x^*/P^*$. Defined as the relative price of exportables in terms of the general price level, the internal price structure S is also the relative price of exports and nontradeable goods. To show this, write the general price level as a weighted geometrical average of the respective prices of the two goods, i.e.,

(3) $P = P_n^a P_x^{1-a}$

where P denotes general prices, P_n nontraded goods prices, P_x exportable goods prices, and the weights a and 1−a denote the shares of the two goods in the gross domestic product. Dividing both sides of this expression by P_x and inverting the result yields

(4) $P_x/P = (P_x/P_n)^a = S$

which says that the internal price structure S is equivalent to the relative price of exportable and nontradeable goods weighted by the latter's share in the gross domestic product.

Stated this way, the price structure variable measures the internal opportunity cost of producing exportables such that a rise in S means that a country will have to give up more nontradeables per additional unit of exportables produced. And, when combined with the terms of trade, it also measures the opportunity cost of transforming nontradeables into imports by way of exportables. Thus if Q_n/Q_x represents the quantity of nontradeables given up to produce a unit of exportables (the internal price structure) and Q_x/Q_m is the quantity of exportables sacrificed to obtain a unit of imports (the terms of trade), it follows that the product of these ratios $(Q_n/Q_x)(Q_x/Q_m) = Q_n/Q_m$ shows the domestic nontradeables cost of obtaining imports by means of exports. In this regard the price structure variable represents the *indirect* terms of trade just as the relative price of exports and imports represents the *direct* terms of trade.

Being a real relative price, the internal price structure is affected by real economic variables such as intersectoral differences in productivity, tastes, and the degree of market power. For example, if productivity (and hence output) is advancing faster in a country's export-producing sector than in the rest of the economy, the resulting rise in the relative supply of exportables will lower their internal relative price thereby altering the price structure. Likewise a reduction in the degree of market power in the export sector relative to the rest of the economy will result in a fall in the relative price of exportables and a corresponding change in the internal price structure. Similarly, a shift in demand away from a country's exportable good to its nontradeable good will lower the internal relative price of exportables and alter the structure of prices.

Before proceeding to the third building block of the model, it should be noted that substituting equation 2 into equation 1 and solving for the exchange rate yields

$$(5) \quad E = T \frac{S}{S^*} \frac{P}{P^*}$$

which expresses the exchange rate as the product of the terms of trade, relative price structures, and the purchasing power parity ratio of national price levels, respectively. Regarding this expression three points should be made. First, it recognizes that factors other than national price levels affect exchange rates. In particular, it says that the purchasing power parity ratio of national price levels is *a* determinant but not *the* sole determinant of exchange rates. In this respect it differs from the simple monetary approach, which identifies the exchange rate with the purchasing power parity determinant alone.

Second, equation 5 specifies the terms of trade and relative price structures as the constituent components of the real (price-deflated) exchange rate. That is, since the real exchange rate is by definition the observed exchange rate divided by the purchasing power parity ratio of national price levels, it follows that the real exchange rate R is the product of the terms of trade and relative internal price structures as can be seen by writing the equation as $E/(P/P^*) = R = TS/S^*$. This real exchange rate changes with shifts in the terms of trade and internal price structures. It also undergoes temporary changes when sluggish price adjustment prevents national price levels from responding as fast as exchange rates to changes in underlying economic conditions.

Third, the equation shows that the strict purchasing power parity condition assumed by the monetary approach holds only if the real exchange rate R is unity. This can be seen by rewriting equation 5 as

$$(6) \quad E = R \frac{P}{P^*}$$

which says that the exchange rate will equal the purchasing power parity ratio of national price levels only when the real exchange rate is one. But the real exchange rate will be unity only in the special case in which both countries produce a single identical traded good (or standard basket of traded goods) such that commodity arbitrage will render the real price of this good everywhere the same. In all other cases the real exchange rate can be expected to possess a value other than unity. Hence we conclude that the strict purchasing power parity condition postulated by the monetary approach rests on the special assumption of a one-good world.[6]

QUANTITY THEORY OF MONEY

The third building block of the model is the quantity theory of money which links general prices P to national nominal money supplies M and real money demands D. Written as follows

$$(7) \quad P = M/D \text{ and } P^* = M^*/D^*$$

the quantity theory says that the general price level in each country is determined by the demand-adjusted money stock, i.e., by the nominal stock of money per unit of real money demand. Written in the form $M/P = D$, the quantity theory also expresses the condition of money market equilibrium according to which the price level adjusts to equate the real (price-deflated) value of the nominal money stock with the public's real demand for it thereby clearing the market for real cash balances. Note that equation 7 implies that the purchasing power parity ratio of domestic to foreign national price levels is determined by relative national money supplies and demands. Here is the essence of the simple monetary approach to exchange rate determination, namely the extension of the quantity theory of money to the open economy under floating exchange rates.

MONEY DEMAND FUNCTIONS

The fourth component of the model consists of money demand functions linking the demands for foreign and domestic currency to the expected future rate of change of the exchange rate. Money demand is assumed to be a function of four variables, including (1) real income (a proxy for the transaction demand for money), (2) nominal interest rates (the opportunity cost of holding money rather than bonds), (3) expected future rate of inflation (the anticipated depreciation cost of holding money rather than goods), and (4) expected rate of change of the exchange rate (the anticipated rate of return from holding foreign money rather than domestic money). In what follows, however, all but the last of these money demand determinants are suppressed and real money demands D in both countries are treated as a function solely of the anticipated future rate of change e of the exchange rate, i.e.,

(8) $D = D(e)$ and $D^* = D^*(e)$.[7]

Equation 8 emphasizes the crucial role of exchange rate expectations in the determination of current exchange rates. It implies that exchange rates behave as efficient asset prices, being extremely sensitive to expectations of future conditions and adjusting instantaneously to changes in those expectations. In particular, it states that money demand functions provide the channel through which expectations influence exchange rates, i.e., expectations determine relative demands for the two currencies and therefore also the exchange rate between them. Thus a rise (fall) in the expected future rate of change of the exchange rate will, by raising (lowering) the expected yield from holding foreign rather than domestic currency, shift demand to the former (latter) thereby depreciating (appreciating) the current exchange rate. In this way current exchange rates are determined by exchange rate expectations operating through the channel of relative national money demands.

COMPONENTS OF THE EXCHANGE RATE

The foregoing elements can be combined into a single reduced form expression by substituting equations 2, 7, and 8 into equation 1 and solving for the exchange rate. The resulting expression is

$$(9) \quad E = T \frac{S}{S^*} \frac{M}{M^*} \frac{D^*(e)}{D(e)}$$

which says that the exchange rate is composed of the product of four groups of factors, namely the real terms of trade, relative internal price structures, relative nominal money supplies, and relative real money demands, respectively. Of these four components, the first two comprise the real exchange rate and the last two the underlying determinants of the nominal or purchasing power parity exchange rate. More precisely, the terms of trade and relative price structure variables account for real influences affecting the exchange rate through nonmonetary channels. By contrast, the relative nominal money stock variable accounts for purely monetary influences affecting the exchange rate through monetary channels (i.e., through money supplies). Finally, relative real money demands account for real and expectational influences affecting the exchange rate through monetary channels (i.e., through money demands).

Regarding the effect of these four determinants on the exchange rate, the equation predicts that a rise in each will tend to depreciate the exchange rate and a fall to appreciate it. That is, the equation predicts that a country's currency will depreciate upon:

1. a worsening of the terms of trade (i.e., a rise in the export cost of obtaining imports),
2. a rise in the relative price structure reflecting an increase in the nontradeables cost of producing exportables,
3. a rise in the relative money stock due to a faster rate of monetary expansion at home than abroad, and
4. a rise in the demand for foreign relative to domestic money due, say, to a rise in the expected future rate of depreciation of the exchange rate.

Conversely, the equation indicates that the exchange rate will appreciate given (1) an improvement in the real terms of trade, (2) a fall in the nontradeables cost of producing exportables, (3) a reduction in domestic relative to foreign money growth, and (4) a rise in domestic relative to foreign money demand reflecting improved prospects for the value of the domestic currency.

APPLICATION OF THE MODEL

Having outlined the augmented monetary model, the next step is to use it to answer certain questions arising from exchange rate experience in the post-1973 era of floating exchange rates. The first question is: What has caused the large exchange rate fluctuations observed in recent years?[8]

The model outlined above identifies three sources of exchange rate disturbance, namely

- real shocks operating through the terms of trade and relative internal price structures,
- monetary and real shocks operating through money supplies and demands, and,
- changes in exchange rate expectations operating through relative money demands.

All three types of shocks were prevalent in the turbulent 1970s and all three contributed to exchange rate movements. Real shocks occurred in the form of oil embargoes, changes in international demands, commodity shortages, tax and regulatory burdens, shifts in commercial policy, productivity growth differentials, and the like. Monetary shocks occurred in the form of divergent money growth rates and frequent sharp shifts in short-term policy targets. Also, during this period uncertainty about future developments became more intense. The policy surprises and the associated increased uncertainty about the future induced large and frequent changes in exchange rate expectations. Channeled through real money demands, these expectational changes were immediately embodied in the price of foreign exchange which jumped to its new equilibrium level consistent with the altered expectations. In short, the events of the 1970s indicate the extent to which disturbances can affect exchange rates. Given the abundance of shocks, surprises, and uncertainties in the post-Bretton Woods period it is small wonder that exchange rates moved as much as they did.

EXCHANGE RATE VOLATILITY

The second question refers to the high degree of short-run (daily, weekly, monthly) volatility exhibited by exchange rates. With respect to volatility, Frenkel [5; p. 23] and Flood [3; pp. 10–13] note that since the adoption of floating exchange rates in early 1973 exchange rates have displayed a degree of variability far exceeding that of national price levels and sometimes approaching that of stock prices quoted on the securities exchanges. And Artus and Young [1; p. 26] argue that exchange rates have been much more volatile than their underlying economic and financial determinants (e.g., money growth rate differentials, real relative prices, inflation differentials and the like). Why are exchange rates so volatile?

Exchange rates are more volatile than their basic economic determinants because they depend not only upon the current value of those determinants themselves but also upon expectations of the entire future paths of those determinants. This expectational factor magnifies the impact of unanticipated changes in economic conditions on the exchange rate. Those changes affect the exchange rate directly and also indirectly through their effect on expectations. In particular, by inducing shifts in exchange rate expectations, disturbances to underlying economic conditions may engender large and frequent movements in exchange rates. For example, unforeseen changes in monetary growth rates may, by altering expectations of future monetary conditions, produce disproportionally large changes in current exchange rates. Viewed this way, exchange rate volatility is seen to stem from large and frequent shifts in exchange rate expectations operating through relative money demands.

In this connection, the model stresses that exchange rates are efficient asset prices dominated by expectations of the future and extremely sensitive to new information (announcements, rumors, unforeseen events, policy surprises and the like) that alters those expectations. Consequently, when new information appears it is immediately discounted into the market price of foreign exchange which jumps to its new equilibrium level consistent with the changed expectations. Since new information abounds by definition in periods of turbulence and uncertainty, it follows that exchange rates will exhibit a large degree of volatility in such periods. The 1970s constitute a prime example of such a period. Given the economic shocks, political upheavals, policy surprises, and uncertainty that dominated that period, the observed volatility of exchange rates is no mystery. That volatility reflected the large and frequent shifts in expectations induced by the shocks, surprises, and news of that period.

SOURCES OF DEPARTURE FROM PURCHASING POWER PARITY

The third question is: Why have exchange rates since 1973 failed to conform to the predictions of the purchasing power parity theory?

That theory predicts that exchange rates will move over time as the ratio of nominal national price levels so as to leave the real value of money and its counterpart, the real price competitiveness of goods, everywhere the same. These predictions have not held up well in recent years. On the contrary, as Jacob Frenkel convincingly demonstrates in his paper "The Collapse of Purchasing Power Parities During the 1970s" [4], exchange rates have frequently deviated sharply from purchasing power parities and in many cases these deviations have persisted with the passage of time. What caused these deviations that have produced such large discrepancies between the external and internal values of currencies?

The model suggests that deviations from purchasing power parity occur for two reasons. One is nonsynchronous movements of exchange rates and price levels due to sluggish price adjustment; exchange rates adjust much faster than national price levels to changes in underlying economic conditions. Being efficient asset prices, exchange rates are extremely sensitive to unforeseen changes that alter expectations of the future. By contrast, national general prices are composed largely of commodity prices reflecting past and present conditions as embodied in existing contracts and are therefore relatively unresponsive to unforeseen changes in economic conditions. Consequently, when changes occur, sensitive exchange rates adjust immediately whereas sluggish national price levels lag behind. The resulting differential speed of price response causes a temporary divergence from purchasing power parity. It follows that in turbulent periods like the 1970s, when shocks and surprises occur frequently, exchange rates will deviate from purchasing power parity much of the time.

Sluggish price adjustment is not the only source of deviation from purchasing power parity, however. The model suggests that real structural changes in tastes, technology, and market structure also play a role. Operating through real relative prices, these structural changes necessitate real equilibrium changes in the exchange rate and thereby produce systematic divergences from purchasing power parity. In terms of the exchange rate equation $E = RP/P^*$, real structural changes generate movements in the real exchange rate R, thereby necessitating equilibrium shifts in the market exchange rate E relative to the purchasing power parity ratio of national price levels.

To illustrate how real structural changes produce systematic deviations from purchasing power parity, consider a hypothetical case in which the United States exports wheat to OPEC in exchange for oil. For convenience, assume that the monetary authorities are stabilizing general prices in both countries so that no exchange rate disturbances arise from that source. That is, all shifts in money demand (due, for example, to productivity-induced increases in income) are accompanied by corresponding changes in the money supply so as to leave general prices and purchasing power parity unchanged. Now suppose that OPEC forms a cartel and quadruples the price of oil. The rise in the price of oil relative to the price of wheat means that the United States now has to export more wheat than before to obtain a barrel of imported oil. The resulting worsening of the U.S. terms of trade and the consequent rise in the real exchange rate causes the dollar to depreciate relative to OPEC currencies despite no underlying change in purchasing power parity. In short, a real shock in the form of increased market power induces a real exchange rate depreciation relative to the unchanged purchasing power parity.

As another example, suppose that U.S. demand shifts away from fuel-inefficient Cadillacs to fuel-efficient Toyotas, thereby raising the price of the latter relative to the price of the former such that more Cadillacs have to be given up in trade to obtain a Toyota. As before, general price levels are assumed constant. The resulting worsening of the U.S. terms of trade with Japan causes a real depreciation of the dollar relative to the yen necessitating an equilibrium shift in the exchange rate relative to the unchanged purchasing power parity.

Finally, suppose that Canada's export productivity doubles relative to U.S. export productivity, thereby rendering Canadian exports half as expensive as before in terms of U.S. exports. The resulting improvement in the U.S. real terms of trade causes the U.S. dollar to appreciate against the Canadian dollar despite no change in the purchasing power parity. The same thing would happen if productivity were advancing faster in the U.S. export sector than in the domestic nontradeables sector, thereby rendering exportables cheaper in terms of nontradeables. The resulting reduction in the real cost of transforming nontradeables into exportables and thereby into imports would strengthen the external value of the U.S. dollar on the foreign exchanges. In both cases the U.S. would experience a real exchange rate appreciation and a corresponding departure from purchasing power parity.

These examples illustrate how real shocks such as productivity growth differentials and international shifts in demand can induce systematic departures from purchasing power parity. In this perspective there is nothing mysterious about the failure of exchange rates to move in conformity with national price levels in the post-Bretton Woods era of floating exchange rates. Given the abundance of real shocks in that period (e.g., oil embargoes, commodity shortages, diverging productivity growth rates, shifts in international demands, changes in commercial policy, and the like), persistent departures from purchasing power parity were to be expected.

RESIDUAL VALIDITY OF THE PURCHASING POWER PARITY DOCTRINE

The last question raised by recent exchange rate experience refers to the residual validity of the purchasing power parity doctrine. What remains of the doctrine given the departures from purchasing power parity? Is it still a useful guide to exchange rate behavior? Does it still have something to teach us?

Regarding the validity of the doctrine the model presented above yields the following conclusions. First, the purchasing power parity doctrine can be expected to hold in the long run when the source of exchange rate disturbance is predominantly of a monetary origin. Such nominal disturbances have no lasting impact on the real exchange rate and therefore leave the purchasing power parity price-exchange rate relationship intact. Second, the doctrine is unlikely to hold in the short run since exchange rates tend to adjust to changes in underlying monetary conditions more quickly than national price levels thereby causing temporary divergences from purchasing power parity. Third, nor will purchasing power parity hold exactly in the long run when the source of exchange rate disturbance is of a predominantly real origin. Such real shocks alter real relative prices and thereby loosen the linkage between price levels and exchange rates postulated by the doctrine. What this means is that although the purchasing power parity doctrine is a reliable guide to long-run exchange rate movements originating in the monetary sector, its forecasting accuracy diminishes when real shocks affect exchange rates.

Note, however, that the purchasing power parity doctrine remains a useful tool even when real structural changes produce systematic disparities between exchange rate movements and changes in national price levels. It continues to be useful because it identifies divergent rates of price inflation as an important source of exchange rate movements and points out that this source could be eliminated if countries would pursue stable noninflationary monetary policies. That is, it specifies unstable monetary policies as a prime cause of exchange rate movements and stresses that this cause could be removed if countries would practice monetary stability. It also serves as a reminder that policies that strengthen the internal value of a currency will also strengthen its external value on the foreign exchanges. And, in stressing that exchange rates are endogenous variables determined by underlying monetary conditions, the doctrine yields the important insight that exchange rate depreciation per se cannot be inflationary because it merely reflects rather than creates underlying inflationary pressures. For these reasons the purchasing power parity doctrine remains a useful analytical tool.

POLICY IMPLICATIONS

Having employed the augmented monetary model to interpret recent exchange rate behavior, it remains to outline the policy implications of the model. At least three policy implications stem from the augmented monetary model. The first is that it is impossible for countries to peg both the external and internal value of their currencies in an inflationary world subject to real economic shocks. As a result, floating exchange rates may be necessary for countries desiring to stabilize general prices.

To see this, recall the real/nominal exchange rate equation $E = RP/P^*$. It is obvious from this expression that it is impossible to peg both the exchange rate E and domestic prices P if the real exchange rate R and/or foreign prices P^* are changing. Given foreign prices, a rising real exchange rate means that a country that wishes to stabilize its domestic price level must be prepared to abandon fixed rates and let its currency depreciate on the foreign exchanges. Similarly, given the real exchange rate, rising foreign prices mean that a country that wishes to pursue domestic price stability must let its currency appreciate on the foreign exchanges. Under these conditions only floating exchange rates are compatible with domestic price stability. For this reason, floating exchange rates may be necessary for countries wishing to achieve price stability in an inflationary world also subject to real economic shocks. Given price stability as the overriding policy goal, pegged exchange rates would be inferior to floating rates.

A second policy implication of the model is that proposed purchasing power parity policy intervention rules should be rejected.

Such rules would require the authorities to intervene in the market for foreign exchange to insure that exchange rates conform to the purchasing power parity path of national price levels.

Such intervention rules are singularly ill-advised. They wrongly assume that policymakers can and should eliminate all real exchange rate changes. To be sure, real exchange rate changes stemming from erratic macroeconomic policies can and should be eliminated by pursuing stable, predictable policies. But real exchange rate changes stemming from fundamental structural changes in national economies should be accepted. For, as noted above, such changes generate changes in real relative prices that require equilibrium shifts in exchange rates relative to purchasing power parity. An intervention rule that ties exchange rates rigidly to national price levels in accordance with purchasing power parity ignores the need for such real exchange rate changes. It also fails to recognize that, because of sluggish national price levels, real exchange rate changes may be necessary to accomplish adjustments that would otherwise be achieved by movements in national price levels. For example, real exchange rate changes may serve the useful role of providing a temporary outlet for monetary shocks not accommodated by price level movements.

The model's third policy implication is that, short of obtaining a coordinated international program to equalize inflation rates in the trading world, the best way to reduce exchange rate fluctuations is to pursue a stable and predictable domestic noninflationary monetary policy. Not only would such a policy strengthen both the internal and external value of the currency, but it would also contribute to exchange rate stability in at least two ways. First, it would eliminate the unstable monetary growth that is a direct cause of exchange rate fluctuations. Second, it would exert a stabilizing effect on exchange rates via the expectations channel. This is so because market exchange rates are dominated by expectations of future monetary policies and these expectations themselves are influenced by current monetary policies. It follows that stable monetary policies will induce expectations of future policy stability and thereby exert a stabilizing influence on current exchange rates.

Note, however, that a stable domestic monetary policy alone would not eliminate all sources of exchange rate fluctuations. On the contrary, fluctuations could still result from unstable policies abroad as well as from unavoidable real disturbances. But stable monetary policy would eliminate one source of exchange rate variability, namely that produced by erratic and unstable domestic monetary policies. In short, while domestic monetary policy can do little to stop exchange rate disturbances originating from the real sector or from unstable policies abroad, it can stop one source of disturbance, namely that emanating from the domestic monetary sector.

CONCLUDING COMMENTS

This chapter has presented an augmented monetary model of exchange rate determination and has used it to address certain questions raised by recent experience with floating exchange rates. The chapter's main conclusion is that real as well as monetary factors affect exchange rates and that they do so through nonmonetary channels, i.e., through real relative prices. The simplest version of the monetary approach ignores this, however, and for that reason must be augmented with a real exchange rate component if it is to account for all factors affecting exchange rates. Without this modification, the simple monetary approach is capable of accounting only for nominal movements in the exchange rate.

Even so, however, the simple version of the monetary approach remains a useful analytical tool. It provides a reliable guide to long-run exchange rate behavior when the source of exchange rate disturbance is of a predominantly monetary origin. It reminds us that excessive monetary growth is a primary source of exchange rate depreciation and that one can eliminate this source by adhering to stable non-inflationary monetary policies. It also reminds us that exchange rates and price levels cannot be treated as independent, unrelated variables since policies that affect one tend to affect the other in the same way. It notes that since exchange rates themselves are determined by monetary policy they cannot be treated as independent policy instruments. And, in stressing that exchange rates are endogenous variables determined by underlying monetary conditions, it makes the important point that floating exchange rates cannot be inflationary since they reflect rather than generate inflationary pressures. In so doing, it effectively refutes the popular argument that floating rates cause inflation. These propositions remain valid even when real exchange rate changes occur. For this reason the monetary approach remains a useful analytical tool.

NOTES

1. For recent expositions of the monetary approach see Bilson [2], Frenkel [6], and Mussa [8].

2. In other words, the price level equates money supply and demand by deflating the real value of the nominal money stock to the level people desire to hold.

3. According to the purchasing power parity doctrine, this condition ensures that the common currency price of a standard basket of goods is everywhere the same so that there exists no arbitrage advantage to buying in one market over another. It also ensures that the real (exchange rate adjusted) purchasing power of both currencies is everywhere the same so that there exists no incentive to switch from one currency to the other and both moneys are therefore willingly held. The purchasing power parity doctrine argues that if these conditions were violated, goods would be cheaper in one country than another and one currency would be overvalued and the other undervalued on the foreign exchanges. The resulting rush to convert the former currency into the latter in order to purchase goods where they are relatively cheap would quickly bid the exchange rate back to the purchasing power parity at which no advantage exists to converting one money into the other.

4. This is the conclusion reached by Kreinin and Officer [7; pp. 39–40] in their survey of empirical tests of the monetary approach. Of the 10 studies surveyed, at least 7 yield mixed or inconclusive results concerning the monetary approach. See also Stockman [10; pp. 675–76] who notes that the monetary approach has performed no better than simple purchasing power parity explanations and that "there remain substantial short-run variations in exchange rates unexplained by the monetary approach."

5. Note, however, that the monetary approach does capture the effect of real shocks operating through the real income determinant of the demand for money. That is, the monetary approach captures the income effects but not the relative price effects of real disturbances.

6. See Sakakibara [9; p. 204] for a discussion of this point.

7. Equation 8 enters exchange rate expectations directly into the money demand function on the grounds that such expectations constitute the anticipated depreciation cost of holding one currency over the other. The same result can be derived indirectly by assuming (1) that the demand for each currency is determined by the nominal interest rate on securities denominated in that currency, (2) that international nominal interest rate differentials equal the forward premium on foreign exchange (the interest rate parity condition), and (3) that the forward premium equals the expected rate of depreciation of the exchange rate. This latter interpretation views the expected rate of change of the exchange rate not as the cost of holding one currency over the other but rather as the relative opportunity cost of holding either currency instead of securities. Both interpretations yield the same conclusion, namely that expectations of future exchange rates influence current exchange rates through real money demands.

8. See Artus and Young [1; pp. 25–33] for a discussion of these fluctuations.

REFERENCES

1. Artus, Jacques R., and Young, John H. "Fixed and Flexible Rates: A Renewal of the Debate." Working paper No. 367. NBER Working Paper Series. Cambridge: National Bureau of Economic Research, June 1979.

2. Bilson, John F. O. "The Current Experience with Floating Exchange Rates: An Appraisal of the Monetary Approach." *American Economic Review: Papers and Proceedings*, 68, No. 2 (May 1976):392-97.

3. Flood, Robert P. "Explanations of Exchange-Rate Volatility and Other Empirical Regularities in Some Popular Models of the Foreign Exchange Market." Working paper No. 625. NBER Working Paper Series. Cambridge: National Bureau of Economic Research, February 1981.

4. Frenkel, Jacob A. "The Collapse of Purchasing Power Parities During the 1970s." Working paper No. 569. NBER Working Paper Series. Cambridge: National Bureau of Economic Research, October 1980.

5. ——. "Flexible Exchange Rates, Prices and the Role of 'News': Lessons from the 1970's." Report No. 8020. Center for Mathematical Studies in Business and Economics, University of Chicago, June 1980.

6. ——. "A Monetary Approach to the Exchange Rate: Doctrinal Aspects and Empirical Evidence." *Scandinavian Journal of Economics* 78, No. 2 (May 1976):200-24.

7. Kreinin, Mordechai E., and Officer, Lawrence H. *The Monetary Approach to the Balance of Payments: A Survey*. Princeton Studies in International Finance, No. 43. Princeton: Princeton University, International Finance Section, 1978.

8. Mussa, Michael. "The Exchange Rate, the Balance of Payments and Monetary and Fiscal Policy under a Regime of Controlled Floating." *Scandinavian Journal of Economics* 78, No. 2 (May 1976):229-48.

9. Sakakibara, Eisuke. "Purchasing Power Parity and Currency Substitution." *The Economic Studies Quarterly* 30, No. 3 (December 1979):202-18.

10. Stockman, Alan C. "A Theory of Exchange Rate Determination." *Journal of Political Economy* 88, No. 4 (August 1980):673-98.

14

MAJOR HISTORICAL MODELS OF THE MONETARY APPROACH TO EXCHANGE RATES: A SUMMARY SURVEY

This chapter ends the book and completes the discussion of the third case considered by the monetary approach, namely the case of the open national economy operating under floating exchange rates. In discussing this case, the preceding six chapters have examined in some detail the monetary approach to exchange rate determination, focusing particularly on its analytical content, its evolution over time, and its role in public policy debates. It is now time to summarize what we have learned.

Two main lessons emerge from the preceding chapters. First, the monetary approach to exchange rate determination is hardly a new development. On the contrary, it has a long history dating back more than 200 years. Second, since its origin, the monetary approach has evolved through a succession of analytical models of increasing rigor, precision, and complexity. Each successive model built on the foundations of earlier models and laid the groundwork for still later ones. Each additional model contributed a new component to the monetary approach, enriching its economic content and expanding its policy implications. In this respect at least, each marked a milestone in the evolution of the monetary approach. On the basis of the discussion of the preceding chapters, at least six such models crucial to the historical evolution of the monetary approach can be distinguished. As shown in Table 1, they include the following:

1. the simple prototype model;
2. the strict quantity theory model;

3. the real/nominal exchange rate model;
4. the cash balance model;
5. the standard monetary model; and
6. the rational expectations model.

These models are summarized below in order to indicate their contribution to the historical development of the monetary approach.

SIMPLE PROTOTYPE MODEL (1760s)

As noted in Chapter 10, the first and simplest monetary exchange rate model was presented by the Cap political party during the mid-eighteenth century Swedish Bullionist controversy over the cause of the fall of the external value of the Swedish currency on the foreign exchanges. This model says only that the exchange rate E is determined by the exogenous nominal money stock M and that causation runs from the latter variable to the former. Written as follows

$$(1.1) \quad E = E(M)$$

this model ignores the influence of foreign money stocks on the exchange rate and provides no details about the transmission mechanism linking money with exchange rates. Nor does it specify the precise mathematical form of the equation relating money to exchange rates. This failure to specify the exact functional form of the money/exchange rate equation renders the model incapable of yielding the standard monetarist homogeneity proposition according to which a ceteris paribus change in the money stock produces an exactly equiproportional change in the exchange rate. Nevertheless the model does yield two important monetarist policy conclusions. The first is that the exchange rate is an endogenous variable determined by monetary policy and not an exogenous variable reflecting external real disturbances to the balance of payments. This conclusion follows from the model's specification of money as the single most important determinant of exchange rates. The second conclusion stemming from the model is that monetary overexpansion is the chief cause of and monetary contraction the appropriate remedy for a depreciated currency. The idea that the exchange rate is primarily a monetary phenomenon and that rapid money growth weakens and slow (or negative) money growth strengthens a currency on the foreign

TABLE 1. Major Models of the Monetary Approach

Model	Authors	Components
Simple Prototype Model	Cap Political Party (1760s)	MER
Strict Quantity Theory Model	Strict Bullionists (early 1800s)	QTM PPP
Real/Nominal Exchange Model	Moderate Bullionists (early 1800s)	QTM PPP TOT
Cash Balance Model	Cambridge School (early 1920s)	QTM PPP MDF
Standard Monetary Model	Mundell-Johnson (late 1960s)	QTM PPP MDF
Rational Expectations Model	Keynes, Robertson, von Mises (early 1920s) Mussa, Bilson (mid 1970s)	QTM PPP MDF REH

LIST OF SYMBOLS

Abbreviations:
- MER = unspecified money/exchange rate relationship
- QTM = quantity theory of money
- PPP = purchasing power parity relationship
- TOT = terms of trade or real exchange rate
- MDF = money demand function
- REH = rational expectations hypothesis

Variables:
- E = exchange rate
- M = money stock

Dependent variable	Relevant explanatory variables	Exchange rate equation
Exchange rate	Domestic money stock.	$E = E(M)$
Exchange rate	Relative money stocks.	$E = KM/M^*$
Exchange rate	Real exchange rate or terms of trade. Relative money stocks.	$E = TKM/M^*$
Exchange rate	Relative money stocks. Relative money demands.	$E = (M/M^*)\ (D^*/D)$
Exchange rate	Relative money stocks. Relative real incomes. Relative interest rates.	$E = (M/M^*)(Y^*/Y) \times (i/i^*)^a$
Exchange rate	Relative money stocks. Relative real incomes. Expected future values of these money and income variables, these expectations being based upon all available information including observed money growth.	$E = (M/M^*)(Y^*/Y) \times \left[\dfrac{r + m^e(m, I)}{r^* + m^{e*}(m^*, I)}\right]^a$

K = constant coefficient on money stock
T = terms of trade
D = money demand
Y = real income
i = nominal interest rate
a = interest rate semi-elasticity of demand for money
r = real interest rate
m^e = expected future growth rate of money per unit of real income
m = observed money growth rate per unit of real income
I = available information
* denotes foreign country variable

exchanges is of course the essence of the modern monetary approach to exchange rates. For that reason the Caps' model may be regarded as the simplest prototype of modern models of the monetary approach.

STRICT QUANTITY THEORY MODEL (EARLY 1800s)

The second analytical model instrumental in the development of the monetary approach combines a rigid version of the quantity theory of money and the absolute version of the purchasing power parity doctrine to reach the conclusion that exchange rates are determined by national money stocks operating through national price levels. As enunciated first by the Swedish academician P. N. Christiernin and later by D. Ricardo and other British members of the strict bullionist school, this model in its simplest form consists of the following three equations:

$$P = kM \tag{2.1}$$

$$E = P/P^* \tag{2.2}$$

$$P^* = 1 \tag{2.3}$$

The first equation is the strict quantity theory of money according to which general prices P are rigidly linked to the money stock M by a constant k consisting of the ratio of the turnover velocity of money to real national output, both regarded as fixed constants in the model. The second equation expresses the absolute version of the purchasing power parity doctrine, according to which the exchange rate E equals the ratio of domestic to foreign prices P/P^* as required to keep the real value of money and the real price competitiveness of goods the same everywhere. The third equation assumes that the foreign price level P^* is an exogenously fixed constant that, for convenience, can be normalized and set equal to unity. Substituting the first and third equations into the second yields

$$E = kM \tag{2.4}$$

which says that except for the fixed constant k the exchange rate is determined solely by the domestic money stock. It was on the basis of this model that Ricardo, Boyd, and other strict bullionists attributed the depreciation of the British pound during the Napoleonic wars solely to the inflationary policies of the Bank of England.

A precursor of the modern monetary approach, this model possesses several key characteristics of that approach. First, it identifies the quantity theory and the purchasing power parity links in the transmission mechanism running from money to exchange rates. In so doing, it incorporates the two main ingredients of the modern monetary approach. Second, it enunciates the neutrality of money concept and extends it to the open economy under floating exchange rates. In particular, it asserts that purchasing power parity tends to maintain the real relative price of goods and the real value of money the same everywhere such that exchange rate movements have no lasting impact on real economic variables. This neutrality proposition is of course a key tenet of the modern monetary approach and represents an extension of the quantity theory of money to the open economy under floating exchange rates. Third, the model expresses the money/exchange rate equation in an explicit mathematical form that possesses the monetarist homogeneity (that is, equiproportionality) property according to which the exchange rate varies equiproportionately with the money stock. Indeed, it was on the basis of this homogeneity property that the strict bullionist writers concluded that the rate of exchange rate depreciation constituted both proof and measure of an equivalent rate of excessive monetary growth and of the need for a corresponding rate of monetary contraction. This view survives today in the form of the assertion that exchange rate movements provide a precise indicator of the degree of monetary ease or tightness and a reliable guide for the policy authority.

Its ability to generate strong policy conclusions notwithstanding, the strict bullionist or Ricardian model had some severe limitations, however. Focusing solely on the domestic monetary stock, it ignored other factors affecting exchange rates, namely foreign money stocks and real relative price (that is, terms of trade) changes stemming from temporary departures from purchasing power parity. The omission of these variables prompted John Wheatley and William Blake to incorporate them into an extended version of the Ricardian model.

TWO-COUNTRY VERSION OF THE STRICT QUANTITY THEORY MODEL

As noted above, the Ricardian version of the quantity theory model took the foreign price level and money stock as given constants and concluded that the exchange rate moves with domestic prices and money alone. Wheatley, however, extended this analysis by considering variations in foreign, as well as domestic, prices and money stocks. In so doing, he concluded that exchange rates depend upon *relative* (domestic compared to foreign) money stocks rather than on domestic money stocks alone. To obtain this result, Wheatley replaced the equation $P^* = 1$—equation (2.3) of the Ricardian model—with the alternative equation $P^* = k^*M^*$, stating that the foreign price level P^* is determined by the foreign money stock M^*. Substituting this equation into the Ricardian model yields the exchange rate equation

$$(2.5) \quad E = K(M/M^*)$$

where K is the ratio of the constant coefficients k and k^* linking domestic and foreign money stocks to domestic and foreign prices. This equation states that foreign as well as domestic money stocks affect the exchange rate such that a depreciation of the external value of the domestic currency can stem equally from falls in the foreign money stock as well as from rises in the domestic money stock.

The chief policy implication of Wheatley's model is that domestic money growth per se need not depreciate the exchange rate if the foreign money stock is also expanding. In particular, the exchange rate will appreciate if the foreign money stock is expanding faster than the domestic monetary stock and will stabilize as long as both money stocks are changing at the same proportional rate. In postulating that the exchange rate depends on the ratio of the two national money stocks, Wheatley advanced the monetary model one step closer to the modern version, which holds that *relative* national nominal money stocks are a dominant determinant of exchange rates.

REAL/NOMINAL EXCHANGE RATE MODEL (EARLY 1800s)

The third monetary model emerged when William Blake and other members of the moderate bullionist school incorporated a real exchange rate (or terms of trade) component R into the quantity theory model to account for temporary departures from purchasing power parity. Written as follows

$$(3.1) \quad E = RK(M/M^*)$$

Blake's model accepts the quantity theory model as a long-run equilibrium condition that need not, however, hold in the short run. More precisely, his model recognizes that real shocks operating through the balance of payments may cause the real exchange rate R to deviate temporarily from its equilibrium value of unit at which purchasing power parity prevails and the market exchange rate E is at the level dictated by relative money stocks. That is, his model permits real shocks (and the associated departures from purchasing power parity) to affect exchange rates in the short run through the real terms of trade component R. The model insists, however, that the real component is self-correcting and quickly returns to its equilibrium value of unity. When this happens, purchasing power parity is restored, and the observed market exchange rate returns to its path dictated by relative money stocks as predicted by the strict quantity theory model. As viewed by Blake, the chief analytical significance of the self-correcting real exchange rate is that it provides an automatic adjustment mechanism that ensures the stability of purchasing power parity equilibrium. In so doing, it supports the conclusions of the quantity theory model.

From his model Blake drew two monetarist policy conclusions. First, since in the long run the real exchange rate is self-correcting and automatically returns to its equilibrium level consistent with purchasing power parity, it cannot be the source of persistent exchange rate depreciation. Only the purchasing power parity exchange rate can remain permanently depreciated. And since that exchange rate is determined by relative money stocks, it follows that persistent exchange rate depreciation is a sure sign of an excess relative issue of currency, just as the quantity theory model insists. Second, the self-correcting real exchange rate ensures that no policy intervention is needed to correct an under- or overvalued currency on the foreign exchanges. Intervention is unnecessary, since the external value of the currency will automatically correct itself and will return to the level dictated by underlying monetary conditions. In short, Blake's doctrine of the self-correcting real exchange rate underlies and strongly supports the policy views of the monetary approach.

One characteristic of the Ricardo–Wheatley–Blake line of monetary models is the failure to identify real money demands as a factor affecting exchange rates. Far from being specified as key determinants of exchange rates, money demands were treated as fixed constants and subsumed in the constant coefficient linking money stocks to exchange rates. This neglect of money demands was rectified in the cash balance model developed in the 1920s, however.

CASH BALANCE MODEL (EARLY 1920s)

The fourth monetary model instrumental in the evolution of the monetary approach specifies relative real money demands as a key determinant of exchange rates. An extension of the Cambridge cash balance approach to price level determination popularized by A. C. Pigou, J. M. Keynes, and D. H. Robertson in the 1920s, this model replaces the constant coefficient k (that is, the velocity/output ratio) in the rigid quantity theory equation $P = kM$ with the inverse of the real demand for money D. The resulting price equation is

$$(4.1) \quad P = M/D$$

which says that the price level is determined by the demand-adjusted money stock—that is, by the nominal stock of money per unit of real money demand. As noted by Keynes, Robertson, and Ludwig von Mises in the early 1920s, this equation also states that the price level clears the market for real cash balances by equating the real (price-deflated) value of the nominal money stock to the level that people desire to hold. Assuming a similar price equation holds abroad and substituting both equations into the purchasing power parity relationship yields

$$(4.2) \quad E = (M/M^*)\,(D^*/D)$$

which says that the exchange rate is determined by relative nominal money supplies and relative real money demands, respectively. In particular, equation 4.2 predicts that a rise in the relative demand for a currency will strengthen that currency on the foreign exchanges, and a fall will weaken it.

Except for the omission of the underlying determinants of real money demand, equation 4.2 is virtually the same as the modern monetary approach. It embodies the monetarist homogeneity (that is, equiproportionality) postulate. It explicitly recognizes relative real money demands as a key determinant of exchange rates. In so doing, it provides an additional channel besides relative money supplies through which underlying economic disturbances can influence exchange rates. Moreover, it conforms with the modern monetary interpretation of the foreign exchanges, according to which the exchange rate achieves international monetary equilibrium by clearing the market for real cash balances in both countries so that both money stocks are willingly held. Consistent with this interpretation, equation 4.2 implies that the exchange rate equalizes the real purchasing power of both money stocks such that both are willingly held. What the equation does not do, however, is to specify the underlying determinants of the demand for money. This is done in the standard monetary model described below.

STANDARD MONETARY MODEL (LATE 1960s)

The next monetary model specifies the underlying determinants of the relative money demand component of the exchange rate equation $E = (M/M^*)(D^*/D)$. In so doing, it identifies the *ultimate* (as distinct from the *proximate*) determinants of exchange rates. Although this model dates from the 1920s when Keynes, Robertson and von Mises expressed money demand as a function of real income, its modern formulation owes much to R. Mundell and H. Johnson, who restated the monetary approach in the late 1960s and early 1970s. Identifying real income Y and nominal interest rates i as the chief determinants of money demand (and denoting the interest elasticity of that demand by the exponent a), the standard monetary model may be summarized as

$$(5.1) \quad E = (M/M^*)(Y^*/Y)(i/i^*)^a$$

which says that the exchange rate is determined by three sets of factors, namely relative nominal money stocks, relative real incomes, and relative nominal interest rates—all regarded as exogenous variables with the last two operating through relative real money demands. The particular variant of this equation typically employed in empirical work on the monetary approach is the log-linear expression

$$(5.2) \quad e = (m - m^*) + (y^* - y) + a(i - i^*)$$

where e, m, m^*, y, y^* are logarithms of the exchange rate, domestic money stock, foreign money stock, domestic real income, and foreign real income, respectively, i and i^* are the domestic and foreign nominal interest rates, and a is the interest elasticity of the demand for money, this elasticity assumed to be the same for both countries.

As written, equation 5.2 embodies the standard homogeneity property according to which an increase (decrease) in the relative money stock produces an equiproportional depreciation (appreciation) of the exchange rate. The equation also predicts that a rise in a country's real income and/or a fall in its interest rate relative to that of its trading partners will appreciate the exchange rate. That is, it argues that anything that reduces the relative supply of and/or raises the relative demand for a currency will strengthen that currency's external value on the foreign exchanges. In predicting that rises in income and falls in interest rates will strengthen a currency by increasing the demand for it, the monetary approach runs counter to the traditional balance of payments analysis of exchange rates. The latter analysis associated rising income and falling interest rates with balance of payments deficits and thus predicts that they should weaken, not strengthen, the currency on the foreign exchanges. By contrast, the monetary approach predicts that these changes should strengthen the currency. Much of the interest in the modern monetary approach stems from the disparity between its predictions and those of the rival balance of payments approach.

A key feature of the standard monetary model is its treatment of the nominal interest rate variables in equation 5.2. Those interest rates are treated as exogenous variables, when in fact they are endogenous variables determined by the same real and monetary factors that determine exchange rates. The inherent endogeneity of nominal interest rates is stressed in the rational expectations monetary model described below.

RATIONAL EXPECTATIONS MODEL (MID-1970s)

The rational expectations model constitutes the sixth and the most recent contribution to the evolution of the monetary approach. Although the essentials of the model were foreshadowed in the work of Cassel, Keynes, Robertson, and von Mises in the early 1920s, the most recent version of the model derives from the work of M. Mussa and J. Bilson, who reformulated it in the mid-1970s. The model endogenizes the nominal interest rate differential of equation 5.2. It does so by expressing the interest differential as a function of exchange rate expectations, which are assumed to be formed, consistent with the predictions (that is, mathematical expectations) of the model itself, from forecasts of future excess money supplies. The result is that exchange rates are seen to be determined not only by current excess money supplies (that is, money supplies per unit of real income), but also by expected future values of those same monetary variables, these expectations being based upon all available information, including the observed behavior of the money stocks. In this way, the observed conduct of monetary policy, foreign and domestic, provides the data from which rational expectations of future monetary policies and hence future exchange rates are formed. And once formed, these expectations are immediately discounted into current spot exchange rates, which adjust instantaneously in response to new information about changed circumstances.

In short, the rational expectations model adds another channel through which excess money supplies influence exchange rates. Those monetary variables not only affect exchange rates directly through the quantity theory channel stressed in the standard monetary model, but also indirectly through an expectations channel running from observed current excess money supplies to expected future excess money supplies to exchange rate expectations to nominal interest differentials and thence to exchange rates themselves. At least two versions of the rational expectations model exist.

The first utilizes the Fisher real/nominal interest rate relationship to define the nominal interest rate as the sum of the expected future rate of inflation and the real rate of interest, respectively. It then treats the real rate of interest as a given constant equalized across countries by integrated world capital markets such that the nominal interest differential stems solely from expected inflation differentials alone. Via rational expectations, the expected inflation differential is shown to be determined by differential expected rates of money growth per unit of real income. The result is an equation expressing the exchange rate as a function of current and expected future excess money supplies with the latter viewed as being determined by rational forecasts of future monetary policies. Chapter 8 presents a model of this type.

A second version of the rational expectations model utilizes the interest parity condition to convert the interest rate differential into the expected rate of change of the exchange rate via the following route.[1] First, it asserts that the interest differential equals the forward premium on foreign exchange (the interest parity condition). Second, it argues that, under certain plausible conditions (such as risk neutrality, no transactions costs, rational use of information, and competitive markets), the forward premium on foreign exchange equals the expected rate of depreciation of the exchange rate. Via this route, the interest differential is shown to be equivalent to the expected rate of depreciation of the exchange rate. Having shown this, the model then identifies the determinants of the expected rate of depreciation itself. It does so by applying the rational expectations hypothesis according to which exchange rate expectations must be the same as the predictions (that is, mathematical expectations) generated by the model itself. Those predictions indicate that the expected rate of exchange rate depreciation depends solely upon expected future values of relative national money stocks per unit of real income. Substituting these results into equation 5.2 produces the conclusion that the exchange rate is determined by current and expected future income-adjusted money stocks. In short, both versions of the rational expectations model arrive at the same conclusion, namely that the exchange rate depends upon the current and expected future magnitudes of the exogenous money and income elements that determine money supply and demand.

The rational expectations model yields at least two implications not found in the simpler monetary models. The first is that exchange rates may be more volatile than their underlying monetary determinants, since those determinants affect exchange rates both directly through the proportional monetary channel and also indirectly through the expectations channel. In other words, the expectations factor augments and intensifies the impact of the direct monetary effect on exchange rates. As a result, small changes in the underlying monetary determinants may produce magnified changes in the exchange rate. On the policy front this implies that a stable monetary policy would contribute to exchange rate stability in at least two ways. First, it would eliminate the unstable monetary growth that is a direct cause of exchange rate fluctuations. Second, it would exert a stabilizing effect on exchange rates through the expectations channel. This is so because exchange rates are affected by expectations of future monetary policies and these expectations themselves are influenced by current monetary policies. It follows that stable monetary policies will induce expectations of future policy stability and thereby exert a stabilizing influence on current exchange rates.

The model's second conclusion is that exchange rate changes stem largely from *unexpected* changes in money stocks per unit of real money demand. For, according to the rational expectations view, *expected* changes in these variables should have little or no impact on exchange rates, since those changes have already been fully anticipated and discounted into the exchange rate. Having been foreseen in advance, such changes entail no disappointed expectations, no surprises, no new information to discount into the exchange rate. By contrast, unexpected shifts in demand-adjusted money stocks should, indeed, affect the exchange rate. Not having been foreseen in advance, they produce forecasting errors that constitute new information that the market discounts into the exchange rate. In this manner, they alter the exchange rate, which adjusts to incorporate the new information represented by the monetary surprises. The policy implication is clear: exchange rate stability requires stable, predictable monetary policies. Being predictable, such policies would eliminate the unforeseen monetary shocks that are a major source of exchange rate fluctuations.

CONCLUSION

This completes our summary survey of the major analytical models of the monetary approach to exchange rates. As shown above, these models were instrumental in the historical development of the monetary approach. From the simplest prototype model to the most recent rational expectations framework, each contributed new components to the monetary approach, thereby enriching its economic content and expanding its policy relevance. In this respect at least, each model played a crucial role in the evolution of that approach. This evolutionary process undoubtedly will continue as the monetary approach undergoes further elaboration, refinement, and modification. Additional refinements might include (1) the incorporation of terms of trade and price structure variables into the model along the lines of Chapter 13 and (2) a better identification of the sources of real exchange rate disturbances to account for departures from purchasing power parity. One might also extend the model to include policy reaction functions describing the exchange market intervention behavior of the monetary authorities as well as their efforts to neutralize (sterilize) the effects of such intervention on the domestic money stock. Then too, the monetary model needs a clearer conception of the appropriate money supply and demand measures to include in its empirical equations. For, as pointed out by M. Mussa,[2]

> It is not clear . . . that the theoretically and empirically relevant definition of the money supply for use in analyzing nominal income, real output, and the price level is also the relevant definition to apply in discussing exchange rates. It may be, for instance, that interest bearing deposits held by large corporations are of far more importance in determining the exchange rate than currency and demand deposits held by the general public. Further, the model of the demand for money that is most useful in explaining the behavior of exchange rates may be different in important respects from the model that is most useful for other purposes. Specifically, in explaining the behavior of exchange rates, it is important to give prominence [as does the rational expectations model] to the expected rate of change of the exchange rate as a determinant of the relative demand to hold foreign rather than domestic money.

Whatever the modifications, however, the monetary approach undoubtedly will continue to be useful not only because of its analytical tractability and its capacity for yielding strong policy conclusions, but most of all because it serves as a powerful reminder that money supplies and demands are major proximate determinants of exchange rates.

NOTES

1. J. Bilson, "Recent Developments in Monetary Models of Exchange Rate Determination," *IMF Staff Papers* No. 2 (June 1979):201–23.

2. M. Mussa, "Empirical Regularities in the Behavior of Exchange Rates and Theories of the Foreign Exchange Market," in vol. 11 of the Carnegie-Rochester Conference Series on Public Policy, a supplementary series to the *Journal of Monetary Economics* (1979), pp. 9–57.

BIBLIOGRAPHY

Adarkar, B. P. "The Theory of International Prices." *Indian Journal of Economics* 15 (April 1935).

Angell, James W. *The Theory of International Prices.* New York: Augustus M. Kelley, 1965.

Arkin, Marcus. "The Economic Writings of David Hume—A Reassessment," *Essays in Economic Thought*, edited by Joseph Spengler and William R. Allen. Chicago: Rand McNally and Company, 1960.

Artus, Jacques R. and John H. Young. "Fixed and Flexible Rates: A Renewal of the Debate," NBER Working Paper Series, Working Paper No. 367, June 1979.

Barbour, D. *The Theory of Bimetallism.* New York: Greenwood Press, originally published in 1885, first Greenwood reprinting, 1968.

Barro, Robert J. "A Stochastic Equilibrium Model of an Open Economy under Flexible Exchange Rates." *Quarterly Journal of Economics* 92 (1978).

Bilson, John F. O. "Recent Developments in Monetary Models of Exchange Rate Determination." *IMF Staff Papers* 26 (June 1979).

——. "The Current Experience with Floating Exchange Rates: An Appraisal of the Monetary Approach." *American Economic Review: Papers and Proceedings* 68 (May 1976).

——. "Rational Expectations and the Exchange Rate." Unpublished manuscript, Northwestern University, August 1976.

——. "The Monetary Approach to the Exchange Rate: Some Empirical Evidence." Unpublished manuscript, Northwestern University, October 1976.

——. "The Monetary Approach to the Exchange Rate: Some Empirical Evidence." *IMF Staff Papers* 25 (March 1978).

——. "Rational Expectations and the Exchange Rate." Ch. 5 in *The Economics of Exchange Rates: Selected Studies*, edited by J. Frenkel and H. Johnson. Reading, Mass.: Addison-Wesley, 1978.

Bladen, Vincent W. *From Adam Smith to Maynard Keynes: The Heritage of Political Economy.* Toronto: University of Toronto Press, 1974.

Blake, William. *Observations on the Principles Which Regulate the Course of Exchange and on the Present Depreciated State of the Currency.* Originally printed in London, 1810, reprinted edition, New York: Burt Franklin, 1969.

Blaug, Mark. *Economic Theory in Retrospect.* Homewood, Ill.: Richard D. Irwin, 1968.

Bloomfield, Arthur I. "Adam Smith and the Theory of International Trade." *Essays on Adam Smith*, edited by Andrew Skinner and Thomas Wilson. Oxford: Clarendon Press, 1975.

Bodin, Jean. "Reply to the Paradoxes of Malestroit Concerning the Dearness of All Things and the Remedy Therefore." In *Early Economic Thought*, edited by Arthur E. Monroe. Cambridge: Harvard University Press, 1924.

Boorman, John T. "The Evidence on the Demand for Money: Theoretical Formulations and Empirical Results." In *Current Issues in Monetary Theory and Policy*, edited by Thomas M. Havrilesky and John T. Boorman, Arlington Heights, Ill.: AHM Publishing Corp., 1976.

Bordo, Michael David. "John E. Cairnes on the Effects of the Australian Gold Discoveries, 1851–73: An Early Application of the Methodology of Positive Economics." *History of Political Economy* 7 (1975).

—— and Anna J. Schwartz. "Clark Warburton: Pioneer Monetarist." *Journal of Monetary Economics* 5 (1979).

Bowley, Marion. *Nassau Senior and Classical Economics.* London: Allen and Unwin, 1937.

Branson, William H. "Monetarist and Keynesian Models of the Transmission of Inflation." *American Economic Review* 65 (May 1975).

Bresciani-Turroni, Costantino. "The 'Purchasing Power Parity' Doctrine." *L'Egypte Contemporaine* 25 (May 1934). Reprinted in his *Saggi di Economia.* Milan: Giuffre, 1961.

——. *The Economics of Inflation: A Study of Currency Depreciation in Post-War Germany* (1931), translated by Millicent E. Sayers; with a Foreword by Lionel Robbins. New York: Augustus Kelley, 1968.

Brownell, Francis H. *Hard Money.* New York: American Smelting and Refining Company, April 1944.

Cairnes, John E. *An Examination into the Principles of Currency Involved in the Bank Charter Act of 1844* (London, 1854). New York: Augustus M. Kelley, 1966.

——. *Essays in Political Economy.* London: Macmillan and Company, 1873.

Cannan, Edwin. *Money: Its Connexion with Rising and Falling Prices.* London: P. S. King and Son, 1935.

—— (ed.), *The Paper Pound of 1797–1821: The Bullion Report.* New York: Augustus M. Kelley, 1969.

Cantillon, Richard. *Essai Sur La Nature Du Commerce En General*, edited by Henry Higgs. London: Macmillan and Company, 1931.

Cargill, Thomas F. "Clark Warburton and the Development of Monetarism Since the Great Depression." *History of Political Economy* 11:3 (1979).

Cassel, Gustav. "The Present Situation of the Foreign Exchanges." *Economic Journal* 26 (March 1916).

——. "Further Observations on the World's Monetary Problem." *Economic Journal* (March 1920).

——. *Money and Foreign Exchange after 1914.* New York: Macmillan, 1922.

——. *Post-War Monetary Stabilization.* New York: Columbia University Press, 1928.

——. *The Theory of Social Economy.* New York: Augustus M. Kelley, 1967.

Cesarano, Filippo. "Monetary Theory in Ferdinando Galiani's *Della Moneta.*" *History of Political Economy* 8 (Fall 1976).

Chandler, Lester V. *The Economics of Money and Banking.* New York: Harper and Brothers, 1948.

Claassen, Emil M. "World Inflation under Flexible Exchange Rates." *Scandinavian Journal of Economics* 78 (1976).

Collery, Arnold. *International Adjustment, Open Economies, and the Quantity Theory of Money.* Princeton, N.J.: Princeton Studies in International Finance No. 28 (June 1971).

Connolly, Michael. "The Monetary Approach to an Open Economy: The Fundamental Theory." In *The Monetary Approach to International Ad-*

justment, edited by Bluford H. Putnam and D. Sykes Wilford. New York: Praeger Publishers, 1978.

—— and Taylor, Dean. "Testing the Monetary Approach to Devaluation in Developing Countries." *Journal of Political Economy* 84 (August 1976).

Daugherty, Marion R. "The Currency-Banking Controversy: Part I and II." *Southern Economic Journal* 9 (July 1942–April 1943).

Deane, Phyllis. *The Evolution of Economic Ideas*. Cambridge: Cambridge University Press, 1978.

DeJong, F. J. *Development of Monetary Theory in the Netherlands*. Rotterdam: Rotterdam University Press, 1973.

Dombrecht, M. "The Monetary Approach to the Balance of Payments under Fixed Exchange Rates: A Survey." *Tijdschrif vorr Economie en Management* XXIII (1978).

Dornbusch, Rüdiger. "Alternative Price Stabilization Rules and the Effects of Exchange Rate Changes." *The Manchester School of Economic and Social Studies* 3 (September 1975).

——. "Devaluation, Money, and Non-Traded Goods," *The Monetary Approach to the Balance of Payments*, edited by Frenkel and Johnson. Toronto: University of Toronto Press, 1976. Also in *American Economic Review*, 63, December 1973.

——. "The Theory of Flexible Exchange Rate Regimes and Macroeconomic Policy." *Scandinavian Journal of Economics* 78 (1976).

——. "Monetary Policy under Exchange Rate Flexibility." NBER Working Paper Series, Working Paper No. 311, January 1979. Also in *Managed Exchange Rate-Flexibility: The Recent Experience*. Boston: Federal Reserve Bank of Boston, October 1978.

—— and Dwight Jaffee. "Purchasing Power Parity and Exchange Rate Problems: Introduction." *Journal of International Economics* 8 (May 1978).

Eagly, Robert V. "Adam Smith and the Specie-Flow Doctrine." *Scottish Journal of Political Economy* XVII (February 1970).

——. "The Swedish and English Bullionist Controversies." *Events, Ideology, and Economic Theory*, edited by R. V. Eagly. Detroit: Wayne State University Press, 1968.

——. *The Swedish Bullionist Controversy.* Philadelphia: American Philosophical Society, 1971.

Edie, Lionel Danforth. *Gold Production and Prices before and after the World War,* Bloomington, Indiana: Indiana University Studies, Study No. 78, Vol. XV (March 1928).

Einzig, Paul. *The History of Foreign Exchange.* London: Macmillan, 1962.

——. *The History of Foreign Exchange* (second edition). London: Macmillan, 1979.

Ekelund, Robert B., Jr., and Robert F. Hebert. *A History of Economic Theory and Method.* New York: McGraw-Hill, 1975.

Ellis, Howard S. *German Monetary Theory 1905–1933.* Cambridge, Mass.: Harvard University Press, 1934.

Eshag, E. Prime. *From Marshall to Keynes.* Oxford: Blackwell, 1963.

Fausten, Dietrich K. "On the Humean Origin of the Contemporary Monetary Approach to the Balance of Payments." Paper presented at the 53rd Annual Conference, Western Economic Association, Hawaii, June 20–26, 1978.

——. "The Humean Origin of the Contemporary Monetary Approach to the Balance of Payments," *Quarterly Journal of Economics* (November 1979).

Fetter, Frank W. *Development of British Monetary Orthodoxy, 1797–1875.* Cambridge, Mass.: Harvard University Press, 1965.

—— and Derek Gregory. *Monetary and Financial Policy.* London: Irish University Press, 1973.

Fieleke, N. "The International Transmission of Inflation." *Managed Exchange Rate Flexibility: The Recent Experience.* Proceedings of a Conference, Federal Reserve Bank of Boston, October 1978.

Fisher, Irving. *The Purchasing Power of Money.* New York: Macmillan, 1911.

Flood, Robert P. "Explanations of Exchange-Rate Volatility and Other Empirical Regularities in Some Popular Models of the Foreign Exchange Market". NBER Working Paper Series, Working Paper No. 625, February 1981.

Frankel, Jeffrey A. "On the Mark: A Theory of Floating Exchange Rates Based on Real Interest Differentials." *American Economic Review* 69 (September 1979).

Frenkel, Jacob. "Adjustment Mechanisms and the Monetary Approach to the Balance of Payments: A Doctrinal Perspective," *Recent Issues in International Monetary Economics*, edited by E. Claassen and P. Salin. Vol. 2, of Studies in Monetary Economics, North Holland-Amsterdam, 1976.

——. "A Monetary Approach to the Exchange Rate: Doctrinal Aspects and Empirical Evidence." *The Scandinavian Journal of Economics* 78 (1976).

——. "Purchasing Power Parity: Doctrinal Perspective and Evidence from the 1920's." *Journal of International Economics* 8 (May 1978).

—— and Clements, Kenneth. "Exchange Rates in the 1920's: A Monetary Approach." NBER Working Paper Series, Working Paper No. 290, October 1978.

——. "Flexible Exchange Rates, Prices and the Role of 'News': Lessons from the 1970's." Report No. 8020, Center for Mathematical Studies in Business and Economics, University of Chicago, June 1980.

——. "The Collapse of Purchasing Power Parities during the 1970s." NBER Working Paper Series, Working Paper No. 569, October 1980.

—— and Harry G. Johnson. *The Economics of Exchange Rates, Selected Studies.* Reading, Mass.: Addison-Wesley, 1978.

—— and Harry G. Johnson (eds.). *The Monetary Approach to the Balance of Payments.* Toronto: University of Toronto Press, 1976.

—— and Harry G. Johnson. "The Monetary Approach to the Balance of Payments: Essential Concepts and Historical Origins." *The Monetary Approach to the Balance of Payments*, edited by J. A. Frenkel and H. G. Johnson. Toronto: University of Toronto Press, 1976.

—— and Harry G. Johnson. "The Monetary Approach to the Balance of Payments." *The Monetary Approach to the Balance of Payments*, edited by J. A. Frenkel and H. G. Johnson. Toronto: University of Toronto Press, 1976.

—— and Carlos A. Rodriquez. "Portfolio Equilibrium and the Balance of Payments: A Monetary Approach." *American Economic Review* (September 1975).

Friedman, Milton. "Commodity Reserve Currency." *Essays in Positive Economics.* Chicago: University of Chicago Press, 1953.

—— and Rose Friedman. *Free to Choose.* New York: Harcourt, Brace, Jovanovich, 1980.

——. "The Political Economy of International Monetary Arrangements." *Dollars and Deficits*, edited by Milton Friedman. Englewood Cliffs, N.J.: Prentice-Hall, 1968.

—— and Anna Jacobson Schwartz. *A Monetary History of the United States.* Princeton, N.J.: Princeton University Press, 1963.

Fry, Maxwell J. "A Monetary Approach to Afghanistan's Flexible Exchange Rate." *Journal of Money, Credit and Banking* 8 (May 1976).

Genberg, A. H. "Aspects of the Monetary Approach to Balance of Payments Theory." *The Monetary Approach to the Balance of Payments*, edited by J. Frenkel and H. G. Johnson. Toronto: University of Toronto Press, 1976.

Genberg, Hans, and Swoboda, Alexander K. "Causes and Origins of the Current Worldwide Inflation." Discussion paper, GIIS-Ford Foundation International Monetary Research Project, Graduate Institute of International Studies, Geneva, Switzerland, November 1975.

Gervaise, Isaac. *The System or Theory of the Trade of the World.* Baltimore: Johns Hopkins University, 1954.

Giffen, Robert. *The Case against Bimetallism.* London: George Bell and Sons, 1892.

Girton, Lance. "SDR Creation and the Real-Bills Doctrine." *Southern Economic Journal* 41 (July 1974–April 1975).

—— and Don Roper. "The Evolution of Exchange Rate Policy." *The Monetary Approach to International Adjustment*, edited by Bluford N. Putnam and D. Sykes Wilford. New York: Praeger Publishers, 1978.

—— and Don Roper. "J. Laurence Laughlin and the Quantity Theory of Money." International Finance Discussion Papers No. 103, Board of Governors of the Federal Reserve System, March 1977.

—— and Don Roper. "J. Laurence Laughlin and the Quantity Theory of Money." *Journal of Political Economy* 86 (August 1978).

—— and Don Roper. "A Monetary Model of Exchange Market Pressure Applied to the Postwar Canadian Experience." *American Economic Review* 67 (September 1977).

Gootzeit, Michael J. *David Ricardo.* New York: Columbia University Press, 1975.

Graham, Frank D. *Exchange, Prices, and Production in Hyperinflation: Germany, 1920–1923.* Princeton: Princeton University Press, 1930.

Grampp, William D. "The Liberal Elements in English Mercantilism." *Essays in Economic Thought,* edited by Joseph Spengler and William Allen. Chicago: Rand McNally and Company, 1960.

Great Britain. *Parliamentary Papers* (Commons). "Report from the Select Committee on the High Price of Gold Bullion," (No. 349) III, 1810.

Gregory, T. E. "Introduction," in Tooke and Newmarch, *A History of Prices,* Vol. I. New York: Adelphi, 1928.

Grice-Hutchinson, Marjorie. *The School of Salamanca: Readings in Spanish Monetary Theory, 1544–1605.* Oxford: Clarendon Press, 1952.

Grubel, Herbert G. "International Monetarism and the Explanation of World Inflation." *Weltwirtschaftliches Archiv* CXIV (1978).

——. *Domestic Origins of the Monetary Approach to the Balance of Payments,* Essays in International Finance No. 117, Princeton, New Jersey, Princeton University, International Finance Section, 1976.

——. "Ricardo and Thornton on the Transfer Mechanism." *Quarterly Journal of Economics* 75, LXXV (May 1961).

Haavelmo, Trygve. "Wicksell on the Currency Theory vs. the Banking Principle." *Scandinavian Journal of Economics* 80 (1978).

Haberler, Gottfried. *The Theory of International Trade: With Its Applications to Commercial Policy.* London: Hodge, 1950.

——. *A Survey of International Trade Theory,* Special Papers in International Economics, No. 1, July 1961, International Finance Section, Department of Economics, Princeton University, 1961.

Haney, Lewis H. *History of Economic Thought* (fourth and enlarged edition). New York: Macmillan, 1949.

Hardy, Charles O. *Is There Enough Gold?* Washington, D.C.: The Brookings Institution, 1936.

Hawtrey, Ralph G. "The Bank Restriction of 1797." *Economic Journal* 28 (March 1918).

——. "The Gold Standard and The Balance of Payments." *Economic Journal* XXXIV (March 1926).

——. *Currency and Credit.* London: Longmans, Green, 1934.

——. *Trade and Credit.* New York: Longmans, Green, 1928.

——. *The Art of Central Banking.* New York: Augustus M. Kelley, 1962.

Hayek, Friedrich A. "A Commodity Reserve Currency," *Individualism and Economic Order.* Chicago: Regnery, 1948.

——. *The Constitution of Liberty.* Chicago: University of Chicago Press, 1960.

——. "Introduction." *An Enquiry into the Nature and Effects of the Paper Credit.* Fairfield: Augustus M. Kelley, 1978.

——. *Law, Legislation, and Liberty, Volume I: Rules and Order.* Chicago: University of Chicago Press, 1973.

Heckscher, Eli F. *Mercantilism* (2 vols.), authorized translation by Mendel Shapiro. London: Allen and Unwin (1931) (1935 English edition).

Hegeland, Hugo. *The Quantity Theory of Money.* Goteborg: Elanders Boktryckeri Aktiebulag, 1951.

Heller, H. Robert. "International Reserves and World-Wide Inflation." *I.M.F. Staff Papers* 23 (March 1976).

Henderson, Hubert. "The Function of Exchange Rates." *Oxford Economic Papers I* 1 (1949).

Henneberry, Barbara and James G. Witte. "The I.M.F. Gold Auction: More Bitter Fruit from Bretton Woods." Paper prepared for presentation at the Annual Meetings of the American Economic Association, Atlantic City, New Jersey, September 18, 1976.

——. "Variable Gold Parities from a Classical Viewpoint: Hume Versus the Monetarist." Unpublished manuscript, Indiana University, November 1974.

Hicks, John. *Critical Essays in Monetary Theory.* Oxford: Clarendon Press, 1967.

——. "Thornton's *Paper Credit* (1802)." *Critical Essays in Monetary Theory,* edited by Hicks. Oxford: Clarendon Press, 1967.

Hollander, Jacob H. *David Ricardo: A Centenary Estimate.* Baltimore: Johns Hopkins Press, 1910.

——. "The Development of the Theory of Money from Adam Smith to David Ricardo." *Quarterly Journal of Economics* (1911).

Hollander, Samuel. *The Economics of David Ricardo.* Toronto: University of Toronto Press, 1979.

Hume, David. *Writings on Economics,* edited with an introduction by Eugene Rotwein. Freeport, N.Y.: Books for Libraries Press, 1955 (reprinted 1972).

Humphrey, Thomas M. "A Monetarist Model of World Inflation and the Balance of Payments." *Economic Review* 62 (November/December 1976).

——. "The Monetary Approach to Exchange Rates: Its Historical Evolution and Role in Policy Debates." *Economic Review.* Federal Reserve Bank of Richmond, July/August 1978.

——. "The Quantity Theory of Money: Its Historical Evolution and Role in Policy Debates." *Economic Review.* Federal Reserve Bank of Richmond, May/June 1974.

International Monetary Fund. *The Monetary Approach to the Balance of Payments.* Washington, D.C.: International Monetary Fund, 1977.

Isard, Peter. "The Process of Exchange Rate Determination: A Survey of Important Models and Major Issues." Federal Reserve Board, International Finance Division Discussion Paper No. 101, January 1977.

——. *Exchange Rate Determination: A Survey of Popular Views and Recent Models.* Princeton Studies in International Finance Section, May 1978.

Iversen, C. *Aspects of the Theories of International Capital Movements.* London: Oxford University Press, 1935.

Jager, H. "The Global Monetaristic Variant of the Monetary Approach to the Balance of Payments: An Empirical Study of the Netherlands." *De Economist* 126 (1978).

Jastram, Roy W. *The Gold Constant: The English and American Experience, 1560–1976.* New York: John Wiley and Sons, 1977.

Jevons, W. Stanley. *Investigations in Currency and Finance,* edited by H. S. Foxwell, London: Macmillan, 1884.

——. *The Theory of Political Economy* (fourth ed.). London: Macmillan, 1924.

Johnson, E. A. J. *Predecessors of Adam Smith.* New York: Augustus M. Kelley, 1965.

Johnson, Harry G. "Elasticity, Absorption, Keynesian Multiplier, Keynesian Policy, and Monetary Approaches to Devaluation Theory: A Simple Geometric Exposition." *American Economic Review* (June 1976).

——. *Inflation and the Monetarist Controversy.* Amsterdam: North-Holland, 1972.

——. "Mercantilism: Past, Present, and Future." *The Manchester School* (March 1974).

——. "The Monetary Approach to the Balance of Payments: A Nontechnical Guide." *Journal of International Economics* 7 (1977).

——. "The Monetary Theory of Balance of Payments Policies." *The Monetary Approach to the Balance of Payments*, edited by Jacob A. Frenkel and Harry G. Johnson. Toronto: University of Toronto Press, 1976.

——. "The Monetary Approach to Balance of Payments Theory." *Journal of Financial and Quantitative Analysis* (March 1972).

——. "The Monetary Approach to Balance of Payments Theory: A Diagrammatic Analysis." *The Manchester School* (September 1975).

——. "The Monetary Approach to Balance of Payments Theory and Policy: Explanation and Policy Implications." *Economica* 44 (August 1977).

——. "Money and the Balance of Payments." *Banca Nazionale Del Lavoro Quarterly Review*, Rome (March 1976).

——. *Money, Balance of Payments Theory and the International Monetary Problem.* Essays in International Finance, No. 124. International Finance Section, Department of Economics, Princeton University, November 1977.

Jonson, P. D. "Money and Economic Activity in the Open Economy: The United Kingdom, 1880-1970." *Journal of Political Economy* (October 1976).

Kalamotousakis, George J. "Exchange Rates and Prices: The Historical Evidence." *Journal of International Economics* 8 (1978).

Katseli-Papaefstratiou, Louka, T. *The Reemergence of the Purchasing Power Parity Doctrine in the 1970's.* Special Papers in International Economics, 13, Princeton University, International Finance Section, December 1979.

Kemp, Donald S., and D. Sykes Wilford. "Exchange Rates and the Balance of Payments in Latin America." *Business Economics* XIV (September 1979).

Keynes, John Maynard. *Monetary Reform.* New York: Harcourt, Brace and Company, 1924.

——. *A Tract on Monetary Reform* (1923). Reprinted in the *Collected Writings of John Maynard Keynes.* London: Macmillan for The Royal Economic Society, 1971.

——. *A Treatise on Money* (2 vols.). Cambridge: Macmillan and Company, St. Martins Press (first edition 1930, this edition 1971).

Khan, Mohsin. "Inflation and International Reserves." *IMF Staff Papers* 26 (December 1979).

Kindleberger, Charles P. *International Economics.* Homewood, Ill.: Richard D. Irwin, 1968.

——. *The World in Depression.* Berkeley: University of California Press, 1973.

Krause, L. B. and Salant, W. S. *Worldwide Inflation.* Brookings Institution, Washington, D.C., 1977.

Kreinin, Mordechai and Lawrence Officer. *The Monetary Approach to the Balance of Payments: A Survey.* Princeton: Princeton Studies in International Finance, No. 43, November 1978.

Laidler, David E. W. "Thomas Tooke on Monetary Reform." *Essays on Money and Inflation,* edited by D. E. W. Laidler. Chicago: University of Chicago Press, 1975.

——. "Price and Output Fluctuations in an Open Economy," in *Essays on Money and Inflation.* Chicago: University of Chicago Press, 1975.

——. "Expectations and the Behavior of Prices and Output under Flexible Exchange Rates." *Economica* (November 1977).

——. "Adam Smith as a Monetary Economist." *Canadian Journal of Economics* 14 (May 1981).

—— and A. R. Nobay. "International Aspects of Inflation: A Survey," edited by E. Claassen and P. Salin. *Recent Issues in International Monetary Economics,* Vol. 2 of *Studies in Monetary Economics.* New York: North-Holland, 1976.

—— and Michael Parkin. "Inflation: A Survey." *Economic Journal* (December 1975).

Laughlin, J. Laurence. "Gold and Prices, 1890-1907." *Journal of Political Economy* 17 (May 1909).

——. *Money and Prices.* New York: Scribners, 1919.

——. "Prices and the International Movement of Specie." *Journal of Political Economy* 10 (September 1902).

——. *The Principles of Money.* New York: Scribners, 1903.

——. "The Quantity Theory of Money." *Journal of Political Economy* 32 (June 1924).

——. "A Theory of Prices." *American Economic Association Publications* 6 (February 1905).

League of Nations. *The Course and Control of Inflation: A Review of Monetary Experience in Europe After World War I.* Geneva: League of Nations, 1946.

Leigh, Arthur H. "John Locke and the Quantity Theory of Money." *History of Political Economy* 6 (Summer 1974).

Letiche, John M. *Balance of Payments and Economic Growth.* New York: Augustus M. Kelley, 1967.

——. "Isaac Gervaise on the International Mechanism of Adjustment." *Journal of Political Economy* 60 (1952).

Locke, John. *Several Papers Relating to Money, Interest and Trade, etc.* (1696). New York: Augustus M. Kelley, 1968.

Low, J. M. "An Eighteenth Century Controversy in the Theory of Economic Progress." *The Manchester School* (September 1952).

Machlup, Fritz. "Summary of the Discussion on Frenkel." *Recent Issues in International Monetary Economics,* edited by E. Claassen and P. Salin. Amsterdam: North-Holland, 1976.

Magee, Stephen P. "The Empirical Evidence on the Monetary Approach to the Balance of Payments and Exchange Rates." *American Economic Review: Papers and Proceedings* 66 (May 1976).

Marget, Arthur W. *The Theory of Prices* (2 vols.). New York: Augustus M. Kelley, 1966.

Marshall, Alfred. *Official Papers.* London: Macmillan and Company, 1926.

——. *Money, Credit and Commerce.* New York: Augustus M. Kelley, 1965.

——. "Remedies for Fluctuations of General Prices." *Memorials of Alfred Marshall,* edited by A. C. Pigou. New York: Augustus M. Kelley, 1966.

Mason, Will E. "The Monetary Rule: Whence It Came and Where It Went — And at What Cost Was It Lost?" Unpublished manuscript, Pennsylvania State University, 1978.

Mayer, Thomas. "David Hume and Monetarism." Paper presented at Western Economic Association, 1978.

McCloskey, Donald N. and J. Richard Zecher. "How the Gold Standard Worked, 1880-1913." Paper presented at the Annual Cliometrics Conference, University of Wisconsin, April 27, 1973.

——. "How the Gold Standard Worked, 1880-1913." *The Monetary Approach to the Balance of Payments,* edited by J. Frenkel and H. G. Johnson. Toronto: University of Toronto Press, 1976.

Meiselman, David. "Worldwide Inflation: A Monetarist View." *The Phenomenon of Worldwide Inflation,* edited by Meiselman and Laffer. Washington, D.C.: American Enterprise Institute, 1975.

—— and Arthur Laffer (eds.). *The Phenomenon of Worldwide Inflation.* Washington, D.C.: American Enterprise Institute for Public Policy Research, 1975.

Meltzer, Allan H. "Monetarist, Keynesian, and Quantity Theories." *The Structure of Monetarism,* edited by Thomas Mayer. New York: W. W. Norton, 1978.

Metzler, Lloyd A. "The Theory of International Trade." *A Survey of Contemporary Economics,* edited by Howard S. Ellis. Philadelphia: Blakiston, 1948.

Michaely, Michael. "Analysis of Devaluation: Purchasing-Power Parity, Elasticities, and Absorption." Seminar Paper No. 112, Institute for International Economic Studies, Stockholm, Sweden, October 1978.

Mill, James. *Elements of Political Economy* (third edition revised and corrected), 1844. London: Bohn; New York: Augustus M. Kelley, 1965.

Mill, John Stuart. *Principles of Political Economy.* London: Longmans, Green, 1926.

Mints, Lloyd W. *Monetary Policy for a Competitive Society.* New York: McGraw-Hill, 1950.

Mises, Ludwig von. "Balance of Payments and Foreign Exchange Rates" (1919), in *On the Manipulation of Money and Credit,* translated by Bettina Bien Greaves and edited by Percy L. Greaves, Jr. Dobbs Ferry, N.Y.: Free Market Books, 1978.

——. *Stabilization of the Monetary Unit—from the Viewpoint of Theory* (1923), in *On the Manipulation of Money and Credit,* translated by Bettina Bien Greaves and edited by Percy L. Greaves, Jr. Dobbs Ferry, N.Y.: Free Market Books, 1978.

——. *The Theory of Money and Credit.* Irvington on Hudson, N.Y.: Foundation for Economic Education, Inc., 1971.

Monroe, Arthur Eli (ed.). *Early Economic Thought: Selections from Economic Literature Prior to Adam Smith.* Cambridge: Harvard University Press, 1924 (1965 edition).

——. *Monetary Theory Before Adam Smith.* New York: Augustus M. Kelley, 1966 (originally published in 1923).

Mun, Thomas. "Englands's Treasure by Forraign Trade." *Early Economic Thought,* edited by Arthur Eli Monroe. Cambridge: Harvard University Press, 1924 (1965 edition).

Mundell, Robert A. "The Monetary Consequences of Jacques Rueff: Review Article." *Journal of Business* 46 (1973).

Mussa, Michael. "A Monetary Approach to Balance of Payments Analysis." *Journal of Money, Credit, and Banking* (August 1974).

——. "The Exchange Rate, the Balance of Payments and Monetary and Fiscal Policy under a Regime of Controlled Floating." *Scandinavian Journal of Economics* 78 (May 1976).

——. "Macroeconomic Interdependence and the Exchange Rate." *International Economic Policy: Theory and Evidence,* edited by R. Dornbusch and J. Frenkel. Baltimore: Johns Hopkins University Press, 1979.

——. "Empirical Regularities in the Behavior of Exchange Rates and Theories of the Foreign Exchange Market," in Vol. 11 of the Carnegie-Rochester Conference Series on Public Policy, a supplementary series to the *Journal of Monetary Economics* (1979).

Mundell, Robert A. *International Economics.* New York: Macmillan, 1968.

——. *Monetary Theory: Inflation, Interest, and Growth in the World Economy.* Pacific Palisades: Goodyear, 1971.

Myhrman, Johan. "Experiences of Flexible Exchange Rates in Earlier Periods: Theories, Evidence and a New View." *Scandinavian Journal of Economics* 78 (1976).

——. "Balance of Payments Adjustment and Portfolio Theory: A Survey," edited by E. Claassen and P. Salin. *Recent Issues in International Monetary Economics,* Vol. 2 of *Studies in Monetary Economics.* New York: North-Holland, 1976.

Nicholson, J. Shield. *A Treatise on Money.* London: Blackwood, 1888.

Niebyl, Karl H. *Studies in the Classical Theories of Money.* New York: Columbia University Press, 1946.

Nurkse, Ragnar. *International Currency Experience.* League of Nations, 1944.

O'Brien, Dennis P. *The Classical Economists.* Oxford: Clarendon Press, 1975.

Officer, Lawrence H. "The Purchasing-Power-Parity Theory of Exchange Rates." *IMF Staff Papers* 23 (March 1976).

Ohlin, Bertil. "The Future of the World Price Level." *Index,* Stockholm, 1927.

——. *Interregional and International Trade* (revised edition). Cambridge: Harvard University Press, 1933 (second printing, revised edition, 1968).

Papaefstratiou, Louka T. K. "The Reemergence of the Purchasing Power Parity Doctrine in the 1970's." Economic Growth Center, Yale University Center Discussion Paper No. 312, May 1979.

Parkin, Michael. "Comment on M. Mussa, 'The Exchange Rate, the Balance of Payments and Monetary and Fiscal Policy under a Regime of Controlled Floating.' " *Scandinavian Journal of Economics* 78 (May 1976).

——. "A 'Monetarist' Analysis of the Generation and Transmission of World Inflation: 1958–1971." *American Economic Review* (February 1977).

——, I. Richards, and G. Zis. "The Determination and Control of the World Money Supply under Fixed Exchange Rates, 1961–1971." *The Manchester School of Economics and Social Studies* (September 1975).

Patinkin, Don. *Keynes' Monetary Thought.* Durham, N.C.: Duke University Press, 1976.

——. *Money, Interest, and Prices* (second edition). New York: Harper & Row, 1965.

Peake, Charles F. "Henry Thornton and the Development of Ricardo's Economic Thought." *History of Political Economy* 10:2 (1978).

Petrella, Frank. "Adam Smith's Rejection of Hume's Price-Specie-Flow Mechanism: A Minor Mystery Resolved." *Southern Economic Journal* 34 January 1968).

Pigou, A. C. *Industrial Fluctuations* (second edition). New York: Augustus M. Kelley, 1967.

Putnam, Bluford H., and John R. Woodbury. "Exchange Rate Stability and Monetary Policy: A Case Study." Unpublished manuscript, Federal Reserve Bank of New York, August 1976.

Putnam, Bluford H., and D. Sykes Wilford (eds.). *The Monetary Approach to International Adjustment.* New York: Praeger Publishers, 1978.

Reisman, David A. "Henry Thornton and Classical Monetary Economics." *Oxford Economic Papers* 23 (March 1971).

Ricardo, David. *The Principles of Political Economy and Taxation.* London: J. M. Dent, 1917.

——. *The Works and Correspondence*, edited by Piero Sraffa. Cambridge: Harvard University Press, 1951.

Rist, Charles. *History of Monetary and Credit Theory.* New York: Augustus M. Kelley, 1966.

——. *The Triumph of Gold.* New York: Philosophical Library, 1961.

Robbins, Lionel. *Robert Torrens and the Evolution of Classical Economics.* London: Macmillan, 1958.

Robertson, Dennis H. *Money.* New York: Harcourt, Brace, 1922.

——. *Money.* 2nd ed. New York: Harcourt, Brace, 1929.

——. *Money.* 4th ed. Chicago: University of Chicago Press, 1963.

Roper, Don. "Peter Temin, Did Monetary Forces Cause the Great Depression? A Review Article." *Journal of Monetary Economics* 4 (1978).

Rostow, W. W. *British Economy of the Nineteenth Century.* Oxford: Clarendon Press, 1948.

Rothbard, Murray N. "New Light on the Prehistory of the Austrian School." *The Foundations of Modern Austrian Economics,* edited by Edwin G. Dolan. Kansas City: Sheed and Ward, 1976.

Rowe, J. W. F. "An Index of Industrial Production." *Economic Journal* 37 (June 1927).

Rueff, Jacques. *The Age of Inflation,* Gateway Editions. Chicago: Henry Regnery, 1964.

——. *The Monetary Sin of the West.* New York: Macmillan, 1972.

St. Clair, Oswald. *A Key to Ricardo.* New York: Kelley and Millman, 1957.

Sakakibara, Eisuke. "Purchasing Power Parity and Currency Substitution." *The Economic Studies Quarterly* 30 (December 1979).

Salerno, Joseph T. "The Monetary Approach in the Eighteenth Century." Unpublished Working Paper (no date).

Sayers, R. S. "Ricardo's Views on Monetary Questions." *Quarterly Journal of Economics* 67 (1953).

Schumpeter, Joseph A. *History of Economic Analysis.* New York: Oxford University Press, 1954.

SeKine, Thomas T. "The Discovery of International Monetary Equilibrium by Vanderlint, Cantillon, Gervaise, and Hume." *Economia Internazionale* XXVI (1973).

Senior, Nassau William. *Three Lectures on the Transmission of the Precious Metals from Country to Country and the Mercantile Theory of Wealth* (1828), reprinted by London School of Economics and Political Science. London: Houghton Street, Aldwych (no date).

——. *Selected Writings in Economics.* New York: A. M. Kelley, 1966.

Silberling, Norman J. "Financial and Monetary Policy of Great Britain during the Napoleonic Wars: Ricardo and the Bullion Report." *Quarterly Journal of Economics* 38 (November 1923–August 1924).

Smith, Adam. *An Inquiry into the Nature and Causes of the Wealth of Nations,* edited by Edwin Cannan. New York: Random House, 1937.

——. *Lectures on Justice, Police, Revenue and Arms.* New York: Kelley and Millman, 1956.

Sowell, Thomas. *Classical Economics Reconsidered.* Princeton, N.J.: Princeton University Press, 1974.

——. *Say's Law.* Princeton, N.J.: Princeton University Press, 1972.

Spengler, Joseph J. "Richard Cantillon: First of the Moderns." *Essays in Economic Thought,* edited by Joseph Spengler and William R. Allen. New York: Rand McNally, 1960.

Staley, Charles E. "Hume and Viner on the International Adjustment Mechanism." *History of Political Economy* 8 (Summer 1976).

Stockman, Alan C. "A Theory of Exchange Rate Determination." *Journal of Political Economy* 88 (August 1980).

Swoboda, Alexander K. "Monetary Approaches to the Transmission and Generation of Worldwide Inflation." Discussion paper, GIIS-Ford Foundation International Monetary Research Project, Graduate Institute of International Studies, Geneva, Switzerland, March 1975. Also in L. B. Krause and W. S. Salant, Worldwide Inflation, Brookings Institution, Washington, D.C., 1977.

Taussig, F. W. *International Trade.* New York: Macmillan and Company, 1927.

——. *Principles of Economics* (2 vols.). New York: Macmillan, 1911.

——. "Wages and Prices in Relation to International Trade." *Quarterly Journal of Economics* (August 1906).

Taylor, W.L. *Francis Hutcheson and David Hume as Predecessors of Adam Smith.* Durham, N.C.: Duke University Press, 1965.

Thornton, Henry. *An Enquiry into the Nature and Effects of the Paper Credit of Great Britain.* Fairfield: Augustus Kelley, 1978.

Tooke, Thomas. *A History of Prices,* Vol. IV. New York: Adelphi Company, 1928.

——. *An Inquiry into the Currency Principle* (second edition, 1844). London: London School of Economics and Political Science, 1959.

Tsiang, S. C. "The Monetary Theoretic Foundation of the Modern Monetary Approach to the Balance of Payments." *Oxford Economic Papers* 29 (November 1977).

Vanderlint, Jacob. *Money Answers All Things.* London, 1734; reprinted by Johns Hopkins Press, Baltimore, 1914.

Vickers, Douglas. "Adam Smith and the Status of the Theory of Money." *Essays on Adam Smith*, edited by Andrew Skinner and Thomas Wilson. Oxford: Clarendon Press, 1975.

——. *Studies in the Theory of Money, 1690–1776.* Oxford: Augustus M. Kelley, 1968.

Viner, Jacob. *Canada's Balance of International Indebtedness, 1900–1913.* Cambridge: Harvard University Press, 1924.

——. "Mercantilist Thought." *International Encylopedia of the Social Sciences*, edited by David L. Sills, Vol. 4. New York: Macmillan, 1968.

——. *Studies in the Theory of International Trade.* New York: Augustus M. Kelley, 1965.

Walker, Francis A. *International Bimetallism.* New York: Holt, 1896.

Warren, G. F., and F. A. Pearson. "Relationship of Gold to Prices." *Journal of the American Statistical Association*, Supplement (Proceedings), Vol. 28, 1933.

Whale, P. B. "The Working of the Pre-War Gold Standard." *Economica* (February 1937).

Wheatley, John. *Remarks on Currency and Commerce.* London: Burton, 1803.

——. *An Essay on the Theory of Money and Principles of Commerce.* London: printed for T. Cadell and W. Davies, Strand; W. Bulmer and Company, Cleveland-Row, St. James, 1807.

Whitman, Marina von Neumann. *International and Interregional Payments Adjustment.* Princeton Studies in International Finance, No. 19, 1967.

——. "Global Monetarism and the Monetary Approach to the Balance of Payments." *Brookings Papers on Economic Activity* 3 (1975).

Wicksell, Knut. *Interest and Prices.* New York: Augustus M. Kelley, 1965.

——. "The Influence of the Rate of Interest on Prices." *Economic Journal* XVII (1907); reprinted in *Economic Thought.* New York: Random House, 1965.

——. "International Freights and Prices." *Quarterly Journal of Economics* (1918).

——. *Lectures on Political Economy, Vol. II, Money.* New York: Augustus M. Kelley, 1971.

Wilford, D. Sykes. *Monetary Policy and the Open Economy: Mexico's Experience.* New York: Praeger Publishers, 1977.

Winch, Donald. *James Mill: Selected Economic Writings.* Chicago: University of Chicago Press, 1966.

Winch, D. N. "What Price the History of Economic Thought." *Scottish Journal of Political Economy* (November 1962).

Witte, James G., and Barbara Henneberry. "A Monetary-Real Approach to Balance of Payments Theory: Old-New Synthesis for Old-New Problems." Unpublished manuscript, Indiana University, April 1977.

Wood, Elmer. *English Theories of Central Banking Control, 1819–1858.* Cambridge: Harvard University Press, 1939.

Wu, Chi-Yuen. *An Outline of International Price Theories.* London: Routledge, 1939.

Yeager, Leland B. *International Monetary Relations.* New York: Harper & Row, 1966.

——. *International Monetary Relations: Theory, History, and Policy*, 2nd ed. New York: Harper & Row, 1976.

Zapoleon, L. B. "International and Domestic Commodities and the Theory of Prices." *Quarterly Journal of Economics* 45 (November 1930–August 1931).

ABOUT THE AUTHORS

THOMAS M. HUMPHREY is a research officer and economist at the Federal Reserve Bank of Richmond, where he edits and writes for the Bank's *Economic Review.* Author of the book *Essays on Inflation* (first published in 1979 and now in its second edition), he has also published articles on the history of monetary theory in *History of Political Economy, Southern Economic Journal, Atlantic Economic Journal,* and *Banca Nazionale del Lavoro Quarterly Review.* In addition to his scholarly publications, his *Economic Review* articles have been reprinted in anthologies, festschrifts, financial periodicals, and newsletters. He holds a Ph.D. degree from Tulane and B.S. and M.S. degrees from the University of Tennessee. He has taught at several southern colleges and universities, including Auburn, Tulane, Virginia, Mary Washington, and Virginia Commonwealth.

ROBERT E. KELEHER is a senior financial economist with the Federal Reserve Bank of Atlanta. He holds a B.S. in Economics from the University of Illinois and a M.A. in Economics from Northern Illinois University. His Ph.D. in Economics is from Indiana University. Before coming to the Atlanta Federal Reserve Bank he was a bank economist at First Tennessee National Corporation in Memphis, Tennessee. His interests are in the areas of monetary policy, international economics, regional economics, and "supply-side" economics. In addition to publishing in the *Economic Review* of the Federal Reserve Bank of Atlanta, he is currently responsible for national economic analysis at that bank.